IRELAND, IRISHMEN AND REVOLUTIONARY AMERICA, 1760–1820

Rudeness and Promise in the Immigrant's America: Washington D.C. in 1794

IRELAND,
IRISHMEN
AND REVOLUTIONARY
AMERICA, 1760–1820

David Noel Doyle

Published for
The Cultural Relations Committee of Ireland

by

THE MERCIER PRESS

Dublin and Cork

In memory of my mother
Eileen Mary Doyle
1916-1966

The aim of this series is to give a broad, informed survey of Irish life and culture, past and present. Each writer is left free to deal with his subject in his own way, and the views expressed are not necessarily those of the Committee. The general editor of the series is Caoimhín Ó Danachair.

David Doyle lectures on United States history in University College, Dublin. His other publications include *Irish Americans, Native Rights and National Empires*, New York 1976; *America and Ireland 1776-1976*, Westport, Conn. 1980 (with Owen D. Edwards); *The Irish Americans* 42 vols., New York 1976 (with L.J. McCaffrey and others).

Contents

ENVOI

When some years ago the Cultural Relations Advisory Committee of the Irish Department of Foreign Affairs, of which the writer had then the honour to be Chairman, was casting around for ways in which Ireland might fittingly mark in lasting form the Bicentennial of American Independence, it was our good fortune to find in David Doyle a young historian able and willing to take a fresh look at the relations between our countries and peoples in that pregnant age of world history.

Ireland, Irishmen and Revolutionary America, 1760–1820 contains in the first place its author's findings on Ireland-colonial shipping and on Irish indentured servants. These findings his Introduction passes over too modestly, for they include substantial original research in which we are presented not just with sets of thesis-type statistics but also with a close scrutiny of a very complex situation.

While pride of place must always go to original research, in the commissioning of this study we had in mind too that the frontiers of knowledge may also be extended by a critical re-interpretation of information already accessible. Here again the author has made his own distinctive contributions. In tossing up the whole, so to speak, to obtain a better view of it, he has it come down, not quite with a new dimension, but in a somewhat different shape. The role of Ireland and Irishmen in the American Revolution will henceforth be seen as forming much less of a pattern, or patterns, than has hitherto been thought to have been the case.

For the rest, among the work's many virtues, including a limpidity of narrative not always associated with scholarly excellence, one particular feature merits special mention in even the briefest of send-offs. For the sake of the general reader it may be recalled that, with such exceptions as Lecky, MacNeill, Curtis or Kenney, up to half a century ago much of the writing of Irish history fell to men (there have been few women in the field) who were primarily journalists, not researchers. With the founding, in 1936, of the Ulster Society for Irish Historical Studies and of the Irish Historical Society (incidentally, in that order) and the first issue, in 1938, of their joint journal, *Irish Historical Studies,* this situation was changed utterly. Irish historical writing has since then been fully in the hands of professional historians whose prime quality is a disinterested approach to their subject. To that goodly company David Doyle is a worthy addition. With him there is no upholding of ethnic or religious pietisms, indeed no faintest trace of partisanship. Here we meet on their own terms Scotch-Irish, native Irish, 'Old English' Irish, Dubliners of various levels of society, countrymen (some of them Irish-speaking); here we see them exert a greater or lesser influence upon that eighteenth century rendezvous of the west, whence from a population less than that of Ireland there was to spring the nation and people destined to become the leaders of the free world of two centuries later.

In short, in having David Doyle undertake the present task we builded even better than we knew. The study he has produced is not only worthy of its theme but will most assuredly bear further fruit. As one directly involved from the start in that renaissance of Irish history, as it has been called, which took off in the thirties, let me congratulate him on a solid original contribution to American roots and a stimulating insight from a fresh angle into the Irish-American heritage. *Nár lagaí Dia thú, a Dháithí.*

Tarlach Ó Raifeartaigh.

INTRODUCTION

It was a pleasure to turn directly from the pointilliste technicalities of Ph.D. study on Irish America and American life in the 1890s, to the broader and more eventful canvas of their revolutionary half-century a hundred years before. Perhaps the contrast in conditions between the state of the American Irish in the two periods prompted the underlying thesis of the work:—that the American Revolution was genuinely revolutionary if the condition of the Irish, both short-term and long-term, is examined. Before 1776, Irish Catholics in the colonies were a servant class of a widely proscribed religion. Irish Presbyterians were a secondary caste, tolerated, but widely disliked, even by so fair a man as Benjamin Franklin. By 1800, Irish Catholics were immigrating to the United States as a land more favourable to them than their own. Irish Presbyterians had established a political preeminence there, relative to numbers, that contrasted sharply with the defeat of their cousins in the United Irish movement, who had tried unsuccessfully to breach Anglican hegemony at home. General scholarship about the American revolutionary era must take into account these remarkable changes. Not in changing the condition of blacks or of women—for therein, general improvement would have been so unexpected as to be ahistoric,—but in its remarkable amelioration of the status of all Irishmen, the revolution vindicated the belief of the men of the time that their commitment to human equality was not merely rhetorical. The impact of the revolution upon Ireland, too, needs to be re-studied, for few of the extant generalisations have proved satisfactory: my central thesis indicates it may have been greater than even the suggestions in chapter six imply.

I have lived roughly equal thirds of my life in the Dublin area, near Belfast, and in four US cities. I hope I have done justice to my findings on the distinctiveness of the Ulster tradition in America and in Ireland, yet also revealed grounds for considering it a cognate part of the rest of the Irish story. In this I have been moved by scholarship, and by experience, rather than by political outlook: my Ulster Catholic friends, long before the present tragic troubles, always worried that I took my Ulster Protestant friends too much on their own terms. This may have been no bad beginning for scholarship, while being perhaps not a full recipe for the politics of today.

This work was hurried too rapidly for my taste, due to an original BiCentennial commitment which I failed to keep. But it may thus offer a fresh and unified view of a body of materials which have accumulated in the past twenty years, so rich in publication; or it may at least stimulate other scholars to realise that this is a fascinating field, which raises a whole series of questions afresh. It is really a group of essays in explanation and reinterpretation; a definitive study of the subject was excluded by my terms of reference. But it has so engrossed me that I would wish I had been able to work more extensively upon it. In only two areas, that of Ireland-colonial shipping, and that of Irish indentured servants, could I do extensive primary source research, which I hope later to extend and publish in full. For the rest, I have been completely reliant upon published scholars, many of whom deserve to be better known. That I am a beginner in eighteenth century studies has doubled my debts to them.

Brevity caused me to abandon one topic which, on examination, seemed peripheral and minor: that of armed Irish Loyalism, canvassed critically in Charles Metzger, *Catholics and the American Revolution*, 237-265, in Oliver Snoddy, "The Volunteers of Ireland", *Irish Sword*, 7, (1965), 147-159, and in Michael O'Brien, *A Hidden Phase*, 187-194. In annotation, I have aimed at bibliographic completeness, since the field has not been organised heretofore, and given specific citations for most quotations but only occasional events. There are two exceptions: I have annotated the chapter on the Irish in the American Revolution rather more fully, because it is the core of the work, and covers more ground than the rest; and I have indicated the sources on the Irish chapter six sparingly, since few American readers will have the resources to pursue it deeply, and Irish scholars, on the other hand, will find the indications I have given more than sufficient.

Teaching and lecturing publicly in both the United States and Ireland has convinced me that in both cases it is best to assume little knowledge about the one by the citizens of the other. I may therefore present certain American issues too simply for American readers who enjoy lavish complexity in their revolution studies. I will certainly irritate those here who enjoy their Irish history told with full attention to the terminology of the time: this honourable tradition places too much strain upon intelligent Americans who like to read about several countries, rather than give detailed attention to one. Hopefully, the two stories placed in juxtaposition may spark off thoughts which would otherwise be lost, and thus my deliberate fault here be compensated.

Several times, despite illness, my wife insisted that I remain committed to this project. Thus its appearance owes first to her courage. Beyond that my thanks are many: to the late J.G. Simms, a great 18th century scholar,who gave it meticulous attention; to Dr. T. O'Raifeartaigh, who has painstakingly supervised the production of a decent ms. and who smoothed many bureaucratic tangles; to E.R.R. Green, Alden Vaughan, Betty Wood, and James McGuire, who read and commented on various aspects of the first draft, and provided me with many leads; to Edith Johnston, Professor Patrick Corish, Stuart Bruchey, Kevin Danaher, Kevin O'Neill, John Smith (TCD), Cyril White, Eric Foner and A.N. Sheps for conversations and exchanges which enlightened me; to my brother Greagóir Ó Dúill for translating much Irish material; to Audrey Lockhart for wide use of her work before its publication. I am especially grateful to those whose readings of events so conflicted with my own as to force my mind to deeper study: notably J.C. Beckett, Owen Dudley Edwards and Maurice Bric. Financial support came from University College, Dublin, the Irish Cultural Relations Committee, and the Irish Scholarship Board, which together made possible my work at Columbia University where the body of this was researched and written in 1976-77. T. D. Williams, James Shenton, Alan Davis, Dennis Clark, John Lawton, Con Howard, Eithne Woods, Ina Foley, and others ensured that the wheels of support kept turning at various points in a hectic year; Theodore Wilson, Richard McKinzie and David Katzman carried much of my teaching in that time. Members of my own family, and of my wife's, intervened at vital moments to keep things going, one way or another, as did certain close family friends. I am more than usually conscious of how much this owes to all of them.

David Noel Doyle
University College, Dublin,
March 1980

Illustrations

The publishers wish to thank the New York Public Library for permission to reproduce pictures from the I.N. Phelps Stokes Collection of American Historical prints.

IRELAND, IRISHMEN AND REVOLUTIONARY AMERICA 1760–1820

Prologue

Roger Lamb as a boy in Dublin, had played dare-devil by running the rigging of the masted ships docked along the Liffey quays; as a youth, wild and vicious by his own account, he had joined gangs in Long Lane and Kevin Street feuding violently with short swords. Of poor but industrious Protestant parents, the youngest of eleven children, he fled into the British Army from shame at the age of sixteen, joining the Ninth Regiment of Foot, in 1773. Ruthlessly ill-treated in training, he thought of desertion, until terrorised into remaining on seeing his first flogging of a fellow recruit: "I cried like a child." Only the friendliness of a sergeant, who had him to his table and had him tutor his children, made this wrenched-up adolescent year bearable.

Three years later he was in Quebec, fascinated by its customs and its social system, where tenants were often richer than their *Seigneurs*. Within a year, he was marching south of Lake Champlain with the army of General 'Gentleman Johnny' Bourgoyne, burdened by the 'extraordinary measure' of the foot-soldier's baggage: sixty pounds of provisions, arms, blanket and the rest. The great flocks of passenger pigeons, the wild diversions of the army's painted Mohawk allies, the endless stretches of lonely forest, the desertion of the poorly-trained, hungry, frightened and double-minded Colonial Loyalist allies: he observed much despite his burden and his youth. At Ticonderoga he had the plain soldier's first experience of war: "Such terrible scenes cannot but harrow the recesses of his heart, and . . . even common humanity will make him suffer sorrowful pangs for the destruction and agony of the brave enemies overthrown." The mounting ruthlessness of the war between 'kindred relations' appalled him; such as the gratuitous murder of a helpless foraging party of his colleagues in a potato field or later the stabbing of prisoners in his column, as they were marched across wintry and 'fanatical' New England to Boston after the surrender of Saratoga.

Three years later again, after a remarkable escape from Boston by sea south to British-held New York, and re-enlistment in another regiment, the Royal Welsh Fusiliers, he found himself in the heart of the second great campaign of the war, that between Clinton and then Cornwallis for the Empire against Nathanael Greene and his subordinates in the Carolinas and Virginia, which was to culminate at Yorktown. Few common soldiers can have seen so much: he was present at the first great British defeat and at the final one. Shocked that the Carolinas planter regarded his slaves as the Irish 'Grazier and Farmer does here his livestock', he yet approved their 'hospitality, urbanity and enlightened minds' . . . those in Charleston at any rate.

The brief and observant respite on the coast was followed by months of arduous campaigning. He was overjoyed to be part of the army that defeated General Horatio Gates at Camden in the up-country on 16 August 1780, since 'three years (excepting two months and a day), had elapsed since he was made a prisoner at Saratoga by General Gates.' He was especially pleased as the commander of the key centre division at the battle was Francis Rawdon, heir to the Earl of Moira's estates in County Down, a fellow Irishman, as yet but twenty-five, and one of the most brilliant of British commanders in the war. Rawdon, commanding Loyalist Colonials from the Carolinas and the Loyalist "Volunteers of Ireland" from Pennsylvania and New York, ordered a medal struck to mark the victory. Patriotic pride did not distort the young Irish sergeant's view. Lord Cornwallis himself reported back to London four days later, "Rawdon (whose capacity and zeal for service I cannot too much commend) saw the necessity of contracting his posts and securing Camden."

Ahead of Lamb lay the fateful invasion of North Carolina under Cornwallis himself, the jettisoning of supplies at Ramsay's Mill (which struck the young soldier as a strange tactic in hostile country), and the defeat at Guilford Courthouse: a campaign condemned by another one of Cornwallis' key Anglo-Irish subordinates who accompanied it, General Charles O'Hara, as one which had not "produced one substantial benefit to Great Britain" but had "totally destroyed this Army." It was not for mere sergeants to be so outspoken: doubtless Lamb felt the same. Not surprisingly, in both his *Journal* of the war, and his later *Memoirs*, Lamb skirted over the final gruelling march to Yorktown, 1,500 miles to final defeat.

The fighting in South Carolina, after Camden, degenerated into ruthless irregular warfare. The area of the Waxhaws on the North and South Carolina border, settled only fifteen years before by Ulster migrants, was harassed into rebellion by Banastre Tareleton, 'the Green Dragoon', who rightly did not trust protestations of loyalty born of convenience rather than conviction. In the ensuing troubles, young Andrew Jackson had his first experience of war. As a thirteen year old 'messenger' under his relative Major Crawford, he witnessed the action at Hanging Rock. The next year, scarred by a dragoon's sword on the face, he was brought as a prisoner to Camden with his brother Robert. Andrew was young, irrationally anti-British, quite undisciplined and yet remarkable. Two years before, he had participated in his first cattle-drive; he had varied his smattering of learning in Francis Cummins' private academy with cock-fighting, rigorously pursued. In excitement, he lapsed into the Ulster accents of his mother (his father had died in 1767, shortly after Andrew Jackson's birth and two years after the family's emigration from Co. Antrim to America). Fearing for the safety of her reckless sons in the crude British jail in Camden, Elizabeth Hutchinson Jackson from Carrickfergus went to plead with the British commander for their release; none too soon, for both had contracted disease. Amazingly, the British commander agreed. But was it perhaps because the young and confident Lord Rawdon was moved by the intense manners and Scots accent of his own native Ulster? Mrs. Elizabeth Jackson later died while nursing American prisoners in British-held Charleston. Andrew Jackson, with piercing blue eyes, face as long as a Lurgan spade, high shock of red hair, and lonely resolution, would embark on the career of frontier soldier, land-speculator, professional English-hater, southern politician, and national hero, that would lead him to the Presidency by 1828, and make of him a symbol of the political reconciliation of the older Ulster Irish stock in America and the incoming thousands of Catholic Irish.

Among the 171,000 sailors recruited and pressed into Britain's Royal Navy during the American War was a wild, restless and voluble Kerryman, Owen Roe O'Sullivan. He was the greatest of the popular Gaelic poets, judged by his influence upon the traditions of Munster subsequently; he transformed the restrained measures of his bardic predecessors into a torrent of colourful language which brightly lit a world of deepening poverty. Today we miss in it any forthright treatment of the themes of O'Sullivan's real experiences as schoolmaster, migratory harvester, sailor, potato digger, and soldier; but these were the daily diet of his audience, who preferred the embroidered braggadocio of his rhymes of drinking, brawling and loose-loving. Fleeing an enemy, he found himself in the British Fleet bound for the West Indies in 1782, which was to prevent a repetition of the disaster of Yorktown, i.e. to avert the allied naval might of France, Spain and Holland, from seizing Britain's West Indian empire. O'Sullivan, with many other Irishmen, enjoyed the release of battle when Admiral George Rodney finally closed with the French Admiral De Grasse off Les Saintes, a rocky bird-crowded archipelago in the Leeward Islands. For O'Sullivan, the subsequent victory was easily explained: 'Rodney's guns and Paddy's sons' made the French turn tail, when "The seas were all of crimson dye,/Full deep we stood in human blood,/Surrounded by a scarlet flood,/But still we fought courageous." O'Sullivan perhaps under-estimated the improvements in the guns he helped to handle: gun tackle to enable oblique fire, streamlined priming to speed re-loading, and generally better cannon were the real causes "We plied our 'Irish pills' so hot,/Which put them in confusion." Moreover, he and his fellow Irish officers and recruits were lucky in that the death rates from scurvy, malaria and yellow fever (the real killers in the West Indian operations) were unusually low due to the high calibre of Admiral Rodney's medical officers. O'Sullivan survived to return to Kerry to boast the tale, until killed in a fight two years later with the servants of a farmer he had insulted. Commended by his captain for bravery, O'Sullivan had done something to save the remnant of Britain's North American Empire, and vindicate 'Erin's glory.' A strange irony for one who in his Gaelic poetry wished to see the whole tribe of Anglo-Irish "boors" routed out of his land!

The American experiences of Lamb, O'Sullivan and Mrs. Jackson underline the confusion of Irish inter-relations with the American Revolution. Sergeant Roger Lamb actually saw two Maguire brothers re-united with each other after

Saratoga: they had fought on opposite sides, the American Maguire having emigrated years before. It is indeed a paradox that Irishmen seem to be everywhere in this era; and yet their presence is as fragmented as it is ubiquitous. Subsequent chapters will attempt to picture the framework of such strange contradictions, and then to make fuller sense of the Irish participation in America's birth as a free nation. It is at once clear that Ireland was not an independent state itself, nor had it a homogeneous or unified people. Yet little is really predictable: the original Hutchinsons and Jacksons had come to Ireland under the aegis of a master-scheme to render it safe for Britain against the likes of native O'Sullivans: in the western hemisphere, in a matter of three generations, the roles were reversed in these instances.

Nonetheless there were patterns. In the British Parliament in the 1770s, the most skilful opposition to the American War came from Isaac Barré, Richard Brinsley Sheridan, Edmund Burke, and William Petty Lord Shelburne (whose father had changed the family name from Fitzmaurice in 1751), all Irish born. This disparate group influenced opposition leader Charles James Fox, through his sister-in-law Mary Fitzpatrick, daughter of the Earl of Upper Ossory and her brother Richard, Member of Parliament, dandy, actor, Foxite. Richard himself served with conspicuous lack of enthusiasm in the American War in 1777–78 in the Pennsylvania campaign, and returned to fuel the arguments of the pro-American group with his experiences. A 'Whiggish' Irish connection in British politics, hostile to metropolitan domination of an empire that included Ireland, sensitive to the slights which London's inner social cliques could visit upon all provincials, and increasingly concerned for the privileges and prosperity of their native Kingdom of Ireland, thus focused the misgivings of those in England who scrupled to crush the Americans by brute force. That all of these Irishmen were of the Ascendancy class whether by birth or choice, rather than of the common Irish, defeated and reduced for a century, indicates how on the eve of the American Revolution the simple polarisations of Irish politics and society outside Ulster between conqueror and native, Catholic and Protestant, lord and peasant, were breaking up: a movement accelerated by the American Revolution.

For Ireland in the years 1775–1800, the tragedy was to be that this movement proved incomplete, that the new fluidity was inadequate to the years-deep permafrost of Irish history that lay beneath a thinly flowering spring of liberal and inclusive patriotism. For Irishmen in America, on the other hand, there was by 1800 the conviction that the spring of their new nation was burgeoning irreversibly into summer.

The irony was complete in the figure of Lord Cornwallis: decent, intelligent, somewhat stumpy in gait, vigorous and unpredictable, this Englishman presided over a series of defeats in America, culminating in the loss of the Thirteen Colonies. Fifteen years after that loss, he was Lord Lieutenant of Ireland, the King's Viceroy, charged with preventing the loss of that other British possession, then in widespread insurrection. He was to succeed, and among his instruments was one of his subordinate officers from the Carolinas and Virginia campaign, Dubliner Sir Henry Johnson. An inefficient colonel at Yorktown, later inspector general of recruiting in Ireland charged with raising thousands of Irish countryfolk to fight the French Jacobin menace, Sir Henry now had the chance to redeem his reputation. At New Ross on 5 June 1798, he defeated the onslaught of the army of Irish insurgents, and broke the momentum of the Irish uprising in the south. Perhaps because of his English prejudices, Cornwallis still thought the fifty-year old Anglo-Irish commander 'a wrong-headed blockhead.' No Irish Revolution was to follow the American in a century.

Chapter 1

Ireland and America in Contrast, 1760-1800

The worlds of Ireland and America were closely enough connected from before the 1760's right through the American Revolution. Yet American independence was achieved, and that of Ireland completely lost, between 1775–1800, the first by force of arms and by the Treaty of Paris in 1783, the second by a series of political and revolutionary failures, culminating in the Act of Union of 1800 that abolished the separate Irish Parliament and made Ireland part of the United Kingdom. Before we deal with trans-Atlantic Irish-American connections, and before we discuss the important role of Irishmen in the American Revolution, and look more closely at the failure of the revolutionary impetus in Ireland, we must look at each society in turn, to set the scene of those events. That two worlds, so closely inter-related by trade, emigration, and events were yet so contrasting, greatly accounts for the emergence of America, and the disappearance of Ireland, as political nations in these years.

Both Ireland and the Thirteen Colonies held overwhelmingly farming populations in 1775. Through towns, market systems and the English language, both were increasingly engaged in trading their agricultural surpluses. Both were under-peopled by the standards of today's crowded planet: Ireland with about 3.7 million individuals and the Colonies with 2.4 million human beings, about a fifth of them black men who were slaves. Both were controlled ultimately by Great Britain, which had around 7 million people. Dramatically unlike today, Ireland had twice the white population of the Colonies, something that should be borne in mind throughout this essay. Again, melodramatically unlike today, of any ten white men in the Anglo-cultural world of the North Atlantic (Britain, Ireland, North America and the British West Indies), approximately four were English, three were Irish, one was Scots or Welsh, and two were colonials in the western hemisphere. And of the ten, to look at it another way, nine would have been countrymen (if not actually farmers in their right). Today, of course, in the same Anglo-Atlantic world of over 300 million people of every race, a group of ten men would include seven Americans, two Britons, and either one Canadian, or West Indian or Irishman. And eight of these ten would be townsmen or city-folk. Of course there would be a considerable Irish strain amongst those in Britain and

North America.

The very different relative dimensions of the world of Britain, Ireland and the Colonies in 1775 forcibly reminds us that Ireland was then a much stronger element in trans-Atlantic history than it is today. Secondly, the considerably smaller populations everywhere involved in the Age of the American Revolution underline the degree to which the creativity (or the failures) of relatively small numbers of men could yet shape the history of tens of millions afterwards. Leading townsmen like Benjamin Franklin, Robert Morris or Sam Adams in America, or like Henry Flood, Wolfe Tone and Henry Grattan in Ireland moved in an urban world smaller than that of the cities of Colorado or of Munster today. Then as now, however, towns were the pivot on which the world turned. Though then so small in size, yet their very fewness in the 18th century gave those who controlled them a leverage over an accelerating human history, a leverage difficult to imagine today. Certainly the more prominent businessmen in Denver or Cork today would not dream of exercising the influence which came naturally to the leaders of wealth and opinion in the Dublin or Philadelphia of 1775. In short, the size of the stage has little to do with the greatness of the actors upon it. But the eyes of vast and populated countrysides were drawn to those small stages: Dublin with around 180,000 people, Cork with 80,000, Belfast with 15,000; and in the Colonies, Philadelphia with 40,000 souls, New York with 25,000 and Boston with 16,000. And the actors within them had the conscious "feel" of still manageable communities: they were not dwarfed by vast, rival yet interlocking metropolises. Moreover, they were generally men younger and more dynamic than the leaders of the surrounding rural provinces, beneficiaries of talent and forcefulness rather than inheritance. They were largely Protestant (Anglican, Quaker and Presbyterian-Congregational), if somewhat secularised. These characteristics were in Ireland overshadowed by the defects of their country cousins (peerage, gentry and others), and their constructive merits hampered and obscured by their benefiting from the narrow politics of ascendancy. In both societies, as their roles multiplied, so they gained in political confidence.

A mass of farmers, comparable populations, the relation to an Anglo-cultural Atlantic world: these generalities almost exhaust the similarities between Ireland and the Thirteen Colonies in 1775. As the landscapes of each come into focus, it is their differences which strike home to the eye. Let us take Ireland first.

In one view, Ireland was a sister Kingdom of Great Britain, sharing the same King, united in joint Imperial interest against all other great powers, sharing the same State religion (anglican or episcopalian protestantism), its politically most powerful families intermarried with those of England. George Berkeley, the Anglo-Irish Bishop and philosopher, could rhetorically question "whether the upper parts of this people are not truly English by blood, language, religion, manners, inclination and interest?" These "upper parts" were basically the descendants of a garrison aristocracy of English officers, speculators and adventurers imposed upon Ireland in the wake of successive defeats in the 16th and 17th centuries. The entire country had been parcelled out in large, medium and smaller estates following the expropriation of successive sections of the native population, so that by 1775 over 90% of the land was ultimately owned by Anglican landlords. However these included a significant proportion of native families which had "conformed" politically and religiously to secure privileges, possessions and local eminence; such as certain Butlers in Kilkenny, Fitzmaurices in Kerry, O'Briens in Clare, or Fitzpatricks in Laois, a process that had gone on spasmodically for over 100 years when it was rendered systematic by provisions in a law of 1704 prohibiting Catholics from purchasing land, or leasing it at length, providing that eldest sons who conformed to Anglicanism inherited sole title to their father's estates, regardless of the claims of their Catholic siblings or the wishes of the owner. However, even non-Anglican *Protestant* landowners also tended to conform, such as the Scots Presbyterian Montgomerys in Donegal.

For the Anglican establishment had legal monopoly of all national political power, of entry to the professions, of military officerships, of university and most secondary education, of almost all local power: the court system, the county administrations, the town corporations, the customs and excise establishment were almost all exclusively Anglican "closed shops" by the 1740s. In short, Anglicanism was the corporate badge of the ruling class, the distinction of all those supposed to harmonise Ireland's fortunes 'in the protestant interest' with the demands of London's ruling establishment. That (before 1760) they accepted such a client role for the most part goes far to explain their having that ethos of irresponsibility for which they were often criticised by the best of their own caste. Their view of this general role, however, did not lead them to any easy acquiescence in London's day-to-day demands. They remained difficult to manage, agreeing only on their broad role. Why they accepted it was another matter: it had much to do with the fact that it placed an entire people in their power: "During the eighteenth century colour and slavery were not the only badges and methods by which a small minority kept a large majority in subjection." Or in the more explicit terms of a second scholar: "It was this colonial attitude—the attitude of the man who felt and enjoyed his superiority over the native—which was paramount among the landowners of Ireland . . ." An entire body of legislation, 'the Penal Laws,' sustained and amplified the resultant "ascendancy" of this class by rendering Anglicanism the title to membership within it; defining Catholicism as the mark of official subordination, social debasement, and economic disability; and leaving non-Anglican protestants in a fluid yet galling no-man's land.

Socially, this ascendancy of landowners found expression in a crude form of manorialism: all legal titles to the use and possession of land ran back to these owners; a majority lived on demesnes within their estates, and rented out the rest. They presided over their localities through manorial or leet courts, through Anglican vestries which had administrative responsibilities, through the other aforementioned official bodies, but perhaps most importantly through a network of influence, power and intimidation. This they exercised by their control of the final source of livelihood (the land), their access to official agencies of repression (such as the militia and the courts), and by their command of bodies of often unscrupulous servants. After 1760, rising pressure of population upon the land gave them the added advantage of being able to play competitive tenants against each other. All landed families exercised their powers differently: many behaved with judiciousness and restraint, perhaps most tended to respect the rights of traditional families of tenants and sub-tenants on their estates. A minority such as the Fosters in Louth, the Osbornes in Tipperary, the Gregorys in Galway attempted to improve the standard of farming and the general level of life among their tenants. Such were the exceptions. One visitor commented that an Irish landlord could scarce invent any order his tenants dare refuse to obey: a charge graphically evidenced in the order book of Tipperary landowner Thomas Otway, who operated a system of fines, penalties and threats so scrupulously demanding that it reduced the labourers and cottiers who worked for him to virtual peonage. That nowhere in the country was the system essentially different meant that there was little impetus to moderation among this ruling class: in areas of Eastern Europe such as Ukraine, where not dissimilar systems operated, sparsely inhabited regions in contiguous territories meant that the oppressed could continuously flee. Such a prospect mellowed some of the lords there toward leniency. In Ireland, even in Ulster where there was an unwritten tradition of relatively fairer play vis-à-vis tenants, the passage of the 18th century demonstrated lenient or just treatment to be very precarious, and very much a matter of revocable custom. The Irish landlord was confident his tenants could not flee elsewhere. Thus was the whole country networked with patterns of domination: the Farnhams in Cavan, Beresfords in Waterford and Wexford, Brownlows in Armagh, Chichesters in Antrim, Fitzgeralds in Kildare and hundreds of others were lords in every sense, whether their titles were in the English or the Irish peerages, or in neither. Even the "good" landlords, as the century progressed, tended to operate according to rationalising or non-traditional conceptions of what was good for their estates, so that their discriminations (between efficient and inefficient tenants) seemed oppressive to their supposedly grateful tenantry. As for the mass of them, they deserved the common view that they lived for gun-sports, racing, the drunken companionship of their fellows, and the hope that they might eventually accumulate enough money (or marry it) so that they could join those of their class who lived in London, the absentees.

Nonetheless, the very existence of such a homogeneous class over the whole country meant there was a group which of necessity took an island-wide view of things, and put it to work at least occasionally, not merely in matters political, but in public works, economic improvement, and the making of a common Anglo-Irish cultural standard. This latter became the chief avenue by which Ireland related to the world of rapid innovation outside. It was not the only one: Catholic Irish connections with France played a lesser part. But if the political economy and social ethos of the Protestant ascendancy was reactionary by the standards of most contemporary West European aristocracies, nonetheless that ascendancy acted as the chief doorway to a wider world, a world in which the notion was spreading that man could systematically improve his earthly habitat, and mitigate the mean and greedy calculations of a politics of scarcity and fatalism. This was indeed the paradox of the age. That the Irish Catholic gentry on the eve of their final extinction had looked toward the same culture (during their short Indian summer under James II in 1685–91) suggests it might not have been otherwise had an alien Anglican ascendancy never been imposed: in the 18th century throughout Europe a politico-cultural cleavage between landlords with expensive modern tastes and traditional peasantries was general.

The existence of a coherent national ascendancy had a second vital effect. However cumulatively and fragmentedly, it tended to produce reactively a *common* sense of oppression, a shared and popular feeling of nationality, which ultimately became the basis of Ireland's modern self-consciousness. Before the 18th century, 'Irishness' and the conscious sense of it certainly existed, but it was occasional, largely unspoken, fissured by the persistence of territorialism and ethnic subdivision between Gaelic Irish and medieval English immigrant descendants. Scholars working in Gaelic literature and in Catholic sources tend to reach a different estimate of it than those working with the English State Papers. The contradictions in the assertions of Cecile O'Rahille, P. J. Corish and J. C. Beckett are not insuperable if one realises that the political and even the religious factors were not then the key determinants of public behaviour among the Irish which they later became, so that 'Irishness' found only fitful political expression. Instead loyalty to family and possession was the crux of the prominent man's calculations. This explains the deviousness, the hedging of positions, the playing for the protection of any master (even an English king), who should guarantee position and possession. That historians working in English sources particularly have found little clear evidence of political nationality in the 17th century is not surprising: English was for leading Irishmen the language of equivocation, self-protection, perhaps of the main chance, but much less frequently of their loyalties. The sweeping attack of outside adventurers upon the landed possessions of these men, an attack which used a highly indiscriminate equation of politics and religion as its instrument, swept away the refuges of subterfuge, of mixed loyalties, of straightforward family pride, by which many Irish magnates repeatedly sought to avoid the dilemmas posed. The equation of Irish native=Catholic=disloyal (and its reverse combinations) also swept away the distinctions which the Catholic 'old English' tried to maintain between themselves and the Gaelic Irish. If successive English monarchs from Henry VIII to William III sought to avoid the application of so crude an index of loyalty to their person for Irishmen, the bulk of the 'protestant interest' in Ireland found it simplified their fears, greatly increased their estates, and neatly tied up their politics. Disloyalty always meant confiscation of land and position.

But the effect of this was to render permanent among the Irish the contrary positions: Protestant=English=oppressor. Fourth generation Anglo-Irish gentry in 1775, moving to a more tolerant and comprehensive patriotism, were to the Gaelic-speaking countryfolk 'Sassenach' or 'Gaoill', interlopers still, and hereditary enemies. Strangely, however, this vague reactive politicization coincided with some persistence of the older view, that a man's public behaviour must be primarily dictated by the exigencies of his family's livelihood. This explains why "conforming" families like those of the Protestant Butlers, of Edmund Burke, or of Dr. James O'Donnell of the Glens of Antrim were apparently not ostracised by their Catholic kin; why even such spokesmen of the native tradition as the poets Piaras Mac Gearailt and Andrew Magrath could turn to Protestantism. A recent study by David Miller shows that Catholicism was not as strong in traditional Irish society in its formal forms as it has been since the 1840s in English-speaking society in Ireland. Patterns of Mass-going among emigrants in Britain and America in the 1850's confirm this: only at most one-half available adults attended, when account is taken of incapacity due to illness, aging, child-bearing and child-care. Active bishops in Ireland such as James Murphy, John Troy, and James Butler were aware there were serious pastoral problems. Thomas Moore, the poet, believed after a Munster journey that peasants were able to steel their consciences to agrarian crime because of their openness to the shibboleths of Deism. And the traveller who came closest to them, the young French noble hiker De LaTocnaye, said of such religious change, that the peasants "always judge such actions and their motives in a matter-of-fact, common-sense way".

LaTocnaye went on to note, however, that when the religious defector openly sided with the government, the common attitude changed to one of much hostility. Indeed it seems clear that it was the proscription from power and prosperity that most rankled with the Irish Catholics as a whole. True, this in turn led them to a more vivid re-estimate of the value of their religious faith. However, unlike other oppressed Christian peoples such as the American black slaves or medieval Italian peasants and more recent European groups, they did not produce a literature (derived from Old Testament prophecy) asserting the ennobling and redemptive value of collective suffering, and devoid of bitterness toward their enemies. Instead, such themes . . . where they occur at all . . . seem perfunctory, ritualistic, and as impatient of suffering as they were expectant of self-righteous revenge. Already by the 1780s and '90s, pseudo-religious political prophecy was finding its way into print:

> In the latter times many alterations will happen; *Bearla* [English] will be spoken in every house, and there will be a Sir in every district (titles multiplied); the Goill will become Gheil and the Gheil will become Goill. The descendants of Milesius [the Irish or Gheil] shall be persecuted with unfeeling tyranny . . . [But] When the foreigners shall be guilty of the crimes which brought the Milesians low, the batallions of the Goill will be defeated, and Eire shall be her own.

While young and vital christians like Edmund Rice and Nano Nagle, reared in merchant comfort in Waterford and Cork, were being moved to new understanding of their Catholic convictions in the light of late 18th century humanitarianism, the impoverished multitudes who moved them to compassion were too reduced and defeated to share such true christianity, except on the most fitful basis. Indeed, generally, Catholicism was well on the way to becoming an ideology of collective self-assertion among the mass of those who could not and would not "cross the culture line" (as light mulattoes once did in America and Africa) into the advantaged world of Protestant Anglicanism. In that sense the remark of Dr. John Hotham, in 1777, that the Roman Catholics cherish their religion above all else, can be understood. That it often penetrated more deeply was the fortunate side of it; even the minds and hearts of the poor are riven with complexities. Ultimately it was the political prostitution of Anglicanism in Ireland that produced a politico-sectarian Catholicism in response: that both Christian faiths were elsewhere already strangely linked by the influences of a Christo-centric pietism was a fact the average Anglo-Irish Anglican or peasant Catholic would have found irrelevant to his quarrels. Yet St. Francis de Sales' writings had influenced both William Law and Joseph Butler, the formative thinkers of anti-deist Anglican revival in England, and through them perhaps, remotely, John Wesley; while among the reading Catholics of Ireland, De Sales and his English disciple, Richard Challoner, were the key guides to those seriously concerned with 'the devout and holy life.' The political uses of religion were much more exciting, and much less demanding, than such lonely integrities of the spirit. It was a rare Irishman of any tradition who could then conjecture, as did Bishop Berkeley, that an internal, invisible communion linked good Roman Catholics and the 'sincere Christians of our Communion', which to him, as to other 18th century Anglo-Irish Anglican Churchmen, was 'the Church of England'.

The increasing polarisation of politico-sectarian division as the century advanced strangely coincided with relaxation of the anti-Catholic laws. Protestants who sought to enforce them were increasingly regarded as eccentric. After 1746, the organisational life of Catholics had proceeded apace, not merely for purposes of worship, but for those of education, and even for economic purposes such as the circumvention of restrictions upon their practice of urban trades. The reasons are complex and still unclear. Growing toleration apart (and subsequent history would cause one to doubt its extent), the very debasement of the Catholic population was perhaps so general that the ruling ascendancy felt inclined to allow them the bauble of their popish superstitions for consolation and the maintenance of order. Whatever the case, pseudo-religious animosity was growing nonetheless and the reasons are most likely to found in the sphere of livelihood and population.

The Catholic population of Ireland was generally desperately poor. To Arthur Young, who travelled Ireland in 1776–7; Richard Twiss, who travelled it in 1775; Edward Willes, who journeyed earlier in 1757–64; De LaTocnaye who travelled later in 1796–97 and many others, the virtual destitution of the mass of the native population over wide areas was the central observation to be made and the beginning of political reflection upon Ireland's problems. Each claimed that matters were apparently much improved on previous years: but then these were usually their first visits, and it is normal for the articulate and privileged in unjustly stratified societies even today to palm off the embarrassing persistence of outsiders as to the prevalence of poverty, with self-congratulatory remarks to the effect that things were much worse for the poor and/or the natives before our time. In fact historians simply do not know whether this improvement was true or not at this time, and the evidence is contradictory.

But the poverty was often graphically experienced: poor farmers making bridles and reins out of straw; swarms of children naked or half naked; girls taking the lice from each other's hair; adults scratching the itches of malnutrition; the complexions like 'smoked ham' or yellowed parchment produced by windowless and chimneyless cabin interiors; towns filthy and oppressive. Above all 'the universal dejection of mind visible in the countenances of the lower sort.' It has recently been contended that there existed a growing middle class of Catholics removed from the ravages of poverty: but this was very small. The very historian who decisively established the existence of a class of Catholic shippers, wholesalers, produce merchants and exporters has given us a list of Dublin "middle-class" Catholics who registered their loyalty in 1778–82; and the vast majority of them (over 1,000 out of 1,250) are petty shop-keepers, chiefly inhabiting Dublin's old inner city, elsewhere described by a contemporary: "nowhere anywhere can compare with the quarters where the lower classes vegetate." Speaking of precisely this class of small traders, Richard Twiss commented: "The indigence of the middle-class of people is visible even in Dublin."

The majority of Irish people were country dwellers. Here conditions varied from region to region, even from estate to estate, but they were generally bad. Again, there was a rural middle-class of larger livestock farmers, of "middlemen" who took land on long leases at cheap rates and re-rented it dearly for short terms; of various jobbers and dealers. Outside Ulster, the mass of these were Catholic. Their ethos was a compound. Part of it was the old irresponsibilities of later Gaelic society which allowed local strong men to enjoy the profits of land without either owning it *or* using it (usufruct). Most of them justified this on the spurious ground that they were clan sub-chiefs and so wise an Anglo-Kerryman as Lord Shelburne, though he did not like their lifestyle, was taken in by their argument. The other element in their outlook was emulative: they learnt the worst lessons which the Anglo-Irish landowners had to teach, convinced that to be a man of weight and substance was to be a leisured parasite: Lord Kenmare, himself one of few Catholic nobles left by the 1760s, wrote of the

pride, drunkenness and sloth of the middling sort among the Irish. Every one of them thinks himself too great for any industry except taking farms. When they happen to get them they screw enormous rents from some beggarly dairyman and spend their whole time in the alehouse of the next village. If they have sons they are all to be priests, physicians or French officers.

Seen in this light, it is peculiar yet revealing that the poor, in search of champions, joined the wailing against the insults to which these splendid drones were subjected by the Anglo-Irish: they too lamented Art O'Leary, the classic half-sir and Austrian mercenary depicted by implication in Kenmare's passage. Of course there were busier and more honourable and constructive men than those who caught the eye of Kenmare or Arthur Young: the farmers and jobbers who made the Cork butter market or the Ballinasloe livestock fair among the largest in Europe. Generally speaking, the countryside could ill afford any middlemen interjected between itself and the landlords; it was too poor. On the other hand, it enjoyed too few rural entrepreneurs such as were behind its great markets, and many of the Irish Catholic merchants drawn abroad engaged in the sterile and non-innovative wine trade from their bases in Bordeaux and Nantes. Of the other proportions of the talented tenth who migrated to the Continent, the bulk of them became mercenaries, and were drawn to most archaic aspects of European military and court life, just as few of the many Irish priests and teachers abroad figured in the exciting efforts then proceeding to reconcile the claims of reason and humanity with the elemental truths of religion.

In short, the combined rural and urban Catholic class which was not poor cannot have numbered more than a few score thousand families (in a Catholic population of 3 millions which was rapidly rising); and its precarious unreality is suggested by the pursuits of those of its children who escaped to Europe. The mass of the Catholic poor who remained are a vast mystery to historians, as indeed are the common people everywhere in the 18th century, from Lancashire weavers to Carolina's slaves. Were the mass of the Irish desperately poor, or only relatively and varyingly so? Were they consciously and resentfully poor, or did their recent forebearers' past, as migratory cabined herdsmen and as poorly clad and housed labourers, make them feel that their 18th century conditions were tolerable and even adequate? Were they universally depressed, ignorant, prone to crime, and of low morale, or were they spirited, keen-minded and knowledgeable, controlled by conscience and community standards, and essentially self-respecting? Were their conditions of life improving or regressing, improving with the quickening of agricultural prosperity and the spreading supplementary incomes provided by the great linen and woollen trades; regressing with increasing population pressure upon a land system which was also hardening in its demands (rents, terms, leases), and with a standard of agriculture which was almost everywhere poor and under-productive? Was the vibrant folk life whereby the lives of the people were diverted by a vast traditional lore, by collective custom, by song, dance and ballad to a remarkable degree a sign of continuing group vitality; or, like the Ghost Dance religion of the plains Indians in the 1880s–90s, was it a series of ritual movements and incantations against the cold of defeat? (The great and sympathetic student, James Mooney, claimed he derived his understanding of the Dance from his Irish background). Were they a-political or had they keen insight into the politics of national welfare? "The great bulk of the people were restricted by poverty to political speculations of the simplest kind" argues R. B. McDowell; but the contemporary De LaTocnaye, writing of the people of the poorest province (Connacht), had said, though no radical:

> It is a mistake to think the peasant of this country so ignorant or so stupid. Misery, it is true, does stultify him and make him indifferent. Yet I declare it is among the people that I find indications of a disposition to do everything that could render society happy and prosperous, where it has been possible to inspire him with the interests of their country.

In short, almost everything about the mass of Irish folk (1760–1820) is debatable, and sources can be found to put each contradictory position in turn. Only on the broad outlines can there currently be any certainty. The land system *was* appalling, by any standards: the mass of the people were small farmers, cottiers (who received or hired a few potato acres in return for labour or for enormous rents paid to the farmers), permanent farm labourers, migratory labourers, and beggars.

Growing numbers of competitors and rising opportunities to market produce and thus pay higher rents were apparently enabling more forceful countrymen to persuade landlords to lease directly to themselves, while simultaneously multiplying the shoals of the landless. The hierarchy of snobberies that fragmented the Irish countryside in later years perhaps already divided the people along the line of these groups, although it did not fully coincide with it: men of good family (and the rural memory was very long) were still respected although poor. Contrarywise, however, well-being overcame every stigma, even that of illegitimacy . . . excepting that of being an outsider! High rents, county taxes, payments (tithes) to the alien state church, fines, and extra-legal 'considerations' to men of power forced the mass of countryfolk into reserving rising monetary incomes to meet these demands, and towards finding food and clothing outside the realm of money: growing potatoes, making clothing. Any surplus ready money was invested in pigs or cattle, as investment against higher rent demands, or in renting small acreages for wheat or oats cultivation. By the 1780s, some money was being ploughed into bettering living standards. The remarkable spread of domestic textile production across much of the country (not merely in Ulster as once thought), helped these latter processes, but to less extent than they should: for it was widely recognised that the cost of rent kept pace with the rise of textile income 'to the summit'. And population, increasing one half million per decade from 1760–1800, constantly subverted such gains also.

What can be safely asserted, I feel, is that politico-economic consciousness was rising, whatever the standard of living. The traditions of past tribal subsistence were fading. Livelihood was increasingly perceived by the people as a whole as a central issue, with rents, livestock, markets, and political structures seen as an inter-connected whole. Of course they did not understand these things in economic terms as did only a small minority of townsmen; theirs was a highly *political* economy, but Ireland was a hyper-politicised society, and even the educated, argued visitors like Young, Twiss and LaTocnaye, shared the same bias of mind. Young felt that a majority in the Irish House of Commons could not understand the basic economics of an issue like crop bounties. It is certainly instructive that the great movements of peasant violence: Whiteboy, Steelboy and Oakboy ventures in systematic subversion of the rural establishment in Munster and Ulster, were ultimately related to issues of enclosures, evictions, rent increases, and tax and tithe demands. Ultimately, too, it is hardly coincidence that the two most bitterly fought and well organised uprisings during the 1798 Rebellion were in Wexford and North Down, precisely the regions which in Arthur Young's view stood out from the generally atrocious levels of farming, housing, and nutrition in South-East Ireland and over most of Ulster. That the spirit of economic improvement among the common people found such a nemesis where it was most pronounced perhaps shows that in the circumstances of ascendancy and manorialism, economy was inevitably political.

Was the experience of Irishmen, as we have implied, a common one? Outside of their responses to the common conditions imposed on them by the ascendancy, the answer must be largely No! Hector St. John Crèvecoeur, the French consul who would later help Irishmen establish the first Catholic parish in New York, noted in 1782: "The Irish themselves, from different parts of the kingdom are very different. It is difficult to account for this surprising localization. One would think, on so small an island, an Irishman would be an Irishman; yet it is not so: . . ." Regionalism played as large, or larger, a part, in Irish life, as it did in the Thirteen Colonies, then each so distinct. But the Thirteen Colonies were essentially mono-lingual and mono-cultural, everywhere adhering to variant Americanizations of English language, law and custom. This was not so in Ireland.

Richard Twiss noted in 1775 that while the peasants were fluent in English, Irish was nonetheless generally used, except among the better sort. And Irish language and traditions were the bulwark of localism. The more prosperous dairying areas of Munster, the better-off herding areas of east Connacht spoke Irish generally as did the poorer areas of those provinces. English was the language of the towns, and the predominant language with those areas in Leinster within easy access from Dublin (six hours ride, or a 50 to 60 mile radius). A great crescent of traditional society, stretching from Donegal and the Tyrone mountains through Fermanagh, Cavan, Monaghan, north and west Meath, south Armagh, south Down, and north Louth, thirty to forty miles wide, separated the English-speaking plantation settlements of north east Ulster from the Anglo-Irish heartland in east Leinster. This factor has never been sufficiently emphasised by historians. The south and west Ulster culture belt was profoundly traditional: remnants of Brehon law in relation to fosterage, grazing, and marriage were still fitfully applied. Truly archaic native farming practices were still followed. Poets like Art MacCooey, Peadar Ó Doirnín and James Woods enlivened its mind. The old women of the area spoke of its inhabitants as the Irish, to them everyone else in Ulster was Scots; and the Irish and Scots fairies fought regularly every year to control the magical realms of Ulster.

Essentially, Catholic and traditional society was fragmented, with Gaelic preponderant yet waning in three separate blocs: Connacht, Munster and south and west Ulster. The land of the settler stocks was also divided. Belfast was twelve hours and more away from Dublin. It lay across territory recently 'an absolute uncivilised country', its people still seeming 'much on a rank with the American savages' excepting their Catholicism, as Edward Willes put it with English misunderstanding (though LaTocnaye said the same in 1797). This helped to ensure that the peculiarities of culture and temperament which prevailed in the English-speaking parts of Ulster, originating in settlement by Scots Presbyterians, were still preserved. In native society, localism was even more intense, so that girls were reluctant to marry outside their localities. This spirit was intensified by the differing experiences of changing patterns of livelihood: a south Down shoemaker was mortified that a girl rejected his suit as that of a poor man and an outsider, and replied (as the Gaelic poet had it):

> Louth girl of a tribe of brutes
> Who do not understand playfulness nor live in a valley,
> You keep your doors shut to emphasize refusal,
> Unlike the fort which I live in.

How can we sum up this strange society, or multi-society, that was later 18th century Ireland? On the one hand, quays were crowded with exporting vessels; the towns full of planning and building; the gentry and middle-class were re-housing themselves in gracefully-doored urban terraces and fine country houses (to replace the ramshackle and underfurnished piles of before 1760); private banking, brewing, distilling, glass-making, and a host of crafts flourished; the farm produce or provision trade booming, and the linen and woollen trades increasing; the English language spreading yet the native traditions still vital, both cultures receptive to outside influences: for example, Gaelic poets like Brian Merriman and Seán Ó Coileáin to the innovations of Robert Burns and Thomas Gray; the gentry had relaxed the anti-Catholic laws; there was a shift toward a more humane view of the poor, the criminal, the mentally ill and the sick, among sections of the ascendancy. On the other hand, there was poverty and degradation which need not be again detailed, but which found expression in a literary savagery which can only have been the tip of the iceberg of the violent outbursts in the night meetings of the Whiteboys: "I would tie you up with a hempen rope and I would drive my spear into your paunch" or "I forgive all the plunderings that Death has ever done, since he has laid low David, that clod, the devilish old bum-baliff".

The ironies were epitomised in Dublin. Arthur Young in June 1776 admired its recent beautiful buildings, marks of the new prosperity and of the rising pride of the 'Protestant nation': Leinster House, the National Parliament, Trinity College, the Rotunda, its clubs and assembly rooms; he listened to the eloquence of its political leaders in its House of Commons; he enjoyed its good society. Yet he could not wait to get away: "walking in the streets there, from the narrowness and populousness of the principal thoroughfares, as well as from the dirt and wretchedness of the *canaille*, is a most uneasy and disgusting exercise." Perhaps we today can understand it best if we do not think at all in terms of Ireland; for our minds continuously debate the rival images of poverty/oppression versus wellbeing/justice for the society as a whole. Nor, in fact, should we think of it in modern Western terms at all. Instead, its contradictions are illumined by the experience of countries like Peru and Ecuador from the 1890s-1930s. Prosperity based upon inadequate foundations, controlled by smallish urban and landowner cliques of cosmopolitan culture, makes possible the rapid introduction of the public monuments, the transport systems, the higher education, of the outside world. But the mass of the people find that their very engagement in the spiral of development, as miners, cultivators and labourers, is offset by the skewered nature of socio-political reality: they remain poor. Aristocratic 'liberals' play at the sophisticated discipline of representative government, but the cost of their tastes cancels the benefit to all which should accrue from the combination of growing national wealth and rational government. With a civilised Lockean ethos among themselves, such elites apply a vicious Hobbesian one to the mass of the poor pressing in on their world. For cocoa, and coffee, or guano we may read beef, butter and linen; for Guayaquil or Lima, Cork or Dublin; for the 70% and more Indian and mestizo, native Irish; for the white Hispanic elite of landowners and their *latifundia*, the Anglo-Irish lords and gentry and their estates; for Spanish language and law, English, for Quechua and Indian tradition and fading memories of an Inca past, Gaelic, Irish tradition, and confused memories of Gaelic lordships. Of course such outlandish analogies cannot be carried too far; but it is better that we think in such exotic terms to understand 18th century Ireland, than that we read back in any way resonances derived from the experience of 20th century Ireland. These analogies do bring home how an unjust elite prosperity could co-exist with general and servile poverty, in a country in which lord and countryman inhabited different worlds, alien ways.

One final contradiction can be understood another way. The unquestionable gaiety, keenness and vitality noted of so many of the poor coincided with all the marks of misery. The difference was surely one between generations. A young and growing population danced and sang, and like the young Carleton was full of hope. Early marriage and young children averted early cycnicism, despite the horror of confining poverty. As multiple children turned to burden, as the struggle intensified to hold a lease on some land, or to keep any income above rent costs, a colder view set in. This is not conjecture. Looking back in 1847 upon the Irish commoner before he had been affected by Daniel O'Connell, one of them, now American, wrote:

> He was a suspicious, shrinking man: . . . He seemed to be thinking, and contriving, constantly, without any apparent motive. You felt you could not open your heart to him;

for he never did to you; if in low rank, he plied you with transparent flattery; if he was of middle life, he was breaking off the conversation mysteriously. And old men, his contemporaries, who have gained his confidence, and reached the bottom of that deep, dark, narrow heart, have declared that they could find in it no human faith, or hope . . . let him be as honest as he might, yet in political enterprises they dare not trust him; sheer despair had laid him open to corruption.

Edmund Burke had characterised him similarly in a letter to Fox in 1776. His determination in middle age, to secure for his droves of children skill and literacy in English, mathematics, book-keeping, and even the dancing skills and deportment of a gentleman, through the instrument of a multitude of ill-equipped, popular and often costly schoolmasters, must be seen too against this. Not the love of intricacy and learning so much as a desperate effort to give the young the chance of a better life than he himself enjoyed, was at the bottom of it.

Recent accounts detail the process whereby a small farmer class gradually entrenched itself on the land, forcing the landlords into a form of dependence upon them in the absence of other capital than rent, and forcing thousands of their fellows into landlessness in the absence of adequate acres for all. These accounts could be misread. It is questionable whether there was a rational strategic advance. Instead the adjustment of some to securer patterns of tenancy and market production may have been a more reluctant, bewildered and driven process than behavioural narratives suggest, patterning as they do myriad acreage and tenancy transfers into vast coherent changes. These changes proceeded from manifold attempts to avoid or lessen impoverishment, and were probably hedged with misgiving, bargained from weakness, and blind to wider implications. The patterns were closely affected by past regional traditions, as in Ulster and the Old English areas of Leinster. They were countered by widespread attempts to prop up the position of the poor by those who were almost poor. There is little evidence, before the 1820s, that countrymen accepted that their cooperation with market forces helped act as a solvent of rural community, much to suggest they believed the contrary.

This picture of the calculating Irishmen, pursuing livelihood through every thicket of difficulty, in fact of constant defeat, is found in between the lines of Gaelic poetry (as Louis Cullen has shown); it is found in Edmund Burke's most realistic work: the letters he wrote to and for the vast clan of his Irish Catholic relatives, Nagles, O'Donovans, and Nugents; it is found above all in the estimate which his priests made of the temptations besetting his soul. In the Irish proverb, the man without a stratagem was no better than a pig; priests were concerned lest the Hobbesian world he inhabited forced him into stratagems of violence and injustice. It was a pastoral realism, not Jansenism, which caused Archbishop James Butler of Cashel, often troubled by Whiteboy outrages, to pen that summary of the Tridentine decree upon sin, which echoed in the Maynooth and Baltimore catechisms for the next 180 years: that original sin darkened the understanding, weakened the will, and induced in the soul a strong inclination to evil. In 18th century Ireland, perhaps inevitably so!

The very earliest school geographies, readers and histories in independent America spoke of Ireland as another world: a world of poverty, of foreign conquest and oppression, of superstition and debasement. From 1800–1840s, the lesson did not vary. This, itself, points to the singularity of American expectations. It is with relief that one turns to the world of their origins, the America of the 18th century.

Two things would have at once impressed anyone from Ireland arriving in the Colonies. On one hand, there was no general impoverishment nor servility among the white population. On the other hand, outside of Philadelphia, New York and a few rural estates, there was none of the sophistication of building, dress, horse-team, and manner which cross-lit the fore-stage of Irish life so anomalously. An Irishman's reaction to America would therefore very much depend upon whether he was one of the privileged or even of better merchant stock (such men would tend to see the colonies as rude and uncouth, however promising); or upon whether he was of the common sort (for him, the self-reliant manners and freedom from pressing want of his American counterpart would have seemed almost miraculous). Benjamin Franklin emphasised this truth in pamphlets, one published in Dublin in 1784, the other in London in 1786:

> Whoever has travelled thro' the various parts of Europe, and observed how small is the Proportion of People in Affluence or easy circumstances there, compar'd with those in Poverty and Misery; the few rich and haughty Landlords, the multitude of poor, abject, and rack'd Tenants, and the half-paid and half-starv'd Labourers; and view here the hap‚ ‚ Mediocrity, that so generally prevails throughout these States, where the Cultivator works for himself, and supports his family in decent Plenty, will, methinks, see abundant Reason to bless Divine Providence.

Perhaps Franklin had in mind particularly Ireland, among those 'parts of Europe' which so unfavourably compared with the 'happy Mediocrity' of his own Pennsylvania: certainly this could be a capsule version of his known reactions to it, following his visit to Ireland in 1771. For as he had then written: "The chief exports of Ireland seem to be pinched off the backs and out of the bellies of the miserable inhabitants." Contrariwise, in the Colonies, "The great Business of the Continent is Agriculture" and the involvement of the mass of the people in this wholesome and progressive pursuit as their own masters, banished vice by outlawing idleness, promoted virtue by energising all men in healthy self-interest and family service, prevented the emergence of a caste of exploiters bent upon luxury and oligarchy, and was the basis of a republican culture of simplicity and mutual respect among a growing population.

As a contemporary of such Europeans as Justus Moser, Otto Litken, and Anders Chydenius, Franklin was well aware of the geographic base of America's good fortune, as of Europe's misfortune: in Europe population was outstripping the means of agricultural subsistence, allowing the rich to prey greedily upon the desperate; in America, as Franklin argued in his *Observations Concerning the Increase of Mankind* (1755), numbers would safely double every twenty-five years given the Colonies' vast extent of unsettled but potential farmland. Nor was Franklin wrong. The Colonies had around 10 people per square mile in their settled areas in the 1770s, fewer than three people per square mile in terms of the territories ceded by Britain in 1783. In contrast, Ireland had a population of around 140 people per square mile in this same year, rising to as many as 350 per square mile in certain densely packed rural districts (South Armagh, Cavan, for example). For an Irishman, the Colonies must have seemed an insupportably lonely place, as one poet said.

There can be no doubting Franklin's estimate of the result of this contrast. Land cost as much in Ireland to rent one acre for only one year, as it did to buy an acre of cultivable but unfarmed land in America, for good. Annual rents per acre varied from 10 to 23 shillings in the Coleraine district of Ulster, rising to 31 shillings around Dublin in 1776. In Coleraine and Dublin districts in frontier Bedford county, Pennsylvania, in 1783, despite land speculation, land *cost* between 2 and 10 shillings per acre *for permanent possession*. Improved land, however, or land already farmed, which was more comparable to the Irish acres, cost anywhere from 20 to 200 shillings per acre throughout the settled States in the 1770s, depending upon the accessibility of markets by track or river. On the other hand, it was all but impossible for farmers to *buy* land in Ireland: even as late as 1843 Daniel O'Connell's nationalist Repealers themselves moved swiftly to crush William Conner's agrarian populism, in the name of landlord rights!

Relative social equality and popular well-being were not the only consequences of cheap land and the absence of landlords. The entire social pyramid was radically altered. Outside the Southern plantation areas, 40%–70% of all mature American men were farmers, mostly owner occupiers; 15%–30% were labourers and servants; 10% were artisans; 10% were merchants, physicians and the like. The *small* farmer in America owned from 40 to 200 acres of land (in Ireland, he held under 20 acres); the medium farmer, from 200 to 500 acres in the Colonies (in Ireland, from 20 to 60 acres); the large farmer, from 500 acres to several thousand (in Ireland, from 60 acres upwards). The 'wealthy' Irish grazier or stock-raiser with 250 acres was the social equivalent of the 2,000 acre stockman of the Carolinas Piedmont, or the 1,000 acre tobacco planter of the Chesapeake Bay area.

Moreover, obviously, everything the American farmer made in profit after the expense and effort of either improving his cheap land, or paying off a settled farm, was his own. Even if he farmed for his household, rather than for market, he could expect to attain middle life with around 100 acres, a frame house, serviceable clothes and good clothes, a decent set of tools, implements and firearms, a good horse, perhaps a draught ox or oxen team, some cattle and pigs, a labouring son, an indentured servant (or in the south, a slave 'hand' or two), and a certain real social position. Those who farmed for market, along the river valleys in the North, in large and small Southern coastal plantations, usually lived considerably better. Linen and woollen manufacture, furniture carpentry and other handcrafts, brewing, tobacco curing, clothes making, and other tasks, could be carried out on most medium and large farms, from products of that farm. Costs of necessities, except in terms of long hours of labour, were thus held low; in Ireland in the 1770s, their high purchase price was generally a matter for despair, excepting only yarn and cloth in areas of domestic spinning and weaving. Timber for fuel, building, and handcrafts was freely available on almost everyone's land in America. In Ireland, the almost complete absence of trees (which forcibly struck Englishmen), meant that furniture was rudimentary (two stools, a table), and that heating was very expensive outside of the peat-bog areas. The mass of Americans were 80 to 300 acre farmers. The mass of Irishmen were labourers, cottiers with under 5 acres, and small farmers with under 15 acres: men who could not really save, for whom all gains were precarious, for whom any social position was that granted in evening gatherings by the 'boys'.

Labourers, seamen and schoolteachers in America (the three most poorly paid callings), were usually young men bent upon a stratagem of saving, acquiring skills, and then purchasing a farm: and so of acquiring 'an easy and honest competency.' Seven out of every ten landless workers in Lunenburg county, Virginia, did do so in their lifetime: an area typical of the newer regions settled by most Irish immigrants, as by migrants from more settled districts, where there was less land available for such a transition. Moreover, labourers were not as such a caste set apart, despised and exploited by farmers of all grades (as was the case increasingly in Ireland); only the unmarried, shiftless, drifting older labourer, content never to follow the accepted scheme, but instead reliant upon whisky, hunting and fellowship for his comfort, was distanced socially and permanently.

In long-settled areas, the social pyramid was hardening; there were families of established wealth and position; styles of life, standards of living, taste in housing, clothing and the accoutrements of horsemanship were more closely modelled on those of England's middle class and gentry, as these were shown to them by governing British officials, by merchants and sea captains and by their hosts and hoteliers of their own journeys to Britain. Such men would have found it easy to relate to the more businesslike of the Anglo-Irish gentry, and to Irish merchants, sharing with them a similar outlook, culture and behaviour. Only the latter's contempt for inferiors would have amazed them. While devout believers in the division between 'the better sort' and "the common people", the elite in America had travelled less far from its unpretentious middle-class English 17th century antecedents, than had their Anglo-Irish counterparts, and was also inclined to respect the custom of a country in which even the simplest men were elevated to a certain dignity, if partly because of their scarcity value!

Only in New York's Hudson Valley, in sections of the Chesapeake Bay and Virginia Tidewater country, in the plantation coast of South Carolina, and in the chief towns (Boston, New York, Philadelphia, Williamsburg, Alexandria, Baltimore, Charleston) was such social differentiation far advanced, however. Even in those areas, a majority of the white population died leaving some property, as they had lived in some comfort. To Franklin, the American city threatened the bucolic mediocrity that was America with the spectre of over-population, resultant dependence upon factories, and shaper social cleavage, but it was vindicated by its being a microcosm of American virtue, as well as by being a source of stimulus, sophistication and diversity. Modern study corroborates his views: the American city had a leisured and almost aristocratic elite (as had the plantation country), but the essential fabric of city life (as also of much plantation country), was that of energetic, enterprising middle-class folk, often self-made men, of distinctly middle-brow outlook and limitations.

On the other hand, there was little of the drastic and general destitution that disfigured the life of many Irish cities (except those towns, such as Coleraine, Bandon, or Castlebellingham, which took care to run out the vagabond poor so that the problem never developed). Only an entire lack of international perspective can cause a young American historian to comment lately: "By the eve of the Revolution, poverty had blighted the lives of a large part of the population." By his own figures and tables, he shows by this he means that the two in a hundred Philadelphian householders who paid no tax, and left no property in the 1720s, had risen to ten in a hundred by the 1760s-70s! And even the bulk of these (unlike their Dublin counterparts), were employed, if fitfully, had access to reasonably cheap food, and were the object of real public concern. In Ireland, only the then-small Presbyterian Belfast, with its Charitable Society founded in 1752, could match such concern: elsewhere, as LaTocnaye wrote bitterly of Cork, the better-off hardened their hearts by scoffing at the peculiarities of the poor. In Dublin, perhaps as many as sixty-five per hundred were poor in a sense stronger than that of Philadelphia: a people dressed in rags and fed on gruel, potatoes and (if lucky) the odd rabbit.

A people, however, is more than its structures of subsistence. The very success of revolution in comparatively comfortable, and progressive, America, and its failure in Ireland, where the causes for discontent were so very much more general, suggests no easy connections between livelihood and politics in either case. The life of the mind of communities prompts their politics, and shapes the landscape in which their interests are seen, in which possibilities stand clear. Here we come upon one of the great unknowns of the relations between Ireland and the Colonies: the relative degree and character of the mental life of each. We have indicated something of the controversy as to the animation of mind of both countryfolk and gentry in Ireland. Debate about that of the colonies is no less intense.

It is possible to gather together, distil, and exhibit 'the marrow of puritan divinity' as it was presented in the pulpits of Congregational New England, Anglican Virginia and Presbyterian New Jersey, and create the impression of a strange and intense world of practical dogma, of theories of the church with political repercussions, of transformations of the soul with individualist overtones, of holy convenants which made human society more organic and responsible. It is possible to abstract the comments of a multitude of colonial 'Gazettes' (Maryland's, Virginia's, Pennsylvania's) and of manuals of 'husbandry', law, and medicine, and schematise a vigorous and progressive world in which the aphorisms of the French Enlightenment and of Scottish Common Sense found in America a novel, strenuous, and cumulative application to every field of earthy human endeavour, linked by a common language of human preoccupation in the task of subduing a wilderness. Perry Miller and Merle Curti have done so in each case, each followed by a host of offshoots and disciples. Yet there remains a strong doubt. Just as the brothers Grimm could reconstruct the dying and tattered fragments of the story-traditions of exhausted and hungry peasants, into a closed and vibrant scenario, so too such concentrated abstraction creates an unreal picture.

J.P. Brissot de Warville, the Marquis de Chastellux, J.D. Smyth, Roger Lamb and Charles Stedman, the authors of five key works published upon revolutionary America in Dublin from 1784 to 1811, create a very different composite picture of the mental life of America at that time. Though they comprise two French allies of the Revolution, and three pro-imperial enemies of it, their pictures largely agree, and correspond in turn with the essential picture presented by Franklin, and by David Ramsay, even with that painted by implication in Gilbert Imlay's panegyric to the Kentucky territory, the three fullest pro-American works published in the same years, in Dublin. Only Crèvecoeur's *Letters from an American Farmer* (Belfast, 1783), paints a different picture: "The American is a new man, who acts upon new principles; he must therefore entertain new ideas and form new opinions" or again, "Americans are the western pilgrims who are carrying with them that great mass of arts, sciences, vigor and industry which began long since in the east." But Crèvecoeur agreed that the chief population of the British Americas was in the middle colonies; and here his estimate of their people's character came close to that of native Pennsylvanians Franklin and Charles Stedman. Franklin's 'happy mediocrity' was filled out by Stedman: Pennsylvanians were "farmers robust, frugal, persevering, and industrious: but of rude and unpliant manners, with little penetration and less knowledge." To Crèvecoeur, "Industry, good living, selfishness, litigiousness, country politics, the pride of freemen, religious indifference, are their characteristics." To Smyth, a somewhat Americanized British officer, the inhabitants of the same region (specifically western Maryland and Lancaster county, in Pennsylvania) though their industry had transformed the region, were dull and narrow: "they have no idea of social life, and are more like brutes than men."

Almost all 18th century intelligensia (of every nationality), were Lockeans in their psychology and in their theories of society: the environment, natural and contrived, made men what they were. For Arthur Young in Ireland, the improving landlord or farmer could not but transform the very mentality of the peasants around him (*Tour,* 1:462): "In a wild or but half-cultivated tract, with no better edifice than a mud cabin, what are the objects that can impress a love of order on the mind of man? He must be wild as the roaming herds, savage as his rocky mountains; confusion, disorder, riot, have nothing better than himself to damage or destroy: . . . but when great sums are expended and numbers employed . . . it is impossible but new ideas must arise, even in the uncultivated mind." Similar ideas shaped the above authors' responses to the American cultivator. The sublimity of his natural environment, which ennobled him (as Imlay argued most forcibly), was offset by loneliness, ceaseless toil, and the general absence of leisured and cultivated society: this constricted him. Even Imlay wrote his *Description of the Western Territory* to try to persuade London gentlemen to settle in it, that the spirit of emulation might transform the natural nobility of its inhabitants into real sophistication! Even so, Roger Lamb specifically repudiated Imlay by name as a romanticist of rural America. And even Crèvecoeur joined Smyth, Stedman, de Warville and de Chastellux in agreeing that among the inhabitants of frontier regions 'remote from the power of example and the check of shame, many families exhibit the most hideous parts of our society.'

Even more than Ireland, however, America was regionally sub-divided. The New England region was one of poor small farms, of still vigorously Puritan commitments, with a third of its people engaged in trade, shipping, fishing and lumbering, with the mind of its people alert, enterprising, narrow, illiberal, and penetrating. The central colonies, with their sophisticated cities and towns, was a region of dull and egalitarian farmers producing great wheat, flour, linen-seed, and beef surpluses. The coastal south had vigorous and educated plantations alternating with areas gone to seed through luxury, indolence, soil exhaustion, and over-reliance upon slaves. In the interior, from south to north, conditions were more uniform, with frontier isolation giving way, to lesser or greater extent, to more settled, ordered and yet relatively self-sufficient communities. These divisions were so described in the sources published in Ireland, chiefly in the 1790s; nor has modern scholarship essentially altered these characterisations.

In short, the Colonies were unfinished, rudimentary, laborious places for the most part. Over large areas, loneliness, and the absence of a dense social life, had not dissimilar effects of mental depression which poverty induced in Ireland. Only in New England and the towns did more ordered and concentrated settlements produce among common people a lively mental life as intense as that pursued by Irish countryfolk. It was a Pennsylvanian domiciled in Charleston, David Ramsay, who correctly admitted that Masssachussets and Virginia . . . with traders and the planters so untypical of the nation as a whole . . . were the prime movers in the revolution that created a nation. But, as we shall see, the same Ramsay (whose *History of the American Revolution* was also published in Dublin, in 1793), would argue that the Revolution was revolutionary, that it was the central event that galvanised a nation of prosaic rural localities into one of unprecedented mental activity among simple folk.

Moreover, such popular mental life, however "selfish" and "narrow" (in Stedman's terms), was quite unlike that of Ireland. It was almost obsessively purposive and practical, the realm of prayer apart. Rural "tall stories" were no counterpart to the Irish folk's vast canvases of hero-tale and magic-tales, folk-custom and verse creation, ritual and dance that interpenetrated with ideas and conversations on livelihood, politics, landlords and crops in ways which subtly altered both as time progressed. Colonial Americans "as an independent people, with half a continent to civilise, . . . could not afford to waste time in following European examples, but must devise new processes of their own" argued Henry Adams in 1889, a theme so brilliantly detailed by Daniel Boorstin seventy years later. To Adams, such a severe realism constrained the American mind, where to Boorstin it released it from European dogma. Whatever the case, supposedly Americans were happy in that they could obey almost literally Freud's so-called Reality Principle, bringing their imagination into close conformity with the demands of their existence: Benjamin Franklin was the key exemplar of this tendency.

As for Ireland, even the boldest and highest forms of its intellectual life seem to partake of that strange dualism we noted of its common people's habits of thought. This enabled its genius to cast question marks over the iron box of Enlightenment environmentalism which had so possessed the higher mind in America . . that of the circle of Thomas Jefferson: Rittenhouse, Rush, Priestly, Peale and Paine. For in Ireland, Jonathan Swift postulated that all social custom was arbitrary; Edmund Burke that politics and social classes were a matter of organic vision; and George Berkeley, that reality itself was precariously dependent upon the ideal process of God's mind. It was heady almost modern stuff, and a far cry from the naive and progressive functionalism of Jefferson's circle, confident that God had long since left a completed America to the genius of man. The Irish ideas could scarcely beget confidence in revolution, the American could scarcely beget anything else.

Chapter 2

Ireland and America in Connection: Empire, Merchants and Sailors, 1730–1776

The more immediate connections between Ireland and the American colonies in the eighteenth century were human and prosaic: the goings and comings of merchants and ships' masters, of emigrants and servants, of officials and soldiers. This human traffic was regular, constant and increasing, although it lacked the density and frequency of later Irish American links. Nonetheless by the 1770s around one in ten ships leaving the major American ports was bound for Ireland; and perhaps as many as one in five white Americans, certainly at least one in six, was of Irish origin south of New England. Such facts reflected more than the geography of Atlantic sea-routes and the chance-taking of businessmen or the accidents of adventuring ambition which those routes suggested. They reflected the growth of the British Empire, by circumstances and design, through the years since 1660. The Empire was the great yet vague formal connection, binding colonies and Ireland under the common final authority of the English kings. It expressed, furthered, and sometimes limited the more natural and immediate flow of people and goods between Ireland and America. England and Ireland, the lucrative 'plantations' (as colonies were still called) of the sugar-rich British West Indies and the sparse-peopled North American coastline were all interwoven in the fitful calculations of English statesmen and networked by the rigging and spars of the empires' merchant ships. After a general glance at this imperial context (so important also to understanding the contrasting political struggles of Irish and Americans against Britain after 1760), we shall look in turn at the activities of a handful of representative Anglo-Irish imperial officials in America, at the activities of merchants involved in Irish-American trade, and in the next chapter at the experience of the emigrants from Ireland, drawn from its then distinct peoples, whose lives in America went beyond the links of empire to furnish one of the sources of a new, non-imperial, American nationality.

From the Restoration of England's Charles II in 1660, English leaders were preoccupied with the problems of good government, public order and measured political freedoms in a more systematic fashion than had been customary before the frightening experience of Civil War against the background of a disordered Europe in the preceding twenty years. In a surprisingly modern way, some among them realised that the problems were broader than those of the relations of crown and parliament, court and gentry, merchants and customsmen. Thomas Povey, John Locke and Lord Shaftsbury, a merchant, scholar and top politician respectively, pressed schemes of national greatness upon the King's councils and informed opinion. These linked the regulation and expansion of foreign trade, the encouragement of manufactures, the employment of the poor, the development of British shipping and the exploitation and extension of Britain's overseas territories. Domestic peace, improved international security and growing prosperity would result. The military and naval costs of international position would be less burdensome and provocative with increased national wealth: they had been a key element in setting Crown and gentry at odds in the past. Virginia and Barbados, Ireland and Massachusetts, Jamaica and Maryland, were all considered subordinate props, and naturally so, aiding the all-important goal of England's happiness, to benefit from it where they might, but to contribute to it wherever practicable. New possessions or colonies, in India, Africa and the Americas . . . notably New York (1664), the Carolinas (1663), Pennsylvania (1682) and Georgia (1732) . . . were settled and established in the same context.

England, then, was the centre. Elsewhere was the periphery. To us today the scheme sounds ominously repressive: the very concept of 'imperial' has an unhealthy ring to it. Yet it did not seem so at first. The general idea implied the development of the colonies; and so that enterprising individuals might be drawn to them, there must be a certain liberality in their treatment. The American (and Caribbean) colonies were early given representative government: appointed royal governors and their councils were to govern in tandem with local assemblies modelled in structure upon the English parliament, with both upper and lower houses. Their tasks were supposedly quite restricted, yet they grew. In Ireland, the Anglo-Irish gentry were not deprived of their Parliament of Lords and Commons, even though the situation of that parliament had changed so drastically since the early seventeenth century, when it had been partially representative of all the peoples in the country. Economically, the most appropriate productive trades of the periphery were encouraged rather than discouraged: indeed this was central to the whole design. Finally, the political class in Ireland and the majority of the colonial populations were 'Englishmen' as they themselves boasted. Subordination to the sovereignty of the Crown of England was something not lightly disowned by them, however they might contest its precise jurisdiction. The hidden and emotional bond of empire was Englishness; only as it declined, could the repressive possibilities of the system be scrutinised without sentiment. As long as men in Jamestown or in Cork thought themselves essentially English, the imperial connection was more than the sum of its parts.

The formal imperial scheme of the 1660s, however, was not pressed with the decision and resolution normal to public policy today. Implementation was partial. There was no large bureaucracy charged to continuously guide, study and revise its application to changing circumstances. The central elements were codified in a series of policy decisions on colonies, and parliamentary measures on trade (the Navigation Laws), largely completed by 1720. Thereafter the colonial and navigation 'system' and the vague and generalised English mercantilism it expressed became part of the scenario of the very unhectic eighteenth century. Possessions were added desultorily before 1756, few of any real size. There was a tendency to simplify all colonial governments under a common 'royal' form of governor/council/assembly, whereas previously many had been the semi-private baliwicks of great companies and 'proprietors'. Legislation amended the Navigation Laws occasionally, sometimes tightening and sometimes loosening their applications, even as similar extra constraints or new privileges were granted by London to Irish traders. The colonies themselves developed steadily yet leisurely. Yet the system had its reality. Merchants, officials, colonial planters' factors and agents, members of Parliament, landed gentry with overseas interests or relatives in the colonies, ships' owners and bankers, exercised a fitful supervision over the empire through interlocking membership in Parliament, the Board of Trade and Plantations, the exchanges and clubs of London and Bristol, and generally through membership of England's still accessibly intimate ruling circles.

The unity they imposed was not due to any continuing fidelity to the plans of John Locke or Benjamin Worsley. Rather their patterns of behaviour assumed and thus embodied a crude imperial mercantilism. Their continuing business caused them to use their political influence, manipulate their overseas connections, puff up the supposed imperial value of their American interests, or protect their home markets in ways which gave content to the 'system' and exploited their influence upon the Crown, its central symbol. Indeed from its very beginnings the system had been shaped, despite its inspiration, by the special concerns of men who had more influence than they had vision: even contemporaries around 1700 lamented the self-interested inconsistencies of English 'mercantilism' almost to the extent that historians have charted them! Merchant polemicists for strong imperial control of the 'plantations' often had direct interests in both Irish and American trade, as had John Cary of Bristol or Samuel Clement of London.

Apart from this, however, the broad impact of the geography of the North Atlantic basin itself, and of England's possessions within it, together with the stable provisions of the original Navigation Acts, set the limits within which the merchants pursued their ventures and the theoreticians of Britain's greatness outlined their hopes. As a result, the vigorous self-pursuits of the former wove the fabric of the latter's dreams. And the stuffs of that fabric were the great 'staples' of the North Atlantic trade, the key resources of the new empire, and the basis of the colonial economic development we have mentioned. These included codfish, furs, timber and naval stores, grain, flax-seed, tobacco, rice, indigo (a dye-stuff), cotton, sugar and logwoods (to list them in order of their production from the Newfoundland banks south along the American seaboard to the Caribbean). Without these 'staples' the leisurely pace of the trans-Atlantic connection would have been becalmed altogether. As it was, the considerable activity it took to produce these goods, and to transport them and turn them to profit by trade unquestionably quickened the very mentality of those so engaged, and determined that the English-speaking world emerge as pacesetter of modern business practice.

Ireland and the Colonies under English Sovereignty, 1660–1760

Without the staple trades, the colonies might all but have completely disappeared from the day-to-day considerations of English government figures. Their chief concerns, as the memory of Civil War receded and the trans-Atlantic Anglo-Dutch wars for trade and wealth were succeeded by a long series of continental wars with France, were again almost wholly European and traditionally political after 1690. The visions of Locke and Shaftesbury were useful adjuncts, and little more, to the framework of policy-making. But for the trade factor, North America, remote and largely unknown, was seen only as another arena for armed Anglo-French rivalry, an outrider to the predominant political passions of Englishmen, domestic where they were not European. Ireland, on the other hand, was seen foremost as a key element in England's European security. Its role in the trans-Atlantic connection London perceived as unimportant, even though, as we shall see, Ireland's trans-Atlantic connections were restricted even within the Navigation and colonial systems. In fact, one of the persuasive arguments of Anglo-Irish patriots was to be that whereas they dutifully co-operated with the central goals of British policy with regard to Ireland . . . to keep it firm in England's interests in the European rivalries . . . yet they were debarred from full participation in the benefits of the trans-Atlantic system, despite the relative unimportance of Irish-colonial connections to English statesmen. But it is these trans-Atlantic connections which form the main body of this chapter. The irony of the subject lies in this fact, that Ireland and North America were important to English statesmen in separate connections as a rule. Thus, for example, there is no large body of official British papers linking London's colonial and Irish policies. Ireland and North America, if linked in trade, common empire and the flow of emigrants, were thus linked by the back-doors of private connection and incidental acquaintance rather than through the front-door of explicit and continuous public policy in London. In a real sense, many Irishmen and Americans were of necessity more conscious of empire than were most Englishmen.

There are those who would put the story of these imperial connections further back than we intend here, centring them in the late 16th and early 17th century, rather than in the 18th century. Some argue that Britain's subordination of Ireland from Tudor times shaped her approach to the colonial plantations which she settled almost concurrently with her 'plantation' in Ireland of large numbers of Protestant settlers. From Walter Raleigh down to

William Penn, over a period of almost one hundred years, key personnel active in the plantation of Ireland were also active in the settlement of the American colonies. Certain forms of plantation, by huge land grants to proprietors, or to chartered companies, expected to populate and develop them in return, were also common to both areas. Initially, also, certain land-use patterns of incoming English settlers were also similar. Nonetheless the differences were crucial: Ireland was being garrisoned for security, America developed for profit, even if the profit motive was not absent in Ireland, nor the political one absent in the colonies. There was no counterpart in Ireland of the settlement of New England by autonomous religious zealots; nor any counterpart in America of the granting of much of Ireland in estates to Cromwellian soldiers and adventurers. The settlement of Ireland assumed a defeated, docile and white population which would remain the body of the country's workforce. By contrast, only when climate and craft pride among the lower folk they had brought with them thwarted the labour expectations of the early masters of Virginia and the Carolinas, did they turn to alternative, forced sources of labour supply: slaves and indentured servants. Elsewhere, from Pennsylvania to Maine, even initially in Barbados and Georgia, it was assumed that the colonies would be developed by white labour, stimulated by the offers of land as a stake in the wealth they were creating, whereas only in east Ulster did such a pattern prevail in the plantation of Ireland. Precisely because economic development of a harsh and demanding terrain was the goal in America, aristocratic pretension could not be allowed to inhibit settler energies there, as experience rapidly taught.

Likewise, another parallel proves thin and unconvincing. One might expect London's royal councillors and ministers to think of Ireland when it came to designing forms of subordinate government for the trans-Atlantic colonies. If they did, their conclusions can only have been that the cases were too dissimilar to prove useful. There were occasional flurries of comparison. Quashing the attempt of the Governor of Barbados to reject commands from the royal Privy Council patented under the Great Seal of England, Secretary of State Sir Henry Coventry reminded him that the governors (Lord Lieutenants) of Ireland never did so, yet surely Ireland "might pretend a little before Barbados". In 1677–78, London considered imposing upon both Jamaica and Virginia a law modelled upon "Poynings' Law in Ireland": the law of 1494 (later amended, and amplified by precedent), which subordinated the Irish Parliament to the English Crown by requiring it to submit all proposed legislation to London for approval before its final passage. The Virginians were apathetic, but the Jamaican burgesses fought the proposal bitterly with the simple case that distance alone would render the colonies ungovernable if vital laws had to depend on a process involving two long voyages and a lengthy deliberation in London. In the event, the victory proved crucial, for otherwise "the Lords of Trade would probably have extended it to the other royal province thereby permanently placing the American provincial assembly on the same inferior plane as the parliament of Ireland". Distance, expediency,

James Logan (1674-1751)

indifference and the feeling that how the colonies ordered themselves did not much matter as long as they delivered their staple wealth, convinced most English ministers (apart from a few like Lord Halifax from 1748–52) to allow the colonies more latitude in reality than they possessed in law. In contrast, closeness, a troubled history, internal divisions and European implications compelled English ministers to use their legal powers in Ireland to the full, and to go beyond them whenever expedient.

Others argue there was a connection between the way in which Tudor and Stuart Englishmen viewed the native Irish, and their later treatment of black slaves and American Indians in the colonies. Certainly they viewed the 'wild' Irish with contempt and hostility, but political enmity accounted for much of this. There was the usual prejudice and incomprehension where differing ways of life meet in a tense situation, and the misunderstood traits of the more traditional Irish herdsmen and clan leaders were ascribed to the Irish as a whole, despite the efforts of more fair-minded men such as Barnaby Rich to argue that most Irish, like the English, were civil and industrious. Certainly there are analogies and parallels between the way in which those English adventurers active in both Ireland and the colonies . . . such as Francis Drake, Humphrey Gilbert and George Carew . . . regarded the natives of both places. Put most simply, both were unEnglish, and from the narrow perspective of England's insular postmedieval culture, therefore uncivilised. Again, such rationalisations are normal wherever imperial pretension seeks to justify dominance over other human beings. But specific anti-Irish stereotypes were rarely applied to the Algonquian and Muskhogean tribes, peoples of the American forests, apart from obvious dependence upon the same English language terms to describe migratory clans and their divergences from common English habits. Whereas the English in Ireland tended to assimilate 'conforming' Irishmen, Indians and blacks were not so treated in the colonies despite a few initial experiments. In short, the gulf between English and Irish was relative and even passable, that in the colonies almost total. To argue that English excesses in Ireland led the way to those of black enslavement and the anti-Indian wars is to forget that antiforeignism, religious hostility and habits of inequality were normal among all early Europeans, the English perhaps somewhat more than most. A better case might be made that later domestic English prejudice against the English who migrated to Ireland and the colonies was similar, and that this affected their estimates of the rights and liberties of their overseas cousins. The assumption was a double one: that only an inferior species of Englishmen generally went abroad, and, whether he went to Ireland or the colonies, he became contaminated by the wildness or 'incivility' of those places. Even a friend of Irish prosperity such as Sir Walter Harris argued in 1691 that much of the island's poverty owed to the reckless character of its English immigrants, and eighty years later such views were still general. England's views of the American English were similar: Doctor Samuel Johnson was somewhat exaggerating them when he snorted that the colonials were fit only for hanging.

Yet despite the contrast in how they were treated and regarded, Ireland and the colonies had governments which were broadly similar, although operating very differently. This was ultimately because the legislative, administrative and legal institutions of both societies were derived from English example. Moreover those of the colonies were developed at the same time as those of Ireland were refined to match the new situation in which the victorious Anglo-Irish shaped them to their exclusive use after 1691. Simultaneous changes in the British examples on which both were modelled set the context in which these alterations occurred. Institutions are in fact habits: the habitual ways in which a society conducts its political, legal and other affairs. Seen thus, it was natural that Englishmen and their descendants in Ireland and the colonies conduct their public business in English forms. Despite all the rhetoric about colonial assemblies being created at the behest of the King's Gracious Majesty and by His Royal Prerogative, despite the centrality of the Crown in the forms of Anglo-Irish government, these overseas English expected public affairs to be conducted and financed in consultation and agreement with their wishes. Indeed, the tendency to regard institutions as more than collective habits deepened this conviction. Eighteenth century men regarded them (practically, if not explicitly) as analogous to their Christian Churches: vehicles of Providential order, freighted with ancient sanctions and authority. This explains the insistence and self-confidence with which they pressed their views, as we have seen those of Barbados and Jamaica do so early on. The colonials of Massachusetts bitterly resisted the destruction of their local government in favour of direct rule by royal viceroys in the 1680s. Those of Pennsylvania wrested the right of legislation from their proprietor Penn as early as 1696. Around the same time, the Anglo-Irish grew highly touchy about their influence upon the direction of Irish affairs, in face of English legislation upon them, as witness William Molyneux's strong rejoinder in *The Case of Ireland's Being Bound by Acts of Parliament in England Stated* (1698).

What were the institutions of England upon which those of Ireland were undoubtedly modelled in structure, and which these expatriate English (if we may so term them) used as grounds for their own claims to autonomous 'liberties'? What were the changes in England so closely affecting them? The King and his ministers shared sovereign authority over England and ultimately over the empire in tandem with the Lords of the realm and the elected and representative Commons. Theoretically the ministers were but arms of the Crown, and hence the simplification that England was ruled by King, Lords and Commons, or by their combination for legislative purposes, "the King in Parliament". In practice, Lord and Commons reflected the interlocking interests of a common but heavily factionalised ruling class, with great landowners controlling or attracting lesser gentry, lawyers and office-holders (placemen). A largely deferential lower and middle-class population responded inertially to the course of affairs charted by these men. Increasingly, however, the Crown's authority was diminishing as its powers were exercised more directly by its ministers in cabinet, usually coalitions of the most powerful men in the country, who derived their strength from control over majority elements in parliament. Thus direct royal authority over the colonies and Ireland, for example, was waning at the very time in which the Board of Trade and elements in Parliament were using the Crown's name to impose changes upon them. However, the change could be exaggerated: the sort of men who acted as royal councillors in the formative period of the imperial vision, in the 1660s and 1670s, were now more active in their own right. For the rise of the cabinet after 1700 and of the power of Parliament from 1689 were aspects of the same process whereby England was now governed by the will of its wealthy more clearly. The connections were open. Key ministers were now members of the Commons (royal councillors were not in the past). The Commons initiated legislation now without opposition, controlled its own proceedings and privileges, and levied and supervised the appropriations and accounts vital to the functioning on the country's government (then, as now, always growing more expensive by the year).

Yet the legal basis for these shifts in power away from royal authority under Queen Anne and the Hanoverians particularly was very inadequate: collective habits were changing, but not the law itself. Together with the factionalisation of the ruling class, this made for continuing ambiguity and even stalemate in the process of government. What helped was the fact that the more independent members of the Commons regarded the national interest and the King's business (as defined by his ministers) as roughly the same and deserving of support as a rule. Secondly, ministers tended to facilitate, when they could, the private business or interests of all those groups in the country not explicitly opposed to them: this was easier in an age when foreign policy and war was the chief cabinet preoccupation, so that the government had no essential economic or other internal programmes to pursue at the expense of commercial, farming or manufacturing groups. Finally, government was lubricated by generous dosages of political patronage and arm-twisting. Everything was used: the honour of reception at Court, the award of army commissions and church offices, the word to chancery judges to facilitate the transfer of landed estates, the favour of ministerial attention to a host of lobbyists for local legislation and to a swarm of careerists for promotions, places and pensions. In a society of five million or so, heavily stratified, such informal procedures went far toward ensuring the political coherence and ministerial control which the absence of adequate political parties, clear domestic policies and clarity in government structure might seem to make impossible. If the cabinet was increasingly answerable to Parliament, its programmes dependent upon majorities in the Commons, yet, too, it was still a Crown executive, using the considerable prestige and prerogatives of the King to ensure itself those very majorities.

All this affected the colonies and Ireland in manifold ways, important and unimportant. Above all, the confusion of the system in London, its questionable legitimacy (even on its own legal terms), and its ultimate dependence upon free-wheeling arrangements among prominent men, emboldened the shrewder colonial and Anglo-Irish men of talent to exploit the ambiguities of their own institutional relations with London, and play upon the structural confusion within their own local governments.

Patronage, the magic of the Court, and the prestige of the metropolis were considerably less effective at a distance to prompt obedience. The local governments, as said, were copied from the English model. In the colonies, the governor represented the authority of the Crown, and was its chief executive. He retained powers the Crown in England had lost: in addition to appointing executive officers, he appointed judges, creating special courts where he saw fit, vetoed legislation repugnant to the Crown's interests, and convened and dismissed the local Assemblies. Beneath him was an advisory council, modelled upon the old royal Privy Council in England, but lacking its past size and prestige, and entirely without the importance of the newer cabinet in England. This advisory council largely coincided with the upper house of the colonial Assembly, which was the counterpart of Parliament. But because the council/upper house bore little or no real analogy to the House of Lords, the councillors were a handful of prominent merchants and planters who hoped to get something out of the Crown's representative by associating with him openly, and were not necessarily even a representative cross-section of their fellows, much less its recognised leaders. The House of Lords was still in England the epitome of the nation's aristocratic structure and territorial power. The *arrivistes* of colonial councils, with their studied gentility and recent wealth, did not naturally command their society. As a result the lower house of Assembly was the more naturally a cross-section of local interests and personalities: indigenous, confident, contentious and assertive, as sure that it was in substance a Parliament as the Governors were contemptuously determined it was not. In Ireland, on the other hand, the parallels were more exact. Ireland too had Crown, Privy Council, Lords and Commons. But Ireland also had a Governor, the Lord Lieutenant, who summoned Privy Council and Parliament, headed the executive and the armed forces in Ireland, appointed the judiciary, and represented the Crown of Ireland (i.e., the English King) and its prerogatives much more effectively than did the colonial governors. In Ireland, too, the Privy Council, Lords and Commons much more closely represented the organic structure of an aristocratic and gentry society than was the case in the colonies, where the English-style three-fold institutions presumed a social structure that did not exist.

The change toward cabinet and parliamentary power in England affected the workings of these colonial and Irish systems closely. The governors after 1700 were almost always representatives of the dominant factions in English political life at a given time, and often pressed policies dictated by the needs of those factions to maintain themselves. Yet they were also, in a sense, diplomats charged with sustaining the imperial *status quo* by ensuring support for English policy among those whom they were sent to govern. Since colonial governors spent only, on average, five years in their post, and Irish Lords Lieutenant were often resident in London for much of their term, they were in a weak position when it came to balancing these dual objectives. Their narrowly political and broadly national tasks continuously conflicted. They usually extricated themselves by relying upon local men of power. For two generations, Ireland was ruled by an inner group of councillors known as the 'Undertakers' who functioned as an informal cabinet, handling patronage, managing parliament, keeping London abreast of what was practical, and reminding the nervous Anglo-Irish gentry of where their ultimate security lay: in Britain. These 'Undertakers' and their successors were drawn from powerful families such as the Ponsonbys, Boyles, Conollys and Beresfords and from leading Anglican prelates. In the colonies, less successful efforts to counteract the growing power of the local assemblies were made, by reliance upon such leading families as the De Lanceys and Van Cortlandts in New York. The more successful colonial governors (such as William Gooch in Virginia, 1727–49) were those who worked with the local and fluid power structure as they found it, rather than trying to create a group of supporters lacking wide natural influence. In Ireland the threat that a resurgence of native Irish strength might occur and lead to the negation of Anglo-Irish land titles was the hidden stick of Undertaker influence. Its open aspect was the shared assumption of Undertakers and the gentry that the fund of public offices and rewards used to manage the latter remain an Anglican monopoly: but, derivatively, this too depended on the maintenance of a post-Conquest solidarity with Britain. In the colonies the hope of gaining some of the vast ungranted lands of the Crown was the chief carrot that drew many local politicians and speculators within the orbit of British designs, even into a governor's party on occasion. Pressure from the political masters back in England to prevent the emergence of over-strong families in Ireland and the colonies, to force compliance with unpopular Westminster legislation of local importance (such as laws curbing Irish and colonial trade with the West Indies) or to press local Acts in England's interests, and directives to 'pack' the administrations in Ireland and the colonies with young Englishmen in search of a job or a lifestyle: all this constantly subverted the divide-and-manage tactics of building up local pro-London groups.

On the whole the task was treated with greater seriousness in Ireland than in the colonies because of its greater importance. The leading Irish families were absorbed into the patronage and marriage networks of the English nobility, their younger siblings into the clientship arrangements which led to English jobs. In the colonies there was no local aristocracy to be so treated, though there might be the wealthy pretence of one. Nor would the English create one. Whereas loyal and dutiful Anglo-Irish officers, public servants and gentry were regularly dubbed 'Sir' by the King, only one Virginian in a century was knighted.

While the Anglo-Irish political nation could be bribed, beguiled and managed and rewarded from the top down, the elite of non-aristocratic governors' councillors and friends in the colonies were too mundanely a part of their local society to emerge as a permanent pro-English caste to which all upwardly mobile Americans might aspire. Other actions than the failure to

George Croghan (1720-1782)

reward pro-London Americans adequately with title and estate underscored the different importance given Irish and colonial affairs. Colonial business remained in the hands of the Board of Trade, a desultory body of royal advisers, which reported to the government minister primarily concerned with England's relations with the south European powers (the Secretary of State for the Southern Department); the attempt of Lord Halifax to streamline the Board's authority, giving it direct control of the colonies, was treated indifferently in the late 1740s by the cabinet. Initially designed to put the merchantilist-imperial vision of the colonies into action, it degenerated into another body of special pleaders and placemen, often by-passed by influential Englishmen with colonial concerns. Irish affairs, on the other hand, were supervised directly by the cabinet itself, and sub-committees of the House of Commons, the Lords, and the Cabinet, and even of such bodies as the Board of Trade, were regularly deputed to scrutinise Irish business relevant to their fields of executive, legislative or advisory concern. Thirdly, there was marked difference in calibre in the Englishmen sent to handle Irish affairs and those sent to the colonies. A remarkable number of cabinet ministers had already served as expatriates in the uppermost ranks of British government in Ireland. Between 1745–1770. Lords Chesterfield, Dorset, Devonshire, Bedford and Hailfax served as Lord-Lieutenant in Ireland and had gone on to cabinet rank in London. At lesser levels of government, interchange of officials was even more common. On the other hand, the succession of weakish men sent to the colonies only furthered the momentum whereby relative English indifference led to growing colonial power. It may also have expressed a fatalistic conviction that colonies so far-flung, so socially unacceptable to able aristocrats, and so cannily indifferent to all previous English strategies for their control, were virtually impossible to shape to cabinet concerns. As Thomas Barrow has shown, even the skeletal controls of the old imperial and navigation systems before 1756 were widely ineffective. Perhaps Halifax, with his knowledge of Ireland and his lone desire (before that year) to tighten things up in the colonies, may have mused that the colonies might have been more potentially useful to England had defeated Indians there been as numerous as the native Irish throughout Ireland!

In both Ireland and the colonies, the very politics so obvious in the management of the local societies by their governing figures drew attention to the discrepancies between the theory whereby their inhabitants were the subjects of the Crown, and the reality whereby the changing institutions of English politics had placed them directly under clearly self-interested English political factions. Indeed both Ireland and the colonies were now open to direct pressure from those English interest groups most narrowly concerned in overseas affairs. Between 1660–1720s, Irish and colonial lobbies had flourished at Court, in the clubs of Tory and Whig politicians, at Westminster itself. Thereafter, their access to Crown and political parties had apparently become more informal and fragmented. Partly the elaboration of a more specifically imperial vision caused the devaluation of independent overseas representation. Partly the settlement of English political life into a new equilibrium dominated by Whiggish parliamentary and cabinet groupings meant that there was no longer need for Crown and gentry, Whigs and Tories, to use Irish and colonial spokesmen as make-weights in their arguments. Partly, as often in the cycle of English concerns, Ireland and the colonies suddenly seemed distant and tiresome, domestic politics and pleasure under the first Hanoverians and Walpole the more consuming. Whatever the cause, English attention to Irish and colonial agents diminished at precisely the point at which specific English interests were having their way with parliament on Irish and colonial matters. This, however, is a matter greatly in need of fuller study. Certainly this indifference was not for lack of Irish and colonial representatives in London noisily trying to make their voices heard. But these were left to watch with irritation as the newly predominant upper classes there gave free reign to those lobbyists who desired protection from Irish and American trade competition or who wished for 'places' over the Atlantic or the Irish Sea for sons in need of fortune or station.

This multiple convergence of trends, emergent first in the 1690s, fully operative by the 1730s and 1740s, led to blunt questions. Had this London parliament, then, the same right to supervise Irish or colonial affairs as the Crown unquestionably had? Since Crown and Parliament were in law inseparable as to their legislative authority, the question should have been academic rather than real. But it greatly pleased a legalistic generation who thought of rights in terms of precedents and history. And in the absence of a realistic theory of interest-group politics, it offered an arcane yet serviceable framework in which the new changes could be discussed. Relatedly, both the Anglo-Irish and the colonials began to press for a widening of the rights of their local parliament or assemblies along the same lines as the English parliament's broadened powers, and to question the privileges of the royal executive precisely in those matters in which Crown prerogative had lately been restricted in England. The claims were countered in English official circles by a constitutional assumption that such demands were groundless and that the claimants were subordinate peoples. To each group involved, their own tactics were persuasive and their own arguments sensible.

But the results were different in each case. By the 1750s, the colonial assemblies had practical control over the appointment of many executive officers, over the terms and salaries of judges, over the distribution of land grants, over the right to vote and the creation of new constituencies, over the local militias, over the finances of government generally (levying taxes, appropriating revenues, disposing of surpluses, appointing the local treasurers), over the definition of their privileges and dignities. The room for leverage through patronage open to the governors diminished as a result. In Ireland by contrast, despite efforts in 1753 and 1769, the House of Commons never won its case that the financial power of the government of Ireland was its own. It never managed to pass Place Bills (such as passed in the colonies) to exclude Crown office-holders from among its members. It could not prevent

English administrations from repeatedly using Ireland's official revenues for their own political and patronage purposes. If it failed to ensure its own control over Ireland's money supply (again by contrast with the colonies) it did manage to prevent the imposition of unwelcome currencies, although this was of little use in generating that credit so much more easily obtained under the inflationary activities of American assemblies. If it failed to ensure its full financial autonomy, however, it was sufficiently regarded that British governments or Parliaments never attempted to impose direct taxation upon Ireland. Yet the real measure of its weakness was the fact of its enforced acquiescence in the Declaratory Act of 1720 whereby the Westminster Parliament explicitly avowed its authority to legislate for Ireland.

In the colonies, royal authority was persistently weakening although in theory the local assemblies were little more than county or borough corporations. Its lack of institutional and local sources of power disadvantaged it in the struggle against vigorous local communities more and more defining their interests in their own terms. In Ireland, royal authority was strengthened by the fact that the local Privy Council and executive were a powerful first arm of the English administration, had a broad range of patronage powers and were not too distantly isolated from London. It was doubly strengthened by the second arm, that was the English administration itself. The local arm vetted the measures of Ireland's Parliament sent to London for approval: London could then further alter or even veto them. But, most crucially, royal or cabinet authority in Ireland could rely upon the existence of many Anglo-Irishmen of integrity who believed the fortunes of their class rested entirely upon a cordial co-operation with England in the subordinate role to which they had been assigned. That the field of aspiration and frame of reference of so many of them was English or imperial, rather than locally Irish, further emphasised this. Sentiment and the politics of anti-Catholic ascendancy apart, the limited opportunities of the country meant there was little of that convergence of self-interested ambition and local loyalty which American revolutionaries could later take as axiomatic to their own vast land.

Two final points heighten the contrast between Ireland and the colonies within the imperial structure. If Irishmen were pressing for the full rights of expatriate Englishmen, they did so more mutedly than did the colonists. Jonathan Swift, Robert Molesworth and a few others followed Molyneux in criticising the abuses of English authority and its tendency to by-pass the liberties of Anglo-Irish institutions through a regime of corruption. But they never attained the pitch of passionate conviction, nor won the general audience, which similar critics achieved in the colonies. Already by the 1730s literate colonists were familiar with the English libertarian and right-wing critiques of the new cabinet system, seeing in it one new threat to the Liberty that was the precarious heritage of all Englishmen everywhere, against the background of a world in which Turkish tyranny or French despotism was the more normal expression of the inherent evil of men's hearts. Most Anglo-Irish gentry were doubtless too realistic, and too consciously compromised by their relationship to the outer limits of that new system, to be self-righteous partisans of political virtue. Nonetheless they shared some of the same central assumptions, except that for them not the cabinet in London, but the millions of minions of the Papacy that surrounded them, were the more imminent threat. Instead of a Peter Zenger re-printing in New York the libertarian arguments of 'Cato's Letters' against the local governor (1733), Anglo-Irishmen were more likely to read pamhleteers discussing the expediency of challenging the ministry on minor points, given the persistence of their obligations to the empire.

A forgotten yet crucial aspect of Ireland's relationship with the colonies sprang from precisely those obligations. A notable number of Anglo-Irishmen attained high position in the English administration of North America before the revolution. The full measure of these connections remains to be charted, but their importance and implications must be understood. To take some key examples. William Cosby, the insensitive governor of New York who had prompted the polemics of Peter Zenger, was an Anglo-Irishman with links to the vast Newcastle network in English politics. Admiral Sir Peter Warren, of Warrenstown, Co. Meath, owner of much of Manhattan, asked the Duke of Newcastle for the same governorship in 1745 (unsuccessfully), and married the sister of the leader of the great De Lancey faction in New York itself. His nephew in turn, Sir William Johnson of Smithstown, Co. Meath, went to America in 1738 as manager of the De Lancey-Warren estate on the Mohawk, became an Indian trader, a chief of the Mohawks, diplomat to the Iroquian confederacy during the Anglo-French wars of 1755-63, a major military commander in that crucial area south of French Canada, and ultimately superintendent of Indian affairs in the northern colonies. Coarse, vigorous, eloquent, an able linguist and soldier, he contrasted sharply with his aristocratic uncle, and ultimately had eight children by the sister of the chief of the Mohawks, Molly Brandt, and died as the American revolution gathered momentum. Much further south, Arthur Dobbs of Dobbs Castle, Co. Antrim, former surveyor-general of Ireland, became governor of North Carolina in 1754. In Ireland he had been unusual: an improving landlord, concerned to develop both his estates and the country as a whole, yet again, with special capacity to insinuate his way to preferment by cultivating the 'Undertakers' and thus securing the attention of the Prime Minister in London, Robert Walpole. In North Carolina, Dobbs, if an improvement on his predecessors, was too consciously Anglican, too high-handedly the governor, too slighting of local opinion, to be successful, despite imaginative schemes of regional development. Impulsive, passionate and obstinate, like Johnson he flouted social norms by marrying a local Carolina girl of seventeen, when he himself was seventy-three! Finally, most importantly, are two men who never came to America. George Montagu Dunk, Lord Halifax, we have already met. His long-term Dublin mistress, Mary Faulkner, was a notorious 'placemonger', using Halifax's connections to place Dubliners throughout imperial society, some in the American colonies. More vitally, the first Secretary of State for the colonies during the final years leading to the breach with America was Lord Hillsborough, of Hillsborough, Co. Down, an Anglo-Irishman of wide English connections, a friend of George III when he was Prince of Wales, an English M.P. at age 23, comptroller of the royal household in 1755, president of the Board of Trade under Grenville in 1763 through 1765 (the years of the Stamp Act Crisis against the colonists), and colonial secretary and again president of the same Board from 1768, when he pressed for that hard line toward the Massachusetts Assembly which accelerated the final breach. George III remarked of him that he "did not know a man of less judgement" although it must be said that his American policies coincided in general with the convictions of most Englishmen of the time, from the King to Grenville and Pitt (his Prime Ministers). In 1770, under the new Circuit Court Act for South Carolina, he appointed a Dubliner, Thomas Gordon, Chief Justice, and two other Dubliners associate justices, with a Welshman and a Scotsman to make up the full bench.

These cases remind us of two crucial facts. As beneficiaries of the empire, many successful Anglo-Irishmen became part of the imperial structure against which the colonists would later rebel. Earlier we had more occasion to stress the relatively pro-colonial role of Edmund Burke, Lord Shelburne, Issac Barré and others amongst such Anglo-Irish figures in London; we must not forget that they too were successful beneficiaries of empire. Shelburne the Kerryman and Hillsborough the Ulsterman, both imperial Londoners by choice, did not disagree upon the value of the empire or upon whether the American colonies ought to remain within it. They disagreed on the methods to achieve this latter object, the former plumping like Burke and Barré, for conciliation, the latter for coercion. It was a dialectic that continuously divided their counsels as to how to handle their own subject population, the native Irish. Secondly, as Irishmen, denizens of a relatively poor island thrown into an openly careerist, even cynical, age, all these figures from Cosby and Warren to Mary Faulkner and Hillsborough, believed that the colonies were a good source of extra livelihoods for clients and relatives.

As a result, wherever they gained patronage power in the colonies, or over colonial appointments, they created knots of Anglo-Irish expatriates. The career of Joseph Murray, the distinguished New York jurist and protégé of both Warren and Cosby (the latter to become his father-in-law), member of the Governor's executive council, chief pleader for his prerogative (except when the Cosby–De Lancey connection was out of power!), and a founder of King's College, now Columbia University, exhibits the trend: Murray was born in Co. Laois around 1694, presumably Catholic, but became a pillar of Episcopal piety in New York. Even more striking was the way in which Warren's kinsman Sir William Johnson used his superintendency of Indian affairs to create a network of Irish relatives as officials along the western frontiers of the colonies, they in turn appointing further kinsmen as deputies: George Croghan of Roscommon in western Pennsylvania, Dr. John Connolly in Virginia, with Thomas Smallman, Edward Ward, Daniel Clark and others as the secondaries and traders. Almost all of them, like Johnson, Croghan and Connolly, were former Catholics from the Irish midlands, following the example of the connection's head, Warren, in a conformity to Anglicanism. They were the more careful since Catholicism was associated by most colonials with Franco-Indian terror in the area of their jurisdiction. This prototypical 'Irish' interest, dealing with western lands and the Iroquian confederacy at a crucial juncture (from the Seven Years' War through the early phases of the Revolution), continued to recruit relatives from Ireland, and by politics and marriage, effect a remarkable connection between past and future down to the end of the century: the Croghan connection inter-married with that of the pro-American immigrant, Colonel James O'Hara, who in the 1790s became the founder of industrial Pittsburg with his establishment of a glassworks.

This forewarns us against the easy assumption that the Anglo-Irish (or conformed native Irish) in official positions all became Tories in 1776. Since calculation was the basis of their conformity in the past, calculation as easily became the basis of a new Americanism. Croghan and his network, skilled in convincing dubious colonials that they were not pro-French Papists disguised (between 1756–63), shed their loyalty to the Crown as skilfully. But others felt more deeply—Sir John Johnson, Sir William's own son, commanded a regiment of provincials after 1776, appropriately named 'Johnson's Greens'. Thus it is not surprising that the largest numbers of Irish-born loyalists existed (as Wallace Brown has shown), in coastal South Carolina and in New York, precisely the areas in which the patronage networks were most active (a factor he missed). A network of gratitude created by Dobbs and Cosby, Johnson and Hillsborough, withstood to some degree the shifting calculations of career in a world up-turned, and withstood too the fact that most Irish immigrants were strongly pro-revolutionary. Indeed, like the South Carolina Dublin judges, or like James Stirling, (the Anglo-Irish poet awarded a Customs' Collectorship in Maryland in 1755, on the basis of his versified vision of what the Empire might be), imperial Irishmen appointed in opposition to local wishes, played a role in exacerbating the coming crisis between Britain and the colonies. The very fact that the mass of these placemen were expected to be or become Anglican, however, effectively separated them from the mass of their immigrant fellow-countrymen, Presbyterian and Catholic. It may even have had the paradoxical effect of diminishing the numbers of ordinary Anglo-Irish immigrants from mid-Ulster and elsewhere prepared openly to identify with Anglicanism, for few did as will be shown.

Merchants and Sailors

In 1754, Henry Stevenson of Baltimore opened one of the richest houses in the area, 'Stevenson's Folly', from the profits of his Irish trade (which continued from 1747–1759, largely in wheat and flour), and thereby 'laid the foundations' of the city's 'commercial consequence' as his obituary put it. Eighty years later, the diarist Philip Hone noted how remarkable it was that "the three men who held the most distinguished places in the great community of merchants which imparted wealth, splendour and character to Baltimore have all died within a year . . . Alexander Brown, Robert Oliver and William Patterson might at one time have been considered the royal merchants of Baltimore, as the Medici of old were in Italy." Brown, Oliver and Patterson were all Ulstermen, trained in the rudiments of merchandising in their native country. But the contrast is essential. Stevenson, an American subject of the British Empire, built his fortune upon the Irish connection. Oliver, Brown and Patterson each came to America as agents of that connection, but each turned his attention by 1780 almost completely to America's British, Carribbean and European trade, and to America's internal development. From the 1730s to the 1780s, Ireland played an important role in the preparatory phase of America's commercial growth, but with the latter's sustained expansion from the 1790s, the relative importance of Irish trade so declined that not even those who came to develop it (such as Oliver), remained in it. Once an independent America began to exploit the full economic possibilities of its resources, the limitations of a small island as partner to that growth became evident.

Nonetheless for fifty years American Irish trade had been the crucial substance which filled the lightly woven basket of their imperial connection. Its importance was five-fold. At a time when the economies of the middle colonies were weak, with surprisingly little trade between them and Britain, the Irish connection contributed considerably to their growth. The Irish economy likewise benefited considerably from the trade. Relatedly, it was an important element in the rise of those cities engaged in it: New York, Philadelphia, Newcastle (Delaware) and Baltimore on the one side, Cork, Newry, Belfast and Derry particularly on the other. Fourthly, it was an important complement to other trade connections which should otherwise have been more difficult or have created adverse trade balances: that of the middle colonies with the British Isles generally, that of Ireland with the West Indies. Finally, the trade furnished the routes and resources of Irish emigration in the 18th century, and also more specifically helped provide America with trained immigrant merchants.

A glance at some figures is the swiftest instruction in these facts. From 1731–1750, usually up to ten ships a year sailed from New York to Irish ports, and a similar number from Baltimore. Trade with Philadelphia was brisker: before 1750, between fifteen and thirty vessels went from there each year to Ireland. Trade from Boston, however, was virtually negligible, as was that from the southern ports: Charleston or Hampton, Virginia. Nonetheless fewer than fifteen vessels usually went from New York to Britain in the same period annually, and no large number from Baltimore. Often fewer sailed from Philadelphia to Britain than to Ireland. The pattern of incoming sailings was rather different, with very many more coming from Britain to these ports than from Ireland. With rising trade and population, sailings had increased heavily by the eve of the American Revolution, but the pattern had not changed.

Baltimore in 1752

Sailings between New York, Philadelphia and Britain, the West Indies and Ireland 1769–72

New York	To Britain	To West Indies	To Ireland	From Britain	From West Indies	From Ireland
1769	47	125	30	41	179	18
1770	46	189	29	39	226	19
1771	45	194	27	63	220	13
1772	39	199	19	61	208	11
Philadelphia						
1769	27	202	32	46	214	32
1770	25	243	49	42	221	26
1771	27	230	25	71	232	16
1772	23	268	24	63	247	12

Source: *Historical Statistics of the U.S., Ser. Z.*

(It should be noted that vessels bound for the Caribbean were usually smaller than those trading across the Atlantic).

Obviously, the exports of the middle colonies (of which New York and Philadelphia were the chief ports) sent to the British Isles went quite disproportionately to Ireland, especially when considered in terms of the relative populations of Ireland and Britain. In short Ireland was a good market for mid-colonial produce. Throughout the eighteenth century, except for amounts, the goods sent did not vary from those exported to Ireland in 1770: 305,000 bushels of flaxseed, 150,000 bushels of wheat, 3,500 tons of flour, 8,000 gallons of rum, 333,000 feet of board and 2.8 million barrel staves, most of which came from Pennsylvania and Virginia. England derived much of its timber from the Baltic, and grew sufficient wheat at home, importing any shortfall from Europe. It consumed scarcely any flaxseed. Yet American imports from the British Isles came equally disproportionately from England: chiefly manufactured goods of all sorts from textiles and clothing to ironware, firearms, clocks and crockery. The Irish market enabled American traders to draw on London or Bristol merchants through bills of credit often arranged by the Irish merchants whom they supplied, and thus helped offset the middle colonies adverse balance of trade with England. Put another way, Ireland itself gained an inadequate trading return from the goods it took directly from America. This was even more true if one considers its indirect imports. The Navigation Laws obliged Ireland to import tobacco, sugar, indigo and certain other items through British ports if they originated in the British empire. A certain portion of its sugar came through French ports on the continent, but all the tobacco came through Britain. By the 1770s, Ireland was consuming one third of all tobacco imports to Britain. In this sense, Ireland was an important market for the southern colonies also.

Ireland also sent products and produce to the colonies. As a Philadelphia merchant wrote indiscriminately: "Your country produces servants Beef, Pork, Soap, Tallow & Candles which I believe would all anser . . . they will always command the cash." By the 1760s Ireland was legally exporting over five pounds of beef, two of pork and one and a half of butter yearly for every man, woman and child in the colonies. Since much of the population was still coastal, and specialising in other forms of agriculture, these three chief imports were readily marketable, fetching high prices in the middle colonies especially, and often competing very successfully with local produce of inferior quality. This export pattern had developed in response to the restrictive Navigation and Cattle legislation of the 1660s and in relation to the demand for bulk food from the plantation colonies from the Chesapeake Bay south to Jamaica, but had invaded even sections of the mid-colonies market. In addition, much of the outward-bound trans-Atlantic trade of the empire depended upon Ireland to provision its ships: English ships' masters found it cheaper to victual for the long voyage west by calling at Cork than to do so in England. Other Irish goods found their way to the colonies, many of them through Britain (as required of nearly all but provisions and linen by the Navigation acts), through French Atlantic ports, by direct smuggling, and amongst cargoes of largely British manufacture. When Robert Oliver arrived in Baltimore in 1783, he brought a legal cargo of linen, gloves, hats, combs, threads and other dry goods to sell for Belfast merchants. Almost a century before, Irish vessels were trading Irish rugs, stockings and friezes (coarse woollens) illegally into Maryland, together with linen, hats and other goods. Again, the mixture of over-specialization along an accessible sea-board with crude domestic production of clothing and other goods in those areas, made well-finished and fashionable Irish products attractive to colonial buyers for over a century.

Yet the precariousness of these two pillars of Irish trade with the Americans should be noted. As American population rose, communication improved with the interior and along the coasts, and resources were exploited and talents mastered, Irish trade proportionately declined. Dairying and beef production which took hold in Connecticut, Pennsylvania and the Carolina Piedmont, had by the 1780s seriously diminished Irish imports as a proportion of American consumption, and made inroads into the provisioning of the French and English plantations in the West Indies, hitherto a virtual Irish monopoly where salt meat was concerned. Likewise as America could establish manufacturing patterns after 1790 or so, Irish soap, candles, friezes, tinware and lesser goods inevitably gave way. Only where a trade was rationalised and technically innovative, on the model of the new industrial–commercial patterns of Britain, could Irish goods continue to have an impact on an American market still largely unorganised and decentralised: this was the case with linen and butter production. Overall, however, Ireland maintained an important trade with America throughout the 18th century, selling approximately as much in value (though not in bulk) as it consumed. Indeed, had it sustained the momentum of this earlier relationship, employment opportunities for its people and an enhanced capacity to buy and consume more American flour and wheat would have had beneficial effects as its own rural society overpopulated and decayed. Ironically, the patriotic efforts of Irish parliaments to keep Irish interest rates low had the effect of alienating the American profits of Irishmen away from Ireland, as the case of the immensely wealthy Anglo-Irish Warren family demonstrated.

There are indications that Irish-American trade has been under-estimated in the standard studies and statistics, for they are based upon analysis of customs' house returns for incoming vessels at the major ports, as indeed is the table included above. These usually focus upon 'direct sailing' statistics, i.e. vessels, and therefore trade flow, are assumed to originate in the port of last call before entry into the American port under study. But in the eighteenth century, many brigantines and ships from Londonderry to Philadelphia called first at the Delaware ports of Lewes and Newcastle, and are thus listed under inter-American trade: likewise, ships for New York would put in at Perth Amboy in New Jersey, and those for Baltimore or Annapolis at various piers or wharfs in Virginia on the lower Chesapeake. Likewise, since Irish exports to America were few (other than linen), but those to the West Indies were heavy, Irish vessels sometimes engaged in a triangle trade, carrying provisions to Barbados or Jamaica, and thence carrying sugar and molasses, together with some Irish servants, north to the mid-colonial American ports. Occasionally, too, Irish vessels would enter American ports with direct cargoes from Lisbon and Madeira. Only detailed study could determine the extent to which such patterns would alter the general impression of eighteenth century Irish-American maritime connection.

The most colourful aspect of the trade was that of smuggling, although the evidence for it is obviously scattered, so that opinions differ as to whether it constituted an important addition to the official tally of trade. Down to 1765, most of the tea, spirits and tobacco smuggled into Ireland came from French ports to the Isle of Man, whence they were brought into Ireland by small wherries, vessels too small to have engaged in direct trans-Atlantic activity. Nonetheless, even before that time there is evidence of direct if sporadic illegal trade between Ireland and colonies as widely separate as Maryland and Maine. In 1731 William Pepperrell and Charles Apthorp ran two brigantines of goods from Kittery in Maine to Ireland. Illegal Irish woollens were offered for sale in colonial newspapers in this period.

All of the tobacco coming from France via the Isle of Man was of clandestine American origin, as was some of the rum (which for Irish taste, noted a Philadelphian, should 'be high enough to sink Oyl'). After 1763, the volume of Irish American trade was increasing and with it the number of vessels engaged in it. Not surprisingly, most of the evidence of smuggling dates low Candles, to be sold by JOSIAH HEWES, in Chesnut·Street.

THE *Partnership of* William *and* Andrew Caldwell, *being expired, those who are indebted to them, beyond the Time of Payment, are desired immediately to pay, to prevent Trouble ; and those who have any Demands, to bring them in to* Andrew Caldwell, *to be adjusted and paid.*

Andrew Caldwell & Joseph Wilson,

Have imported per the Conolly, *from* Dublin, *and the latest Vessels from different Parts of* Ireland ;

A General *Assortment of* Yard-wide *and* 7·8 Linens, *white and brown Sheetings,* 6, 8 *and* 10 *Qr. Diapers,* Lawns, Cambricks, Damask Table Cloths, &c. &c. *They have also lately received, by Way of* New York, *a large Assortment of Woollens, suitable for the Season, printed Linens and Cottons, Silk and Linen Handkerchiefs, a great Variety of plain and figured Ribbands, Sewing Silks, Womens Shoes, Writing Paper, Pins, &c. all which they will sell very cheap for Cash, or on short Credit.*

TO BE LET, and entered upon the First Day of April

Ulster American Merchants advertise Irish Goods

from the last forty years of the century. In 1770, Irish sailors mobbed and injured an exciseman in Philadelphia who had intercepted their vessel on the high seas. Yet probably the bulk of illegal trade still went through French ports: Irish smugglers were highly organised to operate through these ports and the isle of Guernsey, and American connections with French ports were increasingly heavy, legally so after 1783 (or 1776, to Americans). Thus Joshua Johnson of Annapolis, who founded the first tobacco shipping business free of British capital and middlemen, was dealing with several dozen French-based merchants by 1782, including the Franco-Irish houses of the Cumings and Moylans of Lorient, the McCarthys of Bordeaux and James O'Dea of Paimboeuf. Irish smugglers, especially from Rush, north of Dublin, dealt with precisely these ports, and it seems probable that between 1783 and 1793, the bulk of American tobacco consumed in Ireland was illegal: this may also have had the effect of keeping legal prices and duties down, thereby spreading pipe tobacco widely as a popular pleasure. For Americans perplexed by a post-war dislocation and recession in trade, such an outlet was not inconsiderable: up to five million pounds (lbs.) may have been smuggled annually in that decade into Ireland. Generally, however, smuggling only supplemented the legal forms of trade. The fact that there was not more of it through the century suggests that the legal connections were adequate to convey most of what Ireland and America had to trade with each other, notwithstanding the aggrieved protagonists of Irish woollens.

Throughout the century, however, a startling amount of legislation was devoted to the attempted suppression of smuggling, doubtless reflecting more the irritation of the country's rulers at its continuance, than indicating its real dimensions. The laws limited American Irish trade in greater ways too, as we have seen. Under the Navigation Acts and their supplements, only servants, provisions and horses could be directly exported to the colonies from Ireland. In 1705, linen was added to this list, and in 1731 Sir Robert Walpole, rather than accept changes in the prohibition on all Irish woollens exports, permitted all 'Unenumerated' articles to be imported directly from the colonies: timber, pitch, flour, flaxseed, whale-oil and other products chiefly of the middle colonies. The expansion of American Irish trade dates from that time (and most of the cargo of Pepperrell and Apthorp was illegal only by a few months!). Interestingly the Irish lobby in London neither co-operated on this occasion with its American counterparts, nor does it appear to have done so subsequently, although it did act together with the West Indian lobby. Given the fact that both Ireland and the colonies were constrained (if not as oppressed as once thought) by the Navigation Laws, this failure at co-operation is interesting. Official London in the 1730s and even in the 1750s was small enough for most of those struggling for its favours to have at least a nodding acquaintance with each other. It is hard to resist the impression that the Irish and the American agents believed they had few common interests, for in those years the imperatives of interest should have overcome any social distance imposed by Anglo-Irish snobbery. In short, the shrewd and influential merchant communities of both Ireland and the colonies may not have believed that their mutual trade could be improved to advantage in London, or may alternatively have felt that it would take its own course, or may finally have underestimated the potential it achieved between 1765–1776, as later in the 1780s.

The transfer of a merchant class, of mercantile skills, was another consequence of these connections. In an age of trade, indeed, this might be interpreted as the counterpart of today's 'brain drain' of professional people. Initially, Anglo-Irish Quakers played a large role in this migration. Seventeenth century immigrants, they became prominent in Ireland's skilled trades, in the woollen and linen businesses and in retailing and shipping, greatly out of proportion to their small numbers. Restrictions on trade, native Irish hostility, and the contempt and abuses visited upon them by the Anglican establishment caused many to remove again, but not before they had usually consolidated a network of urban Quaker connections in England as well as Ireland. Most went to Pennslyvania, following the track of the most famous of them, Lurgan-born James Logan, Dublin merchant and then secretary to William Penn. Thomas Griffiths, a Cork Quaker, came to Philadelphia via Jamaica in 1716 with an introduction to Jonathan Dickinson. He became a land agent with Logan for the Penns, a prominent merchant, the treasurer of the Free Society of Traders, and ultimately Mayor of Philadelphia, 1729–30 and 1733. Robert Strettell of Dublin, after a long stay in London, brought a cargo to Philadelphia which he used as the foundation for a major business in dry goods. A quiet and deliberative fellow, solid and honest, yet like Logan and many Irish Quakers, he believed in the virtues of defensive war. In 1751, he too became mayor of the city. Others went inland: Robert Millhouse and Samuel Wyly launched a store and grist-mill in the South Carolina backcountry, which became the nucleus of the areas's commerical organisation, and of the town of Camden. The Quaker connection continued important in American Irish links, too: for example, as late as 1794, the New Yorker Isaac Hicks initiated his expansion from dry goods wholesaler to shipping and commission agent by entering into arrangements with fellow Quaker businessmen in Ireland: Harvey and Lecky in Cork, James Holmes in Belfast, Edward Forbes in Dublin. The role of American Irish and Irish Quakers in the Philadelphia/Ireland connection would probably repay examination.

Presbyterian immigrant merchants seem to have operated in the earlier part of the century in a more limited way. Perhaps typically they began like Joseph Read, a maltster from Carrickfergus, who set up a retail business in Trenton, New Jersey, dying with no fortune in 1737: it was left to his son Andrew to move the business to Philadelphia in 1750 and become prosperous. William and Edward Paterson emigrated as tinsmiths to Berlin, Connecticut in 1735, commemorated in contemporary local doggerel:

O what's that lordly dish so rare
That glitters forth in splendour's glare?

. . . . . . Tis a tin pan
The first made in the colony,
The maker, Pattison's jest by,
From Ireland in the last ship o'er
You all can by.

Their brother, Richard, migrated from Derry to Delaware in 1747, becoming a prosperous pedlar, and then small manufacturer. By then, however, much larger businesses were being established by Presbyterians, both in organising the commerical life of the interior as surpluses first emerged (from towns like Frederick, Maryland, and Lancaster, Pennsylvania), and by sharing in the rapid expansion of the seaboard cities. In the 1760s, William Allen and Blair McClenachan of Philadelphia were two of the wealthiest men of the middle colonies; Oliver Pollock, a Coleraine man untypically married to a Catholic and intimate with the Jesuits of Havana, had cornered much of the trade of (then Spanish) New Orleans, and had wide connections in Europe, the Caribbean and the British colonies. Instances could be multiplied.

Finally, burgeoning trade and growing toleration caused members of the Irish and Franco-Irish Catholic merchant and shipping families to turn their eyes to Philadelphia. Stephen Moylan, Thomas Fitzsimons, John Mease, and Richard Meade were the most important among them, Meade being the first to come, in 1732 via Barbados. In New York by 1750s several Irish ship-owners and captains, most notably Daniel O'Brien, were engaged in shipping goods to the West Indies, Portugal and coastally north and south.

Merchants could not function without sailors. Today vast and semi-automated cargo vessels can carry smallish crews. In the 1770s, ships commonly weighed between 50 and 450 tons (against up to 25,000 tons today), so that the crew complement was considerable for the cargoes carried. Under the Navigation Acts, Irish ships and seamen were allowed to participate in the inter-colonial, colonial-English, and Irish-English trades as well as the colonial-Irish trade: in short, to do more than Irish merchants could. Resultantly, a large population of sailors emerged in Ireland, based particularly upon the Catholic lower classes of the southern and eastern ports of Ireland. Their great fear was impressment into the British navy in war-time, which they avoided by many clever contrivances. Many passed into the American merchant service. The ship *Massachusetts* in 1790 carried twenty-six New England sailors and ten Irish out of Boston. The relative numbers of Irish sailors must have been considerably higher in vessels out of New York and Philadelphia, given the part Irish composition, origins and connections of its shipping circles as seen above. The radicalism of the 'Jack Tars' of New York noted by historians in relation to the link with Britain, might have been strengthened by this element. Irish sailors' involvement in smuggling and naval service avoidance (quite apart from their other anti-English traditions, expressed in pro-French privateering activities from 1756–63), would hardly have made of them a conservative element during the sailors' debates on independence after 1773.

John McCusker has shown that between 1734–1776, at least one hundred and sixteen separate Irish-owned vessels registered at Philadelphia, eighty from Ulster ports, twenty-five from Dublin. Many of them had been constructed in Philadelphia. Given the nature of seamen, transference from these ships to American ships in the inter-colonial and West Indian trades would have been natural. More specifically, there is evidence of ships' masters in Philadelphia seeking Irish seamen or Irish servants as trainees: thus immigrant Robert Campbell was indented to William Moore, a mariner in the Jamaica trade in 1746, for example; and runaway notices for Irish sailors were not uncommon in colonial newspapers, as John Madden and Patrick Carvan fled the *Amelia* at Bermuda Hundred in 1769. Seafaring (outside New England) was both squalid and despised, and thus considered suitable to the Irish, as were other such then low status occupations as school-mastering. For the Irish on the other hand, seafaring (like colonial school-mastering) offered at least the relative freedom of mobility and the unpredictable. Nonetheless, occasionally the horror of it all peers out from below the billowing sails: Henry Clark, master of the *Middleton*, advertised for an Irish ship's boy named simply Tom, aged from three to five, who fled his vessel at West Point with two other sailors. That Irish sailors are advertised as fleeing both British and American ships in colonial ports, as frequently as English sailors, may indicate how common was their presence. Moreover, ships' masters were often warned by the owners of ordinary Irish runaway servants to beware lest they attempt to pass themselves off as sailors, and thus leave the colony in which they had been bound. These were but fragments of the broader movement. Many of the vessels recorded by McCusker voyaged repeatedly into Philadelphia, the city's journals reveal, as likewise did those entering Maryland and Virginia harbours. British vessels which provisioned and gathered servants in Cork, Waterford or Youghal probably filled out crew complements there also. The crews of America's biggest trade, the West Indies, drew on the lower class Irish-born and Irish creole population of the islands. All this requires detailed and imaginative reconstruction. One chilling instance may be given among many to illuminate that world. In October, 1744, the all Irish crew of the *King's Meadow,* bound from Jamaica to London with five French and Spanish prisoners, conspired with them, murdered the captain and first mate, and aimed for the Canaries; only their interception by another British vessel caused their capture, the Irishmen being sent for trial in London, the continentals for trial in Virginia.

There was a reverse side to all these connections. It is often assumed that the impact of the American Revolution upon Ireland was indirect: the publishing of pamphlets, the letters from emigrant kin in America, the effect of trade embargo, military recruitment and parliamentary debate. But at that time Ireland even more closely matched the description of it by English chief secretary George Wyndham in the first years of this century: that it was a country governed more than most by conversation. Through networks of sailors and merchants, often linking through the Caribbean and France, more vivid and direct (if distorted) information must have been coming into Ireland about events in America from the emergence of the first anti-British tensions there in 1759 through the Stamp Act crisis, right down through the Intolerable Acts and the early years of the revolution. Conversations now lost to scholarship may well have been the principal route of American influence upon Ireland. Certainly it is known that sea traders such as Belfast's John McCracken (father of United Irishman Henry Joy), earlier gained much of their liberalism from their overseas experiences.

Yet, despite all these connections of empire and trade, one must stress that they were no more than connections. Two thirds of the trade of the American colonies was inter-colonial or with the West Indies. Ireland and the colonies were indeed connected, but were yet different worlds, their day-to-day connections being elsewhere. For Ireland, the more common connections reinforced the reality of British dominion; for the Americans colonies, their more usual links underscored the unreality of that dominion, for they were Western Hemispheric. Not surprisingly, the richest connection between Ireland and America, that of emigrant Irishmen in the colonies, is not straightforward even though vital and humane.

Chapter 3

Mixed Exodus: Emigration from Ireland to Colonial America, 1715-1776

Two Emigrations, or Several?

A committee of the Continental Congress, mulling over possible insignia for the newly independent United States, at first determined upon a composite coat of arms, reflecting Tom Paine's assertion that 'Europe, and not England, is the parent country of America.' It would have included an Irish emblem. The adult generation of 1776 were acutely aware of the Irish element among them, an element which had so well assimilated into the nation's mainstream after the Revolution as to virtually disappear after 1800, until freshly renewed. Two rival camps of Americans somewhat polemically recovered and piously studied the extent and traditions of the pre-Revolutionary Irish America during the peak years of the second Irish America, between 1850 and 1940. While much material is therefore available upon the pre-Revolutionary Irish as a result, it has been too neatly segmented into a large Scotch-Irish (Ulster Scot, or Irish Presbyterian) division, and a smaller Irish Catholic division. We shall observe this division, for it is very well founded, yet suggest its very real limitations. Likewise, there was a competitive respectability at work among the historians of both camps, so that native and settler stock Irishmen have been distorted into forerunners of the Republican businessmen of Pittsburg or the Democratic merchants and lawyers of New York of 1900. Thus both Michael O'Brien and Wayland Dunaway pay negligible attention to the sources on colonial labourers, or indentured servants, although it is there that general historians of colonial American have discovered most consistent evidence of the Irish and Ulster Scot presence, and imparted a sense of reality to an otherwise shadowy immigration.

There is little question that around two thirds of Irish emigration from 1717-1776 was of Ulster origin. The most careful scholar has documented a movement of 100- to 120,000 in those years from the five leading north Irish ports, and admits that others left by other ports, including a minority from southern ports. His work can be extended, as we shall see. American scholars customarily estimate that between 200- and 250,000 Ulster Scots entered America in colonial times. Studies of nomenclature revealed by the first Federal Census (1790) suggest that 9% of the American people were ethnic Scots Irish, a figure later adjusted downwards, but which we shall suggest was somewhat an underestimate. The methods of those studies, however, were considerably more sophisticated than has usually been supposed. If corrections are made, it is probable that the Scots Irish in 1790 were as many as 11% of New Yorkers, 21% of Pennsylvanians, 11% of Marylanders, 14% of Virginians, 13% of North Carolinians, 24% of South Carolinians and 27% of Georgians. Barring general infertility or an unrecorded death-syndrome amongst servants from Ulster, and excluding the possibility that the historians of *Scottish* emigration have been grievously in error, the figures should even be higher (see following, and Appendix One). Certainly, however, there is no question that the movement from Ulster was predominantly an Ulster Scottish, Presbyterian one, although there is good reason to think this can be exaggerated, as we shall see. That the *principal* Irish movement was an Ulster one in general, however, is clear. Yet the southern Irish one was also substantial. Remarkably, if both movements are combined, one discovers that the Irish in America in the period of the American Revolution, between 350,000 and 450,000, were then a considerably larger portion of the white population of around three millions at most, than was the case in 1900, when just five million Irish Americans, migrants and their children, had great cultural coherence, although a fraction of the country's seventy-six million inhabitants. Visibility and power are not always a matter of numbers alone. Yet this should caution historians against dismissing too readily the conviction of contemporaries such as Benjamin Franklin and David Ramsay about the role of the Irish in the politics and armies of the American Revolution.

The history of the Ulster emigration is an oft-told tale. Successive re-tellings have amplified the details, shorn off some of the mythic elements, but confirmed the central narrative. Hence this account of it can be brief, since full and fairly recent accounts are easily available. In 1717-18, the leases of the Scottish settler stock began to fall in. The Anglo-Irish landlords now secure and no longer under pressure to populate their estates, granted new leases on shorter and more costly terms, even holding them up to competitive bidding. The process was repeated again in 1735–9, and again in 1740–41. Rents often doubled and even quadrupled. Native Irish Catholics, prepared to pare their living standards to the bone to regain farms in ancestral localities, often outbid the sitting tenants. It galled Presbyterians to be thus 'put on a level with the Papists': as in modern times, the invasion of one's craft or locality by a people previously despised can lead to bitter uncertainty as to one's own self-esteem, unless the bold leap is made to the vision of a common human dignity. This was then out of the question. High prices, a grave currency and capital shortage, trade stagnation, local scarcity, growing families, the cornering of the market for various commodities, and even famine (as in 1740–41) intensified disenchantment with Ulster. Nor should it be supposed that prosperous eighteentieth century farms (on the model of England's home counties) were left behind. Ulster farms were often fairly rudimentary, techniques poor, crop yields light. Nor is it surprising that America was the destination. Francis Makemie and others from the Laggan in Co. Donegal had helped establish the first (Philadelphia) colonial Presbytery in 1706–7. James Logan, Penn's Quaker secretary, invited his fellow Ulstermen to migrate in 1717, at the very time they were likely to come. As Penn's chief land agent, his invitation carried double force. The relatively inhospitable reception for the Scotch Irish who went to New England between 1718–22 (where they began the frontier settlements of Bangor and Belfast in Maine, Hillsboro county in New Hampshire, Orange country in Vermont, and others) further determined that the mass of migrants go to the middle colonies.

From the northern ports, three thousand left in the first wave (1717–18), fifteen thousand in the second (1725–29), and thereafter a continuous flow, stimulated by the famine of 1740–1 in which 400,000 died in Ireland as a whole. By that date too, emigration was being organised regularly as a business. Shipping companies had agents in all the leading Ulster market towns. Officials, speculators, and land grantees like Governor Arthur Dobbs in North Carolina, William Johnson in upper New York, William Beverly and Benjamin Borden in Virginia, not to speak of virtual chancers like Alexander McNutt, all saw that a stream of propaganda was sent back to Ulster. Ships' captains and agents were not above telling hard pressed Ulster women that their lot would be easier in America, where their work would be lighter, and their husbands would use them better! The growing trade between Philadelphia and Newcastle (Del.) in flaxseed, timber and wheat to Belfast, Derry and Newry meant that captains not engaged to carry linen back, to pick up a provision cargo in Cork, or a goods cargo in England, found the passenger carrying trade an excellent way to make ends meet for the return home. Ulster farmers could often sell the good-will of their tenancy, receive a consideration for their improvements to their farm, and sell their effects, and thus bring a small capital with them, as well as pay for the voyage.

By the end of the Seven Year War in 1763, conditions in Ulster had deteriorated for many, as rapid population growth pressed upon resources. The tendency of the area's small-holders to sub-divide their farms with their sons or brothers, and to meet the competitive rent-bidding by extravagant promises based upon what they and their womenfolk expected to make in spinning and weaving linen, meant that the economy was more precarious as a whole by the 1770s than is usually thought. Arthur Young thought 'their portions are so small that they cannot live on them' and that their reliance upon weaving in turn spoiled their none-too-skilled farming abilities. Certain landlords were also becoming more ruthless, notably the Marquis of Donegall in Co. Antrim, whose evictions and high rent demands forced 30,000 out. A recession in the linen trade, caused by over-expansion after 1763, created a severe crisis, since 'Scarce any of them but are weavers' and therefore rents were 'got from them with great difficulty, depending entirely on their web', as Young wrote of west Antrim. The years 1771–1775 saw the normal Ulster outflow to America of up to five thousand a year rise to over ten thousand a year. After the painful bottling-up caused by the continuance of these circumstances during the American War, the outflow resumed in strength from

1783. Endemic rural crisis in Ulster in the latter half of the century was revealed in upsurges of agrarian violence, whether directed against landlords and officials (the Oakboys in 1764, Steelboys in 1770–1), against each other along sectarian lines (Defenders, Peep O'Day Boys and Orangemen from around 1792–95), or against the state itself (the United Irishmen in 1798).

All of this raises a question about the pre-eminent 'mythic' aspect of the migration: that it was stimulated by Anglican repression of Presbyterianism. Certainly, as we have seen, discrimination did exist, perhaps the more oppressive in its socio-economic aspect (that most landlords were Anglo-Irish and usually magistrates as well) than in any generally proscriptive terms. But the confiscation of farm produce as tithes to support Anglican clergy was a very specific injustice. The question of the collective status of the Presbyterians vis-à-vis native Catholics perhaps gave an edge to resentments which might otherwise have sat more lightly upon them, as similarly lessening constraints did upon the shoulders of English dissenters. Despite the exclusion from civic offices inherent in the Test Act of 1703, general toleration was confirmed by an act of 1719, a state grant for the maintenance of Presbyterian clergy was restored, and by the 1750s, militia officerships and certain local government positions were open to Presbyterians by default. Trade, manufacture and landholding were never closed to them; higher education was available in Scotland; they had powerful lobbies working for them in Dublin. That emigration steadily increased as Anglican pressure upon them diminished indicates its relative independence from such considerations. Scotch-Irish protagonists in the late nineteenth century perhaps strained too hard to fit their ancestors into the accepted mould of Pilgrim Father emigration: that of supposed refugees from persecution, seeking a new Israel for conscience sake. Instead, the emigration was quite similar to that of nineteenth century Catholic Irish countrymen, also seeking economic security unattainable at home. Nonetheless, a pervasive alienation from the Anglican establishment was a contributory factor to the disenchantment that made for emigration, and helped shape the politico-religious traditions of the Scotch-Irish in Pennsylvania, as we shall see. Not surprisingly, the Presbyterian lobbies in London and Dublin exaggerated the religious element in the migration to pressure the establishment into concessions to them, with the argument that the loyalist or Protestant interest in Ireland could not be bled further with safety to the Crown's power.

As nineteenth century emigrants sought the livelihood available in the burgeoning industrial and transportation economy of the urban frontier, so the eighteenth century Ulster emigrants sought livelihood and security on the farming frontier of the Back Country, unless exceptional skills or capital made entry into the maturing seaboard economy (of farm or trade) possible. As the nineteenth century Irish sought power, comfort and familiarity in urban concentration, so too the Ulstermen sought independence, power and familiarity in the *relatively* exclusive settlement of whole blocs of western lands. The patterns of their settlement was quite systematic. The first groups

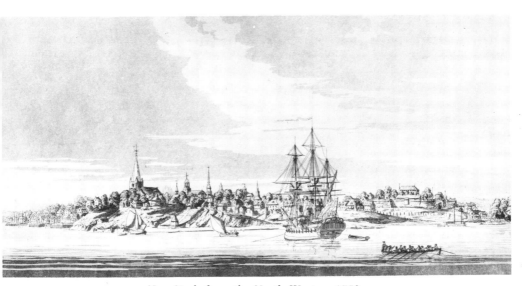

New York from the North West, c. 1770

took what farms were left in the region of the Delaware estuary: the lands that are now west New Jersey, north Delaware, and north eastern Pennsylvania. Smaller numbers spread at the same time into the northern and back counties of Maryland (1717–1730). Thereafter the main tide moved west along the Schuylkill and Susquehanna rivers after 1730, crossed the Blue Ridge mountains, and turned southward along the rich - yet still uninhabited Cumberland Valley. They shared this movement with German settlers, staking out farms county-by-county in an alternating pattern with the Germans: the two groups rarely mixed. As the Beverly-Borden grants became available, and with a friendly governor in William Gooch, the Ulstermen then proceeded further south along the 'great valley' into Virginia, still between the Blue Ridge and the Appalachians (1732–36). In eastern and central Pennsylvania their significant leaders had been clergymen, such as Francis Alison, Gilbert Tennent and others. In the Valley of Virginia, Ulster laymen such as James Patton, John Caldwell and John Lewis assumed community leadership in the absence of clergy. Thereafter, the migration, increasingly a third wave, second generation one, fragmented socially and culturally. By the 1750s, it was filling up the backcountry of North Carolina and spilling onto the rolling and forested Piedmont. In the 1760s, it fanned out onto the South Carolina Piedmont. In both these latter instances it met with other waves of Ulster immigration coming directly through the port of Charleston in response to generous offers of free land (after 1730) to Protestant settlers in South Carolina, and to Governor Dobbs' settlement schemes in North Carolina.

Not until considerably later did Ulster folk cross the Allegheny and Appalachian mountains to the west of the valleys and piedmonts: from the 1760s they moved into western Pennsylvania, as also into West Virginia (as it would later become); in the 1780s, through the Cumberland Gap, into Tennessee and Kentucky. This was almost wholly a second generation movement. It is notable, however, that two areas of the heaviest fighting in the American War were among those settled by the first three waves of migration: west Jersey and east Pennsylvania in the north, and the Carolinas Piedmont in the south, as shall be discussed again.

What sort of people were these settlers? What kind of life did they create? Did they retain distinctively Ulster characteristics and peculiarities? Had they an explicit collective tradition at the time of the American Revolution? These questions are not easily answered, despite their importance. Quite apart from the deficiencies and contradictions in American sources, we know little enough about them even in Ulster. Secondly, it is vital to stress that between the waves of 1717–1730, those of the 1740s–1750s, and those of the 1770s and later, there must have been considerable differences, caused by changing Ulster backgrounds. The earlier settlers were much closer to the Scottish background (many indeed, born in Scotland) and to the hostility towards the native Irish of the era of the Williamite wars and the passage of the Penal Laws: John Lewis had it boasted upon his tombstone that he "slew the Irish laird." (His landlord, strangely, had been one of the few Catholic gentry who kept his land despite the confiscations: Lewis killed him in a quarrel over rent. The usage 'laird' interestingly points back to the traditional lowland Scots resentment of that area's social system). The later migrants came from an Ulster increasingly transformed by rising population, diminishing Scottish connections, changing economy, and more liberal attitudes amongst many of its articulate class: traders, ministers, craftsmen. Historians make clear distinctions between the Irish emigrants of 1825, of 1850, of 1875 and 1905. Strangely, the Ulster emigrants of the eighteenth century are all lumped together. Yet, to take but one example, in the later period, as relative impoverishment grew and emigration was rationalised, by the 1770s as many as two-thirds of Ulster emigrants were going as indentured servants or redemptioners (terms to be discussed shortly), whereas in earlier years most apparently went as free migrants, often organised by locality. Almost all the early migrants went into farming; some of the later farmer-weaver immigrants stayed in Philadelphia and other towns, hoping to turn their trade to a livelihood.

A more vital question arises. Were the Ulster migrants as uniformly Ulster Scot and Presbyterian as has been supposed? To begin to properly answer this would require much more accurate pictures of eighteenth century Ulster and of 'Ulster America' before 1776 than we have. Moreover precisely this question is the one most clouded by filiopietist acrimony in the past in America, and pregnant with political implications in Ireland today. Certain tentative suggestions can be made. T. W. Moody suggested in 1946 that "It may well be that the catholic and protestant emigrations from Ireland were more closely intermingled than has commonly been supposed." The report of the American Historical Association on the *National Stocks in the Population of the United States . . . 1790 (1932)*, compiled under the dispassionate auspices of J. F. Jameson and Marcus Hansen with the assistance of the American Council of Learned Societies, stressed the prevalence of native Ulster Irish nomenclature amongst the areas of 'Ulster Scot' settlement in the colonies: names such as Boyle, Devlin, Doherty, Gallagher, Heaney, Hamill, Keenan, McArdle, McCaffrey, McCann, McParland, Mulholland and Traynor, together with the more obvious (but religio-ethnically more dubious) Maguire and O'Donnell. William Douglass wrote in 1755 that the fall-in of leases "occasioned an emigration of many north of Ireland Scotch Presbyterians, with an intermixture of wild Irish Roman Catholicks." The chief authority on the Valley of Virginia during the Revolution notes that there is much evidence in its county court records that the prosperous Scotch-Irish farmer settlers had native Irish servants. This certainly is the case for those areas for which we have evidence upon runaway Irish bondsmen. Certainly wealthier settlers commonly brought their servants: the Quakers to Philadelphia from Ireland particularly so.

Nor is it simply a matter of Ulster Irishmen of Catholic background. Clearly there were many such, going in client status, if not as bondsfolk, perhaps ingratiating themselves by a change of religion, (as William Johnson's servant Bernard Lafferty presumably did:—for his loyalty he returned to a sheriff's office in Co. Tyrone). In 1715 Ulster had a population of 600,000, one third Scottish stock Presbyterian, with up to 130,000 English stock Anglicans and over 270,000 Irish Catholics. This was following a continuing Scottish migration that brought fresh settlers into Ulster as late as the fifty thousand who immigrated between 1690–1715. Earlier, as a Census of the mid-seventeenth century reveals, native Irish Catholics intermingled with Scottish and English settlers in virtually every townland of Ulster: contrary to most American works upon the Scotch Irish, Ulster was *not* another Scotland, although there were indeed areas of heavy Scottish concentration (north Down, south Antrim) and lighter concentration (south Armagh, west Derry, east Donegal). The earlier eighteenth century migration to America probably reflected both the continuing antagonisms but also the peculiar interdependences of native Irish servants and settler farmers; the later migrations (particularly from Antrim in the 1770s) the clearly Presbyterian Scottish traditions of those special localities. But rural over-population as the century progressed was most intense in areas of seventeenth century *English* settlement, such as north and central Armagh, so that it seems unlikely that this did not also affect the character of 'Ulster Scot' migration. In the eighteenth century the fusion of the English and Scottish elements in Ulster culture (a product of industrialisation in the Lagan Valley from 1800 onward) has not yet occurred, outside some towns: religion, dialect, social customs and farm practices were somewhat distinct for the two groups, settled in different areas. "The number of non-Presbyterian emigrants from Ulster may have been greater than has generally been thought" conceded R. J. Dickson, and evidence supports his intuition. Although he argued it "was certainly greater than the number of the non-Presbyterians who emigrated through" Derry, Portrush, Larne, Belfast and Newry, it actually came through these ports.

   Generally Anglican emigration from Ireland is unstudied. Some indications of its possible volume will be given in the discussion of indentured immigration, but it seems probable, given their favoured status in Ireland, that Anglicans were the most likely to emigrate as free individuals. The role of 'placemen', largely Anglican, has already been indicated, as has the existence of numbers of convert native Irishmen, and of convert Presbyterians: America offered these a certain freedom from reproach (and perhaps self-reproach) their own society would not. They included famous men: Croghan, Johnson, Dulany and James Kane of New York, among former Catholics, and Hugh Gaine among ex-Presbyterians. For obvious reasons, worldly motives were not absent in the earlier conduct of such men in religious matters: nonetheless evidence suggests such a man as Croghan found genuine satisfaction in his later years as an Anglican. For most Anglo-Irish immigrants, however, Anglicanism was the religion of their genuine conviction. Revolutionary soldiers such as Edward Hand and Anthony Wayne were active in starting Anglican communities in Pennsylvania, even if others such as Richard Butler were more indifferent. A large proportion of the Anglican clergy in Maryland was Irish, and a scattering in the Carolinas and Virginia. Some were good, such as Charles Woodmason, a pastor of "great simplicity of character and most unassuming," the chronicler of the back country, or James McCartney, a man "of pious and zealous endeavours," to quote contemporaries on both. The majority were worthless, such as Daniel Earl from Bandon, grandson of an Irish Lord Chief Justice of Queen Anne's time, who won the lines from an irate colonial "A half-built church/And a broken down steeple/A herring-fishing parson/And a dam set of people." In New York and Philadelphia, Anglicans were founders of churches and of the friendly Irish societies, and in the Tidewater plantation country, they shared the religion of the planter majority, as did jurist Peter Lyons in Virginia and the Rutledges in South Carolina. Otherwise the Irish Anglicans who remained visible were either the exceptionally committed or the time-serving, and the task of the former was not simplified by the unpopularity of the latter. Their difficulties can be illustrated from the case of Thomas Barton. Immigrating to central Pennsylvania in 1750, he found many Anglicans without a pastor scattered among the Presbyterians in the Ulster settlements. He himself returned to Britain to seek training and ordination. Upon his return, with the outbreak of the French and Indian War (the Seven Years War), he was appointed a chaplain to the provincial militia, but a mass protest by Ulster Presbyterian officers forced revocation of his appointment, and Barton had to accompany his charges in the guise of a volunteer officer. The Presbyterian ministers themselves (of Donegal Presbytery) were embarrassed, and offered formal apology, but could do little with the trenchant anti-Anglicanism of their laymen. His peacetime ministry to Ulster Anglicans in York, Carlisle and Huntington counties was itself hindered. Irish Anglicans turn up in every status and area in the colonies: but so fragmentedly that one cannot generalise about them: how can one link John Searson, the melancholic and wandering Londonderry merchant of the Jerseys and east Pennsylvania, a Puritan in theology, with the Jarratts, a poor immigrant farming family in New Kent county, Virginia, that was afraid of the local plantation gentry yet lively and content. Can one link these again with John Ormsby, who immigrated in 1752, and attempted a parody of the excesses of Anglo-Ireland on the banks of the Ohio? Ormsby acquired a vast land tract around frontier Pittsburg and let it out to eighteen tenants, presumably Ulstermen, in return for a third of their produce; became a key member of Pittsburg's mercantile plutocracy, and his family were among those who urged the harshest possible measures against the 'Whiskey Insurrectionists' of 1794. Unlike in Ireland, the miniscule Anglo-Irish minority lacked the coherence to establish a secure niche in American life, nor were the rest of the Irish inclined to grant it to them.

Widespread Anglican indifference, when the social props of their religiosity were removed, and Catholic subordination, which we shall see, best explains why Presbyterianism emerged at first as the master institution of the Ulster emigration in America, thus colouring its subsequent history so disproportionately as to be thought by implication only a Scotch-Irish movement, or mostly so. The achievements of Presbyterianism, however, should not be exaggerated. Up to 300,000 Ulster immigrants went to America by 1776. Given high colonial birth rates, survivors and descendants ought to have numbered more in 1800; yet in that year there were·reportedly only fifteen thousand members of Presbyterian churches in the United States, and many of them were of English Presbyterian, New England Congregational and Continental Reformed background. Although other factors were involved in this situation (granted each adult member meant another three to five family attenders), one obvious explanation, that only a majority proportion of Ulster immigrants, not all, were Presbyterians, has never been advanced. Such an interpretation would at least mean that the Presbyterian church had not failed so catastrophically in America as the figures would otherwise suggest!

What of emigration from the rest of Ireland before the Revolution, other than Anglican? Between 1880 and the 1930s, when immigration restriction sentiment defined itself in the United States along the curious lines that the best Americans were those with blood or kinship links to colonial migrants, demonstration that there had been appreciable numbers of colonial Americans of Irish Catholic background seemed vital, and historians such as Michael O'Brien so strained the evidence to prove that there were, that they lost the case with the body of dispassionate observers. More recent and cautious work suggests that indeed there were many such immigrants. The *National Stocks . . . 1790* report demonstrated that of heads of families 4.9% were of native Irish background. Its method was to take a broad sample of representative surnames peculiar to the population of Leinster (such as Moran and Flannery), to Munster (such as McCarthy and Ryan), to native Ulster, and to Scots Ulster (such as Orr and Boyd), and to infer from the relationship between the proportions of people of those surnames in Ireland in the 1890s and the proportions of people of the same names in America in 1790 the probable Irish and Scotch Irish element in the colonial population. The procedure was duplicated for each of Ireland's provinces, in relationship to America, as well, giving virtually identical results. Generally, one is inclined to trust the conclusion. Yet there are two reservations. As the report admitted, it excluded undistinctively Irish and Scotch Irish names. It thereby over-assigned all Munros, Frasers, and Buchanans to Scottish origin, underestimating the Ulster Scot element, but, more importantly, was thus unable to reach any real estimate of the numbers of Anglo-Irish stock Americans, and also underestimated the southern Irish component. For the report failed to recognise the significance of the 'Old English' (medieval originating) element in the Catholic population particularly in Leinster, while admitting "the probability that the numerous English-Irish in Leinster migrated at a greater rate than the Celtic and hence gave that province greater representation in the American population than has so far been established." It was precisely from this province that much of the Catholic migration seems to have come, from the ports of Dundalk, Dublin, Wexford and Waterford. Nonetheless, a double check on such names as Bolger, Flood, Kinsella and Nolan (such as the report carried out), names very representative of the province, probably goes far to balance this error, except in the case of Anglo-Irish Protestants, and the more obvious case of name-changing.

This somewhat technical and dry discussion, however, helps to introduce the more controversial yet sound claim that up to 100,000 emigrants from the south of Ireland, Catholic, Anglican and others, emigrated to pre-Revolutionary America, the majority Catholic. This might seem to contradict the common observation of contemporaries: "An Irish papist will not leave the Kingdom to go to any of our colonies for any prospect of gain" (Edward Willes, 1759), a sentiment repeated by William King, Thomas Newenham, Arthur Young and most colourfully by Samuel Madden (1738): "they are fond of living in their own country and averse to our American rambles." But notably all these were outsiders to the native Irish community.

Young, the most careful investigator, spoke largely to landlords, and was most sensitive (as they were) to the migration of settled tenant 'yeomen' who left with skill, family and some capital. Yet, only in passing, he refers to migration from Courtown and other Catholic districts in Leinster and Munster. More significantly, the upheavals of the seventeenth century together with poverty, urban growth, rise of dairying and beef production, class and land-tenure inequities, attractions of soldiering, regional famines (general in 1740), and other forces in the eighteenth century produced an unknown yet well evidenced floating population among the native Irish. Tenants or prospective tenants, skulking around their ancestral lands (as Protestants tended to put it with distaste), were loath to leave; but there were scores of thousands with little to lose. Many migrated from district to district in search of work or service, thousands going to England (as Dorothy George and others have shown); young men took to the roads for schooling; whole families migrated to the towns, often drawn first by seasonal employment in meat and butter packing; others sought outlets for skills on completion of apprenticeships; youngsters romantically and vainly headed for port cities in hopes of fame or fortune, turning to the sea or the army when else had failed. In a society where old patterns of native subordination had given way to newer patterns of service, clientship and hopeful servility, many fled bad masters and yet sought good ones. Others wandered as journeymen, tradesmen and apprentices, as jack-of-all-trades, petty criminals, and adventurers. It is notorious among census takers today and among social historians of the nineteenth century that society's underclass in every Western or Westernizing society is in a continuous state of desperation, movement and flux: and today American or South African officials cannot account for admitted millions of rural-to-urban migrants, many of them alien. Ireland in the eighteenth century was pre-eminently the society in which such patterns should also be expected to prevail to at least some degree: it is known that the hearth and poll tax rolls for the pre-1760 period systematically underestimate the Catholic populations of Irish towns. Moreover, Ireland (unlike England) had no Poor Law, confining people to their native localities; and, on the other hand, the frequent passage of anti-vagabondage legislation and the Ascendancy obsession with crime, are indicative of a ruling elite anxiously and consciously out-of-touch with their country's underclass. In short, if the majority of Catholics remained tenacious of their localities and fitted into the established society by tenancies, sub-tenancies and employments, however casual, there was a considerable floating population which had drifted from these moorings. The majority of southern Irish emigrants were of this latter type, very different from the Philadelphia Irish merchants, Quaker or Catholic, we met previously. Indeed, the rapid growth of Cork, Dublin, Belfast and Derry presumed the existence of such a class.

Their whole pattern of emigration has to be understood against this background, their routes to America in terms of the patterns of connection described in the last chapter. Before the 1740s (with its intensification of trade), the movement was fragmentary: for example, in 1725, two known vessels sailed from Dublin to Virginia, with 136 passengers and with 115 passenger servants respectively; in 1735, four ships went to Philadelphia and one to Charleston from Dublin with unknown numbers of passengers; with the great eighteenth century Irish famine of 1740-41, there was a marked increase in southern (as northern) Irish emigration to the colonies, with the largest numbers before 1770–76. Most of the passengers were bond servants, pledged in advance to be placed by their captain with a short-handed American planter or merchant; a few travelled with better-off, usually Protestant, Irish immigrants. (An unimportant fraction only consisted of Ulster Presbyterians who found it convenient to sail from the nation's largest port). A third group, other than servants and independent immigrants, was that of transported convicts and vagabonds. The precise dimensions of the general flow, quite apart from the proportions of its various components, are impossible to estimate.

The 'servant' trade from Ireland had been established as early as the mid-seventeenth century. It was a logical corollary to the place the native Irish were expected to occupy in the English trans-Atlantic scheme of things. Down to 1715, Ireland had a net Protestant immigration (English, Scots, Huguenots, Palatines) and an officially encouraged net Catholic outflow. Both Cromwell's circle, and the Restoration circle of Lord Clarendon, encouraged the trade; the Navigation Act of 1663 permitted it. Initially, the majority were sent to the West Indies: "This Illand is the Dunghill wharone England doth cast forth its rubidg," complained Henry Whistler of Barbados. Indeed, colonials had mixed feelings about them. Jamaica discriminately offered an £18 bounty for British immigrants, a £15 bounty for Irish. Virginia and Maryland placed duties upon the importation of Irish Catholic servants, together starting in 1699. The tax was not high, at 20 shillings per head (Va., 1699; Md., 1704 and later 40 shillings). For servants could fetch between ten and thirty-five pounds for their bond years. Pennsylvania taxed all Irish servants in 1729, "probably for religious reasons" as well, and doubtless also because of James Logan's bitter disenchantment with his countrymen as useful inhabitants. The laws of the southern colonies were explicitly "to prevent the too great importation of Papists" as also were increasing restrictions in the Carribbean. But it is noteworthy that the trade was not prohibited. Action was only taken to discourage it where possible alternatives were available. The rise of black enslavement and the African slave trade, rather than legislation, helped curtail it.

Nonetheless, its persistence after the availability of black slaves can be explained. Virginia and Maryland granted 'head-right' land bounties of 50 to 100 acres to those who brought *bona fide* white inhabitants to the territory (the precaution was made necessary because enterprising sea-captains had sold head-rights on their passengers for cash before 1700). In the Carolinas and Georgia, the tendency was to restrict these grants to those bringing Protestant immigrants only, so that the majority of these southern Irish servants and transportees went to Virginia and Maryland. Secondly, the incoming Irish had skills which blacks initially lacked, and which free British immigrants sold to the planters at exorbitant day-rates. Thus a ship load of indentured servants from Dublin in 1749 included a spinner, tailors, a glass-grinder, shoemakers, linen weavers and bricklayers. Runaway advertisements (for servants absconding before completion of their bound terms) mention Irish servants in several colonies as millers, coopers, peruke-makers, plasterers, smiths, and turners; the Mayor of Dublin indented hoziers, a bookbinder, a gardener and others in 1750 for America. Not surprisingly, the only Irishmen such major American planters as George Washington and Robert Carter had on their Virginia estates were skilled craftsmen, such as Daniel Sullivan, who trained Carter's black textile force. Thirdly, white Irish servants, particularly those with some experience of deferential status in a better-off household, were acceptable in the situations of domestic companionship common to isolated Virginia and Maryland farms, from which blacks were excluded by reason of strangeness, prejudice and fear. In short, while carefully confining Irish Catholic immigration, the planters of the southern and Carribbean colonies were inclined by various factors to leave the door ajar to it. They did not open it in welcome, even though John Locke himself wished they would. Hugh Jones, in his *Present State of Virginia* (1724), gives a remarkably accurate over-view of these particulars as Eugene McCormick, Abbot Smith and Audrey Lockhart have reconstructed them from other evidence. He conveys a flavour of their context:

> The Ships that transport these Things [imports from England] often call at Ireland to victual, and bring over white Servants, which are of three kinds. 1. Such as come upon certain wages by Agreement for a certain Time. 2. Such as come bound by Indenture, commonly called Kids, who are usually to serve for four or five years; and 3. those Convicts or Felons that are transported ... abundance of them do practice great mischief, commit Robbery and Murder, and spoil Servants, that were before very good ... though indeed some of them proved indifferent good. Their being sent thither to work as Slaves for Punishment, is but a mere Notion, for few of them have ever lived so well and so easy before, especially if they are good for anything.

Jones too concluded by noting the especially advantageous situation of those brought up to a special trade, (stressing those of smith, carpenter, tailor, cooper and bricklayer), when their term of service or of sentence was over, so that his separate comment on servants as the "worst of Mankind, the Refuse of Great Britain and Ireland, and the Outcast of the People" seems irritable rather than dispassionate. 'Kids' indeed there were: children were desired as more tractable, and served longer terms (sometimes until eighteen or twenty one), so that one reads of one Polly Murphy, who went missing in New Jersey in 1775, a servant 'very near five years of age.' Adults, with usually four or five year terms (unless convicts), found it of advantage to go voluntarily as time passed. In 1745, in Dublin, two inns on the quays, both named 'The New York and Philadelphia Arms' served as clearing houses and shipping agencies for such would-be servants.

As for convict transportation, the Dublin Parliament allowed transportation as a reprieve for the capital offences of stealing less than twenty shillings, ten sheep or two cows in 1703. Four years later, vagabondage was made subject to transportation, an act subsequently renewed. In 1726, merchants were granted twenty shillings for each prisoner they had bound to them (many re-sold the prisoners at a profit). In 1730, perjury was made transportable (and it should be recalled that to the mass of the native Irish, perjury was the only logical way to handle the Anglo-Irish court system, as was mutually understood). Finally, in 1735, vagabondage was made mandatorily subject to transportation. The first acts with transportation seen as a reprieve, were humane by the standards of the time. The vagabondage acts were so inhumane that there is little evidence that they were generally applied even if local assizes might be sporadically severe. By our standards, however, many cityfolk and countrymen were transported to America for paltry offences, others for better cause. At the Dublin Quarter Sessions of 1761, Bart Nailor was transported for murder, Bridget Daly for stealing shoe-buckles. The Kilkenny assizes in 1769 sent Nicholas Shortall to America for taking two shillings, Anstace Henessy for thieving four hats. Mary Donaghue was sent from Cork in 1774 for stealing a silk cloak. Some must have intensely disliked their experiences in bond-servitude in America: Thomas Carroll, a Cork cattle-thief, was executed when he unlawfully returned in 1767 after ten years. A minority turned to crime in the colonies, as did Richard Roche, executed in New York in 1753, whilst others put their choleric spirits to better use: Samuel Crandall, an Irish convict, was ringleader of the anti-Stamp Act Riots in Rhode Island. For the years for which detail is fully available (due to an Irish Parliamentary investigation) it appears that 1,890 Irish transportees were shipped to America between 1736–1743, half of them for crime and half for vagrancy: generalised to the entire period for which transportation was effective, between ten and twenty thousand transportees must have been sent before the Revolution.

After 1740, as said, the general emigration seems to have intensified: in 1755, eleven vessels at least sailed from Dublin, Cork and Youghal to north American ports, in 1765 at least ten, including ships from Sligo and Galway; in 1775, at least nine, including sailings from Dundalk and Waterford. Yet we

do not know of how many passengers most carried. For some it was few. The
Industry out of Cork (1755), with a butter cargo for Virginia, brought only
seven servants. On the other hand, one vessel in 1775 carried one hundred and
fifty emigrant passengers from Dublin. Perhaps a majority of the vessels were
Protestant-owned and captained, out from southern Irish ports, as their names
often loudly proclaimed: the *Freemason, Revolution, Loyalty, Orange,
William and Mary* and probably *Prudent Hannah.* In later years, the growing
Catholic mercantile interest was reflected in ships such as Captain Murphy's
Neptune Galley, Lonergan's *Bordeaux Yacht,* Troy's *Hibernia,* Power's *Duke
of Tuscany,* and Gaffey's *Charlotte.* Although one cannot be certain of these
designations, and cannot infer that unbound paying Catholic migrants waited
until there was a Catholic Irish shipping connection with America, nonetheless
it is safe to say that the emergence of such a connection in so segmented a
society probably had the effect of convincing at least some would be non-
destitute emigrants that not all the colonies were inhospitable Puritan enclaves,
off-bounds to Catholic ambition or adventure. Other evidence of growing
southern Irish interest in America is suggestive. The *Limerick Chronicle* in
June 1772 advertised a Limerick/Baltimore sailing by noting that the latter
was a place "where there is liberty of conscience." The Dublin *Mercury*
doubtless exaggerated when it noted in January 1770 that Irish Papists were
"rumoured" to be selling their estates in great numbers and "retiring every day
to the continent of America, where they can exercise their religion
unmolested—a cursed Falsehood." Growing knowledge and confidence about
America, the spreading anglicization of the country from the east, the feed-
back from the freed servants and Ulster Presbyterians (for the society was not
so segmented to prevent its general diffusion), the effect of soldiers' tales of the
continent on their return home after the Seven Years War: these are some
factors which might account for the beginnings of a larger movement to the
middle colonies, when coupled with the obvious trade and shipping increases.

It is nonetheless virtually impossible to say how many went from southern
ports. A handloom weaving collapse in Cork in 1769, a potato failure in 1765
and a grain failure in 1766–7, the linen depression from 1771 onwards: these
affected more than merely Ulster, and the pressure from rising population was
ever-present. Audrey Lockhart has established that 439 known vessels left
southern Irish ports for America between 1681–1775, the great majority from
Dublin, Cork and Waterford after 1750. Her study, based upon British and
Irish sources, misses many recorded in American records.

The rapid establishment of Catholic parish life in all the major port cities
from Charleston to Boston in the twenty-five years from 1775, as the
liberalisation of law and attitude in post-Revolutionary America made it
possible, probably took place as such older emigrants (with families for whom
they were responsible) emerged from the towns' brickwork to join the post-
Revolutionary newcomers: certainly not all the Irish Catholics so involved can
have been recent arrivals.

We are fortunate in having detailed evidence upon the overall pattern of

Irish emigration to Pennsylvania for 1745–46 and 1771–75, which neither R. J. Dickson nor Audrey Lockhart used (since it was probably unavailable to them). It greatly strengthens the case of the latter as to a fairly large southern Irish migration, and weakens the case against it of the former proportionately. It also demonstates the degree of native Irish participation in the Ulster exodus, and it generally confirms the picture suggested by the *National Stocks, 1790* analysis. This evidence consists in the indenture records of "Servants and Apprentices Bound and Assigned before Mayor James Hamilton, Mayor of Philadelphia" in the 1745–46 year, and before Mayors John Gibson and William Fisher in 1771–73. It is corroborated by an analysis of the hundreds of advertisements for Irish runaway servants issued in colonial journals in the 1740s and from 1768–73. Such evidence specifies Irish, Irish-born, or from Ireland as a matter of course for common sense legal and evidential reasons, and is thus more reliable than that of surname analysis alone, used meticulously in the 1790 census study, and impressionistically by Michael O'Brien. Correlation of this evidence with shipping records and with broad surname analysis, (as but one element among three), is thus fairly persuasive: the indenture records give the particular vessel which each immigrant used, and its port of origin can be established by reference to reports in the *American Mercury,* the *Philadelphia Chronicle,* records of the Philadelphia Customs House, and to Irish sources.

The results are unsurprising. In 1745–46, for example, 529 Irish immigrants were bound to masters in Philadelphia. They had arrived on twenty-two ships, brigs and snows. Obviously other immigrants had come on these ships who were free migrants and hence were not bound. Others had disembarked at ports-of-call before Philadelphia: James Mitchell's *Happy Return* and Joseph Smith's *Catherine,* both from Londonderry, had both called at Newcastle, Delaware, before putting in at Philadelphia in the same week, May 30 to June 6, 1745. Both these factors help explain the smaller numbers of bound servants from the vessels of Ulster origin. What is most revealing, and quite logical, is the extent to which there is a close relationship between the port of Irish origin of all the vessels and the composition of its bound passengers. Thus the *Kouli Kan* from Belfast, an area and city of then virtually complete Ulster Scottish settlement, brought no native Irish servants at all. On the other hand, the snow *City of Cork* from that port brought an almost entirely Munster Irish immigrant group, with a few of 'Old English' background. On the first came William Anderson, John Morrison, Robert Barnett, Charles Stewart, Alexander and Samuel Forrentine, James Low, William Willson and others. On the second, Dennis Horgan, Catherine Irley, Teague Hannan, Daniel Hurley, Owen Quigley, Thomas Connor, Lawrence Mahoney and Joan Sullivan, among others, with Barnaby Grimes, Darby Collings, Anne St. John, and others among the Hibernicized 'Old English' [there were also a couple probably of more recent (seventeenth century) English background, and probably Protestant: George Hill, William Trow]. The imprecision in demarcating the latter groups is small, when the bulk of the servants are clearly native Irish, just as those from Belfast were overwhelmingly Scots-Irish.

The confusion comes with the intermediate ports: but, again, is what one might expect. The bond servants and redemptioners on the ships from Derry and Newry (by far the majority of those sailing to Philadelphia) are ethnically mixed, but remarkably so in proportion to the ethnic mix of their cities' hinterlands. Fortunately there were only negligible numbers of Catholic 'Old English' inhabitants in Ulster: native Irish servants from these ports have native Ulster nomenclature, while those of English and Scottish surnames thereby reveal their direct origin as Anglican and Presbyterian settler stock. Both Newry and Derry served areas in which native Ulster and settler Ulster met (the area of the crescent described in chapter one). Confusingly, they also served areas of both English and Scottish settlement. The *Martha, Happy Return, Catherine, William* and *Belinda* from Londonderry (as its Ulster captains called the city) together brought about 140 servants, approximately 55 Ulster Scots, 70 native Irish Ulstermen, and 15 Ulster English.

Again, it must be stressed that these are servants only; some are ethnically debatable. Nonetheless the roster of John Willson, John Woodside, Allen McDugal, Margaret Boyd, Alexander Stewart and William Wasson is unmistakable on the one side, as is that of Daniel O'Mullan, Francis O'Neill, Hugh Gallagher, Timothy Scannell, Bryan Hammil, Anne McGonagle and Charles Donelly on the other. What is persuasive is less the individual name (in Ulster there were cross-over exceptions on both sides in culture, religion and nomenclature), than the cumulative impact of whole batches of patronymics, often linked with Christian names one or the other side would not use (Fardy Gallagher, from the now obsolete Gaelic Feardorcha, for example, as against Duncan McVea, with Patrick and Hugh as ubiquitous on the native Ulster side as Alexander was on the Scots Ulster side). As to the forgotten seventeenth century English element in Ulster, its presence in the migration is evidenced by such sturdy Puritan names as Ezekiel Bullock and Ephraim Boggs, as well as by less startling examples. What adds a further element of strangeness to all this is the implicit evidence that certain companies or captains clearly encouraged native Ulster Irish passengers (as did those controlling the *Happy Return* and the *Catherine*), others discouraged it (those controlling the *Belinda*, as well as a group of merchandise masters carrying only a handful of servants: the *Sally, Rundell, Griffin, Nancy* and *Pomona*). Interesting too is the fact that a considerably higher proportion of the native Ulster passengers went as freewillers or redemptioners than of the Scots and English Ulster ones. At first sight this suggests greater independence, more money or better chance of contacts, but little other evidence supports this and it would contradict all one would expect. Instead, it seems more likely that the captains and chartering companies, all of them Protestant and usually Presbyterian, on the one hand, and the native Ulster emigrants on the other, did not always sufficiently trust each other to enter into pre-voyage indentures in Londonderry. Ironically, as we shall see, this often meant that these 'freewillers' received better indenture terms upon independent negotiation in Philadelphia, than did those pre-indentured servants disposed of by the captain or his agents. Nonetheless, the vast majority of *all* Ulster immigrants were pre-indentured, and handled in batches in Philadelphia by such agencies as Conyngham and Gardner (which acted for most Derry vessels) or Blair and Irvine (acting for Newry ships), when the captain had other duties as was usual. I have stressed the Londonderry situation, as it is easier to reconstruct. The Newry-Philadelphia pattern followed similar lines, and likewise reflected an ethnic mix, in somewhat similar proportions, although the English Ulster element was proportionately lighter.

The largest number of servant immigrants, however, came in vessels from Dublin: William Rankin's *Dublin Prize* carried at least fifty-six, Benjamin Burke's *Rebecca* thirty-five, Nathaniel Ambler's *George* at least sixty (there were two other *Georges* trading from Ulster and Cork), among others. Despite its volume, this trade was less well organised than that from Ulster: the Dublin vessels lacked agencies in Philadelphia, and the captains disposed of the servants themselves. One suspects the vessels were more likely to be over-crowded, and less healthy, to judge by the relations between tonnage and passenger numbers. The Dublin vessels, too, reflect the ethnic mix of their hinterland of their port of origin, and of the city of Dublin itself. The majority of the servants involved may even have been Dubliners: twenty years later, in the later 1760s, the largest number of Irish runaway servants in New Jersey of specified birth had been born in Dublin, five times as many as those specified as having been born in 'the north of Ireland'. Certainly their nomenclature mirrors that of lower class Dublin in the eighteenth century. What is striking is the paucity of definitely Protestant Anglo-Irish names among them, even though as many as a third of the lower and lower middle classes in Dublin in the 1740s was of that background: at very most only a fifth, and many of these could as easily have been Catholics of Old English background. Few were almost certainly Protestant Anglo-Irish: William Dobson, Richard Hudson, John Corporall, James Hunter, John Walker, Clevell Ormsby, and Mary Radcliffe, among others. But others could as equally have been Catholic 'Old English', an element strongest in Leinster and particularly in areas for which there is evidence for migration: Wexford, Kilkenny, Dublin county and city: servants such as Sarah White, Ella Field, Julian Moor, Honour Howdrick, Ann and Margaret Francis, John Johnson, John Coply were probably these. But the great majority of servants from Dublin were either of native Irish stocks (the very confusion of their regional names testifying to a vast-in-migration to a growing city), or of *unmistakably* 'Old English' stock. Indeed, the intimate mix of these two latter groups suggests that the native Irish and 'Old English' common people, allied politically and religiously since the mid-seventeenth century, had fused into a common population in Leinster by the 1740s . . . but this is the most tantalisingly unstudied question of Irish social history.

Finally it could be noted that very few women were among the native Irish migrants from Ulster, but a significant minority among those from Dublin, with fewer again from Cork. This suggests that traditional and patriarchal control over daughters until marriage was already slipping in the Dublin area by the 1740s, but was still strong elsewhere, particularly in Catholic south Ulster. For the migration as a whole, among all groups and religions, was of the young and the unmarried where bound-servants were concerned. As a whole not 5% of the native Irish migrants were women, almost as few among the 'Old English'. It is certain also, however, that women were not in demand as Benjamin Marshall wrote in 1765. The implications of this for the establishment of an eighteenth century 'Irish America' were very far-reaching. By the 1880s, half of Irish emigrants to America were unmarried women as is well known. This meant there had been as well as a radical change in American demand patterns, a transformation of the attitude toward women in the intervening century and a half, in Ireland: again a subject without any real study. Put bluntly, it meant that firstly, few eighteenth century Irish emigrant men could hope to marry Irish wives, and the very possibility of an 'Irish America' was thus undermined for that century. The exception was the migration of substantial numbers of Ulster Scottish (and some lower-class Anglo-Irish) women, the former more usually as daughters in family 'free' migration than as servant girls on their own. The mystery as to why a migration of southern and native Ulster Irishmen failed to produce a strongly visible Irish American society in the eighteenth, whereas the Ulster Scottish migration succeeding exceptionally in producing a viable 'Ulster America' is largely explained by these facts. Secondly, the strength of American Irish Catholicism in the later nineteenth century was often attributed to the tenacity of the Irish woman's Catholicism. Its weakness in the previous century was not solely due to American unfriendliness: most Irish Catholic males in the colonies married lower class Protestant American girls. By fortunate coincidence, the Pennsylvania marriage records for 1748–1752 survive, precisely the years in which the incoming servants of 1745–46 were completing their bond terms and becoming free to marry. While there is evidence of intra-Irish marriages, suggesting that perhaps the freed servants would have preferred Irish wives, the majority of the men married others than Irish. They had no choice otherwise than loneliness!

However, many of them were drawn from amongst people but informally Catholic in Ireland (above p. 6). Bishop James Murphy, in 1804, spoke of "our illiterate laity" in Monaghan, "nine-tenths of our people owing to their great poverty," who had just learnt basic doctrine "these few years back". At home folk-custom and community beliefs supplemented religious inadequacies, e.g., by specifying alternative Sunday practices when Mass was missed. Without such social buttressing, it is doubtful whether Catholicism, central to their collective identity, would have survived, even had there been Irish wives. Only after 1800 did the Irish Church really undertake the mammoth task of teaching its adherents to internalise and individualise their religion, and thus make them more capable of perseverance after emigration, the social props and folk culture removed. Only thereafter could an identifiable overseas community coalesce around a renewed church-going (below pp. 182-86).

Some Indications of Volume

While there will never be precise evidence for the entire flow of people from Ireland to America in the eighteenth century, the following overall picture seems probable, in accord with both general American, Irish and British evidence, and with the specific evidence of 1745–46 and 1771–73. Known sailings from Ulster ports, chiefly btween 1753–1775, as studied by R. J. Dickson, took up to 120,000 emigrants before the American Revolution. As many as 50- to 80,000 more at the very least travelled to America in sailings principally in the earlier years (to 1763); the 1740s see an average of ten entries a year to Philadelphia from Ulster harbours alone. Perhaps a quarter of this Ulster migration, or almost a half of its indentured and redemptioner passengers, were native Ulster Catholics; but its overwhelming characteristic was that it was a predominantly Ulster Scots movement, managed, shipped and placed in America by Presbyterian agents, ship-owners, captains and emigrant businessmen in Philadelphia and the Carolinas. This finding is clear too from studies of the areas in which they settled, as by analysis of the 1790 census.

As for the rest of Ireland, the flow was considerably greater than has been supposed. Over the colonies as a whole, two thirds of Irish runaway servants were *not* of Ulster Scot or of Anglo-Irish background, a finding as true of Pennsylvania and Maryland in the 1740s, as of New Jersey, Pennsylvania, Maryland and Virginia from 1768–1773, to cite the colonies of preponderant concentration upon which I have collected over five hundred cases. It is held by most authorities that only three or four per cent of bound servants became runaways; bound servants served an average of four years (five years in Maryland) before release; these patterns alone would indicate a heavy Irish immigration to the colonies, for a continuous runaway pattern presupposes a continually refurbished supply of Irish immigrant servants.

If Audrey Lockhart's listing of sailings from southern ports made from British and Irish sources is amplified by evidence for the 1740s and 1770s alone from American sources and correlated with the indenturing evidence of 1745–46, 1771–3 for Philadelphia, the Annapolis returns which show that almost 6,000 Irish came into that part from 1745–1775, and the above evidence of runaway patterns, it is logical to assume that as many as 100,000 southern Irish emigrants came to America from the 1670s to 1776. When added to the native Irish from Ulster, they equalled perhaps two-thirds of the Ulster Scottish migration. Their scattering, the absence of women among them, and other factors ensured for them a certain oblivion in history, partly justified, partly unjustified. One could have expected also a certain re-migration from the fairly heavy southern Irish concentration in the West Indies, where by the 1730s the lower class white population (as the Governor of Jamaica admitted) was preponderantly Irish. Aubrey Gwynn carefully documented the existence of this Hiberno-Creole people. Given the fact that Philadelphia's and New York's chief trade in the eighteenth century was with the West Indies, and that Irish sloop and schooner captains such as William Shagnessy were engaged in it, one might expect additional Irish migration from the West Indies. Oddly, apart from an early flow from Barbados to Georgia and the Carolinas, and a small flow to New Orleans, there is virtually no evidence that there was. Likewise, contrary to expectation, there is little evidence of a flow southward to the middle colonies from the Irish-manned Newfoundland fisheries (supplied with flour and timber from North America). In each case, one discovers only the odd individual. A more notable, yet small flow, seems to have been that of deserters from the British forces in North America after 1756, and from the Royal Navy and British merchant marines.

At most 10% of the southern Irish flow seems to have been Anglo-Irish Protestant; perhaps at most another 10% had already conformed to Anglicanism before, or soon after, leaving the country. Altogether, however, the flows we have examined would safely account for the finding of the national stocks, 1790 study, which maintained that 3.7% of the American population in that year was of southern Irish stock (or 116,248 individuals), and that another 1.2% was of native Irish stock from Ulster. This latter the study admitted might be more, could it be shown that the native Irish in Ulster migrated at a rate approaching that of the Scots Irish from Ulster: certainly there are indications that its flow was heavier than has been thought, chiefly to Pennsylvania (which that study found also was their principal concentration). Since we may suggest a total native Irish flow of 130,000 before 1776 (around 90,000 from Leinster and Munster, up to 30,000 from Ulster), with at most another 10,000 Anglo-Irish Protestant immigrants from the southern provinces, it might seem one ought to claim more for 1790, given normal reproduction pattern and resumed immigration after 1783. However, the inter-marriage factor noted before, the pressures toward acculturation which it did little to prevent, and in fact fostered, seem to mean that the conclusion of the 1790 census analysis is fairly realistic. (Unfortunately, its popularisations in the widely used *Historical Statistics of the United States* and elsewhere lump the native Ulster element with the Scots and English Ulster element).

There is no need to go further, and claim a vast 'hidden Ireland' in the colonies or revolutionary America, as Michael O'Brien used to do, or to claim with greater sophistication (as Richard Purcell did) that disproportionate migration of certain kin groups distorts the 1790 study unfairly. County migration was indeed the norm in the nineteenth century, with unequal numbers of Sullivans and MacCarthys from west Cork, for example, coming to New York, in the great rural exodus. Precisely because eighteenth century migration was *not* a countryside outflow, but stemmed from the Irish melting pot of the port cities, the 1931 study of the 1790 population by representative nomenclature is broadly indicative, if not precisely accurate, as to the native Irish element in the colonies. Indeed what may be termed the Connacht anomaly proves this point. The study found that .8 of Americans in 1790 were of Connacht origin. There is no evidence of any migration from Connacht at all in the eighteenth century, (a couple of sailings from Galway and Sligo excepted, with no record of passengers): but Connachtmen were finding their way to Dublin and London during the century, as to Liverpool and Limerick. These names are thus not evidence for Connacht migration, but for inter-county migration in Ireland, with the tail end of it drifting across to America, some of it from England. Precise regional studies support this general picture. The many essays on the Irish in various colonies by Richard Purcell, despite his reluctance to generalise, reveal a scattered and thin population of individuals, rather than of communities. Where Michael O'Brien found countless 'Pioneer Irish' in New England, the careful if sympathetic Gerald O'Donovan found a mere trace element population. Both Purcell and O'Donovan corroborate the 1790 census study, however unintentionally.

Strangely, it is the Ulster Scots element that has been under-estimated by that study, as it has recently been increasingly ignored by American historians. This must be emphasised, and may be taken as the considered conclusion of a southern Irish historian impatient with the narrowness of much of the Ulster Scottish tradition (while respectful of its distinctive identity). For the facts are fairly obvious. The eighteenth century saw well over the certain 130,000 Ulster Scottish migrants go to America before 1776. There it absorbed a large element of the native Irish migration, particularly of Ulster background, and of the Ulster English migration: perhaps 20,000 native Irish and 20,000 Ulster English men, by absorption, socio-cultural familiarity, inter-marriage, co-settlement and at times the strong arm! On the other hand, Ian Cargill has carefully demonstrated that the maximum Scottish migration to the colonies before 1776 was around 20,000: at the very most 25,000. A Scottish American historian, he had nothing to minimise. The bulk of these emigrants were Highlanders. And indeed the 1790 Census analysis, if it confined itself to findings for Highland names virtually unknown in Ulster (such as M'Kinnon and M'Leod), would have extrapolated the whole Scottish population in the United States in 1790 at between 1% and 4%, or between thirty and one hundred thousand. Instead, working from the relative frequencies of Lowland names in the Registration of Births for Scotland in 1863 and for Ireland in 1893, it concluded that such names as Ross and Buchanan were indicatively Scottish. In fact the migration from the areas of Scottish concentration in Ulster from 1740–1776 was so heavy, that names like Ross, Buchanan and Munro, until then common in east Ulster, virtually disappeared. These are precisely the names which are used to inflate the 1790 Scottish population to a total of 8.3%, or 263,330 individuals, and to claim a vast Scottish population for colonies like Pennsylvania. The 1790 analysis then (somewhat complicatedly) reduces the Ulster Scottish outflow towards native Irish levels, and towards Ulster's proportion of the population of Ireland, working from an original under-estimate of the Scottish element in Ulster, and hence of Ulster Scottish migration. Thus, after first premising about 9% of the 1790 population to be Ulster Scottish, it finally reduces the entire Ulster element to 6% or 190,662, including Ulster English and native Ulster Irish elements. By its reasoning, the Ulster Scottish element in 1790 was around 150,000 at most : no more than the recorded figures for its original migration, considerably less than the Scottish element proper, and with no allowance for reproduction! This simply defies the historical evidence.

A careful colony-by-colony analysis shows how the false assumptions as to the provenance of Scottish nomenclature in America distorts the result for almost every colony but North Carolina. A corrected reading would allow the Ulster Irish (two-thirds of them Scots Irish at least) the majority of the 'Scottish' population of the other colonies. In 1745–46, for example, no Scottish servants at all were bound before the Mayor of Philadelphia, in the same year, not a single ship came from Scotland to Philadelphia, as against at least thirteen from Ulster, and only one went to Scotland (Leith) from that city. In 1771, the *Pennsylvania Chronicle* recorded only four Scottish runaway indentured servants against twenty one English and twenty five Irish. New York and Pennsylvania journals record only two Scottish runaways for all New Jersey for 1768 against fifteen black (slaves), six English and twenty six Irish runaways, and ironically one of the two Scotsmen, William Rynan, had lived for a time in Ulster before migrating again! In Virginia in the first half of 1771, the incidence of Scottish runaways was non-existent, to judge by the coverage of two journals, against that of fourteen Irishmen, three Englishmen and thirty-five blacks. The 'Scottish' population of the colonies proves on examination to have been largely an Ulster one, despite such famous names as John Witherspoon and James Wilson, the President of Princeton and the Signer of the Declaration of Independence. Probably as many as 130,000 of the American population of 1790, at the least, should be withdrawn from the Scottish column and placed into that of the Ulster Scots as acute scholars of colonial America (following Cargill) have long been aware. 'Ulster Scot' America would then number a more realistic 280,000 in 1790, apart from the other Ulster elements it might have absorbed. This figure alone is consistent with its being the preponderant element in Pennsylvania politics during the revolutionary era, the largest single eighteenth century immigrant group, the aggressive and even determinative element in the Irish presence in the colonial and revolutionary period (see Appendix One).

Thus we can safely conclude that the Irish stock population of the infant United States in 1790 was around 447,000 (against the 307,000 allowed previously). Instead of only half of it being Ulster Scottish, up to two thirds of it was, certainly thus if the elements absorbed into 'Ulster America' are accounted for. Of the rest 116,000 may stand as the figure for those of southern Irish background: scattered, intermarried and coherent neither politically, religiously nor culturally. On the basis of the 1745–6 and 1771–3 Philadelphia records, and the runaway records and shipping reports of Pennsylvania, Maryland and Virginia, we are safe in saying that the vast majority of these were of common Irish Catholic background (Gaelic and Old

English). We may also safely repeat that between thirty and forty thousand Ulster Americans were also native Irish in background, and a half of these had not been absorbed into 'Ulster America'. An additional 20,000 unlisted Ulster Americans were of English background, as were ten thousand of the southern Irish. That over a quarter of a million Scottish stock Ulsterfolk are the key to this picture cannot be doubted; with absorption of most Ulster English and many Ulster Irish, perhaps 300,000. This will emerge more clearly with our next inquiry. For the Ulster Presbyterian stock was not only preponderant numerically. It was also concentrated geographically by settlement, as that of the southern Irish was scattered from New York to Georgia by poverty, bond service and the recruiting sergeant.

What then befell both Irish and Scots Irish in colonial America to make this so?

Appendix One

Irish Elements in the Middle and Southern States, 1790
(% of white population)

	1	2	3	4	5	6	7
State (colony)	Ulster, Scots- Irish	Ulster native Irish	Ulster Total	'Scots'	Leinster, Munster, Connacht	Ireland (A.H.A.)	Ireland (revised)
New York	8.3	1.9	5.1	7.0 (3.0)	3.0	8.1 (1.0)	12.1
New Jersey	9.0	3.5	6.3	7.7 (4.7)	3.2	9.5 (1.0)	15.2
Pennsylvania	16.6	5.5	11.0	8.6 (6.1)	3.5	14.5 (3.0)	23.6
Delaware	8.0	4.5	6.3	8.0 (5.0)	5.4	11.7 (1.0)	17.7
Maryland	7.6	4.0	5.8	7.6 (3.6)	6.5	12.3 (1.2)	17.1
Virginia	9.0	3.4	6.2	10.2 (5.0)	6.2	11.7 (1.2)	17.9
North Carolina	8.1	3.3	5.7	14.2 (5.0)	5.4	11.1 (1.0)	17.1
South Carolina	13.6	5.3	9.4	15.1 (10.0)	4.4	13.8 (2.0)	25.8
Georgia	17.0	6.0	11.5	15.5 (10.0)	3.8	15.3 (1.0)	26.3

Notes:
Columns 1, 2 and 5 were calculated by representative nomenclature studies by the A.H.A. Column 3, which a statistical naïve view might expect to be a combination of 1 and 2, was calculated by the A.H.A. on the basis of other stocks present in state populations, and by corrections of the inferred frequency of Ulster Scottish elements (from key surnames) when set against the native Ulster element frequency.

Column 6 thus represents the A.H.A.'s combination of 3 and 5. It might perhaps be noteworthy that Ulster elements are not coterminous with emigration from contemporary Northern Ireland, which the final A.H.A. report assumes: such key Ulster Americans as the Pattons, Lewises and Alison came from Donegal, many of those in New York from Monaghan, and the distinction is meaningless when read back into the eighteenth century, as certainly also for the native Irish from Ulster. This pickayune point might not matter except that from 1924–1930s, immigration quotas were thus falsely based! The Ulster of the A.H.A. study was the historic nine-county province, not merely the contemporary six-county Northern Ireland.

Column 4 gives firstly the A.H.A.'s Scottish elements from assumedly Scottish (proper) nomenclature. In the text I have given the reasons why this is gravely distorted. On the other hand, the assumption that all Scottish immigrants and elements should be combined with the Ulster Scots to present the true proportions for the latter is also false, although it has been done (Leyburn, *Scotch-Irish*, 186n.). Most of them were, but the number varied from state to state, dependent upon previous levels of Scottish immigration. These were significant to the tobacco colonies (Va. and Md.), to New York and North Carolina, and insignificant elsewhere. Bracketed after the 'Scots' element is my estimate of the element of Ulster Scots thus wrongly included: these are of course but estimates, but are based not only upon monographic evidence of Scottish presence (or lack of it), but also on a knowledge of shipping and runaways in the middle colonies from Scotland, based upon a reading of the journals cited in the notes. See also Ian C. C. Cargill, *Colonists from Scotland* (Ithaca, N.Y. 1956); Duane Meyer, *The Highland Scots of North Carolina, 1732–1776* (Chapel Hill, 1961); E. T. Thomson, *Presbyterians in the South, 1601–1861* (Richmond, 1963) and Abbott Smith, *Colonists in Bondage* (Chapel Hill, 1947), 38, 49–50, 180–187, 197–203, 318. That there was no major Scottish Presbyterian force in the development of that church in the colonies (individuals excepted) to counterbalance the Ulster and native American elements, as emerges from any study of colonial Presbyterianism, also makes the A.H.A. figures for 'Scotland' most improbable.

Column 6 gives the A.H.A. total estimate for the combined Irish elements. In view of its admitted virtual non-calculation of Anglo-Irish and Ulster English elements, I added an estimate of these, highest in

Pennsylvania and South Carolina where literary and biographical evidence suggests it (see text) and elsewhere at an additional 10% or so of the general Irish element. See A.H.A. *Report*, 216, 269.

Column 7 offers a conservative and revised estimate of the Irish element in the 1790 population, combining the A.H.A. estimate in column 6 with the Anglo-Irish element, ibid., and the element among the Scots which was probably from Ulster (bracketed, column 4). This table does not take account of two factors: (i) the probability that among the native Irish, a disproportionate section were of the absorbed Catholic 'Old English' of Leinster and Munster: the A.H.A. used largely more specific Gaelic-stock names as less likely to confusion with English immigration, but even in the eighteenth century, these were more common among the Irish speakers less likely to emigrate, and the 'Old English' names were more common amongst the Dublin and Cork dwellers who did migrate disproportionately as bond servants or freemen. The Meases, Meades, Barrys, Conynghams, and FitzSimons, of revolutionary Pennsylvania are suggestive; (ii) the probability that the Anglican Anglo-Irish proper, disproportionately Loyalist (as against the other Irish elements), had many times fled between 1775–1783, so that their proportion in the colonial population was probably higher. Both such adjustments, however, would be minor because of the small margin of probable error in the other (non-Irish) elements shown in the *Report*.

Source: American Historical Association, *Annual Report, 1931*, "National Stocks in the Population of the United States . . . 1790" ed. Howard F. Baker (Washington, D.C., 1932), pp. 232–70 and passim, together with runaway evidence cited in the text.

As this goes to press, Forrest and Ellen McDonald have reported parallel findings on the size of the Irish and Scots-Irish populations. They exaggerate the trouble of separating Scots and Scots-Irish, and of the Irish and some Scots-Irish. Therefore they fuse the three streams, together with some Welsh, into a pan-ethnic Celtic stock. This ignores the distinctive impact of 18th c. Irish experience on the pre-revolutionary mentality of all immigrants from Ireland. Yet their study does confirm the primacy of non-English elements in the southern states: "Ethnic Origins of the American People, 1790," *William and Mary Quarterly*, 38 (1980), 179-199.

Chapter 4

Ulstermen and Other Irishmen in Pre-Revolutionary America

'Ulster America': Activity, Community and Dispersal

The first and crucial point to make is that Ulster Irish and native Irish immigrants lived largely separate existences in America, even in those few colonies (notably Pennsylvania) where they over-lapped. It is vital to stress this, not merely to lay to rest the ghost of nationalist historians who have claimed otherwise, but to draw attention to the light it throws upon the segmentation of Irish society in Ireland itself. Ulstermen and Irishmen remained apart in eastern Pennsylvania and Philadelphia because they were distinct and strange to each other: which suggests that it was not merely British policy, competition for land, or geographic separation which kept them apart back in Ireland (as the United Irishmen would claim two decades later, and as would facilely be claimed by less thoughtful nationalists for another two centuries). Where the two did interact, it was in a situation in which one group was clearly absorbed into the other: as the native Ulster Irish bondsfolk were to the Ulster Presbyterians they accompanied to the Pennsylvania, Virginia and Carolina frontiers, just as servants were to prominent Anglo-Irish and Quaker Irish immigrant families. In Philadelphia, and east Pennsylvania generally, however, by the 1770s, two *separate* worlds of correspondence and friendship, marriage and business partnership, linked together the Moylans, Meades, Fitzgeralds, FitzSimons, Meases and (later) Careys on the one hand, and the Irvines, Johnstons, Dunlops, McHenrys, Reeds, McKeans, Bryans and McClenachans on the other ... to cite only families prominent in the Revolutionary era. Indeed, a study of the correspondence patterns of these families in the papers held by the Historical Society of Pennsylvania not only demonstrates this clearly, but further suggests that each group related more naturally if secondarily to the world of general American connection than they did to each other. The politics of the Revolutionary and post-Revolutionary era would later make this plain, as we shall see.

Recently Irish scholars have begun to revive, with some success in particulars, the argument that in the seventeenth century, Scottish settlers and native Ulster Catholics heavily inter-married. One would expect it from the general intermingling of the peoples revealed by the 1659 census. Nonetheless, only the most childlike racialism of the 1900 sort would infer from such facts that the communities and cultures themselves interacted, and lost their distinct characteristics to produce a composite. Culture and community are not borne along the blood, much less hidden in the genes, but are sustained by conscious and cumulative acts of human choice, as expressed in group behaviour. There is little question that whatever the levels of initial intermarriage, the Ulster Irish and Scotch Irish in Ulster remained separate and antagonistic societies for the most part. Industrialization, the loss of Gaelic among the former, the spread of a common Anglo-Victorian cultural norm in Ireland, and a host of more recent forces, have greatly diminished these differences since 1800 (until they were propped up by the establishment of Northern Ireland). And even in the eighteenth century, as we noted, certain forces were already active to lessen distinctions, such as the spread of toleration, the rise of a shared dependence upon a domestic weaving economy, the attitudes of merchants and so on; more intangibly, the ignorance of Scotland among the ultimately Irish-born Presbyterian population, and the general effect of living in a common, if strained, symbiotic relationship with Catholic Ulsterfolk in a common landscape. Nonetheless, the crucial divergence remained. Inaccurate and even dangerous today, the analogy is apt that sees the Scottish lowlands element in pre-1800 Ireland as not dissimilar to the *pieds noirs,* the lower and lower middle class French *colons* of Algeria in the 1950s: for in the 1770s, the bulk of the Ulster Scots had been in Ireland only the three and four generations that the *pieds noirs* were later in Algeria. Such a people were, at most, but partly Irish (even granted that the very term 'Irish' was in constant flux in the eighteenth century as to its meaning). Their readiness to emigrate in such numbers is suggestive of their conscious ambiguities of position. Ironically, such a proportionately huge migration, when coupled with continuous native Irish population increase, may only have ultimately intensified the insecurities of those left behind, diminishing their capacity to influence the emergent common Irish culture of the nineteenth century. The beginnings of such fears were even reported as far away as Virginia and Pennsylvania. Although detailed evidence is lacking, it appears probable that an even more disproportionate migration seriously weakened the not inconsiderable Ulster Scottish element in the nation's capital: earlier in the century a vibrant Presbyterian circle there, including Tom Drennan (1696–1760), John Abernethy (1680–1740), William Bruce (1700–1755) and Francis Hutcheson (1694–1746) had helped ensure that the city's elite conversation took account of their outlook.

Presbyterianism was unquestionably the strongest overt element in the Ulster Scottish identity in Ireland and America. It both defined and justified their sense of separation. In America, it became the ground of coalition with others of Calvinist persuasion of continental and English background, as we shall see. This alone should be sufficient to rebut any sceptical view that Presbyterianism was only a mask for exclusiveness, or for hostility to the native Irish. Instead, by strange irony, the most irreducibly opposed readings of the Christian tradition thrown up by the Reformation and Counter-Reformation era found themselves in co-existence on a cramped island thousands of miles from either Rome or Geneva: even had there been no political and national differences to compound this situation, mutual distance would have resulted (as it did, for example, in the Montauban region in France as late as the French Revolution). Nonetheless Presbyterianism also became carrier of the Scottish element in the Ulster identity. There are those who claim that Calvinism and Lowland 'Scottishness' were mutually congenial: the one strict, severe, logical, comprehensive; the other dour, calculating, patriarchal, isolated and proudly impoverished. We lack the evidence on pre-Calvinist Scotland to make such assertions justly. They are neat but unconvincing, and scholars today distrust sweeping arguments about either national or denominational personality types. Yet if an intimate connection with Scotland survived both in Ulster and later in Scotch-Irish America, it was through Presbyterianism. John Harrison rightly referred to the "constant intercommunication" of the eighteenth century as crucial. Most Ulster ministers were trained in Scotland, for two centuries. The fundamentalist Covenanters, defeated in 1666 and 1679, and discouraged even by the restored Presbyterian establishment in Scotland after 1690, found an outlet in Ulster. The intellectual and religious trends and fissures of the Scottish church were immediately reflected in Ulster, although the balance of the parties and opinion was more conservatively weighted there. We shall return to the American implications of these connections.

Nonetheless, however vague to us today, other characteristics marked the Ulstermen as Scottish, and may have been given wider scope in Ireland, where they had both political and functional uses. Dialect, customs and traditions were Lowland Scotch for the most part. Kinship connections were at first weaker in Ulster (although rapidly re-formed by new marriages and land arrangements), market towns had to be created, a trader class to emerge, land to be cleared, improved and cultivated: individual energies were thus less constrained, and the prerogatives and power of landlords (and of ministers and elders), were probably less pervasive than those of the lairds and kirk authorities in the Lowlands. On the other hand, the imperative of solidarity, the more intensely felt in face of native Irish campaigns in 1641-2 and 1689-91 and of endemic brigandage into the eighteenth century, meshed with the inherent and intense conservatism of the Ulster communities to offset any real liberalisation before the 1740s. To see the 'Ulster frontier' as preparatory to the American, or to see in the Ulsterman a prototype of America's venturesome and democratic individualism of the backcountry (as is so often done) is far-fetched. The (remotely Scotch-Irish) Kentuckian of the 1790s would have found the townlands of Antrim and Armagh repressive and confined, if yet more disciplined, better lettered and less volubly egotistic, than the thinly peopled Blue Grass counties.

Even so, a certain peasant practicality, a 'dourness' which found encouragement in the cerebral and factual mentality of the kirk, did something to fit the Ulsterman for the tasks of the Pennsylvania and Carolina frontier. But it was not a 'given' (as the same trait, differently shaped, was with eighteenth century German sect immigrants): it was a leaning which could be easily off-balanced. Crèvecoeur perceptively noted that whereas German immigrants were usually successful in farming, and most Scots were, only a minority of Irish were: and given the balance of settlement, he must have meant largely the Scotch-Irish since many were settled nearby in Orange county, New York, not far from his own estate. There was considerable slovenliness in the Ulster countryside as over all Ireland, and partly for the same reasons: the convergence of agricultural insecurity with the still not fully disciplined customs of a fairly primitive people. The incentives to change of immemorial custom were weak. Writers about eighteenth century Ulster speak of its countrymen dropping work at the chance of a rabbit or hare hunt. In the American backcountry, such proclivities had free rein. The tremendous tension between the industriousness favoured by the church and the weight of the past among the peasantry, found expression in the activities of the kirk session courts, which have not been properly studied for either Ulster or Scotland. To believe, as President Woodrow Wilson did (himself of Scots and Scotch-Irish descent and an academic historian), that contact with the Paddy-Go-Easy element in Irish culture had loosened the straight-laced quality of the Ulster Scots and given them a capacity for zest and laughter, is to ignore the record of Scottish Lowland folklore, manners and balladry. Such creative indiscipline was quite indigenously Scottish, as witness the influence of its greatest exponent, Robert Burns, upon the weaver and farmer poets of Ulster shortly afterwards. Indeed Ulster immigrant David Bruce of Pittsburg himself wrote zestful Burnsian verse in Scots dialect in the 1790s under the pseudonym 'The Scots-Irishman'.

Relatedly, American historians have seen in the Ulster immigrant the prototype of the inner-directed commercial and industrial achiever, whether for reasons of hereditary temperament or for reasons of Calvinist formation or both. Dunaway speaks of 'their genius for industry' and a disposition that was 'practical, level-headed, fearless, self-reliant, and resolute.' Not only did few so describe those in Ulster before 1800. Remarkably, travellers through the (Scotch-Irish) frontier districts of America from 1780–1820, particularly Englishmen, commented on the boisterous, assertive, undisciplined and convivial culture of the region as similar to that of the wild Irish in Ireland. (Indeed, as late as 1918, the English folklorist Cecil Sharp described the people of south-western Virginia and northwestern North Carolina in terms of their unhurried, convivial and anecdotal approach to life). The unquestionable association between the Ulster Scot (in America and Ireland), industrious self-discipline, and educated moralism, emerged later in response to the incentives of new possibility, educated ambition and the hope of profit or more comfortable and regular subsistence. Its beginnings may be found among merchants and professional men in Derry and Belfast in the 1750s, (earlier if one looks back to Scotland), and around the same time among their counterparts in Philadelphia, Lancaster, Allentown and Newcastle. Widening horizons then in turn created a market for a more systematic pattern of education among parents ambitious for their children. The Presbyterian establishment responded: its academies and colleges, once founded and impelled by the need to create an educated ministry, were by the 1770s to become the fountain-heads of an academic regimen partly productive of sharp, honest, and innovative clerks and businessmen. The prospectuses, even of Princeton, were by then unashamedly secular. It was not coincidence that William McGuffey, schoolmaster to nineteenth century America through the millions of his textbooks re-printed over three generations, was the president of an Ohio college of the Scotch-Irish dispersion, and himself the grandson of immigrants from Ulster.

The contrast is even more acutely clear in another example. Pittsburg is usually presented as the city, above all, in which the Scotch-Irish 'genius for industry' found its fruition in a mercantile and then industrial establishment almost totally Presbyterian in the late nineteenth century. But in 1794, the outraged Scotch-Irish farmers of the area, alienated partly by the claims to 'their' lands by wealthy 'English' Virginians such as George Washington, but particularly aggrieved by an attempt to tax their massive whiskey production and consumption, had revolted against the Federal Government, after a period of informal resistance to the 'excisemen'. The area contained 570 distilleries, as many as one to every six or so farmers. The stills themselves were treated as a form of capital, the whiskey as currency (besides its massive straight consumption). As in Ulster, whiskey as diversion and as money-substitute over-lapped; as in both Ireland and Scotland, excise was regarded as a tyrannical intervention by government into the realm of hearth and trade. As long as semi-subsistence farming, endemic relaxation with alcohol (not merely in the evenings) and sporadic work-discipline interacted, the world of the McGuffey readers, of sun-up to sun-down discipline, of calculating self-advantage, was in the future. But the nearby river port of Pittsburg, tiny in 1790, yet commanding the Ohio river valley by the connecting Monongahela, was already announcing that new future in the columns of the *Pittsburg Gazette*.

In short, the adjustment of the Scotch-Irish to newer patterns of discipline accompanied the growth of new patterns of work and opportunity, and ultimately the rise of a commerical-industrial climate of opinion. It is questionable whether anything in their make-up predisposed them, rather than others, to that future, and much to suggest the contrary. It is possible that the pre-industrial culture of the entire Appalachian region, from Pennsylvania south to the Carolinas, which survived into the early twentieth century, was even more reflective of the earlier stream of incoming Scotch-Irish than the later commercial-industrial culture which transformed even the farmers of the northern zone of Scotch-Irish settlement, in Pennsylvania, Virginia and Ohio particularly. There was a degree to which the later heavy Scotch-Irish immigration was a transformed one,—from the industrious Ulster of 1770–1830 (when in all as many as 150,000 may have come in, certainly no less than 100,000),—one of weavers, spinners and more competitive farmers.

They settled disproportionately in the established communities of their Americanised cousins in the northern belt, and much less so further south, and may have thus fostered a false and one-dimensional tradition of the relations between the Scotch-Irish and the industrial work pattern. That by the 1820s, the Irish Catholics were the most clearly pre-industrial community in English-speaking experience, has distorted the relationship between the two groups: in America, they too made an even more rapid adjustment in collective discipline to the new circumstances. Thirty years after their main influx (1850–1880s) they forced upon their Church a compromise whereby they would accept a costly Catholic school system only if it had a secularised curriculum modelled upon that of the urban public school, as their priests sadly admitted. Ulster Presbyterian parents had forced the same compromise upon their academies and colleges likewise a generation or so after initial settlement, once they had found their bearings. In this area too, simplistic contrasts between the two immigrations break down.

The history of the Ulsterman in America, then, is less a matter of the working out of hereditary characteristics on the frontier ('the frontiersman *par excellence'*) than of a series of adjustments to changing circumstances within the framework of a received yet still fluid and indeterminate culture. We must look quickly at his several American environments, and his several responses to them.

The great majority of Ulster immigrants were Back Country Settlers: they were pioneers of farming in that great swathe of rolling and timbered country stretching from Western Maryland and central Pennsylvania south to the Carolinas. In such a vast area, with a history of settlement extending over a period of seventy years, farming patterns varied considerably: the first instinct and training of the Ulster farmer (as of any other) inclined him to appraise his skills in terms of the differences in soil, drainage, topography and route accessibility which confronted him. He then laid out his fields and determined on his crops. The heavily glaciated Ulster landscape presented him with a variety of soils and terrains even within one farm, certainly within one area. In the Back Country, there were far longer reaches of uniform conditions. Nonetheless, some evidence suggests that where he could (as in Lancaster County, Pennsylvania), he chose the rolling and drainable hills to the north and south, lightly timbered, and left the heavily timbered central lowlands to the Germans. This certainly followed the farming wisdom of Tyrone or Down, where the low ground was sodden and acid-soiled: but in Pennsylvania, the richest soils were the bottom ones, and they were often naturally drained. Certainly there was more to his choice than a lazy inclination to avoid clearing large numbers of trees (as men like Benjamin Rush of Philadelphia were wrongly convinced): tree clearance was the first major task everywhere. As the farm matured, his tendency was to clear a greater lot of his land, and devote more of his cleared land to grain, than did his supposedly more industrious German counterpart (where they held comparably similar farms). He kept more sheep and horses and fewer cattle than the Germans, and devoted considerably more acreage to flax and hemp: wool, flax and hemp were the basis of his imported traditions of domestic textile production. He usually staked out between 135 and 150 acres, clearing a few acres per year. After forty or fifty years up to fifty acres would be cleared of timber, of which up to twenty acres would be in grain. But there was little increase in his tiny livestock herds: five scrawny sheep ('surprisingly like goats' noted a visitor), five cows, a horse team with one replacement horse. The grain surplus (of wheat, rarely maize or Indian corn) was his cash source by then, together with the whiskey surplus from his rye crop. Occasionally a pig or cow might be fattened for sale, and a flaxseed surplus sold for carriage to Philadelphia, then back to Ulster. This in 1772, if Coleraine, Donegal, Drumore, and Mt. Joy townships of Lancaster County were typical (in contrast to Mannheim, Strasburg and Hempfield townships). The Germans tended to increase their cattle herds, and use grain surplus for their winter maintenance: used to handling severe continental winters, they had not the fear of valuable animals wasted and slaughtered which the Ulsterman had. Further south, in the Carolinas Piedmont, where year-round forage was available through mild winters, Ulster immigrants kept much larger herds: indeed, in the initial stage of settlement, they helped pioneer the open range and cattle drive economy (which would shift west, as the land was divided), improbably among the woods of the Carolinas where Creek and Chickasaw still hunted in formidable bands in the 1750s.

Carl Bridenbaugh wisely swept aside a myth with his considered judgement: "I can find no evidence to support the customary assertion that their Ulster experience made the Lowland Scots better settlers, after the initial stage, if at all." But he was perhaps overly impressed by the judgement of travellers such as Rush, Crèvecoeur, Charles Woodmason, David McClure, and Philip Fithian as to the *appearance* (slovenly indeed) of the Scotch-Irish farms. In Lancaster, and presumably elsewhere, the *substance* of good farming lay with Ulster farmers who now had market outlets and had learnt from every source they could, including the Germans nearby. Arthur C. Lord relates background to Back Country more carefully: the crucial point "was the ability of each man to perceive, through his cultural heritage and by observing his neighbours' methods, the potential of a physical environment, the markets in the area, and to create an agricultural landscape" not European, but unique to the area involved. The Scotch-Irish were inclined to leave the stumps of dead trees in their fields, to use log-barns, to ill-use their sheep, and to appear themselves homespun, even forty years after they took their farm lot. This may have been deceptive, to judge by the central Pennsylvanian and Valley of Virginia patterns. The traditional Ulster (and Irish) reluctance to display prosperity, lest it invite the rapacity of laird, landlord, merchant or tithe proctor; the Presbyterian injunctions against conspicuous ease; the money to be saved if a wife's talents were still exploited long after grain surpluses could acquire imported Irish linens and English woollens, these and other factors inclined the Scotch-Irishman to maintain the threadbare appearance of subsistence farmer after he passed that stage. This, of course, is not to go to the other extreme. Clearly there was much bad farming practice; clearly the vast whiskey consumption, the depression and sloth induced by hard winters in the north and hot summers in the south, and the demoralising distance from easy access to market, also bred a hand-to-mouth absence of routine and calculation in farmers in less favoured regions than those mentioned above, and even in the more awkwardly situated places in good counties. And even in further areas, excellent farmers existed, such as one McMullen, an immigrant, whose farm impressed Fortescue Cuming as the best in the then remote Pittsburg region in 1807.

The variety and extent of the pioneers' tasks were unending. Precisely because they were, they rarely devoted themselves to round-the-clock labour. The temptation to hunt deer, turkey, pigeons, bear, rabbit and squirrel was ever present and offered the chief meat supply: as they had virtually exterminated deer and wolf in Ulster, so now they helped do the same to bear, wild turkey, passenger pigeon and certain deer populations from Pennsylvania south. Lonely families spent whole evenings together, in a custom which German and Anglo-American followers did not follow as systematically and expectedly. It owed its form to the 'cayleying' of Presbyterian mid-Ulster almost certainly. Dunaway, Leyburn and other authorities have missed this connection, as they have also failed to register the role that music played on these occasions. Filling the Back Country, the Scottish and Irish pentatonic mode pre-empted the folk music tradition of the entire Appalachian region, as has been noted by musicologists; moreover, Ulster forms of imagery and narrative ballads shaped both the secular and sacred folk poetry fused onto those tunes. On the other hand, the virtual absence of German folk-music influence is remarkable. In Ireland, the Palatine settlement of 1715 in Limerick, though consisting of five hundred families at most, influenced the folk music traditions of north Munster. The much larger Palatine and Moravian settlements in the Valley of Virginia and the Carolinas have left little trace upon the musical culture of the region. Instead, Scots Lowlands and north Irish balladry spread along the entire settlement belt, subtly altering with time, yet surviving remarkably intact in music and verse in isolated eddies until early in this century. 'Johnny Doyle' became 'Johnny Dials', 'Molly Ban' became 'Polly Van' and similar changes affected Ulster Scots standards like 'Barbara Allen' and 'Lord Randall'. The conservatism and continuity of the musical culture of the area points to the exclusive and familiar culture exchanged over generations of evening visiting in the Back Country. Its ecleticism (with English, Scots and Irish balladry) raises central questions about the tri-cultural nature of Ulster's tri-fold population, and about the degree to which each of the strands of the population participated in the migration. Unfortunately, such was the cultural purism of folk-musicologists in the British Isles from the late eighteenth century until recently (in Ireland interested, even in Ulster, only in native Gaelic material), that we have little convincing evidence on the folk-cultures of Ulster during the era of the

A late 18th c. idealization of back-country development

migration. Current efforts by Ulster scholars are tantalisingly belated: we will probably never discover whether the three Ulster streams pooled their songs after migration or before.

The world of labour was also punctuated by less frequent yet conventional respites. Weddings, flax-pullings, corn-huskings, house-buildings, political gatherings, hay-making and harvesting were occasions for neighbourly gathering, easeful drinking, and rough and even violent sports. The tradition of all-night 'waking' the dead was observed. The intense and indispensable neighbourliness which was the basis for the re-construction of society in the Back Country was grounded in such events. The received standards of group behaviour were enforced by withholding assistance, by ridicule and by outright ostracism or punishment. The first was the most effective: without help, at house or barn raising, at field clearance (log-rolling or stump grubbing), at childbirth or sickness, the maverick settler was severely hampered and isolated. Such men often gravitated into other settlements, moving perpetually, became hunters or trappers beyond the settlement line, or eked out a lonely existence preparing farms for settlement (by erecting rudimentary cabins or shelters and by girdling or felling trees, and then by moving on to do the same elsewhere, for a fee). The manner in which Back Country settlements defined themselves in social form served to exclude the unsociable, and thus to simplify and diminish the roles of pastors and officials when the latter came. Yet this natural 'winnowing out' process worked less effectively as the weight of the American environment told upon the second generation. In the Carolinas, unlike Pennsylvania, a conscious struggle by sober farmers, 'Church people', merchants and the educated was necessary before the American-born 'lower-folk' accepted the constraints of social order. The world of labour, then, was largely a world of family isolation; the interruptions of celebration, politicking and mutual assistance, of conviviality (in every sense) provided the base of community and restrained the exaggerated impulse to an a-moral individualism which threatened the Back Countryman but was little part of the Ulster Scottish tradition. That impulse thus fled ahead, coalescing into pathetic and loose communities of the poor and the wild: ill-fed, drunken, housed in shacks, but always (despite the contrary belief), a despised and smallish minority.

The tasks, however, remained constant, for the majority who undertook to live more substantially and traditionally. Some aimed at the basics, setting a higher priority on sociability; others, "commonly a man of property and good character", were methodical and improving. But the job was the same. They took the log cabin idea from the Germans, changing the ground plan to its Ulster cottage shape, and retaining it after the Germans and their own better class had turned to stone, brick and plank timber homes, modifying the V-notching and dovetailing whereby the Germans and Swedes had joined the logs and altering the materials with which the chinks were filled. The clearing of timber was arduous, the fallen trees seasoned and then burned. They were rolled aside with neighbours later, in the further clearances to extend a farm in settled townships. Wooden fences, variously put together, then lined off the fields. The soil was broken with a primitive light wooden plough, horse- or ox-drawn: both wooden plough and oxen were still known in Ulster. Flax or Indian corn was grown to break the soil effectively the first few seasons, then came the full shift to the preferred wheat and rye. The ground was prepared by harrowing with a triangular wood frame with downward wooden spikes, horse drawn: its shape enabled the harrow to slip past the tree stumps without breaking too often! Seed was broadcast by hand, little weeding was done. Harvesting was by scythe and sickle. Meantime sheep had been sheared, hay had been saved, vegetable gardens (with squash, beans and gourds as well as the more familiar cabbage) were prepared with the hoe, hay saved on the 'in-field' meadow for winter fodder. Indian corn was relegated to smaller acreage, usually on a hill, and cultivated by hoe. Womenfolk usually saw to the 'retting' or drowning of the grown flax. After harvest, the grain (wheat) was threshed by hand-flailing or by treading down with the animals, the ears then gathered and the straw saved for bedding or even, as in Ulster, to thread into harness ropes. The corn was husked, often in community, by hand. Little of this was unfamiliar to Ulster farmers, except the cultivation of Indian corn. Even potatoes were widely grown for food, and oats as a fodder crop. What was distinctive was the unremitting character of the labour: tools and buildings were all made from scratch.

Distinctive too was the heavy summer heat in which it was almost all performed: it is not surprising that the further south the Scotch-Irish went, the more inclined they were to rely upon hunted game, small acreages of corn for subsistence, and upon hogs, often let fend for themselves. Thus there were those who withdrew, as we have noted: "They are very poor owing to their Indolence. They delight in their present low, lazy, sluttish, heathenish, hellish life, and seem not desirous of changing it", wrote fellow Irishman, the Anglican missionary pastor Charles Woodmason, of those in South Carolina in 1767–9. Despite his Anglicanism, he was not so prejudiced as to lie, and indeed championed the Back Country people against their coastal detractors. In 1802, Harm Jan Huidekoper would make similar dispassionate observations in western Pennsylvania; "The log cabins were more shabby, the clearings smaller and more slovenly, the fields more carelessly tilled . . . the settlers were half-starved for lack of proper food . . . Abject poverty held the whole country in its grip". The wonder is not that so many lapsed into such a state of inertial apathy in face of such burdens, but that the majority turned crude Back Country into rural community, cumulatively, collectively and laboriously over a forty year period, and that even for so many of those criticised by Woodmason, Huidekoper, Rush and others, the stage of demoralisation was a temporary one, caused by initial isolation and hardship.

Women played a key role in ensuring that "men of property and character" emerged from sweat and frustration of the log-cabin builders. Their work burden, if anything, was heavier. Fragmentary accounts suggest an elemental and tenacious breed, inured to continuous hardship. As in Ulster, commentators noted that their cabins swarmed with children: they bore ten to fourteen, and saw perhaps half survive, on average, into their teens. The women feared childbirth, and thereafter feared for their offspring. So many other demands were made upon them that many gave only the minimum to motherhood, as Julia Spruill noted, after studying cases of child-abandonment and of children turned apprentice by their mothers (in Scotch-Irish western Virginia largely). "The large number of these indicates that a feeling of parental responsibility did not accompany the general pride in a numerous offspring." Unquestionably, however, the majority had such a sense, and their work underscored it. Women looked after their young, cared for their full families, saw to the drudgery of cooking, scouring, clothes washing, and sewing. She prepared corn for corn-pone or johnny cake by grinding it herself. She looked after the vegetable garden, milked the cattle, churned the butter, hand-moulded candles for winter by dipping the wick in tallow, made soap too from animal grease, baked all bread used. She saw to the full clothing of her family: she retted and pulled the flax; pounded it in a wooden brake to loosen the fibres; scutched or whipped it to separate them; hackled or combed it endlessly to prepare the fibre to the desired fineness. Additionally, she cleaned and carded (or combed) the shorn wool. She spun both wool and flax fibres and then sometimes wove them, although her husband might more often have involved himself in this final skill. The two were woven together to make the linsey-woolsey for summer wear cloth, the wool woven alone for winter wear. She prepared the dyes for the cloth from indigo, madder and various leaves and barks. Up to seventy yards of cloth were produced upon many Scotch-Irish farms in single year.

The mother was also primarily responsible for whatever education and moral training children received, nursed her family members through illness. Gradually, as subsistence gave way (in the more accessible areas), money became available for purchase of clothes and shoes, for household furnishing, cooking irons and ornament. Fulling and grist mills removed some small portion of the tasks of cloth and bread preparation. At all times, however, she was expected to help her husband, when necessary, at harvesting, land-clearance, the dressing of game, the preparation of skins for leather making and so on. Doubtless if her man was himself industrious, devoting extra time to wood-working, furniture making, implement manufacture, leather working and the like, the drudgery of her life was at least a partnership of task with task. If he was popinjay, given to raucous and drunken socialising, to hunting or politicking to the neglect of farm and family and combined this with insisting on the last pound of traditional Ulster wifely duty from her, her existence would have become intolerable. It is not surprising that Woodmason, Fithian, J.F.D. Smyth and others came upon women as apathetic and sluttish as their husbands were slovenly. Increase Matthews, travelling in Western Pennsylvania at a later date (1798), stayed with a family near Chesnut Ridge and wrote "I endeavoured to persuade them that they put too much hardship on their women. In excuse they plead that their business at certain seasons of the year is very urgent. This is truly the case, but not in my mind a sufficient excuse". He had in mind the day-long spreading of flax to dry (after retting), which he saw his hosts' daughters engaged in.

For most immigrant women, however, the observation that patient years of drudgery were in fact leading to the production not merely of their family's necessities, but to that of a farm itself of a substance and productiveness undreamt at home, to a certain homely respect in a growing community, may have offset to some degree the aging and weariness brought on by it all. For their daughters, who did not share the memory of poverty amid closed Ulster horizons, this can have been less so. Few showed any reluctance to marry, despite the Ulster Presbyterian male's unsentimental approach to the matter, even to men who had already buried several wives. In this too they were perhaps elemental, and those raised in the Carolinas were affected by its culture, where it was said of the earlier (English) inhabitants in 1709: "They marry very young; . . . and she that stays till twenty is reckoned a stale maid, which is a very indifferent character in that warm country". If things went grievously wrong, they could desert their husbands, as Mary M'Gehe did her husband Joseph in the New Bern area of North Carolina in 1775, Anne M'Adooe did her husband John in Virginia in 1770 ("after the most tender treatment of upwards of twenty years" he claimed publicly), and as Betsy O'Bryan did her husband Dennis in western Pennsylvania in 1789, evoking his odd comment:

Since she has left me without cause,
I'll give her time enough to pause,
That she may live to see her error,
While I live happy with a fairer.

Others lived not merely more contentedly. Occasionally there is evidence of truly Christian heroism. Catherine Steel of Derry, Pennsylvania, in her 'Life time Raised 19 orphan children', as her tombstone proclaimed, surely winning the respect of her entire community.

For many Ulsterfolk, however, the reality may have been severe, but the ultimate aspirations were towards the gentleman's and lady's way of life, ubiquitously stereotyped in the advice literature of the eighteenth century, plagiarized and localised from London example by the well-to-do among the colonials, and probably all too well remembered by immigrants from the leisured appearance projected by Anglican gentry, and some merchants, at home in Ulster. Some came close to attaining a modest middle-class comfort, though few reached gentility: in all Philadelphia in 1772, only one Ulster Scots Presbyterian, the American-born Chief Justice and merchant William Allen, had the ultimate status symbol of the carriage and horse team. Nonetheless by the 1770s there was a small class, set apart from the farmers we have discussed, who provided the leadership and widening horizons which those farmers and the related rural tradesmen badly required. They were the agents of the change from a subsistence economy through the marketing and professional services they supplied, and became in large measure the political elite of the revolutionary era.

The hall-mark of this class seems to have been its versatility. This was *not* necessarily a sign of Americanisation, although the process was carried farther in America than elsewhere, perhaps. Even in Ulster, incipient capitalists like William Caldwell of Derry were engaged in a variety of pursuits. Those then anywhere forging a commercial world on top of an agrarian society were few enough, able enough, and found time enough to pursue several lines of advantage. Even the greatest merchants in Philadelphia or New York did not engage in more than ten or twelve transactions a day, and success in one venture generated the capital and emboldened the mind for further ones: the Ulstermen who entered these circles behaved similarly. Probably Ulster immigrants were under-represented among the middle class of the established seaboard cities (Newcastle, Baltimore, Philadelphia, Annapolis, New York, Charleston), to judge by the low profile accorded them in studies of the pre-revolutionary era in these cities. Nonetheless there were numbers of them, including the most influential of their own leaders. After 1780, they become more prominent. On the other hand, as suggested already, they were disproportionately active in newer cities and towns, especially in areas of heavier Ulster Irish settlement: Easton and Northampton in east Pennsylvania, Lancaster, York, Harrisburg and Carlisle in central Pennsylvania, Frederick in west Maryland, Williamsport, Staunton and Bedford in Virginia. To simplify, one might say that here especially men became engaged in every activity germane to the creation of their communities and of the Back Country's post-subsistence society.

A few well-known examples make this class alive, shrewd and alert. In the major seaboard cities firstly. In New York, Belfast-born Hugh Gaine (1727–1807) ran a printing house, book-shop, pharmacy, general store and agency at the "Bible and Crown" in Hanover Square from 1759. In 1752, he had launched the *New York Mercury*, which he continued through 1783; in 1768, he became public printer to the province; in 1773, opened a paper-mill on Long Island. He found it useful to conform to Anglicanism, but was never an office-holder. Others such as John O'Kane (1734–1808), a merchant and former Co. Antrim Catholic, and John Patterson, the founder of the *New York Evening Post,* were likewise multiply engaged. In Philadelphia, the Dublin Presbyterian George Bryan (1731–1791), became an importer, ship owner, and wholesaler, then turned to public affairs, at first reluctantly, as harbour commissioner, Assembly member for Philadelphia and as judge of common pleas and of the orphans' court. James McHenry (1753–1816), born in Ballymena and educated in Dublin, helped run an importing and shipping business in Baltimore, then studied and worked in Philadelphia as a physician. Blair McClenachan, his contemporary, was a banker, large-scale ship-owner, and general merchant, active in public affairs and in land speculation, as indeed were most of these Ulster Philadelphians. Similar careers were pursued by Ulstermen in the ports of Delaware, Maryland and New Jersey. An early

Arch Street with Second Presbyterian Church, Philadelphia, 1799

business partnership with a native American, a young start, a family business background (if only as pedlars or drapers), considerable education for the age, a fortunate marriage, a politic personality: these, besides native ability, counted for much in the way such immigrants 'breached' the already established mercantile ascendancy of these cities.

The matter was less difficult, if less rewarding, in the interior. One has the impression that the seaboard Ulster merchants were many times gambling for high stakes: those of a fine house, an estate, leisure and public respect, such as William Allen had already achieved. When these proved slow in coming, many found satisfaction elsewhere, in politics, medicine, law or western development and speculation: thus Charles Thomson (1729–1824) of Maghera, Co. Derry birth, shifted his interests from business to public service even before the revolution, McHenry abandoned it for medicine, Bryan for law and politics. In the interior, however, careers seem to have been more prosaic, although as diverse: the urge to emulate the nearly impossible was replaced by the rewards of escaping and vagariating the Back Country norm. In the journal of Benjamin Rush (1784), one finds a sense of contentment in the Ulster middle class he describes in the inland towns, such as John Pollock, innkeeper and merchant, and John Montgomery, merchant and community leader in Carlisle, and Alexander Lowery, merchant and fur-trader in Marietta. He and other English-stock Philadelphians such as John Penn (in 1786), tended to judge all the Ulster born as rancorous and disagreeable (as indeed some of them in Philadelphia were, such as Hugh Williamson, effective detractor of Franklin). They were surprised to find such country-town businessmen to be easy and agreeable company.

Apart from central Pennsylvania, the class of traders and small businessmen of Ulster birth spread south along the Great Philadelphia Wagon Road down the Great Valley, helping to establish a line of fifteen towns from Frederick in Maryland in the north, through Staunton and down to Camden and Augusta in South Carolina and Georgia, together with some dozen outlying market centres. The commercial network of a wagon road must seem less romantic than that of sea-routes, for historians have never reconstructed it in detail. Presumably in an age so dependent upon personal credit and connection, many of the traders could promise at least a modest stream of manufactures to come along the network, some made locally, since they had kinsmen or fellow-countrymen from Ulster, reliably Presbyterian, back at the fountainhead of it all (in Philadelphia, or Baltimore, later in Charleston and Savannah). J. F. D. Smyth noted of one area along the great road (around Fredericktown and Hagarstown in western Maryland), that the Germans and Irish there "carry on almost every kind of manufacture, as well as a considerable share of trade . . . there is an abundance of mills, forges, furnaces and iron works, all around them," an exaggeration, but an indicative one.

Studies of the Irish American middle class of the late nineteenth century have shown that it was disproportionately composed of those who immigrated as children or young people, who possessed the self-confidence that sprang from long familiarity with the country; or from the second, or American-born generation. While this was perhaps less true in the more rudimentary state of America a century before, nonetheless these same advantages counted for very much. Most Ulster stock lawyers were of these sorts, and law offered the simplest short circuit of the route from adequate living to real affluence: most of its business consisted in debt collection. Moreover, not surprisingly, correspondence patterns suggest that such men, like Thomas McKean, William Paterson and William Allen related to considerably wider circles than did those who immigrated as adults (such as William Irvine or James McHenry). Indeed, their familiarity with a broader spectrum of Americans, their distaste for tribalism, both enabled them broaden the business and political horizons of Ulster America, but also divided them, sooner or later, from the preoccupations of more recent or less favoured immigrants, particularly those in the back country. It is important to bear in mind, however, that by the American Revolutionary era, a considerable portion of rural Ulster Americans had moved beyond the exhaustions of frontier existence, and had the leisure and the educated and monied contacts in business and law, to take a penetrating interest in the crisis.

Youthful Bondage: the native Irish in America

Virtually all the native Irish emigrants to America, and a very high proportion of the Scots-Irish emigrants, spent their first years there as unpaid servants, bound by 'indenture' (a duplicate contract) to a strict form of servitude that might be characterised as a cross between apprenticeship and slavery. At any rate, characteristics of both institutions, whether legal or customary, coloured this servitude: for they were the master types of imposed labour discipline whereby the English settlers in America had first sought to streamline the development of their plantations toward profitability. Various forms of apprenticeship and servitude had been known in England; slavery was largely modelled upon Spanish practice as the English found it in the Caribbean. Indentured servitude itself became by the 1640s the chief form of enforced labour in the colonies, gradually giving to permanent enslavement of Africans from the 1660s onward. But it remained the dominant such institution in the middle colonies throughout the colonial period, and a major supplementary one in Maryland, Virginia and the Carolinas, (for reasons given pp. 62-4). Whatever its supposed legal specifications (and these were much a matter of ancient formulae), this servitude was rapidly shaped to the labour necessities of the new continent: the appeal to law might blunt the resultant excesses, and certainly ensured that the bondage remained temporary, but it did not determine its content. This was rather a product of the regional emphasis of each colonial society and of its economic activities. The majority of bond servants were engaged in agriculture: in the mature areas in the middle colonies in general farm labour, with occasional land clearance; in their newer areas, in arduous lumber work and land clearance principally. In Maryland, the great majority were tobacco plantation hands, as were most of the number in Virginia and the Carolinas, working in the fields with black slaves: even those normally assigned to other tasks would be expected to do field work at certain times. As the eighteenth century wore on, the slave population increased, and planter society became more pretentious, growing numbers were given the skilled tasks of the plantation: smithing, harness making, weaving and even gardening. The farmers of the middle colonies could not afford such diversification of their small kingdoms. Nonetheless, the growth of economic life and of towns (over subsistence) meant that increasing numbers of Irish servants were bound to merchants, artisans, tradesmen and even building labourers in these areas: about one in five in 1745–46, one in four in 1771–73. For most, however, the reality of life was farmwork and fieldwork.

The extreme demands of life in mid-colonial America did not dispose farmers to be particularly sentimental to their families, or even to themselves. The treatment accorded bound servants was hence unenviable. They shared the tasks described in the previous section, without the reward of pay or partial possession, their standard of mean subsistence dependent upon their master's reactions and his surplus. Particularly in the matter of land clearance, there was a tendency to overwork such servants grievously, as there was also at harvest time. For the thousands of Irish and Scots Irish of rural backbround, such drudgery was not unprecedented, although hardly paralleled in its rigour. Moreover, the degradation of a measure of subjection to another's will was the normal accompaniment of farm labour in Ireland even into this century, despite slight pay and theoretic freedom, this being particularly the case for unmarried labourers who 'lived in'. Even the humiliation of close examination as the farmers bought the 'time' of the bound servants in the Philadelphia, Newcastle and other markets, had been presaged in the 'hiring fair' in rural Ireland. But many of the Scots Irish indentured men were not of a class wherein they had had to undergo such a condition at home, being themselves farmers or the sons of farmers, as were a proportion of the native Irish. More painfully many of the southern Irishmen were townsmen, completely unused to such a regimen, and their physiques (as we shall see) very ill-prepared for it, as were the Irish re-migrants from London. The shift in diet, from oatmeal, milk and occasional meat (in the earlier years), from potatoes, less oatmeal and milk (in the later years), and from breadstuffs, beer and dairy produce (for many of the townsmen and Leinstermen) to the monotonous corn or maize dishes and breads (corn-pone and homony) of poorer or less considerate farmer-masters was likewise harsh, as was the shift in climate, to summers hot by Irish standards and winters freezing by the same measure. Nevertheless, diet on the better farms was probably better than in Ireland, climate could be adjusted to by young men, and the evidence of runaway advertisements suggests that the clothing of indentured servants was better than that of the mass of the Irish populace.

Indeed in so far as Andrew Burnaby and other contemporaries and scholars such as James Lemon and Arthur Lord have indicated that standards of farming were good in the south-eastern counties of Pennsylvania in the 1760s–70s, this would suggest a well-managed and fairly industrious servant class: for it was in these counties (Philadelphia, Lancaster, Chester and Bucks) that the overwhelming majority of servants assigned in Philadelphia were working. A considerable number also worked in the improved farmlands of East and West Jersey and in these of the 'Lower Counties' or Delaware. Certainly the continuing recruitment of Irish and Scots Irish labour over a period of fifty years, the absence of systematic complaint against them (such as existed about both slaves and Irish servants in the South), and the relative absence of court cases alleging cruelty by masters (again in contrast with the South), suggest that farmers had found ways to turn their Irish bound labourers into a workforce more helpful than troublesome, more co-operative than coerced. The fact that discontented servants could simply melt away with little chance of recapture, and could mess up their tasks or work inefficiently if angered or underfed (as was commonly noted in Ireland), gave farmers an incentive toward decent treatment. This probably took the form of a certain gruff recognition, as against dehumanising manipulation, together with such common sense devices as permitting the Irish servant man to set his own pace, giving him sufficient food, including meat, allowing him time off and visiting rights to friends on nearby farms, clothing him decently, giving him an allowance for drink (or the money for it). The number of runaway advertisements which evidence drinking and talking back as characteristics of Irish servants in the middle colonies suggest one is not dealing with a class abject and exploited from dawn to dusk.

If economic reasons alone might have ensured minimal decency of treatment, social and cultural pressures were even more persuasive. A considerable minority of servants in the middle colonies, perhaps a fifth, were bound to masters of their own stock, Irish or more usually Scots Irish. Thus Brian Kelly was bound to John Dougharty of Chester county, and Andrew Neelson to Daniel Craig of Bucks county for four years from August 13, 1746. In itself this might not guarantee against ill-usage (it did not in Ireland): but in a situation where the farmers themselves had experienced the loneliness of up-rooting, many had themselves earlier been servants, many had been humbled by the tasks of clearance and cultivation, and many were fellow-Presbyterians in background with their workers, there was better chance of humane treatment. The servants in such situations were strangers rather than foreigners, and strangers of the same faith, customs and class. Contrariwise, the absence of widespread black enslavement and of white gang labour (such as existed in Maryland), and the existence of a growing Scots Irish community (and a smaller native Irish one) throughout eastern Pennsylvania and Jersey, doubtless also helped moderate the treatment given the *majority* of Irish born labourers who worked upon the farms of native Americans, usually of English stock, in the region. In both cases, the bondsman had an opportunity to learn the rudiments of mid-colonial agricultural practices: for many of them, this educative aspect of the system was its one beneficial effect, and considerably so. The fact that few farmers could afford more than one servant (those that could are often listed as gentlemen in the Philadelphia records) meant that the latter must have gained a broad familiarisation with these practices in his four years normal service. For some, this may have meant the stripping of illusions about America, and a determination to find an easier way of life than the farm. For most, however, it led to acceptance of the reality, that "As *America* is a new country, and the settlers generally poor, they are obliged to be very laborious, in order to procure a tolerable subsistence for themselves and their families" (N.Y. *Gazette,* 1768). Over most of the middle colonies, there was the assurance that one's bond labour, even if unpaid, was not enriching a parasitic aristocrat or middlemen, but assisting an unpretentious yeomanry, or even (where Ulster Protestant servants worked for Ulstermen) aiding the man much like oneself. As for the native Irish labourers, though unpaid, their work generally guaranteed them life's necessities. In Ireland, rural and urban labour, fitful and underpaid, was rarely adequate to the cost of such subsistence.

A small minority were fortunate in working for relatives who had migrated before them, such doubtless as Thomas Mullen, his time sold by Conyngham and Gardner to Charles Mullen, a west Jersey farmer in 1746. Others were fortunate in that masters' recognised relationships in acquiring them; Robert McCarroll and Ann Carroll (presumably Irish-speaking Ulsterfolk, to report their names so) bought together by Charles Edgar, a Philadelphia merchant; Marian Henry and her infant son Charles by Joshua Humphreys, a Philadelphia country farmer, and Margaret and Thomas Right by Edward Goff, a Chester county farmer. Brother-sister, husband-wife and mother-child couples were rare among indentured migrants however. Nor were they always respected: Lettice and Oliver Jones were given separate, if relatively neighbouring masters. Particularly humane masters seem inclined to re-unite family members who discovered each other after migration at separate times; thus one is inclined to interpret the re-assignment of John Reardon to Dennis Reardon, a Gloucester county farmer, for the remainder of his term by his initial master, William Hill. That the vast majority of migrants were young and single saved such complications, and was a boon to the farmers involved in the trade.

As noted, however, a surprisingly high proportion of incoming servants (as of apprenticed second generation Irish-and-Ulster Americans) were bound to urban tradesmen and craftsmen. Their numbers are remarkable: of 503 identifiably Irish servants bound between 23 October 1745 and 7 October the next year in Philadelphia, at least 144 were so assigned, 24 of them women (and thus probably house-servants or shop girls). For the rest, they served in a remarkable variety of trades, presumably usually as assistants, and almost all in Philadelphia itself: to sailors, shallopmen, shipwrights, ropemakers, a mastmaker and a sailmaker; to carpenters, joiners, bricklayers and labourers; to shoemakers, hatters, peruke-makers, tailors, fullers, weavers, skinners, leather-dressers and tanners; to chaise and chair makers; to blacksmiths and harness-makers; to millers, brewers, bakers, innkeepers, butchers and merchants generally; with a number, presumably as manservants, to 'gentlemen', and with an individual case to every conceivable variety of Pennsylvanian: a pilot, doctor, surveyor, lawyer and so on. Most were assigned to transportation related trades (marine and equine), to the building trades, as labourers' assistants, and to innkeepers and merchants. This is as the structure of Philadelphia's economy would suggest: but it both may also reflect expertises more general in eastern Ireland (Ulster and Dublin and Cork) than has been supposed, and may further have represented the crucial initial direction adopted by the earliest urban Irish Americans, a direction disproportionately followed in the nineteenth century.

In short, the Irish American working class of 1800–1870, heavily concentrated in transportation and warehousing, seems to have had early antecedents. These Philadelphia patterns (confirmed in the 1771–73 assignments), are paralleled in the more skeletal evidence for New York city, which had a notable bound Irish population from the 1750s. We can safely assume that upon freedom, the majority of these trade and craft assistants attempted independent practice of the same skills: among those acquiring Irish servants in 1745–46 were bricklayer Patrick McCamish, hatter Farrell Reiley, plasterer Patrick McCornish and tailor Dennis Flood. Finally we may note of this class that runaway urban servants were almost unique. Considering they had an easier task to disappear (and more opportunities to adopt the cloak of conscious acculturation to American manners), this can only mean both that they were better treated than those in the countryside, and secondly that they found it advantageous to their future to remain with their masters. The social pressures against grave abuses, however, would also have been strongest in Philadelphia itself, as in other towns.

South of the middle colonies, there was a very different experience awaiting Irish bound labour, generally harsh, exploitative and unrelenting. This was particularly the case in Maryland, where the planter class, driven by debt and gentry aspiration, by diminishing returns and collective cupidity, legislated longer service terms (five years normally for adults only, proportionately longer for youths than elsewhere) and imposed savage penalties for running away and other offences: in Maryland, ten days additional service were required for each day's absence, as against two extra in Virginia, New Jersey and North Carolina, five in Pennsylvania and seven in South Carolina. Court cases of cruel treatment, of insufficient provision for subsistence, and of excessive punishment, are uncommon elsewhere, but less so in Maryland. William Eddis wrote that Marylanders were inclined to exploit indentured servants to the limit of their strength, while relatively conserving their black slaves, since they would have but a few years' service from the servants, and life from the blacks. Throughout the South, the climate was more harrowing for Irish servants and their response relatedly apathetic: Maryland and Virginia, despite planters' efforts, were but poorly and partially cultivated, and much had to do with the absence of an interested, or at least co-operative, workforce. In Maryland, there were six unfree white immigrants to every one free in the eighteenth century, and the balance of importations swung from Irish to English depending upon how severely the laws taxing Irish servants were imposed: over long stretches, apparently, they were not.

The great majority of Irish immigrants to both Maryland and Virginia were from the south of Ireland, many of them coming in English vessels which had provisioned at Cork or Waterford. The majority of transported Irish convicts were also sent to these two colonies, and seem to have had few illusions about what awaited them during their seven or fourteen year terms; in 1773, a brig from Dublin to Baltimore was stranded on Egg's Island, off the Virginia coast, and fifty desperate Irish convicts seized a small craft sent out to aid the vessel, and escaped into Gloucester county. The large numbers of slaves and convicts in these territories, combined with the anti-poor prejudices of their pseudo-aristocratic planters, and the absence of a large population of plain white people with whom the servants might be identified by common anticipation: these factors added to the economic ones to depress the treatment of Irish immigrants in the area. That most of them were Catholic likewise militated against their fair treatment, for we may conjecture that the inhabitants of the middle colonies, who seldom distinguished among types of Irishmen, found *their* usual prejudices mitigated by the fact that Ulster Protestants made up the majority of the Irish among them. Presumably had more Protestants come among the Irish in plantation Virginia and Maryland it would have helped the others there. The *Virginia Gazette* in "A Picture of Europe for 1771" pictured as follows:

ROME. The Pope repeating Homilies; nineteen Cardinals sing penitential Hymns; his Holiness's Hat nodding . . . at a distance, a Spaniard and a Frenchman dancing, after breaking their Chains.

IRELAND. Barefooted; singing the Irish Howl. [Presumably the *caoine* or lament].

In the nature of things, the death rate from 'colonial fever' was highest in these two plantation colonies. They likewise were the sole colonies in which servant women were generally expected to work in the fields. Differently treated, too, were 'Freewillers' or 'redemptioners' (those who paid part of their passage, and sought a master or relative to pay off the rest, or alternatively pledged to make their own indenture arrangements on arrival in America). In Pennsylvania and New Jersey, they normally specified that they be taught the trade of their master (or husbandry) as a condition of service in the earlier years, and in the later served only an average of two years. At all times their service was related to their indebtedness to their sea captain. In Virginia and Maryland, the tendency was to treat freewiller and pre-indentured servants the same. Generally, whereas the middle colonies preserved the sense that the master possessed only the time of the servant, in the South the special circumstances and the prevalence of slavery inclined the planters away from the sense that they had a right to the immigrants service and toward the notion that they had a property in him. Here he was likely to be sold, to be gambled away, exchanged, bequeated by will—and unlikely to be indulged by a court system controlled by the planters. Runaway advertisements suggest, further, that he was less well treated and clothed: 'Negro' clothes, sailor jackets and coarser homespuns seem to have been usual in the area.

Where the exceptional minority in the middle states were town workers, the minority in the plantations were craft-workers upon the largely self-sufficient greater estates. On the Baltimore county estate of Col. John Ridgely and his heirs, these included John Fowloe, the gardener, Joseph Harney and James Roaney, clothes-makers, James Lee, the barber and Charles Doud, fiddler. Since the families possessed of the great estates normally bought their own clothing and furnishings commercially, the value of such craft-workers was that they cut down on the costs of clothing and otherwise servicing the field gangs, in addition to the field work which they themselves did. On many southern estates, the dress of the black slaves, as of the white servants, was produced by Irish weavers and tailors, before the rise of cheap mass production techniques. Among them were perhaps Patrick Clerk, who fled Lawrence Washington of Chotank (a cousin of George!), John Dwyer who ran off from John Atkinson in Fredericksburg and "calls himself an Englishman, but has an Irish accent," or Daniel Ruark, "with many red bumps on his face," who took off from Richard Caddeen of Yeocomico in Westmoreland county, all in the early 1770s, although it is possible such men ran off precisely because the trade at which they expected to labour was perhaps deprived them.

That treatment was particularly bad in Virginia and Maryland is evidenced between the lines of many runaway notices, quite apart from the poorer clothes involved. The printers Purdie and Dixon of Williamsburg conceded the importance of this last matter in their notice for their own runaway Irish apprentice: "we paid £13 for him to prevent him being sent to Maryland and sold", choosing rather "to put him on a footing with the other lads in our Office. He has been well used, and genteelly clothed, which any one may easily discover from the goodness and quality of the Clothes he has taken with him". Clearly, however, young James Carey was not impressed, even by his 'black Silk Cravat.' He was clearly an exception. Cooper John Farrell, "a sickly looking Man" fled from Hobb's Hole Mill with a Scots baker after they "had both been whipped a few Days ago for Hog-stealing and their Backs must still be sore". Underfeeding (implied here) and overwork could also cause the dull mindlessness that led to accident: runaway convict servant John Campbell had a scythe scar on his right leg, and an axe scar on his left shin. The most explicit indication of generally bad treatment (apart from commentators like William Eddis) comes from William Deakins of Georgetown in Maryland, describing the remarkable case of Matthew Savage. Savage was Virginia born, with relatives near Williamsburg, but had found his way back to Ireland, probably to relatives. To return, he indented himself passenger to Baltimore. "But finding he was *American* born, I would not sell him, but agreed to give him liberty to hire himself" so that he could earn the money to buy back his indenture. "He appeared to be very thankful, as I had not treated him as a common servant, and promised to be very industrious".

Evidently treatment in the past had been generally worse than these examples from the 1770s indicate. Nor was bad treatment confined to the planters. Dominick Hogan fled the Petapsco Iron Works in Baltimore county in 1745 with 'an Iron Collar about his Neck'. Henry Kirk, Matthew Jolly and Terence Flanagan, three Irish convicts who fled the same works the following year 'all wear Caps, having their Hair cut off,' Kirk with whipping stripes 'fresh on his Back.' Thomas Haily ran off from Dr. William Lynn of Fredericksburg, 'his hair cut off, and his Head full of Scars,' in autumn 1746. Occasionally freed Irishmen helped the runaways: when Owen Magee fled, his master noted "it is thought a Countryman of his has help'd him to a pair of Shoes". Indeed the fact that clothing and treatment appear to have been somewhat better by the 1770s in Maryland may not be unconnected with the growth of a considerable freed population of Irishmen among the smaller planters, wage labourers and free craftsmen. Enlightened self-interest was also involved: as the North Carolina Act of 1741 requiring decent treatment justified its requirements, "as an encouragement for Christian servants to perform their service with fidelity and cheerfulness". Among smaller planters (the large majority) fear of able-bodied servants was not misplaced: Irishman James Horney (with another Catholic servant, Hector Grant, a Scots Highlander), murdered his master Richard Waters of Kent County, Maryland, gave out that he had gone off, and were not discovered for some weeks.

The native Irish were as well used to abuse as the larger planters were to the habits of command. So perhaps more poignant was the anomalous situation of South Carolina. There the majority of the many Irish plantation servants were Ulster Presbyterians "papists being quite out of repute in Carolina" by the mid-eighteenth century. These emigrants hoped to join the stream of free Ulster people who had gone to the interior directly or indirectly by the Valley of Virginia. A minority of them successfully petitioned themselves out of bondage by appealing to the legislature for land under the colony's Protestant immigration scheme, but the majority were stuck for four or more years in the hot and fever-ridden rice and indigo plantations of the seaboard counties. They arrived in poor condition anyway, since the shippers were not interested in the servant traffic as such, but rather to save on ballast for return journeys of the rice and tobacco transports from Britain. Few Englishmen would travel on the boats, so instead they picked up the more destitute Ulsterfolk, many of these dying and all weakening on the long voyage. "The survivors were in a most pitiful condition when they arrived here," commented Nathaniel Russell in 1767, while Henry Laurens was less compassionate the next year: "The Irish Servants have been a great plague to me" and he had to send the few Catholics among them to Florida. *All* of them "are not worth their homony to me". Eventually he let the Protestants go free, since he could not sell them! Yet even he recognised excesses: he "never saw an Instance of Cruelty in Ten or Twelve years experience equal to the Cruelty exercised upon the poor Irish . . . no other care was taken of those poor Protestant Christians from Ireland but to deliver as many as possible alive on Shoar upon the cheapest possible Terms". The indolent and sybaritic planters of South Carolina, men unlike the driven businessmen of the tobacco country to the north, were yet scarcely less cruel, as a rule. Thus a commentator noted in 1740 that the foreign servants (largely Irish) "have shown a dogged disposition, surly and obstinate, discovering an Aversion to their Masters' Orders".

Indentured servitude, then, in various colonies, and as interpreted by various masters, could vary overmuch. There were servants who were treated as partners and friends, such as George Taylor, who married his master's daughter and ran his foundry in Northampton county, Pennsylvania, beginning a career that would eventually make him one of the Irish-born signatories of the Declaration of Independence (if not otherwise a distinguished politician). On the other hand there were those treated worse than field slaves, for the period of their indentures. In between, there were as many modes of treatment as there were masters. Even ordinarily decent men, finding themselves in complete and often isolated control over another human being, will tend to abuse their power, especially when such exploitation could make the difference between indebtedness and profit, or speed the transition from a hand-to-mouth postfrontier subsistence to a modest comfort based upon wider acres and a wheat surplus. No one who has spoken to Ukranian or Polish deportees who worked upon German farms during the past war, or heard former American soldiers honestly describe how they treated German war prisoners put into work details with their units, can doubt that servitude was rough for most in a considerably less humanitarian century than the twentieth. The insistence with which planters and farmers specify the Irishness of their bond-servants, and their general refusal to make distinctions between Scots Irish and native Irish (both virtually always called Irish) suggest that the key mechanism of exploitation was operative among most of them: the labourer was *other* than the self, a stranger, a foreigner. By calling the Scots Irish only Irish, any difficulties created by his sharing a common Protestantism with his master were overcome. The general absence of personality characterisation (as distinct from physical description) and the rarity even of comment upon habits and mannerisms in runaway notices, suggest that many masters distanced and even depersonalised their servants, the easier to drive them. However, it may be that by definition servants ran away from masters who so treated them, and that such a situation was less prevalent than such notices would suggest. Nonetheless, as the Matthew Savage case illustrates, the Irishness of the servants enabled men to exercise mastery over others without feeling that they were enemies of the *mores* of an American society in which increasingly all of white adult Americans were treated with decency. English travellers around 1800, noted Jane Mesick, believed that "the native laborer in country districts" unlike the redemptioner, was "regarded, not as an inferior, but as a person to be treated with respect and consideration". The tendencies of Irish runaways to claim another name or to deny the 'O' in their name, to lose their accent or other distinctive characteristics, or even to claim that they were of other nationality [as shoemaker Thomas Murphy (alias Newman) did in setting himself forth to be a New Englander!], all tendencies noted by masters, suggests that the Irish themselves were aware of the way in which the society used their Irishness as an excuse for their demeaning treatment. Likewise the strenuous attempts, largely unsuccessful, by Ulster Presbyterians to distinguish themselves clearly from the native Irish, suggests that they too recognised the repressive uses of a caricatured Irishness, for their own *usual* custom in America was to call themselves Irish.

All this said, however, there remained the crucial fact that the law and custom recognised that bond servants were Christian persons temporarily deprived of social freedom and civic rights, and NOT human chattels permanently at the the disposal of their masters. The society's commitment to the humanity of all white people was so great that one detects a certain embarrassment in the use of the foreignness of the servants to obscure this central fact for a time. Neither anti-Irish not anti-Catholic prejudices, however endemic, could overcome the prior recognition of that humanity. This emerged not merely in the fairer treatment in the middle colonies and in the treatment of domestic and certain craft servants in the plantation areas: it was embodied in the law. Everywhere provision for wholesome and competent diet, clothing and lodging was enjoined. The courts permitted servants (unlike black slaves) to testify against their masters, to sue for adherence to the terms of their indentures, and to seek protection, release or resale in cases of cruelty. Early an Irish youth won his contest in a Maryland court for relief from fifteen years service on the ground that it was 'contrary to the laws of God and man that a Christian subject should be made a Slave'. (1661).

Lord Lieutenant Chesterfield, philosopher George Berkeley, James Mac Sparran (Anglican minister in Rhode Island), Lord Sheffield and others between 1745 and 1784 linked the condition of the Irish and the Negro: but the two better informed scarcely did, for MacSparran was comparing the Negro with the Irish at home, and Berkeley's comment deserves quotation as much for its negative as its positive link: "the negroes in our Plantation have a saying, 'If Negro was not Negro, an Irishman would be Negro.'" Sheffield's comment (perhaps based on Eddis) was simple scare-mongering: 'Irishmen, just emancipated in Europe, go to America to become slaves to a negro." Indeed, given the overlap of the workforces, what strikes one in runaway notices is the infrequency with which they mention Irishmen and blacks making common cause: I have found but two examples. Punishment would probably have been more severe for both parties in such cases, and few Irishmen, whatever the sympathies born of a common subjection, a shared hatred of a single master, and a common humanity, can have risked jeopardising the decisively favourable situation they enjoyed as against the blacks in the long term. Blackness alone caused colonial courts to make an *a priori* assumption that a black claiming he was a free person was in fact the offspring of a slave mother. On the other hand, the benefit of the doubt was apparently sometimes granted to Irish servants: Ann Dempsey gained her freedom from the Philadelphia Quarter Sessions in 1753 by claiming that she had been forcibly brought from Ireland and 'Cruelly used on the voyage', and another Irishman got his freedom at the age of twenty-two by showing he had been kidnapped as an infant, as likewise did that celebrated Anglo-Irish victim of victims, young Lord James Annesley, in servitude in Lancaster county from around 1728–1740. That ninety per cent of African slaves imported to the colonies to America had been forcibly kidnapped would have availed them nothing even had they been permitted to sue freely in courts. The clearest evidence of the advantages of Irish status came in 1787. Showing that a law of 1664 had caused the enslavement of her ancestors, Mary Butler, a mulatto woman, successfully sued for her freedom on the ground that she was a descendant of Lord Baltimore's servant, 'Irish Nell', who had married a Negro named Butler, for Baltimore had repealed the law involved in 1681.

Thus, while legislating severely against Popery and often theoretically excluding Irish Papist servants, the colonies treated individual Irish people quite separately from any formulaic revulsion from their creed and homeland. It is difficult to avoid the conclusion that while anti-Irishness served an important use during an immigrant's years of service, upon his liberation he became a beneficiary of the general enhancement of the situation and status of ordinary white people that was normal throughout most of the colonies, if he was a readily useful individual, and did not press his nativity or his religion too hard. To oversimplify, the Irishman, increasingly the victim of overpopulation and a debased political economy at home, was the step-child of underpopulation and a benign political economy in America. This was true whether he was of native Irish stock or otherwise.

What did happen to the indentured servant, the redemptioner or the convict, upon his release? Although one swallow does not make a summer, the number of notable eighteenth century Ulster Americans and Irish Americans who began life as indentured servants is significant. Daniel Dulany, after a Trinity College graduation, went indentured to Maryland in 1703, and ultimately became its attorney general. William Killen, from Co. Clare, also indentured in Maryland, became Chief Justice of Delaware. Mathew Thornton from Limerick, who came to New England as a child, is said to have been indentured, and later became a leading New Hampshire revolutionary, a physician and later justice. Charles Thompson had been indentured after arrival in America at age ten, his father having died on the voyage, and was to become Secretary of the Continental Congress. Thomas Macnamara, a friend of Dulany's from Clare, managed medium rank office in Maryland between 1714–1720, though he had betrayed his original patron, Charles Carroll, by his lechery and violence. Matthew Lyon from Wicklow, future revolutionary soldier and entreprenuer-politician from Vermont, served out his time to Jabez Bacon and Hugh Hannah of Woodbury and Litchfield in Connecticut from 1765–68. The parents of General John Sullivan, Margery Browne of Limerick and John Sullivan of Cork, had been redemptioners from Ireland. These are but the better known examples. At the other end of the continuum from fame to anonymity, we know something of some humbler Irish immigrants who remained Loyalist and recorded skeletal self-histories in the course of pursuing claims against the British Government for their losses. Michael Reading, indentured in Charleston on arrival in 1763, had acquired the relative fortune of £695 through his trade as carpenter by late 1776. John Hennesy, indentured from 1764–68 in the same city, became a carter and small trader on release, and was worth £460 by 1778. Donald Gallagher, after serving his time after 1759 to a New Jersey farmer, had become himself a fairly prosperous tenant farmer by 1775. We have also seen something of Irish traders in Philadelphia.

More persuasive than such scattered cases are the evidences of a very generalised distribution of Irishmen, native and Ulster Scots, in the Census of 1790. On the basis of the Maryland land records of the 1680s alone, and perhaps influenced unconsciously by such sources as Defoe, Hogarth and the anti-poor American gentry, Abbott Smith argued that most indentured servants were uneducated and ill-disciplined, generally a worthless people, who failed to take advantage even of legislation designed to ensure that all freed white settlers could obtain land. The Maryland situation of the 1680s was perhaps anomalous. The servants of that time (post Cromwellian where the Irish were involved) were more ruthlessly treated than afterwards, to judge by the incidence of cruelty cases. The unconscious premise of his assertion may be that the 'white trash' of the Appalachian region had to originate somewhere. But since his work was undertaken, historians of the general southern region have learnt to distinguish a 'plain people', a substantive farming class, interposed between planters and the 'lower people' and to be more careful in drawing harsh lines between the achievers and the impoverished in a situation of general environmental impoverishment on America's first frontier. However, there is little doubt that the majority (though not overwhelmingly so) of freed Irish servants eventually took up land where it was available, in the back country of the colonies: the heaviest Irish concentration on Maryland was in Frederick county, away from the tobacco tidewater of their initial exploitation. That there, and also in the Valley of Virginia and central Pennsylvania, the native Irish took up land in the same counties as the Ulster Scots raises the issue of their mutual acceptance which the interpenetration of their folk-music in these regions does. (This should not be exaggerated: rambling and ragged native Irishmen seem to have been considerably more likely to have been 'taken up' on suspicion of being runaways in Ulster Scot counties, such as Augusta county, Virginia, than elsewhere). Obviously those emigrants, largely from Ulster, who indented themselves to relatives or connections previously in America as a conscious way of getting a start in the country, would upon freedom have joined the mainstream of the young men in established areas now seeking farms in newer areas, where they did not rent, marry or otherwise acquire land locally.

There seems no doubt that the majority of southern Irish emigrants began as indentured servants. Nonetheless among them too there was a considerable free immigration: those taking advantage of the Croghan-Johnson connection in the western borderlands were free men, for example. Such Irish tradesmen as James Cowdy, William Owens, Luke Keating, and Bernard Cory, recorded in the Loyalist claims, immigrated freely. Others, too, like Cory, came after a time in England, freely. Matthew Maher opened his watch business in Philadelphia in 1761, proclaiming in the *Pennsylvania Gazette* that he had "wrought for some of the most eminent watch-makers in both London and Dublin" and had just arrived from Dublin. It is notable that so many of these chose to be townsmen, reflecting perhaps their generally urban Irish background. This seems connected with the fact that all freewillers in the 1745–46 Philadelphia records indented themselves to 'gentlemen' or to urban craftsmen, specifying that they learn the trade as part of their terms of service, and some being prepared to spend longer time in bondage to do so, as Daniel Hiraghty did in accepting a six year term with John Evans, a Philadelphia tailor and John Carroll did in accepting a five year term from William Crosswhite on condition of being taught the 'mystery' of peruke-making. All these facts again emphasise the effect of the situation described in the first chapter: eighteenth century Ireland was proportionately more urbanised than early nineteenth century Ireland, likewise considerably more urbanised than the colonies, and those who had grown up in the exciting if impoverished cities and towns of Ireland were not always ready to sacrifice the self-respect of a craft and the conviviality of a town, for farm labour, even when the rural horizon offered a surer route to a decent competence. The numbers of Ulstermen, too, who chose trade, craft and urbanity was probably considerably greater than has been thought.

To leave on this note, however, would be to distort the picture. Unquestionably, the mass of all servants and redemptioners attempted to gain farms. As Governor Sir Henry Moore noted in New York in 1767 (the city having received at least eight shiploads of Irish servants between 1728–1775, a small traffic, yet making the Irish there the leading bound immigrant group): "as soon as the time stipulated in their Indentures is expired, they immediately quit their masters, and get a small tract of land, in settling which for the first three or four years they lead miserable lives, and in the most abject Poverty, but . . . the Satisfaction of being Land holders smooths every difficulty, and makes them prefer this manner of living to that comfortable subsistence available from . . . the Trades in which they were brought up." Whether they were as unsuccessful as Hector St. John Crèvecoeur believed, or whether they eventually made a passable bargain with the earth is something best left to their own irrecoverable judgement. Returned Irish physician John Brickell, in a Dublin work of 1737 on North Carolina, argued that while few ex-servants immediately became yeomen, some saved and did later, but most remained labourers. In crowded tidewater Maryland, long since divided between planters and yeomen, many freed servants wandered helplessly without bread, and lived in "poverty, want and misery", noted Jesuit Joseph Mosely in 1772. Others, however, moved west and did get land in the back-country. Speaking of both the Germans and the Irish of Frederick county, western Maryland, J. F. D. Smyth wrote: "they are very laborious and extremely industrious, having improved this part of the country beyond conception". Many of these were freed servants. This London cosmopolitan could not understand the calculations that transformed the weary back country into the contenting portion of the ordinary plain folk of peripheral Ireland (north and south), into the hope of former bondsmen whose spirits and capacity survived the exhaustions of servitude and the danger of destitution.

The reactions of the majority of these emigrants to a revolt against the Empire of London were predictable. That so many of them, almost certainly a majority (to judge by the shipping lists of Audrey Lockhart and R. J. Dickson) were recent immigrants, coming between 1765 and 1776, meant that they were sensitive to the waves of political and agrarian excitement which had swept separate parts of Ireland since around 1760, from the Steelboy movement in Antrim through the patriot turbulence stimulated by Charles Lucas in Dublin, to the agrarian, tithe and factional disorders of Co. Cork. There *were* many quiet districts in Ireland in these years: the many emigrants from Londonderry, the fair numbers from Limerick, came from regions almost hermetically sealed (in that era of localisation) from the spirit of harshly politicised discontent. But the great bulk of the migrants came from Belfast, Dublin and Cork, regions predisposed to a rhetoric of confrontation, and carried frustrations which for many may have been intensified by the experience of servitude in America. For the majority who underwent unpaid subjection in these years in America itself, the slogan of Liberty had a real connotation. As the polemics and engravings of the time suggested, as the whig interpretation of political freedom then used by the revolutionaries proclaimed, political servitude was figuratively the chaining down of adult self-direction. Irish experience and American experience combined to make the immigrants respond at once to the idea that Britain was once again about to enchain them in their new home, and deprive them of the homely contents of an untithed farm, of usually rent-free acres, or (if city men), of the remarkable world in which even a labourer could possess an indentured servant, and even an Irish labourer could own a three storey house, as Francis McFarland did in Chester Alley in Philadelphia in 1771. Even as matters were dividing the sentiments of colonial Americans and England, Irishmen were helping to foster the division: a group of 'Irish subscribers' inserted a long whiggish attack on the methods of 'despotism' in the *Pennsylvania Chronicle* (1771) entitled "Thoughts on the Pension List of Ireland" and shortly afterwards (fifteen years before Matthew Carey), 'An Hibernian' proposed a scheme for America's textile independence from Britain in the same journal. Irritable Irishmen and embittered Ulstermen were a useful importation for a country on the edge of revolution. Unfortunately, however, we cannot assume that they all could readily transform their feeling into coherent politics.

the beſt of groceries, he hopes to give ſatisfaction to thoſe who pleaſe to favour him with their cuſtom.

JUST IMPORTED, in the laſt Veſſels from London, and to be ſold on the loweſt terms, for caſh or ſhort credit, by DANIEL TYSON, at his ſtore in Water-ſtreet, a few doors above Market-ſtreet:

A GENERAL aſſortment of European and Eaſt-India Goods, among which are, ſuperfine broadcloths, Wilton cloths, hair pluſh, oznabrigs, ticklenburg, white and brown Ruſſia ſheeting, Ruſſia drilling, Iriſh and Dutch dowlas, Engliſh bed-tick, Iriſh ſheeting, 3-4, 7-8 and yard wide Iriſh linen, Ravens duck, Ruſſia diaper, 7-8, yard wide and yard and 3-8 cotton and linen checks, 10 nail, 11 nail and 3-4 ſtripes, French cotton ſtripes, linen and cotton hollands, bed bunts, cambricks and lawns, muſlin, damaſcus's, mozeens, buckram, brown roles, heſſen, calicoes, nankeens, bengals, half yard and ell wide perſians, ſarſenet, black India and Engliſh taffaty, ſagathys, durants, ſhalloons, rattinets, calimancoes, poplins, Scotch camblets, dorſettees, fuſtians, jeans, thickſets, cotton and wool cards, ſewing ſilk, breeches patterns, men's and women's worſted, thread and cotton hoſe, powder, ſhot, writing paper, black pepper, pewter plates, diſhes and baſons, pewter ſpoons, ſithes, felt hats, knives and forks, ſhoe and knee buckles, quality and ſhoe binding, men's gloves, women's gloves and mitts, ſilk and linen handkerchiefs, black cravats, Scotch and coloured thread, ſilk and hair twiſt, death head and baſket buttons, Morocco pocket-books, horſe whips, &c. &c.

TO BE SOLD,

A VALUABLE Tract of Land, ſituate in Mannington.

An Advertisement for European and East-India goods

Burning of Charleston and Battle of Bunker's Hill

Chapter 5
In a Revolutionary America

General Considerations

Those who try to observe the Irish in the midst of the American Revolution face three large difficulties. Firstly, the evidence of their presence is highly contradictory, and compounded by the fact that few contemporaries distinguished between Scotch-Irish, Anglo-Irish and native Irish. Secondly, their precise roles are dependent upon an analysis of the nature of the American Revolution in the areas of their concentration: a considerably less simple matter than cliché might suggest. Finally the revolution was pre-eminently American: in a sense the first collective and decisive definition of American nationality itself (as against the inertial intercolonial forces which had been long moulding that nationality), and many Ulster Americans and natively Irish Americans participated in it in that spirit. Can their participation be meaningfully discussed in Irish terms at all? Historical studies reflect each of these three problems closely. Where there is precise investigation into the nature of the revolution on a regional basis, certain attention has continued to be given the role of immigrant and second-generation participation. Generally, however the American Revolution has tended to draw scholars essentially national in their emphasis. Despite a fine flourish of 'imperial historians' trying to broaden the framework between 1900–1950, this nationalism of emphasis is now more pervasive than before; whereas ethnic explanations of America's past have made their greatest impact upon our view of the nineteenth century. Additionally, documentation of the parochialism and class-limitations of British politics in the age of the revolution has only served to confirm most American historians of the period in a sympathetic impatience that their revolutionary forebears be done with all that. The resultant and understandable post-European ethos of their work, while certainly true to the attitudes of leaders like Jefferson and Washington, distorts the central facts that a larger proportion of Americans were then European born than at any time since and that American culture itself was far closer to its European antecedents in the eigteenth century than was the case thereafter.

Nonetheless the 'American' emphasis of scholars like John Alden, Douglas Freeman, Dumas Malone, Merrill Jensen and Gordon Wood cannot be lightly set aside. Most white and probably most black Americans by 1776 were native born, with only hazy traditional images of the old world. Scholars can hardly be faulted for their scepticism at the evidence of important (and not merely significant) Irish participation in the American Revolution if much of it was couched in terms so exaggerated as to suggest that the witnesses had little grasp of how American the colonies were by 1776. On the one side we have

British officers. Captain Joshua Pell commented, "the rebels are chiefly composed of Irish Redemptioners and Convicts, the most audacious rascals existing". Dubliner Captain Frederick Mackenzie of the Royal Welch Fusiliers entered in his diary during the Long Island campaign in October 1776: "The chief strength of the Rebel Army at present consists of Natives of Europe, particularly Irishmen:—many of their Regiments are composed principally of these men." Captain Johann Heinrichs of the Hessian Jaeger Corps in British service wrote to a friend, "call it not an American Rebellion, it is nothing more nor less than an Irish-Scotch Presbyterian Rebellion." Lord Richard Howe's secretary Ambrose Serle, reporting as an agent to his former master Lord Dartmouth in September 1776 from New York, noted that 'Great Numbers of Emigrants, particularly Irish, are in the Rebel Army, some by Choice and many for mere Subsistence," and the following year emphasised in his journal that the people of the Newcastle, Delaware, area, largely natives of Ireland, were strongly pro-Revolutionary. He agreed with the Rev. Charles Inglis, an Anglican, that "the Principles of Republicanism had kept pace" with the spread of Presbyterianism. Serle is unusual in that he seemed to understand there was a key difference between the recent poorer Irish immigrant soldiers and the confident and directive role of an Americanised Ulster Presbyterianism. Others thoroughly confused this issue. The leading Pennsylvanian Loyalist, Joseph Galloway, who had failed to keep his colony in the British column, testified before a parliamentary committee in London in 1779 that 'about one-half' the Rebel Army was 'Irish,' and only a quarter of it American. Major General James Robertson testified that he 'remembered General Lee telling me, that he believed half the Rebel Army were from Ireland,' meaning the continental or regular forces of the American Congress. The able and ill-tempered British commander, Sir Henry Clinton, wrote from New York in autumn 1778 a proposal for the London War Office which envisaged promoting widespread Irish desertion, since the "Emigrants from Ireland were in general to be looked upon as our most serious antagonists".

Evidence from the other side, the American, is considerably less persuasive, unless Americans took for granted the presence of the 'Old Countrymen' (as they now more benignly called the Irish of all sorts, perhaps because the very term Irish had had a derogatory ring in the past to them?). Benjamin Rush and Benjamin Franklin agreed upon the key role the Irish played in the revolutionary politics and armies of Pennsylvania, Franklin writing to William Strahan in the aftermath of the period, in 1784, "It is a fact that the Irish emigrants and their children are now in possession of the government of Pennsylvania by their majority in the Assembly, as well as of a great part of the territory." David Ramsay, himself the son of Ulster immigrants yet the most remarkably judicious of early historians of the Revolution, noted that "The Irish in America, with a few exceptions, were attached to independence," and noted of the forces of Pennsylvania that the "common soldiers in that State were for the most part natives of Ireland . . . inferior to none in discipline, courage or attachment to the cause," although he carefully specified in the first instance that 'they were Presbyterians' and therefore 'mostly Whigs'. Henry Grieve, (the companion and translator of the Marquis de Chastellux), who had dined with the Irish merchants of Philadephia at a St. Patrick's Society banquet, argued that 'On more than one imminent occasion, Congress owed their existence, and America possibly her preservation to the firmness and fidelity of the Irish,' although he may well have been swayed somewhat by the society's 'generous libation to liberty and good living' and the warm reminiscences of post-war patriotism. Yet (although he left them unreported) there were grounds for his statement. Nonetheless in all the volumes of material left by the principal actors of the Revolution: Washington, John Adams, Thomas Jefferson, Benjamin Franklin, and James Madison (to take only the most indefatigable penmen), there are no parallels to the sweeping statements of Galloway, Robertson or Clinton. If the Irish presence was so pervasive, America's leaders would have paid it more sympathetic attention: one thinks of Abraham Lincoln's care to consolidate it during the Civil War with his creation of an Irish Brigade under Meagher and his appointment of a full time propagandist to the Irish, Charles Halpine.

In short, the British officers and Loyalists overstated the case. David Ramsay himself correctly set the context for generations of historians by stressing that the principal thrust of revolutionary separatism lay among the overwhelmingly English-descended settlers of Massachusetts in the north and Virginia in the south: yet he was not one to belittle or disparage the achievements of his parents' people! Indeed the very distortions in the British/Loyalist evidence help demonstrate how blind the British were to the reality of a rising American nationality, and helped guide British policy into some crucially mistaken moves. Their assumption that there were scores of thousands of Loyalists in the Middle Colonies and in the Carolinas helped determine their successive and fruitless invasions of these areas in 1777 and 1780 respectively. Back in England, King George III himself, Horace Walpole, and other members of the court and administrative circles clearly believed the whole war was little more than an uprising of rabble-rousing Presbyterians, largely Scotch-Irish: a sort of latter-day Cromwellian outburst against the due civil, ecclesiastical and political order of a sensible and free British empire. Loyalists like Galloway had reason to claim that the rebels were not Americans like themselves: for otherwise they were defining *themselves* out of a nationality by remaining British. More pointedly, the fact that *all* British reports that the rebels were largely Irish came from the Middle Colony campaigns in Long Island, New Jersey and Pennsylvania, is itself instructive of the bias of their vision, although it also clearly confirms the claim of David Ramsay that *in that region* the armies were disproportionately composed of Irish Presbyterians. In other regions, no such claims were made. Roger Lamb, who as a Dubliner should (like Mackenzie) have been the first to comment if large numbers of his fellow countrymen had been among the American forces, never does so, either with regard to the upper New York, or the Carolinas and Virginia campaigns. Anglo-Irish commanders like Lord Rawdon and Guy

Carleton likewise have left behind no soldierly execration about the disloyalty to empire of their compatriots. Even in the middle colonies, perceptive soldier observers like Carl Baurmeister (although he was well aware of heavy Irish immigration to the region), do not specify the Irish as particularly their antagonists. Indeed one suspects that in this region, for complex political advantage, it served commanders to exaggerate the Irishness or Presbyterianness of the *entire* Revolution, to overcome the misgivings which British soldiers and German auxiliaries must have felt in fighting their culture-kinsfolk, the Anglo-Americans and the Pennsylvania Germans. Even Lord Richard Howe and his brother Sir William, we know, had grave misgivings against prosecuting the war with the requisite force because of these factors. Killing Irishmen and Presbyterians was also easier on the conscience!

Irish immigrants, then, were largely concentrated in the region of the Revolution's soft underbelly: the Middle Colonies, rich with trade with the British West Indies and Britain, weakened in national resolve by political division, softened by the growing tendency of their better-off classes to emulate English social distinctions and urban fashions, unfitted for war by the pacifism of the formerly dominant Quakers and of various German sects. It is also possible, although no one has yet suggested it, that the very volume of the Irish influx into the region prompted an Anglophile reaction among many of its inhabitants, just as happened in Henry Cabot Lodge's New England in the 1880s. This certainly seems to have been the case in Kent and Sussex counties in Delaware, shadowed by the prosperity and political acumen of heavily Scotch Irish Newcastle county to the north. By strange irony, then, the Irish may help account for the lack of the fever of independence in the middle colonies, for the rest of the mid colonials realised better than did Virginians or New Englanders that an independent America would not be comfortingly Amer-English in either culture or population. This very unenthusiasm, however, gave the Irish of the middle colonies, particularly the Presbyterians, a role in the revolution in that region very disproportionate to their numbers. In New Jersey, Delaware and Pennsylvania, (and somewhat less so in New York and Maryland), they were at the heart of the revolution. Yet since its engines lay in Virginia and New England, this must not be exaggerated in the broader view. The distance of Washington, of Madison, of John Adams, from a full 'recognition' of this role probably stemmed from their conviction that the middle colonies were only doing their national due; and that, indeed, neither as well, nor as co-operatively, as the national leaders wished.

To understand the reasons why the Irish of the region were pro-American independence almost to a man (whether Anglo-Irish, native Irish, or Scotch-Irish) one can of course look back to the Ireland described in chapter one. But the details and style of their participation, and particularly the predominant role of the Ulster Presbyterian Americans, need more careful telling. It was closely related to the fact that for two intellectual generations, their Irish discontents had been articulated in a way (only recently re-discovered) serviceable to American independence. It was also related to the nature of their recent combative engagement in mid-colonial politics. These elements in turn helped determine that the content of the revolution in the area was generally more radical than elsewhere, if also at times strangely parochial.

The American Revolution was more than a war of independence, although it was chiefly and most simply that. On that, however, the Ulster tradition was unanimous and had been long since carried to America. The radical Whig justifications of the Glorious Revolution against James II, which in mid-eighteenth century Ireland had degenerated into an anti-Catholic cant, had been transformed before that into a creative argument for Protestant colonial liberties on behalf of the Protestants of Ireland by William Molyneux whose work survived to influence the Irish Patriots of the 1780s. His arguments and influence, which extended remotely to America, have been carefully studied in a companion volume to this one by J. G. Simms.

Even more forgotten, but perhaps more crucial was the work of Francis Hutcheson (1694–1746). Born at Saintfield in Co. Down Hutcheson studied at Glasgow University from 1710, but returned to Ireland in 1724 to spend six crucial years in the Dublin circle that included such critics of British misgovernment (though not of the British connection) as Jonathan Swift, William King, Robert Molesworth and Thomas Rundle. There his mind took fire, and Caroline Robbins argues that "Hutcheson's literary reputation was made during his years in Dublin", and his principal ideas moulded there. In 1730, he returned to a Chair at Glasgow, becoming a founder of the Scottish Enlightenment and of a liberalised Presbyterianism. There developing the ideas debated in Dublin circles stemming back to Molyneux, Hutcheson brought them to a radical conclusion. Whereas Molyneux, arguing that Ireland was a separate Kingdom, specifically excluded the North American colonies from his brief that it have English liberties, Hutcheson included them. Boldly developing his thesis that all government exists for the good of the governed, Hutcheson continued:

> If the plan of the mother-country is changed by force, or degenerate by degrees from a safe, mild and gentle limited power, to a severe and absolute one: or if under the same plan of polity, oppressive laws are made with respect to the colonies or provinces; and any colony is so increased in numbers and strength that they are sufficient by themselves; for all the good ends of a political union; they are not bound to continue in their subjection . . . There is something unnatural in supposing a large society . . . remaining subject to the direction of and government of a distant body of men . . . it is not easy to imagine there can be any foundation for it in justice or equity.

It is believed this authentically records Hutcheson's political views as he expounded them throughout his long Glasgow career, even though the precise wording is that published posthumously in 1755. It was certainly prepared as early as 1740, and also agrees with the developing philosophy of his Dublin years.That he always taught so is suggested by the views of his most famous Ulster student, Francis Alison.

Born in Leck in Donegal in 1704, Alison studied under Hutcheson at Glasgow before emigrating to the colonies in 1735. In 1743 he opened a school or academy in Philadelphia, which he later moved to Newark, Delaware, one recognised by the Synod of Philadelphia. Before he did so, 'there was not a College, nor even a good Grammar School in four provinces," wrote contemporary Ezra Stiles of conditions in the middle colonies, other than New York. In 1752 he returned to transform the Latin School of Philadelphia, which became the degree-granting College of Philadelphia, in 1755. There he carried the main burden of teaching for over twenty-five years, until 1779. Franklin, despite the virulence of his relations with most Scotch Irish, excepted Alison, holding him a man of 'great Inguenuity and Learning' despite his theological orthodoxy. Alison was the conduit of Hutcheson's philosophy, indeed, he so revered his Glasgow Irish master's work that he dictated passages of it to his students, including sections on economics and politics. His own views were in thorough agreement with Hutcheson's; the gloss of Dublin suavity was replaced by an Ulster bluntness: "The end of all civil power is the public happiness, & any power not conducive to this is unjust & the People who gave it may Justly abolish it." Years later, Alison would preach to the Continental Congress during its revolutionary deliberations. His virtual monopoly on higher education in the middle colonies outside of the like-minded College of New Jersey (Princeton) was reflected in the fame of his pupils: they included such key leaders of the revolution in the middle colonies as Thomas McKean, Charles Thomson and George Read. The three Ulster American lads actually lived in the Alisons' household while studying secondary and collegiate courses with the Reverend Dr. Francis himself. Alison was irascible and humourless, but it is easy to see this was a result of obvious overwork, for he taught almost every subject: his influence outlasted any distance he created in his students. It is not exaggerating to say that it coloured the whole definition of Pennsylvania's severance from England.

Under Thomas McKean's direction, the revolutionary committee of the extra-legal Conference of Committees of revolutionary Pennsylvania, by-passing the reluctant Quaker-controlled Assembly, drew up in June 1776 its own declaration of independence, to precipitate action by the National Congress, then meeting in Philadelphia. Its wording virtually paraphrased the teaching of Alison and Hutcheson:

> WHEREAS George the third . . . in violation of the principles of the British constitution, and of the laws of justice and humanity, hath by an accumulation of oppressions . . . excluded the inhabitants of this, with other colonies, from his protection . . . and whereas, the obligations of allegiance (being reciprocal between a king and his subjects) are now dissolved . . .

In the event, of course, Thomas Jefferson, with a good and astute respect for the opinions of mankind, re-wrote the Declaration for Congress in the categories of the Deistic enlightenment which had captivated France and

England and had influenced his fellow Virginians. But his earlier drafts showed some influence of the 'Presbyterian' document of the Pennsylvanians, and this latter document, contemporary scholars would agree, was probably closer to the revolutionary reasoning of a largely Protestant and Calvinist America than was that of the liberal Jefferson. Rooted in radical Whiggery, honed in Dublin, fused with Presbyterianism by Hutcheson and Alison, such reasoning was more persuasive to consciences still shadowed by the belief that obedience to Kings was a Christian obligation, than were the glowing phrases about governments as instruments of human equality and improvement which ring more easily on our ears today. The depth of the Protestant colouring of the Revolution cannot be underestimated: Ulster-born Charles Thomson, 'The Sam Adams of Philadelphia' as John Adams called him, recalled enough of Alison's Greek lessons to complete a translation of the New Testament, which with Calvinist orthodoxy Thomson insisted upon calling the New Covenant. Hutcheson and Alison, despite King George and Horace Walpole, demonstrate that the Ulster American commitment to independence was as cerebral as it was temperamental. The famous back-country unilateral Declarations of Independence by the Scotch-Irish of Mecklenburg, North Carolina and of Pine Creek, Clinton co., Pennsylvania are in the same tradition, as are such other documents as the instructions of Augusta co., Virginia, to its revolutionary delegates (to the Virginia preparatory conference to the Continental Congress), and the Westmoreland Declaration of the Hanna's Town community of western Pennsylvania. The very centralisation of Presbyterian polity and of the education of its ministry ensured the maximal diffusion of such views, and of a Dublin influence upon Ulstermen unaware there could be so strange and remote an irony.

Apart from the Independence question, however, the coherence of the Ulster political tradition in America almost completely breaks down. But the American Revolution must first be understood in its other, non-Independence, dimensions before we can establish the Ulster element within them.

These dimensions remain highly controversial. The American Revolution ratified and secured the peculiarities of the American colonial society described in chapter one. There is great disagreement among historians as to how far it further developed these peculiarities. Some argue that the politics of the Revolutionary era consciously polarised conflict between those drifting into hierarchical and European notions of authority and social order, and those aggressively pushing the logic of the American environment towards its democratic fulfilment: as Marcus Jensen puts it, "The American Revolution Within America." Such scholars emphasise that factions and parties emerged within several major states (as the colonies became) with antagonistic interests in the pace of change: that Radicals stressed the interests of ordinary folk (of farmers, mechanics, debtors, cash-short inland merchants and small manufacturers), and of democratic ideologies, in minimising the political power and economic advantages of the wealthy and influential; that on the other hand the rich, together with most professional people, social conservatives and genuine nationalists (these last by no means much different than plain people, except in the matter of convictions) desired that the interests and dynamism of the elite of talent and energy be favourably empowered, and that the political and financial structures of the nation give adequate weight to their judgement. There *were* Radicals who believed that the Revolution was in danger of subversion by the spirit of aristocracy, as they termed these latter trends. There were profound conservatives who regretted every popular manifestation as the beginnings of anarchy. For the former, the revolutionary Pennsylvania constitution of 1776 was the model: for the latter, the Federal Constitution of 1787 seemed a real achievement, if a compromise.

Nonetheless most historians today stress the wide agreement, amongst all parties, that government, both state and national, should be popular, broadly representative, elective, deliberative, and credit-worthy; that it should be safeguarded against self-aggrandisement by periodic change of its officers and by the supremacy of law; and that it be capable of reconciling and encompassing the diverse interests of the community. Within such government there was wide latitude as to whether calculating elites or popular tribunes would have predominant influence, but in none of them (whether the most radical in Pennsylvania, or the most conservative, perhaps South Carolina's) was any one interest, section, or class exclusively empowered. And virtually no one sought that it should be otherwise. Increasingly, for many Radicals it was enough that aristocracy had been rendered impossible, and for many conservatives, that democracy as such was nowhere *formally* ascendent except in Pennsylvania, and that even there it was remarkable how the voters returned leaders of real rank, who understood that society, law and eventually even finance were complex mysteries in need of professional, not amateur, arrangement! Despite the hyperbole of party polemic, the post-1808 'Era of Good Feelings' was anticipated even in the years 1776–1790. This is suggested in the ease with which the radical constitution of Pennsylvania was conservatively altered in 1790, and the relative ease with which the entire nation accepted the new Federal Constitution of 1787. Perhaps because of the tortured history of the emergence of democracy and social justice in Europe some American historians seem inclined to disbelieve this central reality, almost to wish that the rhetoric of parties could be transformed into the blood-stained struggles and reactionary cross-currents that have complicated the modern history of France, Germany and Spain. The majority of them, however, despite individual differences, concur on this overall view.

In short, the views of European contemporaries have been vindicated. Thomas Paine, living in Pennsylvania at the height of its radical-conservative contentions, at first believed them irrelevant, except insofar as they jeopardise the emergence of the independent America of his dream. The Crown had been arbitrary, Parliament unrepresentative and tyrannical, English society controlled by aristocratic cliques, and the mass of the poor left to fend as best they might without voice or influence. The new American constitutions vindicated an entirely new way, and their differences were trivial in comparison. As Colin Bonwick has lately shown, the new America was far from being 'a mirage in the west' to English radicals. Even before the French Revolution, they saw that the American constitutions were antecedent acts of popular sovereignty which limited government, whereas in England the 'Glorious Constitution' was nothing more than the actual organs of government as they were: malrepresentative, hereditable, property-based. Abingdon and Price recognised that the tradition of English radical reform had been decisively challenged: the myth that parliamentary supremacy expressed popular sovereignty, that only the channels of connection between them had to be cleansed, collapsed immediately upon the formation of constitutions in America by popular assembly and ratification. Paine, Jerrold and Cooper went further, and claimed a direct link between popular sovereignty and social reform, linking economic distress with tyranny. It was formerly held that only the French Revolution introduced such ideas to England. Even in France, as Joyce Appelby has shown, an *americaniste* connection emerged *before* its revolution, contending that the *anglomane* belief in mixed or whiggish constitutions with hereditary aristocracy preserved, was no longer a desirable route to reform. English radicals and *americanistes* together saw in revolutionary America the emergence of a new society now guaranteed against decay by popular sovereignty: one based upon generally fair circumstances, religious toleration and rough equality which safeguarded personal independence, hostility to inherited privilege, and yet nonetheless also protected distinctions of ability, energy and accumulated (even inherited) possessions which were socially affordable, natural, and unoppressive in that lavish land. There were, of course, misgivings: even enthusiasts in Europe knew about slavery, indentured servitude, land speculation and crudity. Unsurprisingly, sophisticated Americans like Thomas Jefferson were ready to categorise characteristically American realities in Enlightenment terminology, as though the American social environment had been pre-planned in the offices of an Encyclopédiste. Resultantly, even until lately, the 'Enlightenment' content of the American revolution and its constitutions has been greatly exaggerated, its dependence upon the whiggish and Protestant assumptions of middle-brow British culture (whether of Bristol, Glasgow or Londonderry, as well as Boston and Philadelphia) underestimated even more than the impact of the American environment.

All these points are necessary before we come to discuss the role of the Irish, and particularly Ulster Americans, in the revolution. It would be easy to draw false antitheses between the sectarian radicalism of frontier immigrants from County Antrim and the comprehensive liberalism of Benjamin Franklin or Thomas Jefferson. Ulster Americans were at the heart of the revolution precisely because they were preeminent beneficiaries of the American environment, and carriers of the middle-brow assumptions of the English-speaking world. Even their vociferous parochialism (which at times damaged the solidarity of the revolutionary war effort against Britain) expressed the preeminence of locality as the context of popular preoccupations with which even the nationalists had to come to terms in framing the Federal Constitution of 1787. In America, unlike France, no messianically national culture élite was to ride roughshod over the peculiarities of localities in the aftermath of revolution. For two generations before the Revolution, Ulster immigrants had been practising the proto-democratic promise of political localism virtually everywhere they had settled in real numbers. This prepared them for the politics of the Revolutionary era. We shall examine particularly the pre- and post-Revolutionary politics of the Middle Colonies, particularly Pennsylvania, to fill out this story. Much new work has been done upon the region, and it was the most vital area of Ulster American contribution to the Revolution, as of their largest concentrations. We shall then sketch more swiftly the situation of Virginia and the Carolinas, for the main stories there have not been changed significantly in the past twenty years. If the ideas upon the Middle Colonies represent a new departure, it is only because the detailed studies of recent scholars, taken together, fall into a new configuration: their work is essential.

A generation ago, the Scotch-Irish were fitted into the story of the Revolution in its guise of a revolution *within* America, apart from their role as shock troops of Independence fired with hereditary anti-British feeling. In this view, frontier farmers of little political power, workers, debtors and the poor of more settled regions, together with better-class liberals, had pushed through reforms in the wake of their being called upon to bear the brunt of the struggle against Britain. They had brushed aside barriers to democracy and social equality, sought the abolition of quit-rents and primogeniture, secured vast western lands for further farmer expansion, pressed the establishment of religious freedom, ensured more popular economic programs, prevented lenient treatment of Loyalists, and generally achieved the goals of their pre-revolutionary quarrels with the established élites of the seaboard. They had furthermore, if implicitly, set up the agenda for future democratic advance. As frontiersmen or poorer easterners, the Ulster immigrants and their children were at the heart of this process. Talking of the quarrels between around 1740–1775 in one state, Wayland Dunaway put it, "the fundamental issue between the Scotch-Irish and the Quakers was whether Pennsylvania should be a democracy or an oligarchy," and other scholars then saw this as the unifying issue all along the 1,200 mile Scotch-Irish frontier, from New York south to South Carolina. This view emerged at a time when the impact of frontier experience upon American development was generally overrated, and when likewise the proportions and numbers of Ulstermen there, together with their political liberalism, were much exaggerated. Nonetheless, it still offers the core story of Ulster politics in America . . . or should it be instead, American politics amongst Ulstermen? Let us look first at Pennsylvania and its environs.

The Middle Colonies: an Ulster Revolution?

By the revolution, Pennsylvania was *not* the Scotch-Irish frontier. Benjamin

Thomas McKean (1734-1817)

Franklin told a German professor over a decade before that the Scotch and Irish of the province had abandoned the log-huts of their hunter predecessors for frame and even brick farmhouses. The land beyond the Alleghenies had yet to be settled; that of central Pennsylvania, from Lancaster west to Bedford counties, was the settled core of Ulster America, as we have noted before. In west New Jersey and northern Delaware (culturally and politically tributary to Philadelphia), past Ulster settlement had matured toward an American Presbyterian standard, while yet strongly 'Scotch-Irish' in identity, as Ambrose Serle noted. In its prosperity, it was a long way from the days when it was said of them that they "have sufficiency to live, rather than decency in living" (Rev. George Ross of New Castle, 1727). Indeed, Ulster Americans like Thomas McKean looked down upon the more rustic South Delawareans! Many Ulster Americans had settled as craftsmen, farmers, and traders even in the heartland of Quaker Pennsylvania itself: Chester, Philadelphia and Bucks counties, as well as in the city itself, where there had been few before 1750. It was this very maturation which intensified the level of political preoccupation among them. The relative political apathy of new Ulster settlers on the New York and on the Carolina frontiers has been noted by several scholars: as one put it, when the Revolution came, "they were remote from problems other than those of clearing their land". In mid-colonies, by contrast, patriarchs who could finally relax somewhat, and younger sons who had worked their way, eager-beaver like, into law, trade and semi-gentility, were earnestly political: ambitious to upgrade their entire Presbyterian American community as well as themselves, and to pay back the slights of their Ulster and frontier past. In this respect the Revolution found them as the urban-industrial revolution did the famine Irish by the 1880s: ready for a major thrust to power.

Nonetheless, what they remembered was crucial: past Pennsylvania politics were not merely vivid; by Ulster standards they were still contemporary when the Revolution broke. The key issue was as straightforward as Dunaway put it, but not as he moralised it. It was a struggle for predominance, rather than for democracy versus oligarchy, that engaged both Anglo-American Quakers and the Ulstermen. By the mid-1760s Quakers were but quarter of the province's population, and by the Revolution but 15%, yet had not altered the iron grip which they held on power, chiefly by gerrymandering the western counties out of adequate representation, while over-representing the three 'Quaker' counties and Philadelphia. They feared Presbyterians in terms very similar to Presbyterian fears of Popery and Anglicanism: not without reason, they linked Presbyterianism to the regimes of the Cromwellian Protectorate and the New England oligarchy which had persecuted their ancestors in the previous century. By way of protecting themselves against 'political Protestantism' and despite their unparalleled traditions of toleration, they became oligarchically politico-sectarian themselves. Benjamin Franklin, who considered himself a refugee to Philadelphia from the religious despotism of his native Boston, was the most famous non-Quaker protagonist of their fears. He too linked English Congregationalism and Scottish Presbyterianism as but

George Bryan (1731-1791)

variants of the same theology (which they were), and as both inclining to intolerant oligarchy. That Ulster Presbyterians claimed to have learned the lessons of political proscription at home, and of political toleration in Pennsylvania, did not convince their antagonists: for what seemed more to the point was that between the 1740s and the Revolution, most of them acted consistently as a political bloc. And in Delaware and New Jersey, too, Ulsterfolk tended to act in political unision. But increasingly they did so in close concert with English or Anglo-American Presbyterians, migrant New Englanders, and continental Reformed folk, who had joined Presbyterian churches in the absence of their own; they were inter-marrying, too, on the basis of this. In short, social familiarity and connection, rather than Calvinist design, was probably the main cause of political grouping, even though Presbyterian concerns provided a common language and common preoccupations. From an economic viewpoint, however, disparities were so great that they should have sundered the connection as between the more affluent inter-ethnic easterners and the Ulster-only westerners, were it not that Quaker hostility and later British policy provided issues around which the Presbyterians could actively coalesce.

Before the end of the Seven Years War, Ulstermen had been little engaged in Pennsylvania politics: frontier isolation, farming immersion, minority diffidence and perhaps gratitude were compounded by the rancorous effects of a church split, between New Side and Old Side Presbyterians. All these were disappearing (the Church re-united in 1758), precisely as the ending of the war brought to a head a bitter division between the (now Anglican) proprietor Thomas Penn, a distant Londoner, and the Quaker Assembly. The latter sought autonomy; Penn sought exemption of his own estates from taxation, yet payment of his own quit-rents in scarce sterling (not provincial) currency. At the same time the Scotch-Irish became disturbed by their own discovered powerlessness; they had done more than their share against France's Indian allies under captains like John Armstrong, and now the Quaker Assembly failed to provide adequate frontier militia defence against rampaging Indian bands. It is traditional to equate the sequel to the 'racism' learnt 'on the Irish frontier': the young men of Paxtang in 1763 murdered a group of Christianised Conestoga Indians under Quaker protection. They did so only after wide-ranging murders by irrupting Indians during Pontiac's uprising, and were convinced that the Quakers either encouraged, or were indifferent to such attacks to weaken Scotch-Irish power. Marching eastwards, the Paxton Boys presented a Remonstrance demanding not merely adequate protection, but proportionate political power in the province. Much more was at issue than Indian defence; and even on that subject, Rev. Thomas Barton, the Irish Anglican whose pastorate was repeatedly obstructed by his fellow Ulstermen, nonetheless defended those Presbyterians as genuinely frightened and concerned. The Quakers saw themselves as caught between a vice: Thomas Penn's autocracy to the east, the blood-stained Presbyterians to the west, and could not make reasonable distinctions. Lashing out, they launched an indiscriminate pamphlet war on Presbyterianism as a whole, which had the effect of throwing sophisticated eastern Presbyterians into the hands of the westerners.

Two further developments, now accelerated, were already preparing this. Hoping to by-pass Penn, and achieve the freedom from English interference of royally-governed Virginia, the Quakers had launched a campaign to abolish proprietary government and replace it with direct Royal sovereignty. At the same time, Anglican missionaries in the colonies had stepped up a long-standing desire for an American hierarchy into a full-fledged campaign. Men like Alison, although not unsympathetic, had little respect for the Paxton Boys (who were indeed condemned by the Presbyterian clergy). Instead they saw all three issues as inter-related threats to civic and religious liberty for Presbyterians in the New World. That Anglicanism was the political arm of the Crown, as many believed; that it was certainly linked with office-holding circles in the province, gave body to the suspicion that a major plot was afoot, 1763–68. That the chief architect of the drive for episcopacy, William Smith, was also President of the College of Philadelphia (and steadily Anglicanising it) gave local grievance to vice-principal Alison and the city's Presbyterians, who held the College dear.

Incredibly, in this situation of three-pronged crisis, Lord George Grenville's ministry introduced and passed the Stamp Act of 1765: an ill-fated attempt to better finance imperial government and defence by taxing all official transactions in the colonies. At once the situation of the Quaker Assembly party was undercut: royal government was no longer one of benign neglect, but more oppressive than was the proprietary. Although Quaker leaders like Joseph Galloway tried to keep the issues distinct (as did his agent Benjamin Franklin in London), a massive political re-alignment developed in the region. Some urban Irish Presbyterians like Charles Thomson and George Bryan (previously pro-Assembly, and in Thomson's case, even pro-Indian), together with certain Pennsylvania German leaders and others such as John Dickinson, now detached themselves from the Assembly. They brought leadership and experience to the mass of the Ulster countryfolk. Previously opposition to the Quakers had necessarily coalesced around the 'Proprietary Party,' a core of office-holders, loosely linked with all those who at any given time had reason to oppose the Quakers, as had almost everyone else during the Seven Years' War, or as had Francis Alison from distaste at the secularity and Englishness of Philadelphia's Quakerdom. Now a 'Presbyterian Party' emerged which, while held at bay by the gerrymandered power structure for a decade (1766–1776), nonetheless gradually consolidated a broad constituency around the issues of colonial autonomy, anti-Quakerism, anti-episcopacy and more equitable representation. *Perhaps* because of the nature of this party, so largely 'foreign' in composition, the Anglicans of Delaware and the Quakers of south-eastern Pennsylvania seemed more concerned at their local position than fearful of growing royal control. As a result, the nascent American nationalism of the region became heavily Presbyterian in tone, and Ulster leaders took a key role in attempting to brow-beat recalcitrant Quaker and Anglican merchants into compliance with the non-importation movement of 1765, of 1767 (against the Townshend duties), and again of 1770 and after (against the continuing tea duty, following repeal of the other revenue duties).

That politics in the region were more vertical than horizontal, more a matter of religious-ethnic grouping than class, was demonstrated when Charles Thomson took the lead in the local attempts to enforce non-importation. At first he received no support, and was on occasion bodily opposed, by the largely English-descended White Oaks, the ships' carpenters of Philadelphia (then a great ship-building port); on the other hand, labourers, tinsmiths, house carpenters and servants (disproportionately Irish and German) supported him. Recent attempts to determine lower-class politics in this era have stumbled on these contradictions without adverting to the crucial ethnic dimension, perhaps because of Carl Bridenbaugh's mistaken belief that few foreigners entered Philadephia's workforce. Eventually the imperative of a rising American nationalism swung the White Oaks over to Thomson's Sons of Liberty.

A unified outlook emerged to bind together the disparate nationalities, faiths and issues which made up the nationalist "Presbyterian Party". Francis Alison wrote Ezra Stiles (1769) "our fondness of English fashion and luxury demanded a check, and it is given by Providence in a way that all ranks are loudly called to observe and comply with". Likewise, Charles Thomson believed that the revolutionary crisis had come just in time to avert the corruption of provincial life by the unnecessary stratifications suggested by greed and vanity. Such a diagnosis seemed confirmed by arguments on the other side, such as that of Lloyd's London *Evening Post* (1770) which linked established religion and clear social distinctions as the indispensable foundations of good order. Despite their own growing prosperity, there seems no reason to doubt that Alison and Thomson, or others such as George Byran and American-born Joseph Reed, were sincere in their convictions that aristocracy, privileged religious status, and the abuse of political power were interlocking. It gave them a genuine ground of coalescence with the ordinary farmers and labourers who constituted the bulk of the Presbyterian Party's support, and with the outlook of German leaders like Christopher Sauer. If it stopped considerably short of radicalism in the modern sense (or the old Levellers' sense), it did mean that they were consciously committed to the rough equalities of the New World. It was also quite consonant with the position of most Presbyterians in Ulster and in lowland Scotland, where if there were few aristocrats of their own persuasion, there was also a clear spectrum of achievement and income; and likewise agreed with the 'Common Sense' of the Scottish Enlightenment on such matters. After 1780, however, the looseness of these ideas was revealed as political Presbyterianism fissured.

In the meantime, the emergence of the party co-ordinated the region's pace of anti-British agitation with that of the rest of the country. The network of correspondence set up to combat the drive for an inter-colonial Anglican episcopacy had helped, linking New Englanders like Ezra Stiles and Charles

James Smith (1719-1806)

Chauncy with Alison in Philadelphia, and with William Livingston and the others of the 'Presbyterian Triumvirate' in New York. George Bryan as delegate to the Stamp Act Congress in New York in 1765 had likewise broadened horizons. By 1773, however, and the Boston Massacre, these connections had become regular and completely political. In default of active participation by majority members of the local political establishments, Thomas McKean and George Read in Delaware, Thomson and Bryan, Reed and James Smith in Pennsylvania, networked the region with revolutionary correspondence, and helped create and dominate the local county, city, and township committees of non-importation, of safety, of correspondence. They also travelled extensively to co-ordinate work with the more remote inland county committees, where other figures were active, of Irish background. It would, however, be false to imagine that the movement was solely Scotch-Irish, or that they constituted either its majority or its most radical element (although this has been often stated in the past). As the crisis with Britain approached, leadership in the Presbyterian party so broadened that it is inexact to so describe it. In south-eastern Pennsylvania, the majority of leaders were of English descent: there were as many Irish as Scotch-Irish leaders locally; and in the region as a whole, the most radical leaders, the 'violents' or 'Furious Whigs' looking to the crisis for a chance to re-make society, were not Scotch-Irish: James Cannon, Timothy Matlack, Thomas Young and painter Charles Peale were among the most prominent. Indeed, the political thought of the Ulster American leaders seems at times merely conventional to the age, at others (in McKean's case), correct yet downright unimaginative. The 'exception', George Bryan, was a Dubliner.

Yet it was perhaps enough that the traditions of Hutcheson and Alison were adequate, for America enjoyed a sufficient galaxy of thinkers to extend the horizons of the age: Jefferson, Madison, Jay, John and Samuel Adams, Hamilton, Morris. So too did Pennsylvania in moderates like Dickinson and James Wilson, radicals like David Rittenhouse, Thomas Paine (lately arrived) and the 'violents', sound pragmatists like Robert Morris and Benjamin Franklin. It was as men of *political situations,* not of political construction, that the eastern Ulster American leaders excelled. Charles Thomson has been credited with swinging Benjamin Franklin away from Joseph Galloway and the Quaker moderates toward a proto-revolutionary stance by a single remarkable estimate of the *situation* in the wake of the Stamp Act (which Franklin was inclined to treat lightly at first). Writing to London, 1765, Thomson warned "Should the behaviour of the colonies happen not to square with these sovereign notions (as I fear it will not), what remains but to compel them to obedience,' the conclusion George III finally reached in 1773. It may well be that Ulster tradition did prepare its adherents to see at once the confrontational implication of their politics; and in fairness it must be stressed that unlike all that galaxy of talent mentioned above, the Ulster American leaders, despite high revolutionary civil office, almost all sought a role in the military struggle once independence was declared: Joseph Reed before it, (he too had warned Lord Dartmouth that the enforcement of the Tea Act "must end in blood"), Thomas McKean, John McKinly, James Smith, William Irvine, James Potter and John Armstrong in Pennsylvania and Delaware, and the Lewis brothers in the Valley of Virginia. All could have honourably claimed the press of political and legal services to the revolution to avoid campaigning, although there is also no question that in the more democratic politics now emergent, to have served in arms (particularly as an elected militia officer) consolidated one's political constituency. Except Irvine, Potter and Armstrong, they concentrated on politics after the British withdrew from the Middle Colonies in 1778.

Despite a relatively unradical, certainly untheoretic Scotch-Irish view of politics, however, the Presbyterian Party carried through a political revolution in Pennsylvania in 1776–7. The Ulstermen were preeminent, but neither fully in control, nor fully unanimous, in these developments. One detects a constant tension between the hyper-Presbyterian strain amongst them, pushing at times (it seemed) for an Ulster predominance in Pennsylvania, and the conciliatory arts of mutual adjustment which are everywhere of the essence of politics: this tension at times ran through individuals themselves, at times was more clear in the differences between Ulster Americans from western Presbyterian communities, and the more cosmopolitan easterners. Even before the revolution, the difficulties of building coalition to oppose the Quaker power monopoly, and the normal processes of community life in mixed post-frontier communities, had broadened political skills beyond the sectarian. A study of Lancaster county politics has confirmed this. The enthusiasm of revolution ironically both set the adrenalin of militant self-absorption running, yet also created a whole series of self-broadening exigencies. Unfortunately, non-Ulster Calvinists (English, Scots, former New Englanders and Germans), reinforced this narrower strain, as did the vein of virulent hyper-patriotism unleashed with the British invasion of Pennsylvania in 1777.

What actually happened? Pennsylvania radicalism was a product of the failure of the Quaker assembly to decisively support the Continental Congress (meeting in Philadelphia), in its moves toward militarization and independence. Congressional leaders like John Adams and Samuel Adams encouraged men like Charles Thomson and Thomas McKean to take control of the province through the network of committees. Congress then voted that colonial governments not adequate to the need of the times be formally replaced, well knowing where the impetus would come from (May 1776). The Quaker Assembly then dissolved for lack of support, and the radicals called a convention, to be popularly elected, explicitly for the purpose of creating a constitution rooted in an act of popular sovereignty: the only such case before 1780.

Preparations for the Constitutional Convention were made by a conference of Committees under McKean's chairmanship: it decreed adult male voting rights for all those white resident taxpayers approved by the revolutionary committees as friendly to the Revolution, and it determined on full representation for the western counties. It also made an oath of orthodox Protestant character binding upon all convention members, and one of loyalty to the revolution upon all voters. The result was to throw political power entirely into radical hands. Even moderate Whigs (such as Morris and Wilson) were not elected to the convention, and erstwhile radical nationalists like McKean and Reed found themselves opposed to the constitution which it drew up (both were in military service during the convention). In short, the means to the end of Pennsylvanian support of Independence had now resulted in the most radical constitution in America. Ulster frontier elements, ably led by York lawyer James Smith, combined with eastern radicals such as Bryan, Cannon and Matlack (only the first was Irish) to produce a constitution with a weak, and rotating executive, no upper house at all, and a lower house based on suffrage essentially the same as that once approved for the convention itself and also restricted by the imposition of oaths. They added a 'Council of Censors' which could periodically determine if the constitution had been impaired, and call for popular reform if it had. This Council consisted of one member for each county: a disproportionate power in the hands of the sparsely settled western counties, and a victory for Smith. As Owen Ireland has shown, the Scotch-Irish and their Presbyterian and German Reformed allies then took control for several years of the assembly elected under the new Constitution, enacted and enforced Test Acts and loyalty oaths to exclude all their opponents (moderate Whig as well as Quaker and semi-loyalist) from office, reconstituted the College of Philadelphia as a Presbyterian-controlled University of Philadelphia, interned leading Quakers and Anglicans as loyalist suspects, and denied all non-jurors the use of the courts, or rights to act as merchants, lawyers, physicians or teachers, while subjecting them to double-taxes. To an Irish scholar, it has the familiar shape of the legislation imposed in the previous seventy-five years upon the Presbyterians, even more upon Catholics, by the Anglican establishment in Ireland.

George Bryan, the Dublin Presbyterian closely associated with the new democratic order, yet disapproved of these related and repressive aspects, disfranchising as they did well-disposed German Mennonites and others, such as pro-American Quakers and Anglicans who scrupled to swear permanent allegiance to a constitution they believed defective. Virtually the entire legal profession of Pennsylvania at first refused to serve the courts of the new state of Pennsylvania. Although James Smith had been another of his students from Ireland, Alison voiced the widespread (if inaccurate) view that the government's makers "were mostly honest well-meaning Country men ... intirely unacquainted with such high matters." The Calvinist Assembly multiplied the number of its opponents by oaths and measures which "identified the constitution with the government they had created," (an error made nowhere else in Revolutionary America), and probably thereby considerably increased passive support for the invading English. Nonetheless, its excesses are understandable in that it was a crisis regime, and most of its protagonists had memories of relative political proscription in both Ulster and

Joseph Reed (1741-1785)

in Pennsylvania's past.

Fortunately, after initial misgivings, prominent eastern Ulster Americans like McKean and Reed decided to swallow their distaste and take office under the regime: McKean as Chief Justice, Reed as President of the Executive Council: Bryan served as Vice-President, President and leader of the Assembly. Together they moderated the Assembly's radicalism, dampening the spirit of proscription, ensuring closer co-operation by the province with Congress and the hard-pressed national armies of Washington, creating a basis for dialogue with moderate Whigs on such issues as currency. Accused of opportunism and inconsistency, McKean and Reed were true to their reading of the situation: in Delaware (where he remained a key political figure) McKean had helped engineer a moderate bi-cameral constitution and yet hasten the area into support of the Independence, while recognising that the Scots-Irish were a minority; in Pennsylvania he served a constitution and party for which he had some distaste because it was broadly popular as well as patriotic, whereas the old regime (in his words) was not 'a legitimate agency of power' because it lacked "a full and equal representation of the province". Likewise, in rebuking the pretensions of Anglo-Irish General, Anthony Wayne, Reed gave a key to his change of view: "Property is too casually distributed in this state ever to permit that Aristocratick influence which some wish . . . A popular Government must in the nature of things be most generally agreeable to the People of this State, and . . . I am persuaded this will be the only ruling principle at all times."

In short, the vertical (Presbyterian) organisation of politics in Revolutionary Pennsylvania, if it led at times to a certain archaic Calvinist excess and exclusion, also had the effect of recruiting into that government the more cosmopolitan Presbyterians who could both make their fellow semi-élite Americans aware of the feelings of post-frontier farmers and immigrant workers, but also moderate the impetuses of radical democracy (the repudiation of national obligations, exaltation of the local militia, the incredible disregard for elementary economics). No doubt too Thomas McKean had 'a voracious appetite for place and fees' holding multiple offices in Delaware, Pennsylvania and the national Congress: his multiple leadership redeemed this. Such roles, and the roles of relatively well-educated frontier Ulster 'Constitutionalists', such as James Smith and James Potter, underscore the weakness of past interpretations which saw the whole matter simply in terms of class conflict. That virtually all non-Presbyterian Irish Pennsylvanians of every class and faction became Republicans or anti-Constitutionalists again demonstrates how completely Irish political patterns had re-emerged in the flush of revolutionary America: Generals John Shee, Edward Hand and Anthony Wayne among Anglicans, Thomas Fitzsimons, Stephen Moylan, James Mease, and George Meade among Catholics. Indeed, one of the only frontier anti-Constitutionalist Assembly members, Bernard Dougherty, was almost certainly representative of the lost traditions and politics of the Ulster Catholic migration: he was strongly anti-Presbyterian.

The matter went further than polarisation: the Calvinist assembly, claims one careful scholar, even attempted to 'frame' James Mease and an American Irish Anglican associate, William Wise (although not without some grounds: Mease *was* a greasy character who believed there should be a clear profit in patriotism). Yet again, it cannot be denied that the Ulster Americans had a clearer idea of radical equality than had any of their Irish opponents: before the arrival of Matthew Carey in the 1780s, the Anglo-Irish and Catholic Irish seem to have little comprehension of the implications even of their own good fortunes in making for a new ideology of human possibility. Certainly they produced no leader such as Smith to articulate it.

As the revolution receded, the excesses of the Calvinist coalition reaped their harvest: all their antagonists, from aristocratic Quaker merchants with past loyalist sympathies to frontier Ulster Catholics and German pacifist sectarians, but chiefly Anglicans, merchants, Philadelphia-area workingfolk, and nationalist Continental soldiers and officers, all combined to oust them. The sequel is especially interesting to those who would understand Ulster (or is it human) psychology. Realising the game was up, the new Ulster American country leader, William Findley, canny, fairminded and Ulster-born, approached his rivals behind the scenes and said his people could accept drastic change if it were proposed in the form of amendments to the Constitution of 1776, but would reject abrogation of that document and the writing of an entirely new one. In the event, this was done, and Findley and his associates John Smilie and Robert Whitehill worked within the framework of the *practically* new Constitution (bi-cameral, no Council of Censors; but a generous general suffrage and adequate western representation retained). In public, of course, they continued to inveigh against their 'enemies' who had subverted them by base means: but face had been preserved. These changes (1790) took place against the background of the emergence of national Federalism, and the determination of most eastern Ulster Americans to support it against the diehard opposition of their fellow countrymen in the interior.

From an American viewpoint, the radicalism of Pennsylvania had served its purpose; it had rallied that state to Independence, bringing with it Delaware and New Jersey. In the process, the Scotch-Irish . . . in all their strengths and narrowness . . . had their finest political hour, and their military services kept pace. The fragmentation which they imposed on Pennsylvania, however, narrowed the base of anti-British coalition unnecessarily, and but for their own moderates, would have done so even more. It was a fine basis on which to assert the more radical promise of the American revolution for plain folk, but little ground on which to construct a flourishing trans-Atlantically-connected commonwealth. Ultimately everyone but themselves, from shipbuilding workers to Whigs like Morris and Franklin, from clergy, lawyers and urban dwellers, to erstwhile radicals like Benjamin Rush and James Smith, realised this.

Elsewhere the story was more straightforward, and less dramatic. In the satellite states of New Jersey and Delaware, the Scotch-Irish played a disproportionate role in shifting the local Assemblies to a pro-Independence stance in 1776: in Delaware largely alone, whereas in New Jersey Presbyterian allies included Scottish, Dutch and New England elements. In Delaware, as a minority in an Anglican colony, the tendency of Ulster Americans was to mix leadership with caution: Thomas McKean's famous Lewes speech helped turn south Delaware towards Independence, but George Read, his fellow Ulster American Delaware delegate to the Continental Congress, amazed him by voting against Independence out of deference to the state's climate of opinion. Later they co-operated in the creation of the new local constitution, under which John McKinly, another moderate Ulsterman, became president. Their prosperity likewise had something to do with their moderation; but they enjoyed the special powers of New Castle county, and fought against the removal of the state capital southwards. One gets a marked impression, from Delaware's retention of McKean as its national delegate, despite differences with him, that the south Delawareans, economically bound to Philadelphia yet highly localistic and not very American in outlook, looked upon the Ulster Americans as a link with the regrettable necessities of a wider, and now revolutionary, world. In return, McKean, Read and McKinly did not exploit their advantage within the state. In New Jersey the situation was somewhat different. Although here ethnically also a minority, in combination with other Presbyterians they made up the politically dominant faction in the state. But the Presbyterianism of New Jersey was that of Presbyterians made good: John Witherspoon, the Edinburgh-educated president of the College of New Jersey, William Livingstone, the recent settler from New York battles, and William Paterson, the jurist of Ulster origin, were its leaders. Enthusiasts for Independence, they yet ensured that the state's new constitution was a complex one (against the 'simple' one of Pennsylvania): as in Scottish 'Common Sense' political theory, a representatively popular government was to be balanced by giving due weight to society's elders, the men of property and understanding.

As for New York, we know little: Ulster immigrants, recently come to Orange and Ulster counties, do not seem to have been notably active; some, influenced by the loyalism of local Scottish Presbyterians (with whom they interacted) may have been for the Crown. The City of New York was notoriously Loyalist where its upper classes were concerned. That Presbyterianism was the overwhelming denomination of the area on the eve of the Revolution probably points to considerable immigration of Ulster Americans from Pennsylvania and New Jersey (for much fewer came by sea); and like the Presbyterian triumvirate of the anti-episcopacy and anti-De Lancey campaigns, these Ulstermen probably split three ways with the Revolution: for it, like Livingston; against it, like William Smith; and beyond it, to radicalism, like John Morrin Scott. That none of these three men were Ulster Americans, however, and that they had supported the crushing of an agrarian uprising in the 1760s, may have helped confuse some lower class

Ulster immigrants (who began coming heavily to New York after 1763) but most would have been pro-Revolution as the journalism of John Paterson, and the wobbling away from his Loyalism by Hugh Gaine, suggest.

Revolution in the South

In the south, Ulstermen inhabited another group of worlds. Advantages for change in the middle colonies were good. Continuous immigration, knowledge of the worsening agrarian situation in Ireland, the exchange of journals between New York and Philadelphia and their being read by many Ulsterfolk (as advertisements reveal), the emotions of the anti-episcopacy and anti-Stamp Act campaigns, the good communications linking the main population centres of all the middle colonies: all these account as much as heritage for the relative unanimity on broad issues of the Ulsterfolk of the region. The southern Ulster enclaves, as later, were another matter. They were each of them more isolated from each other, and from the main centres of political and cultural development, than was the case to the north. What is surprising is less the evidence of occasional indifference, than the evidence that here too commitment to the Revolution was widespread, conscious and fundamental. Here too, however, recent local politics coloured the shape and degree of commitment. And nowhere in the South did Ulstermen have the influence upon politics and constitution making that they did in Pennsylvania. Finally, the existence of slavery, of a more virulent indentured servitude, and of neighbouring Indian populations still coherent, powerful and bellicose considerably complicated the landscape for them. In the region as a whole they were frontier people generally, unlike the north where a continuum of Ulster settlement linked western country districts with the culture of the seaboard. In the south, the seaboard was Anglican and semi-aristocratic, its communications running north-south, not east-to-west. This meant that Ulster immigrant communities in the South were probably less Americanised in the cultural sense, while more transformed environmentally in practical matters, than were Ulster Pennsylvanians. This lacks adequate study, however: but reminds us (despite F. J. Turner and Freeman Hart) that for Ulster people the two processes were not identical. The inland southern communities were far removed from the excitements of the Stamp Act agitation in the seaports, from the anti-episcopacy campaign, from the vessels bringing fresh 'exchanges' (newsprints and post) from Dublin and Belfast and Derry. The American nationalist planters of the seaboard spoke and wrote as though they knew little of the Ulster backcountry, and had little idea of which way it would jump politically.

Again, the answer varied somewhat by colony. In Virginia, the Ulsterfolk of the valley of Virginia had long enjoyed good, if distant, relations with the planters on the coast. The House of Burgesses had been careful to increase western representation proportionately as western population grew. Little objection was made when following Ulster precedent, the Presbyterians of the valley took over the local vestries of the Established Anglican church as agencies of government in the absence of an Anglican population. The county court and church sessions functioned as virtually autonomous governments in the region. Nonetheless, service in the House of Burgesses by such prominent valley families as the Lewises kept its leadership abreast of Virginia as whole, while trade linked it northward to Pennsylvania. Although in the nineteenth century, valley chroniclers wrote as though the region had always contained the flower of Ulster emigration . . . civilised and sensible from the start . . . it appears that the sophistication of the years of Woodrow Wilson's childhood (he was born in Augusta county in 1856) was a late product. The simplicity of the early settlers, and the crudity of the frontier was fairly consciously subdued by the better Valley inhabitants from the late 1760s onward. Hunting, indiscriminate Indian killing, heavy drinking, and roisterous entertainment were more typical of the majority in the 1770s: so Fithian's journal and John Ireland's Autobiography reveal. Nonetheless, with no grievances against the gentry who in eastern Virginia led the revolution, the valley people supported it stalwartly, and their proportionate military participation must have been a record. The desire to sweep away the British-protected Indian barrier against their sons' land hunger added an edge to their militant patriotism, but the latter was genuine, for they fought not merely locally but (like their kin in Pennsylvania) throughout the colonies.

In the Carolinas, the crudities of valley life were increased, the effects of protracted Indian warfare were more pervasive and brutalising, and bitter contention with the seaboard power élites weakened the attempts of merchants and better farmers among the Ulster Americans to improve matters. On the eve of the American War of Independence, both Carolinas were thrown into turmoil by 'Regulation' movements in the interior. In South Carolina, the Regulation was basically an attempt by inlanders to reduce to order a countryside suffering an elemental absence of community discipline in the wake of Indian war: attempts were made not merely to suppress predatory criminal communities, but to force men back to ordered farmwork to support families they had left to shift for themselves. The Regulators overreached themselves, and themselves degenerated into arbitrary and brutal patrols, lost the support of the better elements, and were mopped up by provincial troops. Only in 1772, however, was an adequate court system provided by the Charleston Assembly for the interior. Despite almost complete disfranchisement (again by gerrymander) and the recent absence of even skeletal government services, the Scotch-Irish of South Carolina generally supported the Revolution, as did the growing community of Irish-born at Charleston. They were conspicuously active in the campaigns following the British invasion of the state in 1780: at the battles of Camden, King's Mountain and Cowpens they suffered first defeat, and they then helped to break the momentum of the invasion. Familiarity with the semi-guerilla tactics of Indian warfare also made them prominent in the irregular fighting against Loyalists and Indian allies of the British before 1780, and in the invasion's aftermath, under such leaders as John Pickens, Daniel Morgan, William Campbell and Francis Marion. Biographical information suggests that many of the soldiers were second and even third generation Ulster Americans, rather than first.

South Carolina was also the heaviest southern receiving point for direct Ulster immigration, and indeed the most populously Irish southern state (Georgia, proportionately more Irish, was then only skeletally inhabited). Interesting questions are thus raised which have never been adequately studied: were the newer immigrants neutral from unfamiliarity, from timidity, from residual deference to Crown symbols, from shock perhaps at the degree to which in the south (unlike Pennsylvania) Ulster Americans had evolved a secular, loud-mouthed, buck-skinned style? There is little evidence of coherent political activity in the region among Ulsterfolk to match that of the middle colonies or even of the valley of Virginia. Indeed, their leading political champions were not their own: Charles Woodmason, the Irish Anglican pastor spoke for them during the Regulation, and recent immigrant planter, aristocratic Anglo-Irish Pierce Butler from Co. Carlow championed the cause of adequate back-country representation and more equitable taxation during and after the Revolution. On the other hand, the majority of planters of Anglo-Irish birth or heritage were strong partisans of the coastal conservatives: thus the Rutledge brothers and Thomas Lynch, as reactionary in state affairs as they were patriotic nationally. The 'revolutionary' constitution of 1776 conceded very little to the back-country, leaving planter pre-eminence in the state unchanged.

In North Carolina, the Regulation had taken a very different form, which jeopardised for a time Scotch-Irish commitment to the Revolution itself. It was occasioned not by the absence of local government, but rather by the complete corruption of the courts and of policing service by extortioners and hacks. Lacking real political representation in the low-country dominated Assembly, the back-country Scotch-Irish had little alternative but to rise in insurrection. Although we lack adequate information, the class of officials against whom they rose were probably exclusively (or largely) natively American, with relations exacerbated by ethnic tension. The tendency of the governors to believe the worst of the inland people suggests this was the case: the officials were of the same background as the coastal establishment. The Regulator rising was predominantly Scotch-Irish, although not exclusively: Germans, everywhere when ungathered tending to assimilate to the Ulster majority, joined them. Indeed Herman Husband, one of its leaders, would later migrate to Pennsylvania and help lead the equally Scotch-Irish Whiskey Insurrection. He seems to have been one of those chronically impoverished and activist John Brown types of pioneer manqué. The Regulators were crushed at the battle of Alamance in May 1771, by forces led by establishment Ulsterman Hugh Waddell, a scion of the old Dobbs connection. Meantime they had been abandoned and execrated by Presbyterian clergy as had those of South Carolina, and the Paxton boys, before them. This was despite the fact that in

North Carolina the Anglican establishment was imposed to a degree unheard of in Virginia, New York or even South Carolina: only following the Regulation were Presbyterian clergy permitted to solemnise marriages, and as late as 1773, a Presbyterian academy for Mecklenburg county was prohibited by the Board of Trade. Vestries, too, were still Anglican and alive.

Not unnaturally, as E. R. R. Green puts it, when in 1775–6 "the low-country gentlemen and the presbyterian clergy decided on rebellion themselves, they had some difficulty persuading the back-country farmers that times had changed". Governor Josiah Martin believed that these simple people were extremely reluctant to break the solemn oaths they had taken to the Crown on their defeat, and the fact that Presbyterian minister David Caldwell took to absolving the oaths suggests this was the case. For otherwise the back-country had the same reasons and traditions for supporting the revolution as everywhere had the Scotch-Irish: an assertion of their liberties and their Americanness, an opportunity to alter local structures to secure full religious equality and political representation, a chance to repay hereditary grievances against the Anglican establishment of Ulster and North Carolina, and of course the excitement of further western expansion and the sheer hell of officially encouraged violence. Nonetheless their reluctance was considerable: unlike most Scotch-Irish elsewhere along the frontiers, they had recently been sobered by a real military defeat, and knew its costs: enthusiasm for war is usually born amidst the naïvetés of peace (or of easy victories over Indians). As a result the Presbyterian clergy had to drum up their support for the Revolution as a virtually religious obligation. Rev. David Caldwell, in a famous repeated sermon, warned against "The Character and Doom of the Sluggard," surely one of the earliest clerical attacks upon that modern failing, political apathy. Rev. Adam Boyd, editor of the *Cape Fear Mercury*, kept up a patriotic Presbyterian propaganda (the battle won, he then conformed to Anglicanism himself!). The Presbyterian leaders of the Middle Colonies, led by Alison, circularised their co-religionists of the State in the cause. Mecklenburg county scarcely needed such pressure, and was radical, as well as national, from the beginning. Elsewhere, it all seems to have had the requisite effect: while many remained apathetic, many other Scotch-Irish did join the American cause in arms, and very few became Tories, the great fear of the coastal establishment. The colony in fact became the only one in the South to exhibit considerable Presbyterian influence upon the making of its new constitution. The inhabitants of Mecklenburg county instructed their delegates to the Assembly elected to devise the constitution to create 'a simple Democracy or as near it as possible' and to 'oppose everything that leans to aristocracy or power in the hands of the rich,' yet unlike the radicals of Pennsylvania, these Scotch-Irish clearly ordered that the distinction of constitutional forms and legislative measures be clearly maintained: among the latter they of course demanded abolition of the vestries and of marriage restrictions. It should be said that the exact degree of political apathy among the Scotch-Irish as to their revolutionary participation remains controversial: the balance of studies points to the conclusion that support for Independence became fairly general as time went on. The simplicity of many of these people cannot be overestimated: and the early defeat of the Loyalist Scottish Highland emigrants at Moore's Creek Bridge in February 1776 doubtless made vacillating Scotch-Irishmen choose the winning side. Four years later, by the battle of King's Mountain, the interior North Carolina militias were almost wholly Presbyterian.

The native Irish under American arms

Over fifty years ago Michael O'Brien marshalled vast platoons of Irish names from the published muster rolls of the Continental Armies and state militias in an attempt to show that the Scotch-Irish were *not* the backbone of Irish participation in the revolution. But it is in fact unquestionable that they *were*, in the middle colonies and to a less degree in the Carolinas. This does not mean that O'Brien was guilty of pure invention when he painstakingly culled a few hundred each of Kellys, Murphys, McCarthys, Connors and O'Connors, Ryans, Reillys, Doughertys, Connollys, Sullivans, O'Briens and Mullens (to name those for whom he found more than 200 each). Granted that he then guarded insufficiently against re-enlistment of men of the same name in different regiments (and re-enlistment was endemic throughout the war), such figures are in fact quite consonant with what we know of the structure of heads-of-families by name in 1790 (see above, pp. 60, 75). Michael O'Brien's real errors were two: he grotesquely exaggerated the proportions of the Irish in the revolutionary armies as a whole, by inadequately studying everyone else in arms and by an arithmetic enthusiastic rather than exact, and he completely failed to demonstrate to men sceptical of the presence of any but a few score thousand native Irishmen in the colonies why they should all of a sudden rush in whole brigades to take up arms for America. To O'Brien, writing in the heat of the final Sinn Féin claim for independence against Britain, and openly bidding for American support for them by showing how the Irish stood by America in 1776–83, there could only be one motive for military enrolment: a self-respecting and self-sacrificing patriotism. In fairness to him, most American historians (and German-American, and Swedish-American) then wrote in the same vein. But human nature is rarely so unanimously noble, and not any more so among those who drift into paid military service.

The nineteenth century Irish in America did disproportionately enter the armies of the Union, and the Confederacy, as earlier the armies fighting Mexico and later those fighting Spain. They had little enthusiasm for war against other Americans and perhaps even less for war against fellow Catholics: but they went anyway, and their regiments were decimated by heroism and disease. At the same time, the Irish were dying disproportionately in the wars of the British empire. As R. B. McDowell has shown, they constituted almost a quarter of all British forces by the end of the Napoleonic campaigns. They were prominent in the Crimean War and in the Boer War, as in remote campaigns in Africa and India. The motive was nearly always the

John Sullivan (1740-1795)

John Shee

John Barry (1745-1803)

Edward Hand (1744-1802)

same: poverty, and even more than poverty, the sense of a superfluous manhood generated by poverty, a manhood which had the gambler's chance of redemption in the fortunes of war. Michael O'Brien's contemporary, George Plunkitt, pre-eminent observer of the New York Irish, noted acidly that employment generated real patriotism among them, whereas unemployment led to death in the army hospitals (Cuba and the Philippines were in his mind). There were mixed motives for service, but this was the pre-eminent one.

Recall what a Maryland Jesuit said of ex-indentured servants; what Crèvecoeur said of the failure of many Irish. Earlier John Brickell said much the same of North Carolina's ex-indentured servants. Remember that there were few immigrant native Irish girls to the colonies, and that many of the male immigrants from south and west Ulster, from Munster and even from Irish towns then were Irish speakers (runaway advertisements state so). Additionally, visualise the virulence of anti-Catholic prejudice throughout the colonies, recently refreshed by the anti-episcopacy campaign and the conviction that Britain's extension of toleration to French Catholicism in Quebec (the 1773 Quebec Act) *proved* that tyranny and popery were the same. Finally, reflect that poverty and the exhaustions of indentured labour on another man's farm had left little taste for immediate entry to farming, and the answer to O'Brien's puzzle emerges. The Irish did indeed enter the armies disproportionately. Not because they were especially patriotic, but because they could hardly do any better. Service might bring connections, land-grants in the west (a traditional colonial bounty, renewed in the Revolution), perhaps on demobilization a manly swagger and a wife, to replace "the down look" of so many descriptions of colonial Irishmen, and the loneliness brought on by community contempt and an over-abundance of men to women. Service even led to early termination of bondage for immigrants still indentured. All this Captain MacKenzie from Dublin seems to have understood well, perhaps from examining Irish American prisoners of war: and he also illumines why they were recruited so generally.

> They are in general much better able to go through the fatigues of a campaign, and live in the manner they at present do, than the Americans. They certainly have much more spirit, and in some measure make it a common cause with them for the sake of a present subsistence, Clothing & plunder; and the prospect of acquiring some property, and becoming men of some consequence, in case they are successful. The leaders of the Rebellion hold up to them these flattering prospects, and at the same time magnify the dangers they are exposed to if conquered . . . Among so many ignorant people these things have great weight.

What of the Americans? Can reason be found why they might recruit the Irish disproportionately? The difficulties of persuading a nation of self-interested farmers and family men into long-term service were generally recognised by their officers, from Washington down. The problem was not new: it had been the case during previous wars in America. As early as 1740 the Virginia assembly had tried to fulfil military quotas by encouraging the enlistment of "vagabonds" (presumably ex-servants). Manpower shortage was the bane of all American campaigns, and there was a general refusal to recruit negroes, slave or free. The Irish, on the other hand, were traditionally recruited, many servants and ex-servants seeing service during the Seven Years' War campaigns on the frontier. Especially in Pennsylvania, given the conscientious refusal of locals to serve, officers had early filled up company complements with servants, during war tremors in 1711, 1740–42 and 1755–60. In those years, major confrontations on the issue had developed in Pennsylvania between the Quaker Assembly and the royal proprietorial governors: to the former, servants were indispensable property to their masters, to the latter they were the King's subjects, and if Quakers would not serve, then servants must. In Virginia, George Washington himself as a frontier commander adopted the policy of recruiting servants into volunteer Virginia regiments: thus they were not lost to the manpower-short province by long-term regular army enlistment, and he showed a keen understanding of the forces which pressed servants to enlist. He himself enrolled over fifty in that war (these Michael O'Brien has also listed, nowhere adverting to their status!).

During the Revolutionary War, the custom was continued, but with more sensitivity to the feelings of enlistees' masters. The New York Provincial Congress declared they must be compensated, and that no servants could remain in Revolutionary service without their masters' agreement. Pennsylvania's Supreme Executive followed suit, on the declaration of the Continental Congress that all states authorise servant enlistment. In 1778, following protests from the Scotch-Irish farmers of Cumberland county, the Pennsylvania legislature provided compensation to all masters of enlisted servants: many of the servants in Cumberland county would have been native Irish, which may explain why the farmers could complain against the violation of the rights of mankind (i.e., their own), and speak of bond servants as property in the same document! But there was another motive than manpower shortage exciting American leaders: in Virginia, Lord Dunmore had promised freedom to indentured servants as well as slaves who enlisted with the British. "That man will be the most formidable enemy of America if some expedient cannot be hit upon to convince servants and slaves of the impotency of his designs," commented Washington. The expedient was of course that of 1756 renewed: the systematic recruitment of Irish servants. Doubtless, too, masters felt themselves relieved of the obligation to serve by consenting that such a valuable piece of property go free instead, although we have no explicit evidence they felt so.

Thus, (and undistinguished and undistinguishable in O'Brien's sources), there were newly freed servants, and former servants, new farmers, labourers, and urban workers amongst the Irish in arms, as well as numbers of second generation Irish Americans. Few of any of these categories rose to notable rank or position. The exception to this pattern was the infant nation's naval service. The bulk of this was a freelance, privateering navy, with ennobling officerships scattered fairly broadscale. Given the large numbers of Irish sailors in the trans-Atlantic, inter-colonial coastal, and West Indian trades, and the considerable and rising numbers of Irish ships' captains and officers in this business, the chronicle of Irish naval service seems generally credible as O'Brien and others have somewhat sketchily reconstructed it. Here native Irish rise to officership and distinction was also simplified, too, by the very fact of freelance operation: but for Irish land enlistees, the framework of action was predetermined by native American or Scotch-Irish officers who also controlled promotion recommendations (Continental Army). In the state militias, where rank depended upon popularity, even upon election, the fact that Irish soldiers were generally a minority in every unit closed the issue, save in exceptional cases. More importantly, the Irish seaman had previous skills, even of privateering itself, whereas few land enlistees had the experience, or education, much less the habit of command, to mark them for commissions. Indentured servitude cannot have been a good school for anything other than obedience except that its passionate frustration might fuel spirited and violent fighting. Life in Ireland has already inured them to the hardships of campaign.

Old Countrymen or New Americans?

Finally there is the central question raised at the beginning of the chapter: did the colonial Irish of every kind participate in the American Revolution for essentially American reasons, as an aspect of their Americanisation, even as a deliberate act of re-nationalisation (in Noah Webster's sense, not that of today)? Alternately, as W. H. Lecky, George Bancroft and most major subsequent historians argued, did they do so for Irish reasons, as a ritual act of vengeance against British tyranny? Were they, in fact, more Irish or more American by 1776? Either/or propositions are inherently suspect, illuminating as a tool of investigation, but deceiving as a framework for conclusion. In revolutionary Pennsylvania (or Ireland before 1750), they have the flavour of Test Acts, loyalty oaths, and simplistic polarisations, and Claude Levi-Strauss may be correct in seeing in them a regression to the dualistic patterns of primitive tribal thought. Irish tradition, Scotch-Irish experiences in Ulster, reactions to American events, conscious and intelligent choices even among indentured servants—natively Irish speaking—as to where their future lay, decisive political illumination in the wake of bar-room conversations about Tom Paine's *Common Sense* or the latest Alisonian speech of Charles Thomson: all these were factors active among them. That contemporary Americans, British officers, most of the immigrants and their children then themselves thought in terms of slick compartments of nationality and religion simply means we cannot trust the more explicit statements of contemporaries in this matter, and must look at the complex reality in which they lived as men, not as categories. The heat of war and revolution intensified the usual tendency of uneducated men to fail to do their own complexity justice: even George

Action off Mud Fort in the River Delaware, 1777

Washington illiberally excluded all but native-born white Americans from his personal guard, and the vast majority of colonial Americans and Irish immigrants had only rudimentary learning. The answer to this question therefore lies amidst all we have been discussing, wherein British, American, Irish, Scottish and generally western and Christian elements continuously interchanged in the minds and communities of all the Irish-born in Revolutionary America. As E. R. R. Green put it well, the immigrant was not the eighteenth century philosopher's natural man renewing himself entirely afresh in response to America, but someone "practising a European religion, and attempting to realise European ideals in a new country." Can we be more precise? Some indications are useful.

Firstly the Scotch-Irish, immigrating with a culture largely Scottish and a mental landscape largely Irish. Their journalists (John Dunlap, John Paterson, Adam Boyd, Hugh Gaine) demonstrate an immersion in American affairs quite unlike that of leading Irish American journalists after 1840 (D'Arcy Magee, John Mitchell, Patrick Donohoe, Patrick Ford): despite greater attention to Irish news and immigrant-related business than, say, Franklin's *Evening Post,* Dunlap's *Pennsylvania Packet* and the other journals edited by the Scotch-Irish cannot be compared to the nineteenth century *Irish World* or Boston *Pilot.* They are more comparable to the largely post-Irish journals of those interior regions where the Irish were better assimilated from the 1860s: Humphrey Desmond's Milwaukee *Citizen,* William Dillon's Chicago *New World.* But since Dunlap, Gaine, Boyd and Paterson were serving the general populations of Philadelphia, New York and North Carolina, the comparison is not fully convincing. Nonetheless even journals serving the urban Irish *amidst* others in the 1890s, in a comparable way to what they were doing in the 1770s, exploit Irish interests in a conscious way Dunlap and the others did not. Of course, the whole style and function of journalism had meantime changed: the *Journal, Herald* and *Post* of Pulitzer's and of Hearst's heavily Irish New York would have appalled Dunlap and Boyd for other reasons!

Journals, however, were urban; most Scotch-Irish were not, although they might read them. Although evidence shows that virtually nowhere did the Scotch-Irish settle without the presence of a skeletal native American population, nonetheless they settled in concentrations comparable to those of the Pennsylvania Germans, whose retention into the early twentieth century of an entire culture, of language, beliefs, customs, and religious particularism far surpassed any similar achievements of the much larger nineteenth century German immigrations to the American Mid-West. In short, the age of mass schooling, general communications and trade networks by rail and canal, common preoccupations fostered by cheap newsprint, lay in the future. As we have seen, folk-music transmission points to culture retention and transmission among the Scotch-Irish in rural areas. There is evidence of dialect survival: even in Philadelphia, over thirty years after arrival, Francis Alison can use purely Ulster turns of phrase, as when, lamenting that his college was being Anglicanised, he hoped that the College of New Jersey would hold fast for anti-episcopacy: "I should rejoice to see her Pistols, like honest Teagues, grown up into great Guns". Such dialect passed to the American-born: Philip Fithian heard the hard-drinking sons of the Valley of Virginia (which Scots-Irish James McHenry found too isolated for his taste) swear their last 'Half-Bitt' to the oppressed citizenry of poor Boston, and Andrew Jackson, as we saw, used Scotch-Irish accents in his youth. The constant influx of newcomers may have helped ensure such transmission: but it was not alone responsible.

Historians of nineteenth century immigration (themselves largely the children of immigrants), such as Oscar Handlin, Carl Wittke, Arthur Schlesinger, and Theodore Blegen have long maintained that between first and second generation there was massive discontinuity, with the second generation living between two worlds. They based their insight not merely upon study, but upon sociological observation of twentieth century second generations, upon literature, and upon introspection. But between parents rooted in Polish or German or Norwegian speaking countrysides, and children raised amidst the all-pervasive Americanism of industrial Minneapolis, Buffalo, or New York, and schooled in public, or Americanised Catholic, schools, such discontinuity was inevitable. For eighteenth century countryfolk in Pennsylvania, Virginia or the Carolinas, led by Glasgow or Princeton educated Presbyterian clergy and lawyers, schooled by itinerant Irish and Scotch-Irish schoolmasters, isolated in varying degree from the quicker life of the seaboard, cultural survival was not merely more likely: it was probable. The religious and political quarrels of eighteenth century Pennsylvania through the Revolution demonstrate how much this could be the case. Handlin has argued that there was no 'second generation' problem in the eighteenth century because the Scotch-Irish offspring were so thoroughly assimilated: David Ramsay, Rev. David Caldwell or Adam Boyd and so on. Rather there may have been no problem for two reasons: firstly, a much greater continuity between generations, and secondly, the greater receptivity of a colonial, slow-moving, people-short, agrarian America to the similarly British, Calvinist and agrarian culture of the Scotch-Irish. All this clearly requires more study than it has received.

Obviously, then there were regional and generational differences amongst the Scotch-Irish, but less than later American experience would suggest. But what of the different waves of the Scotch-Irish? Did they separate in the way the pre-famine Irish, famine Irish, and Irish immigrants of the 1880s partly seem to have? Again, apparently to less degree than one might expect. The genealogies of major colonial Scotch-Irish families, such as McKean's and others, point to the assimilation of incoming relatives over a considerable period of time, and the inter-marriage of American-born and Irish born. Such patterns, operative also among the nineteenth century Irish, were limited from more general effects by the need of the 'Amer-Irish', who attained a measure of acceptance, to distance their incoming Irish country kinsfolk: educated Irish immigrants were accepted more readily. The general acceptance of the Scotch-Irish meant that they were not placed under the strain of rejecting their kin which was the fate of many nineteenth century Irish-Americans. The bitterness which fissured Irish America in the 1880s and 1890s was thus avoided.

Nonetheless, the great wave of immigration which came on the very eve of the revolution, from 1770–76, fought in a different spirit than that of the older arrivals and their sons. The old Scotch-Irish were clearly fighting for predominantly American reasons. The speeches of their leaders, and the journalism of Dunlap and Boyd, suggest this. More important, the tremendous role of a by now largely American-born and educated Presbyterian clergy in propagandising the revolution took an American framework for the conflict as axiomatic to the change of loyalties prompted by revolt. This was not withstanding the fact that the Hutchesonian doctrines they preached rested upon grounds familiar to Ulster: Loyalism is conditional only upon the loyalty of the Crown to our interests and natural rights.

For the newcomers, Irish memories were as potent as Lecky and Bancroft claimed: "They had fled from the real or fancied oppression of their Landlords" wrote Sir Henry Clinton from New York in 1778. "Thro' Dread of prosecution for the Riots [Steel Boys and Hearts of Oak] which their Idea of that Oppression had occasioned, they had transplanted themselves into a Country where they could live without apprehension; and had estranged themselves from all solicitude from the Welfare of Britain. From their Numbers, however, national Customs were kept up amongst them: and the pride of having sprung in the Old Country, notwithstanding the Connection of Interests, prevented them from entirely assimilating with the Americans".

Again, there are indications of change amongst them. Cultural retention was quite consistent with Americanisation of a sort. Ambrose Serle, speaking of the less isolated seaboard areas (New Castle, Philadelphia and environs were the areas of his experience, together with New York), remarked "these People, being principally *Scotch-Irish* (People from the north of Ireland), . . . could have no opportunity of returning and . . . and living 8 or 10 years, they become habituated to this Country and estranged from their own," a remarkable precision of observation. The intense Ireland-consciousness of post-Famine Catholic immigrants has been persuasively ascribed by Thomas Brown and others less to any reluctance to Americanise (indeed, their enthusiasm was poignant in the matter), as to the rejection and exploitation they encountered in the industrial cities. On the other hand, the readiness of many Americans, (although by no means all, as we have seen of Quakers), to accept the Scotch-Irish largely as they were, meant that they could disengage from past loyalties without necessarily disengaging from their culture. Whether they had always harboured a profound ambivalence about the 'Irish' aspect of their heritage, which might have made the transition easier, seems considerably less likely, although it has often been alleged. Their identity pre-supposed Irish memories.

The radical Constitutionalist 'Sons of St. Tammany' (the parody of Catholic usage was typically Protestant Irish), was founded at James Byrn's tavern in 1772 by lower class Presbyterian (and some Anglican) Irish Philadelphians. It went wild when the toast was taken (in 1783): "The friends of liberty in Ireland. May the harp be tuned to independence and be touched by skillful hands." Whereas they gave three cheers to the other toasts (chiefly American) and thirteen cheers for Washington's, they gave thirteen shouts of joy for the Irish toast, the band breaking into 'St. Patrick's Day in the Morning'. It could have been Patrick Ford's New York a century ahead. *Except* that when its successor society of St. Tammany in 1805 began to recruit large numbers of Catholic Irish immigrants, the society broke up. "We find the order assuming quite new features" ran the complaint, "and the descendants of Kilbuck conversing in a transatlantic tongue [as though] . . . the ancient language of Ireland was that of the aborigines of America." In short, not emigration, but rather the arrival of assertive Irish-speaking Catholics, broke the retrospective Scotch Irish connection with Ireland, just as the political emergence of the native Irish from around 1780 ultimately doomed Presbyterian and Anglican Irish nationalism in Ireland. Backward looking Irish identification, until then, was *not* regarded as inconsistent with the hyper-patriotism of Philadelphia radicalism: for their society ostensibly was dedicated to an ancient Indian chieftain of the region, one who was, unlike St. Patrick, St. George, or St. Andrew (as their ballads put it), as American as one could get! Among the more sedate and prosperous Friendly Sons of St. Patrick, almost all merchants and lawyers, the pretence of inter-religious harmony around trivial and emasculated symbols of Irishness was maintained more easily (as in similar circles in Ireland), partly because the Stephen Moylans and Thomas FitzSimons so fully assimilated to the mores of the city's élite (the descendants of every major Philadelphia patriot Irish family of the Revolutionary era became Protestant: the Moylans, Meases, Meades, FitzSimons,—and their founders had begun the process by intermarriage and conformity). But there was also a political reason: they were all united by artistocratic disdain for the politics of the slovenly Sons of St. Tammany! This fracturing of the Irish identity within Philadelphia itself, with its roots in Irish conflicts of politics and class, was thus intensified by rival commitments within American politics by rival Irishmen.

Just as the patterns of Scotch-Irish politicisation in Ireland found re-expression in the American revolution, so those patterns in turn helped ensure the diminution of their Irish identification. Not so much a hospitable enough America, as an inhospitable group relationship to other Irishmen, determined that the Scotch-Irish forgot Ireland when others arrived in America to claim it. Painfully they learnt the pluralism of America, and accommodated other Protestants within the politics of Lancaster or Augusta counties: German, Anglo-American, Scottish and others. The one people they could not accommodate as equals within that new scheme were the embodied memories of their intransigent Irish past: the Catholic Irish. This in itself is suggestive of how long their 'Old Country' characteristics lived on through their Americanisation. Strange fruit indeed!

What of the native Irish in the colonies and revolution? Isolation and impoverishment had in the past *apparently* led to their chameleon-like disappearance into the wood-lands and communities of America. As young single men, all too conscious of native abuse before the revolution, the impetus to disappear culturally as quickly as possible was strong. But the widespread retention of surnames, the sheer incapacity of an exuberantly convivial people to hide indefinitely, shows the impetus alone was not overwhelming. In the Revolutionary armies they clearly identified themselves as Irish, and forged friendships with their fellow countrymen. Many of them, perhaps even a majority, had been Irish-speaking: almost all those from north and west Ulster who left by Newry and Derry, and many of those who left from Cork, Limerick and Youghal, for the ordinary folk of the hinterlands of these parts were Irish speaking. Even from Dublin, migrant labourers, even servants from nearby Meath and Wicklow, may largely have been so. The bulk of them all would have been bi-lingual: in four hundred runaway advertisements, I have found but two references to incapacity to speak English, and symptomatically one master did not really believe it. John Ryne who ran off in New Jersey, "speaks bad English" as did Robert Hanley, who fled from Salem county in the same colony, both in 1768–69; Peter Murphy was noted for speaking good English although Irish was known as his native tongue. That Luke Gardiner claimed in the Irish House of Commons in 1784 that "I am assured, on the best authority . . . that the Irish language was as commonly spoken in the American ranks as English" is thus not fully false, although very exaggerated. But native Irish assimilation was a more drastic process than among the Scotch-Irish. Before the Revolution, both Catholicism and Irish manners and language were shed for all public purposes in the mere business of daily living, quite apart from the protective reasons. Where such men were concerned, the one decisive impact of the revolution was that it was no longer a question of forced Americanisation among them; as they had emerged to full view in its armies, so hereafter they could Americanise more consciously, about half retaining what they held to be the most valuable part of their heritage, Catholicism. A new openness to the native Irish, and thereby to all non-Protestant immigrants, was not the least among the many social effects of the American Revolution.

Finally, of the Anglo-Irish, despite very incomplete evidence, it can be hazarded that their culture enabled them to assimilate most easily: but not into a generalised America, so much as into the colonial equivalent of the social strata from which they came. As a result, their politics seems to have been *usually* that of the group with whom they were best familiar. Thus for Thomas Barton and the country Ulster Anglicans of the Middle Colonies, a pro-revolutionary stance was probable: but a less radical one than that of the Presbyterians. Generals Shee, Hand and Wayne were hardly untypical. For newcomers who had not been absorbed into Irish or English establishment circles before arrival, but rather affected by the vigorous re-birth of Whiggery in both countries, again pro-Americanism was usual, with General Richard Montgomery (unquestionably the most able of the Irish born officers) the prototype. Among enlightened Anglican immigrants in Whiggish communities, such as Virginia and Maryland, likewise pro-Americanism was probable (as with the Jarratts in Virginia), and the same was certainly true in the Carolinas, as the Rutledges, Thomas Lynch and son, and Pierce Butler demonstrate. But establishment-thought made Loyalists out of Anglo-Irish office holders and of some Anglo-Irish merchants, and of tradesmen to the establishment all along the coast, particularly in New York, Charleston and their environs.

Not all Anglo-Irish were Anglican, however: Anglo-Irish dissenters, descendants of seventeenth century English Puritans and Quakers, and townsmen in Ireland, shared fully the whiggish culture making for revolution, without being compromised by such establishment tendencies. Anglo-Irish dissent virtually disappeared in Ireland, largely through emigration, as well as absoption. Irish Quaker families in Pennsylvania were usually of the pro-war minority (given their experiences in Ireland), and thus produced such figures as the war heroine, Lydia Darragh, and revolutionary diarist, Christopher Marshall. Anglo-Irish Presbyterianism (*not* the Scotch-Irish) gave the Pennsylvania radicals their great slavery abolitionist in George Bryan, who had joined his mother's relatives, the Dennises, in Philadelphia as late as 1752: his father wrote him soon after that he should practise fencing and dancing as routes to gentility, avoid becoming the Rustic or a Tar and make his obligation to God the centre of his life. His successful and indefatigable labours to ensure that Pennsylvania became the first state to abolish slavery (in 1780) in the face of Scotch-Irish indifference, his general moderation, and his spiritual seriousness in politics mark him (in this writer's view), the greatest of all Irishmen in the era of the Revolution. For he combined the high moral intent of Presbyterianism with the sophistication of Dublin and of English dissent, and he remained open to the best currents in his new world (the anti-slavery of Anthony Benezet and the Quakers, the magnanimous democracy of Thomas Paine) while remaining to help lead the Ulster Presbyterians in America from their past.

Chapter 6

Revolutions Frustrated: Ireland, 1760–1800

The American Impact: Patriots and Reformers, 1775–1785.

For an understanding of the source of much of the outlook and behaviour of the Irish in America, and for a clearer grasp of the case that for them America was a truly revolutionary world, a summary, however bald, of events in Ireland necessarily follows.

The forces of rising prosperity and growing confidence amongst Protestants had emboldened them in their long-standing grievances against the British Government (above, pp. 35-37). A 'patriot' party, launched first as an agitation by Dublin apothecary Charles Lucas, exploited the growth of public opinion and the decline of Protestant paranoia vis-à-vis Catholics, to press for liberalised trade and governmental reform. The accession of George III, bringing with it a decade and more of political instability as the young king sought for effective and efficient national leadership amongst contending politicians, weakened the system whereby Ireland was governed, and its Protestant élite managed, by key noblemen. These 'undertakers' now lacked the permanent connections in British politics they had enjoyed in the days of Walpole and of Newcastle. Under Henry Flood, an able, blunt and ambitious lawyer and estate-owner, the Patriots emerged as a small reform group in the Irish Parliament itself, after 1761. Events quickened. At the same time as Charles Townshend was attempting to impose the Stamp Act and other reforms upon the American colonies, he sent his elder brother George to Ireland as Lord Lieutenant with similar objectives: to tighten up direct British control and get the Irish too to pay for a larger share of imperial defence (1767–72). Ironically, this forced the Townshends to make certain concessions to general Protestant opinion (such as provision for more regular elections), and to broaden the base of their political leverage in Ireland, in order the better to concentrate authority, bypass would-be undertakers, conciliate the gentry directly and manage the Irish Parliament. Royal policy thus strengthened the growing patriot opposition by widening the scope of politics. Since the 1750s, popular tumults in Dublin associated with patriot demands had been reported in colonial papers. Americans read them as confirmation of their own drive against taxation without representation. However, whereas the movement in America was widespread, reform agitation in Ireland was relatively confined. The bulk of the Irish gentry wished to be taken account of by the new political order, rather than to control it themselves: and they in turn dictated the

152

political pace of the countryside. Seeing this, Henry Flood himself, unsurprisingly, took office in government in 1775.

By then, however, the second phase of the American crisis was well under way, and it brought independence, international war against Great Britain, and major changes within America. It transformed the balance of conservative and reformist forces in Ireland. On the eve of the American Revolution, a proposal to tax 'absentees'—the holders of Irish estates, both English and Anglo-Irish, who lived abroad and drained their rent-rolls away from the Irish economy—demonstrated clearly how crude cash interests could undermine the Patriot pretensions of many who normally opposed the administration, ostensibly in the Irish interest. Even Edmund Burke, Thomas Conolly, Edward Newenham, Lord Charlemont and the Duke of Leinster opposed it! But it also showed how difficult it was for the government to win popular support by apparently championing a popular measure: too many families related to the governmental machine were party to the absentee system to allow any thorough-going attack upon it. And it demonstrated how unrepresenattive of public opinion were the nominees of the great borough owners. But American events altered, even if fitfully and temporarily, these political forces and calculations in Ireland, and helped effect the 'Revolution of 1782': yet that so astute a leader as Flood could in 1775 abandon popular leadership underscores how indirect this effect was to be.

The American War of Independence eventually weakened Britain, and so provoked Ireland's discontent by curtailing its economy, that the long-range dreams of the reformers became both popular and possible, the freedom of Irish trade and Irish legislation from direct British control. Each was to be but partially implemented, for few Protestants in Ireland were prepared to press matters to the extent that their ultimate dependence on the British Empire would be strained or broken. In that they differed profoundly from the Americans. The American Revolution, on the other hand, dramatised and concentrated forces long gathering in the English-speaking world, toward more representative government, more religious freedom, more popular policy and more national consciousness. It had much less exact effects upon Ireland. Recently the tendency has been to underestimate these influences and effects, yet they too were considerable. The more general forces, and the related arguments for them, were not unfamiliar to educated Irishmen, and had helped fuel the demand of Charles Lucas for parliamentary reform. But they had derived their real immediacy from English example, and had been constrained by the ascendancy privileges of even the poorer Protestants. Now they received the impetus of a revolution that was ordered, distant, propertied and Protestant. The rhetoric of the Irish reformers in the 1780s, both the cautious and the radical, was full of appeals to American precedent, even where inappropriate. Ironically, whereas the American War triggered a political upsurge in Ireland from latent springs, the American Revolution was not properly understood until the 1780s, when 'Irish opinion began to realise that something entirely new was being achieved in the American colonies.' Only then did it help fuel the shift toward radicalism among those unsatisfied with the achievements of 1782, which were more locally rooted.

The initial reactions to the American Revolution were muted. When Benjamin Franklin visited Ireland in 1771, he had found the Patriots disposed to be friends to America, and to see the parallels between them; and Edmund Burke hoped that Ireland might play the part of mediator between the colonies and Britain. Both were to be disappointed. The Anglican gentry, in the midst of a canny series of operations to secure greater recognition from, and influence over, Dublin Castle (headquarters of the British administration), believed that any outward show of disloyalty to the Empire would jeopardise their claims—which were intra-imperial—and in October 1775 in Parliament, naturally declared their support for Lord North's policies. Even the dissenters from the motion (like their Whig counterparts in Britain) favoured conciliation and non-condemnation of the Americans as rebels, thereby indicating that they too saw matters in terms of imperial re-adjustment. Presbyterians in Ulster generally favoured the colonists, who included so many of their emigrant relatives; even so, future reformers like the Rev. William Dickson warned that they were so powerless in relation to the Government that any outward show of support would be foolhardy; while the Dissenting clergy of Dublin repudiated the notion that *they* were disloyal in the crisis. Others were more consistent and courageous. Merchant Irish Quakers, prominently connected with Philadelphia and New York, channelled remarkably generous relief funds to Pennsylvania, New England and the South, 1778–1797, whereas their London co-religionists helped Loyalists only. Dissident minister Rev. William Hazlitt, actively aided American prisoners-of-war confined in Irish gaols: he was a noted radical. But Catholic leaders declared their loyalty as early as September 1775. Nonetheless, amongst all classes aware of developments, an excitement spread rapidly beneath the predictable obeisances of a divided people, so much so that the British administration was grateful to be able to withdraw no more than 4,000 of its Irish forces for war service and feared that it might lose control of the next Parliament, elected in spring 1776. The citizens of Cork, Belfast and Dublin petitioned for peace, disruptions of trade being what was uppermost in their minds.

For the war brought widespread economic dislocation: Ireland's linen trade with America was severed, as was the reverse timber trade, its smuggling trade in woollens and other goods was disrupted by greater naval activity, and in February 1776 its provision (foodstuffs) exports were embargoed by the administration, the better to conserve supplies for the army particularly. This drove prices beyond those ordinary people could afford, increasing hardship. France entered the war in February 1778, Spain in June 1779 and the Netherlands in November 1780, disrupting further legal and illegal trade channels both with the continent and indirectly with the West Indies. Despite the considerable profit engendered for farmers and traders by the army and navy trade, recession amongst urban craftsmen and mechanics was severe when added to the contraction which had begun in 1771 and sent so many emigrants to America (an outlet now removed). The ancient grievances against British trade restrictions were intensified, becoming a general agitation. Simultaneously, the sense of insecurity created by the war led to an upsurge in voluntary armed mobilization amongst Protestants generally. Armed vigilante groups had spread across Munster in the wake of agrarian Whiteboy agitation in the 1760s: counterparts, if better uniformed and disciplined, of the Patrols of the American slave colonies. These were revived in new form in Wexford, Tipperary and King's County (Offaly) as early as 1775–76 primarily to ensure property and Protestants against any lower class Catholic exploitation of the international crisis. By 1778, the movement was spreading rapidly, uniformed Volunteers of Ireland, Presbyterian as well as Anglican, in a short time numbering over 40,000 and presenting themselves as potential defenders of the country against French, later also Spanish, invasion. All over the country, there was indeed a sudden decline in agrarian crime and popular disturbance amongst the rural masses. The excitement of drilling and co-operation, the unusual democratic procedure of most troops (which generally elected their officers), the national self-respect fuelled by the consciousness that their security was now in their own hands, not Britain's, the readiness of the more reformist gentry to use and lead the Volunteers in their quarrels with Dublin Castle, and the remarkable quiet of the Catholic masses coupled with the cautious loyalism of Catholic leadership: all caused the Volunteers to turn from their original tasks to become the spearhead of a renewed and general Patriot agitation for Free Trade and Irish parliamentary independence.

The majority of the Volunteers were middle-class, reformist, yet traditionally Protestant: in the north particularly, ministers led or chaplained many units; William III's birthday and the anniversary of his victory at the Boyne were everywhere the great demonstration days. Self-confidently, 'Volunteer Protestantism' now identified itself with the hopes of an Irish nation which it defined and controlled by force of arms backed by general opinion. The parliamentary Patriots rejoiced in such backing; the gentry who shifted with the prevailing wind made to sound more reformist; the administration's inadequately based mode of controlling parliament directly by general corruption now faltered, then broke down for a time. In Henry Grattan—warm, brilliant and vain—the movement found its man of the hour, while the Dublin and Belfast papers became its organs. In major areas of the country such as Cork county, Down and Meath, factional disputes amongst gentry and aristocrats played into the hands of popular opinion and the Volunteers, weakening conservatives and thus the government. Nonetheless there was never a coherent general national movement such as existed in America, even in Protestant terms. Only within a few years, British statesmen could perhaps too easily write off the Volunteers as an 'epidemical' excitement, and their rapid disintegration following their abandonment by the gentry and the coming of peace should caution those who might see them primarily as national reformers rather than as primarily a wartime popular mobilisation. The bulk of them apparently never broke through to a permanently new conception of politics: incomplete nationalism, deference to the gentry, fear of Catholics, loyalty to the Crown's administrators and division on their specific objectives after 1782 separates their collective ethos markedly from that of most American militia and county and state conventioners of the same time. Hence their achievements under Patriot leadership owed as much to imperial and British factors as to themselves.

The Whig opposition in Britain warned Lord North that he should have another America on his hands if Irish grievances were not remedied. The leading Irish administration officials, on request, gave their opinion as to the source of general economic distress in the war. Copying the Americans, Irish traders and consumers adopted schemes of non-importation of British goods, except in the Volunteer stronghold of cash-conscious Ulster. The Dublin mobs rioted against government policy, and the Volunteers there paraded with their cannons ominously decorated 'Free Trade—Or This'. In several steps Grattan carried the majority of parliament with him in similar demand, more delicately worded. Resultantly, in 1778 the Irish were permitted to export most goods, except textiles and wool, to the British colonies and cotton yarn to Britain, and to fish off Newfoundland. In winter 1779–1780 most further trade restrictions on Ireland were lifted, including those on the export of textiles and wool; she was made a full partner in the imperial trading system, and permitted to trade outside it. She was excluded from the lucrative Indian trade, however, and her exports to Britain could be prohibitively taxed. Nonetheless the gains were important, even if the details were confused and many believed Ireland too industrially retrograde to benefit fully.

In the wake of their success, the Volunteers and the Patriots pressed on toward Irish legislative independence with an enthusiasm which clouded its complex implications. Skilful 'management' by the administration restored governmental control over parliament in time to quash Grattan's first attempt to achieve it in 1780. But just as the news of Saratoga had first inclined London to make concessions to Ireland, so Cornwallis's defeat at Yorktown, the fall of Lord North and the accession to power of the opposition groups which had championed Ireland under Shelburne, Fox, Rockingham, in various combinations from 1782 created an ideal opportunity for the Irish movement. In February 1782, a convention of Volunteer delegates at Dungannon resolved "we know our duty to our sovereign, and are loyal. We know our duty to ourselves, and are resolved to be free". North's viceroy, Carlisle, managed to stave off Grattan's resultant further motion for independence in parliament a week later; but within a month Rockingham had succeeded North, Lord Portland had succeeded Carlisle as Irish Lord Lieutenant, and a parliamentary majority created by bribery and management now gave way to one stampeded by public enthusiasm: Grattan in April 1782 carried his independence motion. Despite serious misgivings, Rockingham and Fox determined to give way. The claim of the British Parliament to legislate for Ireland was abandoned and the control of the British government over Irish legislation was substantially relaxed. Later, her legislative capacity for Ireland was formally renounced.

Irish courts were rendered free from final appeal to Britain's House of Lords in their verdicts; Irish judges were granted life tenure; the army in Ireland was placed under Irish-legislated discipline passed biennially.

Yet nothing was done to ensure the harmony of administrative policy in Ireland, still determined by the British cabinet which appointed Ireland's officials, and the legislation of the newly-free parliament. And nothing was done to ensure that the activities of that parliament, so responsive in 1782 to Protestant public opinion, should remain so, rather than revert, as before, to an arena of the calculus of gentry advantage, over which, as the force of public opinion dissipated, patterns of management could be re-established by the administrators of Dublin Castle. Indeed, the very failure of the reforms of 1782 (to create structures to harmonise administrative and parliamentary interests systematically, and to ensure parliamentary responsiveness to a wider public) almost guaranteed in advance that Britain's cabinets could win their way in Ireland *only* through tactics of management, bribery and division of the opposition, rather than by negotiation with a coherent parliament sure that it had the body of the articulate Irish nation behind it. Irish Patriots such as Grattan and Flood, English Whigs such as Fox and Shelburne were as committed to an imperial interpretation of Anglo-Irish relations as were conservatives in both countries, and likewise believed that the final calls in such matters went to Britain. The Patriots' failure to create a coherent framework for these relationships may have initially been determined by the temporary nature of their prominence in Irish politics—that they took what they could while the going was good—but they proved themselves equally short-sighted during several subsequent Anglo-Irish crises in 1785 and 1788 when they did control a parliamentary majority. By contrast, American leaders who sought a "more solid and constitutional union between the two countries," America and Britain, rather than Independence, as did Franklin in the 1760s and Joseph Galloway in 1773–74, had a much clearer vision of what such a scheme must entail, and recognised that it must rest upon an effectively representative and popular inter-colonial Congress.

For the Patriots were not a fully national movement, but rather only pretendedly so. They were not ready to forge an inclusive party and policy comprehensive of Ireland's dissident interests, to harmonise all these interests with Britain's imperial concerns, and to take office in the Dublin administration to cement such objectives, thereby linking Irish opinion, parliamentary activity and Anglo-Irish interests. Without this, however, they could not give reality to their new imperial status. The realities of Ireland, rather than the designs of Britain, principally prevented this. Indeed it is quite probable that statesmen such as Lord Shelburne and William Pitt, both liberal and imaginatively imperial, would have welcomed such a scheme. But these British prime ministers of the bulk of Ireland's years of semi-independence, 1782–1800, knew it to be impossible, and hence were concerned lest the new and incomplete order would so intensify Ireland's political fragmentation as to make Anglo-Irish relations most difficult, and Ireland almost ungovernable.

The American Revolution owed much of its success to the readiness of all its relative conservatives, such as Washington, Robert Morris, and John Jay, to swallow their inbred conviction that social distinction ought to be reflected in a hierarchic and semi-authoritarian political order. Instead they moved gradually toward a more representational or popular theory of politics, usually via the routes of a comprehensive nationalism and a broadening conception of the nature of political 'interests'. They were helped by the social eminence of many of those embracing more liberal theories, such as Jefferson and Franklin, and even more by the evidence that the revolutionary war and its politics had spurred ordinary Americans, "and set them on thinking, speaking and acting, in a line far beyond that to which they had been accustomed," (as David Ramsay had put it). Even those who believed in a continuing politics of deference took account of this. In Ireland, on the other hand, even the Patriots seemed jealous lest a similar awakening fracture the gentry's near monopoly in social leadership and political intelligence. They were quite aware that such an awakening had occurred even before the rise of the volunteers: the Patriot Lord Charlemont had said of Anglo-Irish financial disputes of the 1750s that "Irishmen were taught to think, a lesson which is the first and most necessary step in the acquirement of liberty", and the agitations of 1778–82 spread that capacity among Protestants of every class, and among many Catholics. The Patriots realised, like their American counterparts, that some form of nationalism was vital to securing their position amongst an aroused people, as to pressing their claims against Britain: but it was a nationalism to be defined from the top down, a strangely artificial though not insincere product. Instead of reconciling fastidious gentlemen to the rising place of their plainer fellow-countrymen in politics, as did the nationalism of Washington and Jay, it sought to reconcile ordinary men to the idea that they should gracefully withdraw from politics, and leave it to the gentry who knew what was best for the nation.

The 1780s saw the establishment of the Royal Irish Academy, the Royal College of Surgeons, the Bank of Ireland, the Dublin Chamber of Commerce, and of a separate Irish Post Office. The same period witnessed the surveying of Irish roads, the projected connection of Dublin with the Shannon via two major canals, the expansion of the capital itself, including the building of its Four Courts and Customs House, a heightened interest in agrarian well-being amongst certain landlords, parliamentary encouragement of textiles production, brewing and grain production, a quickening of literary, musical and social life in polite society, a gentlemanly concern with native Irish traditions and antiquities—and the institution of the Order of St. Patrick. It was all more typical of the enlightened élites of certain Italian and north European provinces than of the ferment of progressive revolution. The failure to construct a political nation comprehending the various segments of society in proportion as they were interested, and the inability to overcome a politics of caste and self-regard, left the British little option than to work with those segments independently, and seduce and direct that self-regard individually. In two areas, those of parliamentary reform and the bettering of the Catholic situation, these failures were most evident, although there were others. In both these areas, the specific impact of the American Revolution was most strongly felt, for they came to a head as knowledge of that Revolution deepened.

In the wake of 1782 Lord Lieutenant Portland warned that now "all sorts and descriptions of men", farmers and labourers, and professionals, craftsmen and workers, Presbyterians and Catholics, were now "unanimously and audibly" pressing claims on Britain, and would have to be separately managed, where management of the Parliament had sufficed in the past. In fact this was hardly true. Since the 1750s the cabinet had paid attention to separate Irish groups, partly as public opinion spread, partly to undercut undertaker and gentry pretensions, partly from imperial necessity. As early as 1768 it was argued that imperial trade concessions were vital to giving Ireland a stake in the quarrel with America: argued by William Knox, supposedly a protégé of George Grenville. This hope was still present during the concessions of 1779–80. Likewise in 1778, the same William Knox, now under secretary for the American colonies, was warning Irish Chief Secretary Richard Heron that concessions must be made to the Catholics to ensure their loyalty.

If it is was natural for the Patriots to champion Irish trade, their relations with the Catholics were more ambivalent. A recent study claims that the whole impact of the American revolution on Ireland was essentially a religious question, that the same Patriots who supported the revolution for Protestant liberty in the colonies, and sought one also in Ireland, were stoutly anti-Catholic; and that their views were reversed by Irish Catholics, who opposed the Americans, and the Patriot programme, and looked to the British for relief. The matter was considerably more complex. Catholics and Patriots were no closed-in monoliths, any more than the notoriously factionalised Dubliners of the time. Certainly the initial steps for reform of the situation of Catholics were taken by politicians associated with the government: Luke Gardiner, Hercules Langrishe and Monck Mason. These were not mere toadies nor office holders; they expressed the conviction of many Irish gentry linked to the Crown that Irish prosperity, imperial security, and natural justice, allied with the good conduct of Catholics, justified extensive change. In 1771, Catholics were permitted to lease bogland; in 1774 to swear fidelity to the Crown (thus bringing them within the outer limits of the constitution); in 1778, in Britain, Edmund Burke, with ministerial encouragement, prevailed on George Savile to bring in a bill for the relief of English Catholics, explicitly as a model for the Irish parliament to follow. Savile was an absentee Irish landowner, and feared that propaganda from Charles Carroll of Maryland and others would entice Irish Catholics from his estates as emigrants. In 1778, a Catholic relief bill was pressed on the Irish parliament by the Government. Patriot Henry Flood, then Vice-Treasurer and in government service, did oppose it: but he had favoured armed suppression of the Americans. Patriot Henry Grattan also opposed it, but essentially because he saw it might be intended as a divisive tactic, as he interpreted the Quebec Act in the Americas, rather than from illiberality. In fact, the Patriots divided: George Ogle, Robert Stewart, Lord Charlemont and pro-American firebrand Edward Newenham joined Grattan in opposing the measure. But others, such as Barry Yelverton, the Duke of Leinster, Denis Daly, Hussey Burgh and Thomas Conolly, supported it, in line with the general trend of the Whiggish liberals in Britain (Fox, Burke, Savile, John Dunning and others). Among popular Protestant spokesmen, if Charles Lucas in the past had been Patriot and anti-Catholic, Anthony Malone had been Patriot and liberal; now, if Newenham was unreconstructed in his political anti-Popery, Dublin radical Napper Tandy was liberal. Even Grattan, Charlemont and Stewart did not dissociate themselves from the growing spirit of toleration for Catholic religious and social freedom; they claimed to fear only that the extension of property rights to Catholics, which was the essence of the Act, would lead inevitably to political power. Newenham's own Catholic constituents declared him a friend of their faith (*Freeman's Journal*, 17/2/1776); obviously a social courtesy, not a political judgment.

The rise of the Volunteers and of wider objectives among the Patriots changed the views of this group. Grattan realised that the British could most easily subvert the independence of the 'Protestant nation' if the latter did not conciliate Catholics but left them to seek redress, as before, from the administration. The new nationalism of the now consciously *Irish* ascendancy could scarcely deny its kinship with the mass of the ancient inhabitants: the Patriots no longer spoke, as in Swift's day, of securing the rights of Englishmen in Ireland, but of the rights of Irishmen. Hence Grattan threw his party behind the Catholic Relief Bill of 1782, which dismantled the body of Penal laws, although leaving Catholics without political power and subject to important further disabilities. Many of those repealed had been so long in abeyance, however, that amongst middle class Catholics, desire was stimulated for a share of power to body forth the formal freedoms of worship, education, association, and property-holding now confirmed. To the Catholic masses in the countryside, the rural power structure unchanged, these matters meant little. The conversion of Grattan and his associates was too belated, too compromised by their continued and growing participation in ascendancy privilege, to swing the body of propertied Catholics behind them, as Grattan had hoped. Anyway, Government supporters had also played an equal role in the Act of 1782. By then, spokesmen on every side took America's toleration for Catholics as a precedent, a touchstone, or a warning that it must be conceded in Ireland.

The relations of the Patriot reformers to the Protestant middle classes and the Presbyterians of the North presents a fairer test of their credentials as a movement of reform. The issues were not confounded by hereditary fears, by an overwhelming arithmetic of animosity against them as with the Catholics. These Protestants were politicised and armed; they shared the same imperial yet now also Irish identities; as Volunteers, they had secured the ascendancy's estates against invasion and native crime, and had ensured Free Trade and independence; they had been generally deferential to the leadership and opinions of the gentry. Now the Volunteers demanded reform of parliament to make it more representative of Protestants generally, and to curb the ability of great aristocrats to determine its membership and of the administration to control it by corrupt practice. In the arguments promoting Catholic rights, Volunteers had played a significant part: particularly those from Presbyterian east Ulster, from both popular and Masonic companies in the bigger Irish cities, and from areas such as east Cork and much of Connacht, where there was a growing Catholic business and grazier class committed to social order against Whiteboyism, and acquiescent in Protestant control of the country. But despite a vocal minority, the vast body of Protestants, including the Ulster Presbyterians, refused to associate Catholics in their drive for parliamentary reform, and supported relaxation of anti-Catholic controls, and occasionally enfranchisement of propertied Catholics only insofar as these objectives were consonant with "preserving unimpaired the Protestant government of this country". They thus weakened their claims, for as Matthew O'Conor, a Catholic near-contemporary pointed out, although himself sympathetic to reform, most Catholics did not see it his way: "They dreaded an increase of power to their former masters, and, therefore, were indifferent to the proposed system of reform".

What was that system? It bore the effects of American revolutionary influences more directly than any other measures of these years, both in the fashion of its proposals, and in its underlying philosophy. The Irish House of Commons was notoriously unrepresentative, even of the 'Protestant nation' itself. In 1775, twenty-four magnates had control of 110 of the 300 seats in the house. In 1783, only 72 of the 300 seats were in any way representative of the Protestants of the constituencies, and fifty-three nobles controlled the election of 124 members. Only in the counties, and not always there, and in twelve towns, were the elections in any way free, although limited electoral rolls and aristocratic influence made even such limited freedom problematic: it was at its best when public opinion was roused, and the gentry seeking to influence the election were divided. In the climate of reform of the 1770s–1780s, this unrepresentativeness was seen as the chief reason why British officials and supposedly corrupt aristocrats could bargain to mutual advantage, ensure the bad government of the country, and flout growing pressure for programmes of national improvement and assertion. As for the 'proposed system of reform,' there were in fact several. The most radical would have enfranchised male Protestant freeholders and most leaseholders in cities and towns, and swept away most 'rotten boroughs' (underpopulated manors or villages represented in parliament by the landlord-owner's nominees). Strict controls would have been imposed on the positions and incomes which members of parliament might receive from official sources. Such schemes were recommended to the reformers by those radical English students of the American experiment, particularly Jebb, Price and Cartwright, with whom an Ulster Volunteer reform convention of 1783 had correspondence. Scores of such schemes were debated at a national Volunteer convention in Dublin in November 1783.

Political realism, and the astute manipulation of the convention by relative conservatives such as Lord Charlemont and Henry Flood, caused the eventual presentation to parliament of a much watered down programme. Not surprisingly, the élitist Irish commons voted at once against even receiving the plan, only the relatively freely elected county members supported it; the borough members opposed it. A large majority of the commons jealously asserted "its just rights and privileges against all encroachments whatsoever". Interestingly, the British administration, by then firmly opposed to any reforms which might render its task 'irretrievably lost' had determined on seeing the Dublin convention 'baffled', as Charles James Fox wrote to the Irish Commander-in-Chief (now none other than 'Gentleman Johnny' Burgoyne of late American disgrace!).

That English Whigs, now in office, Irish upper-class erstwhile reformers, Irish gentry reactionaries and the British administration in Ireland could all combine to frustrate Protestant middle-class reform was partly due to the conviction that enough had already been surrendered (or gained!) in 1782, as well as to the determination of these parties that things were best handled amongst themselves. But fears were intensified by the feeling that the implications of 1782 had yet to be worked out, and that further complication must accordingly be avoided; and these fears were given colour by the fashion of the reform movement itself. Whether it willed it or not, the Volunteer movement was a popular, extra-parliamentary force for change, which seemed by its existence to challenge the legitimacy of established institutions, and in itself had never been given a legal basis. As long as it operated largely under gentry control to curb disorder, protect the country against invasion, and shore up the demands of the Patriot élite, its pretensions were acceptable. Even in the heady days of 1779–1782, however, most members of Parliament had rejected the claim of Volunteer companies and other middle class associations to instruct them, treating their advices solely as constituency information. In 1782 even Grattan had advised the Volunteers to withdraw from politics; and that year, Burgoyne attempted to create a government-controlled militia. But political excitement had gone too far. The Volunteers had expanded to upwards of 80,000 or more; some companies admitted Catholics; in towns, companies of tradesmen and others, and of Catholics, outside gentry supervision, had become common. The fashion of forming associations and holding conventions bespoke an inchoate grouping towards new forms of political life, rooted in middle class self-assertion. In England the counterparts, such as the Yorkshire Association, frightened even many whiggish gentry who sought to exploit them. In the politics of Ireland, armed pressure grouping could only mean the worst to those nervously in command.

The Dungannon convention of 1782 had helped usher in the revolution of that year. The Lisburn and Dublin conventions of the following year committed the Volunteers to reform. But thereafter the fashion rapidly weakened. Attempts to create a national reform convention by such pro-American enthusiasts as Napper Tandy and Edward Newenham in autumn

1784 and January 1785 failed as much from lack of general support as from government obstruction. But in all these, a strong contrast with the situation of American revolutionary conventions is evident. Ignorance, diffidence, uncertainty and residual deference to the very authorities supposedly under challenge marked these conventions of 1783–85. Even moderate radicals such as William Drennan were irritated by the half-hearted calculation of supposed friends of the people as Henry Flood, while those more clearly committed, such as Napper Tandy or Frederick Hervey, the English bishop of Derry and Earl of Bristol, were inadequate and irresponsible. The end of the war, with the treaty of Versailles in 1783, at once strengthened the hands of the authorities immeasurably, and decided thousands of Volunteers that their central purpose, and perhaps only legitimate one, was now gone. With France and Spain at peace, the need to conciliate Catholics, too, was gone, and many Protestants had second thoughts about the recent forcefulness of Catholic life; men like Arthur O'Leary addressing Volunteer conventions, bodies of Catholics in arms, and John Keogh and others pressing for Catholic inclusion in a parliamentary reform. In areas where there were few Catholics, notably Belfast, south Antrim and north Down, certain reformers believed that their cause could be reinvigorated by formal alliance with Catholics: for them, the local manipulation of Presbyterian majority by the Anglican gentry minority was the key question. In Dublin, likewise, the reformers temptation to reinforce the dwindling 'armed property' of the nation by recourse to an 'armed beggary'—the Catholic urban poor—was active. Almost everywhere also, however, Catholic-Protestant tensions were growing in the wake of their mutual disappointments, and fostered both by government policy under Lord Lieutenant Rutland, and by landlords, both Patriot and conservative, concerned for the Protestant constitution. Already, by 1785, Volunteers as well as popular groupings were clashing with Catholic 'Defenders' in Armagh.

Reform agitation was to be reborn in the wake of the French revolution: some Patriots combined again to launch the Whig Club, and, under Grattan, to seek the purification of parliament by restriction of administration influence. More dramatically, radicalism found an entirely new direction in the argument of young Dublin barrister Wolfe Tone that the British connection, so sacred to the Patriots, was the key source of Ireland's discontents, and must be neutralised by a common alliance of Catholic and Protestant. Even his movement, the United Irishmen (founded 1791), however, at first confined itself to the central reform preoccupations of 1783–84: Catholic emancipation and parliamentary reform. The outbreak of war with France caused William Pitt to pressure the Irish parliament into conceding propertied Catholics the vote in 1793, for the same reasons that the Penal Laws had been cut down during a previous war. But despite the efforts of Grattan and others, the insecurity among the privileged everywhere caused by the French Revolution prevented a parallel concession of parliamentary reform. Despite the relative moderation of the United Irishmen before 1794, and the need to conciliate Ireland generally, that insecurity as it affected both British policy and Ireland's ascendancy class, led to increasing repression in Ireland: a revival of reform conventioning in Ulster, a Catholic national convention in 1792, flurries of fresh Volunteer activity, the inadequacy of minor reforms to stem growing public excitement, the turning of sections of the United Irishmen toward an armed separatist republicanism prepared to deal with France, all together gave substance to fear that Ireland might unravel in the midst of the growing international crisis. Repression seemed easier than cautious re-arrangement of the pieces of the Irish puzzle. In collective fear, the ascendancy, Grattan's group apart, had virtually abdicated any constructive role in the crisis. As a result United Irish organisation spread on the one hand, and government oppression, backed by local yeomanry corps and a biased magistracy, on the other. Growing sectarianism and economic pressures exacerbated tensions, and in 1798 several uprisings took place in the Presbyterian North and the Catholic South, more or less under United Irish aegis. They were ruthlessly repressed.

Yet the decade of the American Revolution in Ireland, 1775–85, although often enough slighted by more recent scholarship, has a coherence which the latter decade, 1790–1800, lacks. The French Revolution was so close, so threatening and so emotive, and the condition of Ireland by the mid–1790s so intractable, that the separatist phase of the United Irishmen, and the insurrection of 1798, seem to have been more of a chaotic break with the cumulative history of the century than a progressive development from it. On the other hand, the decade 1775–85 rapidly yet consistently broadened streams of development already active within Ireland: the rise of public opinion, growing toleration for Catholics, increasing sensitivity to the rights of the house of commons both by its members and by English administrators, a growing national pride amongst Protestants which encompassed, at the least, a certain *noblesse oblige* to the body of the nation, the Catholics, and a sense of justice toward Presbyterians. In a twentieth century perspective, the democratic egalitarian and separatist objectives of the United Irishmen after 1795 seem more pertinent to the ultimate Ireland emergent in 1922. And the revolts of 1798 and their aftermath gave a foretaste both of the insurgent Catholic nationalism and of the opposing loyalism of the landed class, from which the future Ireland was to be constructed. But United Irish ideology was in its own time a counsel of despair: a recognition that the middle class rationality encouraged by the American Revolution could find no other outlet in a segmented and impassioned island than in the somewhat spurious unanimity of an Irish Jacobinism, the modernity and secularism of which ignored the depth of separate history and divided religious belief in which each of the Irish segments was embedded. Almost a century was to pass before the Irish ascendancy was to lose its real political and economic hegemony and its related psychological sway over men's minds: a fate determined as much by the development of parliamentary democracy and reformist ideology in Britain as by developments in Ireland. It may in fact be possible that had the seeds implanted by 1785 time to germinate, a more comprehensive and less embittered nationality might have emerged, particularly given the spread of similar reformist trends in British society. The very ambiguity of Ireland's constitution of 1782 might thus have enabled British administrators to compete with the Irish parliament: as happened already with Catholics in 1782 and 1793, as happened with reform for Presbyterians in 1780, as happened for land tenants in 1780, amongst other examples. Again, granted they were largely Protestant landowners, the propertied *did* have a disproportionate amount of political intelligence in this era pertaining to Ireland, or America. Even the reformers of 1785, and later the United Irishmen, as later the Repealers and Young Irelanders, were reluctant to forego their assistance, despite its class biases. Indeed, this accounts for much of the diffidence of reform in these years: as Wolfe Tone said of the Presbyterian middle class: "They were baffled by the superior address and chicanery of the aristocracy". Even in America, the politics of deference survived almost two generations after the revolution, and for similar reasons. Something other than mere toadyism caused an almost entire generation of Irish Catholic intellectuals—Thomas Moore, Sylvester Mahoney, Matthew O'Conor, Denis Taaffe, as well as Daniel O'Connell himself—to lament the lost promise of Grattan's parliament. It may well have been their recognition that in a complex world, an embattled peasant nationalism, heavily Catholic, was not enough.

The American Inspiration: Radicals and Catholics.

Throughout the decade 1775–85, and beyond, ran the vague conviction that America was providing the model of a usable future, if only in certain respects. One must disagree with Owen D. Edwards' statement: "America had not shown the Volunteers and their Parliamentary allies and rivals what freedom meant beyond a mere rhetorical expression," and instead concur with R. B. McDowell's judgement: "Until the end of the century America, the land of liberty, inhabited by a young prosperous and expanding democracy, loomed large in the minds of Irishmen." The body of specific material available to literate Irish opinion on the new nation was very considerable, more so than was to be published subsequently about revolutionary France. John Dickinson's *Letters from a Pennsylvania Farmer* were serialised in Dublin in 1768–9; Crèvecoeur's *Letters from an American Farmer* published in Dublin in 1782 and in Belfast in 1783 (under the name Hector St. John); *The Constitutions of the Several Independent States of America* and related documents, including the Declaration of Independence, were published in Dublin in 1783. Assessments by two leading British radicals, Richard Price and Thomas Cooper, appeared there in 1785 and 1794, and the *Collection of Letters to the Volunteers of Ireland,* by Effingham, Price and other radicals at the request of the Lisburn convention, published in London in 1783, referred extensively to American practices. Sympathetic travel accounts of the new America by two French reformers were also published in Dublin, that of

Francois Jean de Chastellux in 1787, that of Jean P. Brissot de Warville in 1792. David Ramsay's patriotic yet judicious *History of the American Revolution* followed in Dublin the next year, and Charles Stedman's tory but unembittered history of its campaigns in 1794. Gilbert Imlay's panegyric of the birth of agrarian democracy in a romanticised Kentucky, *A Description of the Western Territory,* found an early Dublin printer in 1793. Besides these, the press and pamphlet literature of the period was heavy with American material, much of it concerned to point up lessons and parallels. That few conservative attacks on the new America were published in Dublin: Banastre Tarleton's history of the southern campaigns and J. F. D. Smyth's tour seemingly alone amongst pre-1800 productions, may fairly indicate the balance of popular opinion.

The two flurries of major publication were 1783–85 and 1792–95: the first coincides with the struggle for parliamentary reform, which has been ill-served by historians caught up in glamour of the independence movement. The second coincides with the re-birth of reform fervour following the outbreak of revolution in France. As the very objectives, personnel, and early history of that re-birth indicate, Irish radicals perceived the revolutions as continuous, their implications for Ireland of a piece. In Belfast, radical military carried busts of both Franklin and Mirabeau, Washington was toasted along with the events in France, France and America emblematised as the lights of the rights of man. Given the English language basis of Irish radicalism, it is not surprising that Thomas Paine became something of a hero in Ireland, for he linked the worlds of the American and French revolutions in his life, as he provided a propaganda accessible to them, and directed starkly against the aristocratic Britain of his own early years. *Common Sense* was read in Ireland, although not published there; his *Letter to the Abbé Raynal,* contrasting narrow British nationalism with revolutionary American internationalism and commitment to basic human rights, was printed in Dublin in 1782 probably on the initiative of Charles Thomson; his *Rights of Man* went into at least seven Irish editions in 1791–2, becoming the textbook of the radical revival. The clichés of his principles entered the political balladry of the 1790s, and even the deism of his *Age of Reason,* which appealed to even fewer Irish republicans than American, did not undermine his original impact. Paine, in Ireland as elsewhere, epitomises the inseparability of American and French influences on the reviving resolve to mould a popular polity. The actual English society and its Crown which Paine remembered and hated, against which he pitted idealised republics of America and France, was in fact closer to the experience of men in Ireland than to those in America in 1776 or France in 1791: this must be understood in appraising his popularity.

Underlying all these works was the commonplace that human betterment and political improvement, preferably republican, were interdependent; and the more obvious lesson that the Americans, who had broken the connection with England, were the exemplars of that commonplace. Yet if American example fuelled the reform impulse of 1782–4, as earlier it assisted the gains of

1778–82 and provided some rhetoric of liberty, it may have contributed to a strange malaise underlying much political activity in the entire period: the feeling one gets that to many men a sense of movement was enough, that hard questions need not be too deeply examined. The events of 1778–82 fed this illusion, and the loss of momentum in 1784–85 and again in 1794–95 confirmed it. The pamphleteer of 1779 who claimed *Renovation without Violence Yet Possible* (Dublin, 1779) and the *Dublin Evening Post* writer who claimed violence as the *ultima ratio* the same year anticipated that the implication of the failure to reform in the next fifteen years must be to set things going again in a more bloody way. As rebellion neared, radicals reminded the disaffected that America had extorted its rights by forcing 'an act of justice at the point of a bayonet,' and that France had aided America in this. But the constructive implications even of those American precedents successfully copied were often overlooked. Scholars today recognise that sovereignty was asserted in principle in the assemblies the colonists created to advance their cause or elaborate their new constitutions. The reformist *Belfast News Letter* and the radical *Northern Star* recognised in 1793 that all the gains of the past twelve years had been at least partly gained by delegate meetings, and that popular will could express itself only through conventions given the corruption of parliament. But in 1784 even liberals had disapproved the reform assemblies taking the name of congress because of its American and presumably therefore revolutionary implications. Only a minority of Irish reformers could arrogate to conventions the legitimacy of those forms acquired in America. And in 1793 the administration pre-empted the second chance of such a possibility in Ireland by declaring all conventions illegal.

Just as conservatives saw the implications of conventions more freely than most reformers, so too they saw the logic of religious equality when applied to Ireland. When the penal laws were being relaxed most men agreed with the beneficent example of America: "there every Religion is on an equal footing; yet we see unanimity prevail," wrote a correspondent to the *Hibernian Chronicle* in 1780. But few Protestants, as we have seen, would follow America as far as sharing political power with Catholics. It was perhaps naïve of Wolfe Tone, knowing the very different arithmetic, to point out in 1792 that there "the Catholic and Protestant sit equally in Congress, without any contention arising, other than who shall serve his country best," although not as naïve as George Washington's recommending religious toleration to his anti-Catholic Irish admirer Edward Newenham, the same year. Most Irish Protestants would have followed American example to liberalise their power structures, amongst Protestants, and promote toleration and even goodwill toward Catholics: but not to up-end the whole basis of their politics. Notably, no American informed upon Ireland—John Adams, Benjamin Franklin, George Washington—recommended that they do. They understood that ultimately Ireland was a conquered country, dissimilar from America in that.

The religious issue was closely related to that of social stratification, and here the example of America was likewise inadequate. Irish reformers could envisage the enfranchisement of propertied Catholics because there were so few of them. Even propertied Catholics could not envisage the granting of political power to the propertyless because they were the mass of the people, a dilemma that never arose in America. Theobald McKenna, a Catholic physician reacting against Tom Paine's efforts to universalise human rights, not erroneously remarked of the American constitutional system of the time (1793), that it "labours to palliate what it cannot remedy, the mischiefs of democracy". But he went on to assert a Hobbesian view of reality, not perhaps inaccurately as he might see it threatening his kind in Ireland, "strictly speaking society is the combination of those who *have* against those who *have not,*" a sentiment the more conservative Federalists might feel, but would hardly express so crudely. Equality of condition made advanced political speculation at least allowable in America; in Ireland, deepening inequality caused it to bring almost all constructive political thinking into disrepute by the mid-1790s. Even the United Irishmen could not contemplate an Ireland without landlords, privilege and social stratification: most of them seem to have assumed that middle class Protestants would inherit something of the disproportionate political power of their élite co-religionists, except that they would share it more readily and use it more constructively. Those who found their way to America, such as Hamilton Rowan and Thomas Addis Emmet, were annoyed at the familiarity between classes they found there. It is perhaps not surprising that the few who had harboured the most favourable views of Catholic-Protestant rapprochement and political reconstruction, had their own dreams of a national prosperity which might provide a fresh start. Joseph Pollock of the Newry Volunteers, one of the most persistent optimists of the reform movement of the mid-1780s, believed Ireland to have natural advantages some of which surpassed America's, and a considerable maritime future. Only with such a prospect the American model, gradually applied to reform, toleration and class unity, given British approval, might have helped create a future, rather than a ferment. But international war, the fear of revolution, and the deepening of rural poverty were by 1800 to have so transformed Ireland's horizons, that scholars find difficulty in recapturing the innocence of an era when a Protestant Irish middle class found the America of Crèvecoeur and Paine, of Franklin and de Warville, a programme and an inspiration.

What of the Catholic majority? Recently several writers have claimed that they were indifferent to all this, that, "seeking the most elementary civil rights," they were therefore "unlikely to lose their night's sleep if American Protestants were taxed without representation," those of them who were not "too sunk in poverty and illiteracy to know or care" about it. They were indeed the conquered. But conquest had complicated, not simplified their reactions to events. In chapter one the considerable provincial fragmentation of the Catholic majority has been stressed. This, together with the poverty and linguistic divisions of the mass of them, did conform to their subordinate role 'outside of history', to use the phrase of Albert Memmi about the conquered and colonised everywhere. They thus had no political coherence. Maureen Wall has called them "a nation-wide secret society," which also captures their alienation and the fugitive character of their organisation, but loses this sense of fragmentation. There was, however, an even deeper fissure than all these: that between those who would assimilate in acquiescence to ascendancy control, and those who could never do so: excluded by poverty, tradition, pride, or all three. The urban middle class, however precarious; most of the better-off graziers and farmers; a residual gentry; and above all most Catholic churchmen, fell into the first category. Outside Connacht, these had all made the crucial transition to English language and culture, or were in process of doing so. Acceptance that mass impoverishment and sharp class stratification were ordinances of Providence made acceptable an assimilative thrust which would otherwise have been seen for what it was: an abandonment of their real relationship to native society. The richer subtleties and rewards of everyday society and culture are determined by the alien political élite. Any richness left in the life of the conquered is archaic, undynamic, unrelated to the quickening hour. Unless one has a vocation to serve the poor, in that century a religious matter only; or unless there seem real possibilities of a political revolution in which a native talented tenth can re-graft itself upon the body of the people, the logical and understandable thing is adjustment, acceptance, conformity, pressure for increasing rights beneath the state of domination. For Catholic churchmen, the proscription and improvement of the mass of their people, coupled with the relaxation of formal control on their own activity, had created an ideal situation in which they could cultivate the otherworldly piety of the people, and save their souls. Anything which jeopardised this precarious situation was reprehensible: from below, violence, revolution, wordly aspiration inevitably frustrated; from above, further renewed persecution or control. The acceptance of Protestant Ascendancy and British imperial control for them was logical and not unnatural: comparable to early medieval acceptance of baronial control of church property and appointments, or current acceptance of the *status quo* in Poland or Hungary. A strange alliance of assimilating yet rights-seeking laity in the towns, and the Catholic clergy, both frightened that any false move would bring ruin or setback, ensured that Dublin Castle found superficial allies amongst these two groups whom officials liked for their own comfort to believe *were* Catholics/natives in general.

As late as 1782, amongst the Penal Laws were many which specifically came into effect in war time—relating to the rights of any Protestants to seize Catholic horses, of magistrates to close houses of worship, and so on; and many others, which could be brought into effect at any time, had not been so brought into effect throughout the century except during earlier wars. On top of that the American War brought thousands of Protestants to arm themselves to the teeth. Given all this, as these assimilating groups would see it, acceptance of the administration's line, particularly when it proffered more tangible relief than did these local Protestants, whatever their noises about toleration, seemed both wise and prudent: and had nothing to do with what they thought about America. Of these Lord Shelburne could correctly say "Among the Roman Catholics they not only talk but act very freely on the other (anti-American) side . . . avowing their dislike of a Constitution, here or in America, in which they are not allowed to participate." The initial loyalty address of 1775 was improved on with another in 1778, signed by three hundred such Catholic leaders; by several bishops' pastorals; and by addresses from the Catholics of separate communities, when France joined the war, and Catholics were expectant to reform. Noticeably, the main addresses did not explicitly condemn either the Americans or the French. Several Catholic nobles, such as Lord Kenmare, tried to raise troops for the government. The rhetoric of much Volunteer Loyalism in the wake of war with France, later Spain, was more than a little anti-Catholic, hence the added precaution.

But the acquiescent were not the majority; they were only the vocal. The mass were so alienated that any reverberation of British discomfiture could hardly but please them, although they were in no position to express this feeling as a movement. This was evident in several Irish songs originating in Munster at the time. Thomas O'Meehan, an Ennis schoolmaster, penned some verses in praise of Washington's expulsion of Howe from Boston in March 1776. In them, the vague dream of Franch deliverance become an accurate expectancy that Louis XVI would take advantage of the new war. As the prose translation of key stanzas reads:

Those are stories of good fortune that have come to us from afar over the ridges of the sea,—that the arrogant robbers are wounded at last, the food of eagles and sea-gulls. It is a source of joy and triumph in my eyes that Howe and the Saxons are taken and overthrown forever, and that the sturdy Washington, helpful and brave, is at the head and command of his realm.
The hirelings are screeching, without shelter, without city, without army, without ships on the tide. Verily the boors of Britain before November judgement day suddenly will be under the bondage of Louis.

And the tune to which the song was to be sung, or danced, was re-titled by O'Meehan 'Washington's Frolic.' Another poem, written by someone with a knowledge of the provisioning of the British armies from Cork with Irish meat, recounted how a visionary woman brought news that

the bears of the English-language were overthrown without arms, without clothing, without flocks, without lands; they were thrown into prison in bands . . . by lively Washington . . . and they screeching with the want of meat which the clowns used to be in the habit of eating without limits.

It may refer to the siege of Yorktown, and have been based on information brought back by sailors engaged in provisioning and spread amongst port labourers and packers. Both verse sets indicate clearly how revulsion from the English, rather than detailed knowledge of the American cause, could engender immediate sympathy for the distant revolt.

Thomas O'Brien MacMahon, perhaps, in English, "the only writer of the time who expresses something of the anger natural to a defeated and hardly-treated race", denounced every aspect of the English including their treatment of America, in a pamphlet of 1777, reprinted 1792. Officers of the Irish Brigade of France on leave in Rome in spring 1778 warned Earl-Bishop Hervey of Derry that they planned to invade Ireland. 'Would to God,' wrote another of them, Richard O'Connell, "That we were at this moment 200,000 strong in Ireland . . . I would kick the Members (of Parliament) and their Volunteers and their unions and their Societies to the Devil: I would make the Rascally spawn of Damned Cromwell curse the hour of his Birth!" Catholics in the southern sections, most strongly linked with France, were said to be "in hourly expectation of assistance from France or Spain," Lord Harcourt was informed in 1776: before those nations had joined the war. Thomas Conolly said in the Commons in 1778 that 150,000 Catholics in the same region would join the French if they arrived. 'A Grazier' warned in 1779 that Ireland was divided into two classes, those who would exploit Britain's weakness to extract concessions (presumably the Protestants, as this was their policy) and those "who go much further and declare for independence and an alliance with France," which must either have been a fiction, or, more likely, refer to these Catholics. Notably, the attempt of the assimilating to rouse Catholic recruits for the army was a failure, in large measure. Lord George Germain wrote Sir John Irvine in September 1775, "I find from (Lieut.-Gen) Cuninghame that the Roman Catholics do not enlist for America with the zeal that was expected" and he went on to ask Irvine, the Irish Commander-in-Chief, to explain this to the London military authorities, so that they might take alternative measures for raising troops.

That Catholic opinion was divided amongst those who could benefit from betterment, and those who could never do so, was understood at the time. A letter written from Cork on September 8, 1775, published in the *Pennsylvania Packet* on 27 November, stated explicitly "Though the principal Romanists in Cork and Limerick have formed Associations and offered bounties to such recruits as shall list on this occasion, yet they have very little success; for though the heads of that communion are in the interest of government, the lower class who have not sagacity enough to make proper distinctions, are, to a man, attached to the Americans, and say plainly that the Irish ought to follow their example. . . Many of the draughts that have come here to fill up the regiments ordered abroad, swear that they will not lift a finger against the Americans, among whom they all have relations". The *New York Journal* of 20 August 1775 printed another letter from Ireland: "They have given Lord Kenmare leave to enlist four thousand Catholics for the latter purpose (America), but as yet they have little success. The foolish idea of fighting against their countrymen prevents them." Indeed, it was not the relatives of Lords Kenmare or Cahir, the Catholic nobles who failed to raise troops for America, nor even the relatives of the members of the national Catholic Committee, nor of urban merchants, who had gone in large numbers as indentured servants to America. Amongst the impoverished and the assimilating, not merely was there a vast gulf; there seems to have been incomprehension. Eventually, thousands of them drifted into the British army and navy by 1782, but the reasons were as a-political as poverty itself: "the refuse of the community" said one paper, arguing no decent Catholic would join. The Catholic merchants of the towns, on the other hand, did exceptionally well, as the chief victuallers of the British forces in North America: the rancid quality of their salt beef contributing unwittingly to the demoralisation of the army there. French official intelligence was convinced there would be widespread support if they invaded southern Ireland as part of their strategy of alliance with America: informant Irish emigrés such as Patrick Wall of Myshall, Co. Carlow, exaggerated the support they might expect, but William Bancroft, a merchant friend of Benjamin Franklin, reported realistically to Vergennes in 1779: "nothing leads me to believe that any party or group of men in this country, with the exeption of the Hock-Cutters and the Whiteboys and other outlaws, is disposed to take up arms against the English administration." Even Wall distinguished the Catholic gentry and common people, admitting the latter only to be pro-French. Under De Broglie and Vergennes, several invasion plans were projected from summer 1778 through 1779.

Arthur O'Leary's address to the 'Common People of Ireland' in 1779, warning that the French would never invade except in their own interest, that the Stuart cause was finished, and that 'the poor will be poor' regardless of any change of government, gives evidence that the Catholic leadership was aware of this dual culture amongst their people. "In France, they have poor of all trades and professions. It will be the same here". But the culture he addressed could not listen. As the *New York Journal* said on October 26, 1775, "The common people are industriously kept from a knowledge of public affairs. They know nothing but what the great please to tell them," quotations from a letter from 'M.W.' in Ireland who understood that the poor indeed lived in a separate world from his own—but not one bereft of its own sources of intelligence, despite his misunderstading. A world of gardeners, labourers, domestics, and ostlers must have linked the world of the cottiers and craftsmen to the preoccupations of 'political' Ireland, even granted, as he continued, that "Newspapers since the (Irish) Stamp Act are so high, the poor and middling people cannot purchase them." If Arthur O'Leary's advice thus went unread, knowledge of the crisis must have spread generally—the rise of the Volunteers alone ensured that—to coalesce with earlier conviction that the race of Cromwell would be overthrown, that France would be the source of deliverance, that the America to which so many had migarated as servants was now no more the friend of the English in Ireland and elsewhere. Unfortunately, almost all the political poetry in Irish and English in which these poplular convictions found expression date from the period of the 1798 revolt and after, although a confused ballad from Ulster, conflating several periods, may echo this time: "The jug is on the table/The Duke of York has enough arms/The Frenchman and Spaniard are at the strand/ And I prefer them to the talk of women/ . . . We'll have land without rent from this year on/ And woman of the house, what's your care?" ('S Ó Bhean a' Toighe). Gearóid Ó Tuathaigh has demonstrated brilliantly how the archaic imagery of Irish poetry from the 1790s–1830s could wed the language of eighteenth century Jacobite nostalgia to a grammar of politics which was popular, changing and realistic. Even churchmen who wrote for conciliation in English, may have spoken implicitly from alienation in Irish thereby deepening this counter-culture: as did Nicholas Archdeacon, a dean in Co. Clare, who around 1796 was to compare the original 'leaders of the protestant faith' to women religious who led their order into worldliness and prostitution. Protestants probably had a better understanding of this subculture than they are usually credited with; the *Freeman's Journal* (14 October 1766) had linked "The many extravagant ballad singers which infest our streets both night and day, singing obscene songs, that poison the minds of youth . . . And the great numbers of Popish books lately printed and published . . ." as subversive influences. Attempting to turn Catholics from the army, an item in the same paper (perhaps inserted under Benjamin Franklin's distant Paris aegis), would later assert that Catholics in the army received 500 lashes for as little as being discovered with rosary beads, wondering whether those who forfeited the rights of citizenship for their religion would expose their lives for the pay of a common soldier (13 June 1782). In short, the Catholic masses had not caught up with the subtleties of their lay and clerical leaders: their culture was too alienated.

These distinctions were widely assumed at the time. The 1770s, and again the 1780s, saw serious epidemics of agrarian uprising spread across much of southern Ireland, both in Leinster and Munster. Protestant opinion had divided since 1760s on whether to regard such outbreaks as typically Papist, or typically lower class. In the 1760s, the balance probably tipped toward regarding it as essentially Catholic: a view strengthened by the execution of Fr. Nicholas Sheehy of Tipperary in 1766 for supposed complicity in Whiteboy organisation. As late as the 1780s many still believed this: in 1787, an anti-disturbances coercion bill included clauses to have Catholic chapels in affected areas torn down, a proposal Luke Gardiner and others had had removed as unjust. By then the balance of opinion was seeing agrarian discontent somewhat more clearly for what it was. Nonetheless, the strains on the Catholic community were considerable, especially on those who had something to lose. Thus, the groups of Catholics who came forward to take the prescribed oath of loyalty, and make addresses to the same effect, between 1775–1783, are invariably described as 'respectable', 'the principal Roman Catholics,' 'Merchants and traders' and the like, in press reports of the time. Many statements by the Catholic bishops were also surprisingly explicit, for example that of Nicholas Sweetman, Bishop of Ferns (Wexford), self-denotedly a "professed abhorrer of all lawless disturbers of the public," who prefixed his excommunication of the 'banditti' in 1775, "Whereas the detestable, lawless and unmeaning disturbers of the public, commonly called White Boys, are drawing on us, and our holy religion, the odium of our mild government, and the gentlemen in power in our country . . ." (Dublin *Freeman's Journal,* 3 August 1775). The next year, the co-adjutor bishop of Meath, Dr. Geoghegan, actually shot dead the leader of a White Boy band which raided his home. The outbreaks of the 1780s were directed against excessive dues levied by the Catholic clergy, as against tithes and other ascendancy abuses: Catholic gentry and better farmers were prominent in quelling them; and hence Protestants were less likely to confuse the issues completely. But the condemnations of the 1780s were scarcely less anxious. Likewise, the Catholic Committee took steps to ensure that the Catholic poor did not counter-riot in the cities when news of the anti-Popery Gordon riots came through from Britain, and in 1781 the Catholic bishop of Cork enjoined his people not to riot against, or molest, the troops stationed in the city.

Yet the assimilating classes were not merely passive or servile in their response to the opportunities of the time. As the Catholic Committee reminded the incoming Viceroy, Lord Portland, in April 1782, "At this juncture . . . the rights of mankind are become a glorious topic of enlarged and free discussion," and there is evidence that important members of the Committee used the American situation as leverage for their cause. In October 1777, Charles O'Conor of Belanagare wrote to Dr. John Curry, suggesting that following a British victory they might petition the Crown to open to emigration by Catholics tracts of Maryland and Pennsylvania, as described in a work by 'our Friend, *Ned Burke,'* and use this in turn against the Anglo-Irish: "most probably our Masters would rather repeal all Queen Annes laws relative to us, than admit a general Emigration into that part of the world, where so much would be lost to this nation, and so much would be gained to the Crown . . ." The next year, Sam Laffran of Kilkenny wrote O'Conor in similar vein, promising the threat of mass Catholic emigration to America, if toleration, land and civil rights were offered by the Americans and withheld by the Dublin government. Yet they took genuine interest in the achievement of 1782, even as they curried favour with the Patriots: "while with honest pride as Irishmen, we exult in beholding the national character acquire additional lustre from the universal joy" of those who won the new constitution, they resolved in June 1783. The coverage of Catholic matters in the almost completely Protestant press suggests that Protestants, as well as the Government, were increasingly inclined to appreciate the role the clergy and the respectable played " in reclaiming the people to subordination and order" as the *Dublin Evening Post* said of friar Arthur O'Leary's anti-Whiteboy activities in Cork in 1786.

Bitterly contesting Lord Kenmare's nervous communication to the Volunteer reform convention of 1783, via Boyle Roche, that Catholics did not require the vote, the Catholic Committee had asserted on 11 November, 1783, "That we do not so widely differ from the rest of mankind as, by our own act, to prevent the removal of our shackles." And it is notable that they never formally put themselves on record as opposing the reformist ideology which America, in a sense, was already understood to stand for. Generally, however, they tried to modulate Catholic use of these new currents to their own group advantage, in a way that assumed their control over their own community. In that way, they were both reformers and conservative accommodationists, their initial strategy in the 1770s and 1780s not without analogies to that of Booker T. Washington amongst blacks around 1900 in America. But they could not confine the impact of these broader currents upon their people lower down. The 'lower orders', as Luke Gardiner said in 1787, "have shaken off that restraint, under which they had been heretofore kept by their pastors, and from other collateral causes". They had traditions of their own. In 1778, a mob of them at Philipstown in Co. Offaly, had murdered the hangman of Fr. Sheehy, suggestive of how deeply and far their own preoccupations spread. Given Arthur O'Leary's activities, it is indicative and instructive that the rumour spread that he had conformed to Anglicanism. The bishops of Munster found inexplicable the widespread Whiteboy and Rightboy attacks upon the clerical dues system in 1786, for the priests' standard of living, they held, was modest enough, even admitting that there were greedy and extortionate exceptions amongst them. Is it not possible that the common people found the accommodationism of their erstwhile leaders increasingly unacceptable, when set against what was probably a widening gulf in living standards between Catholic graziers and merchants and the mass of the people (for conditions were worsening in the 1780s)? Possible that the new ideology, however vague its echoes in Munster or Leinster, nevertheless crystallised matters in many minds? William O'Driscoll, supposed self-styled 'Secretary General of the Munster Peasantry' issued a statement thereabouts beginning "Resolved that by the common rights of mankind, the aggrieved are warranted to seek for redress," as the *Dublin Evening Press* reported, 1 August 1786,— a journal that held that the abolition of penal laws governing Catholic leasing of property would exacerbate differences between the poor and the marginally advantaged in the country. When general uprising came in 1798, the Catholic clergy and middle classes, even reformers like John Keogh and Edward Byrne, were almost fanatical in their denunciations. For the common people to riot against dragoons who had attended a mass in Castlebar from curiosity, against priests who rejected the beliefs of the people and conformed, and against outsiders found at prayer-meetings or patterns, was expressive of a sub-culture of primitive revolt. Unlike the post-O'Connell period, when middle class nationalism in Ireland returned to its emotional roots in this folk-consciousness, the 1770s–1780s saw determined efforts by the clergy and middle class to actively exploit the advantages of reconcilation. To the mass of the country people this must have seemed betrayal, given that their sustaining antiforeignism still linked Protestants, Anglo-Irishmen and the English together for certain purposes, distinguishing them for others.

Likewise, and unsurprisingly, even the socially established Irish emigrés on the continent embodied the popular antagonism to Britain, rather than the subtle accommodations of the Catholic Committee. As Richard Hayes showed, the majority of Irish officers in the service of France went over to the French Revolution until their new allegiance was discomfited under the Terror. Many of them had already served in the American war, and been affected by the ferment of ideas it released in French military circles: Dillon's regiment had served with distinction at the siege of Savannah, for example. In 1791, the Legislative Assembly authorised the re-naming of the principal regiments of the Irish Brigade as infantry of the new national army: Berwick's regiment as the 88th, Dillon's as the 87th and Walsh's as the 92nd. While certain commanders defected to the counter-revolutionary allies, the majority remained with these units, notably Thomas O'Meara, Charles Kilmaine, James O'Moran and Arthur Dillon. It is probable that their political attitudes far from being reactionary (as the Convention later maintained) were close to those of many socially conservative but constitutionalist Catholics in America such as Stephen Moylan and Dominick Lynch. They in fact provide the exemplars in life of the spirit of proto-revolutionary alienation which in the hands of Gaelic poets from Thomas O'Meehan to Michael O'Longáin, could connect anti-British tradition, through sympathy for the Americans, to an openness to many of the implications of the French Revolution. And of course France, and the politics of its Irish Brigade, itself gave body to that continuity.

Such alienation was not confined to the Irish-speaking sections of the country, as the 1798 uprisings demonstrated. But it might be thought that it would effectively bar all sympathy between the peroccupations of the mass of the native Irish and the politics of the Patriots. This needs much further study: investigations into popular political culture, such as undertaken for Britain and France at this time, do not exist for Ireland, but those from other countries caution us against assuming the poor to be fully a-political. There are interesting indications. Riots were frequent in Dublin for political reasons, most rioters emanating from the largely Catholic Liberties, a desperately poor area. In 1759 they rioted against the rumour of a union with England, forcing members of Parliament to take oaths to oppose it, as they entered the buildings in College Green. They roughed up Thomas Prendergast, because they thought he was of a Cromwelliam family name; they desisted from drubbing Lord Inchiquin when they heard his family name was O'Brien. Again in 1779 they rioted against a proposed union, as earlier for free trade, and later for independence and again in support of reform. So riotous were they that the Dublin Police Bill, an urban version of the many coercion acts passed from the 1760s onward to control their country cousins, was passed to deal with them. Around 1784, butchers' boys regularly 'houghed' soldiers in uniform: cutting the tendons of their leg as the Whiteboys were houghing the cattle of graziers. It is not impossible that a popular tradition held that bad and all as the politics of the ascendancy was, the direct irruption of immediate British authority—in the shape of a union with England, the coming of its military, or whatever—would be much worse: for so it had been in the 1640s, and the

The Battle of Wexford: New Ross, 5th June, 1798.

1680s. All we know of the way in which oral cultures simplify reality around dramatic, long-remembered events, would incline one to believe that this would indeed be possible. Thus, whereas Matthew O'Conor might be correct in assuming that literate and political Catholics had every reason to support the 'Castle' against the existent ascendancy, or even a reformed one, the populace may have had crude grounds for seeing the Irish Parliament as the lesser of evils, to support the Independence of 1782, with its dreamlike prospect of prosperity, and to comprehend the Americans' independence in that light.

Certainly when the United Irishmen, despite their formal ideology, appealed to the traditional Anglophobia of the countryside, to its Francophile dreams of deliverance, its hatred of Protestantism and its resentment of the ascendancy, their cells multiplied with remarkable speed. Nor were peasants incapable of seeing the relevance of doctrines like the rights of men to their condition: their clergy had assumed of them a capacity to grasp considerably more abstruse doctrines over the previous half-century in which the catechising of the people had spread. Precisely this technique the United Irishmen copied: "What have you got in your hand? A green bough. Where did it first grow? In America. Where did it bud? In France. Where are you going to plant it? In the crown of Great Britain".

In three of Ireland's four provinces peasants died in thousands for that bough in 1798: English-speaking in Leinster, Irish-speaking in Connacht, Presbyterian in Ulster. The ascendancy and the administration together, including Patriots like Charlemont, had all but predetermined that this happen when in 1784–85 and again throughout the early 1790s they had ensured that "The terror of the Papists begins to operate" (Lord Lieutenant Rutland to Pitt, 1784). They had thereby frustrated any possibility that the farmers, shopkeepers and other 'respectable people' of each denomination coalesce in a peaceful political evolution. Contemporary accounts of the sectarian disturbances in Armagh from 1785 onward, written apparently by educated Catholics, emphasise how unexpected was their disruption there of a developing harmony, a disruption particularly distasteful to merchants. Political reform was attempted in 1784, full Catholic emancipation in 1793–95. Both foundered on the inability of most Protestants to trust the Catholic majority, a natural fear which the authorities did not have to create. However they could have actively discouraged it, had they been committed to such reforms. But rising population, land competition and increasing hardship were not merely dividing the poor from each other, Catholic from Protestant in Ulster, journeymen from each other in the towns, they were also dividing the communities within themselves, alienating the hard-pressed from the marginally advantaged, and making the calculations of the 'political Catholics' seem incomprehensible to the rest.

The United Irishmen decided that the solution to the failure of reform lay in exploiting this substratum of popular discontents while creating a middle class movement that would fuse 'political Catholics' with reform Protestants. It was an unbelievably bold and imaginative strategy, but yet a doomed one in the climate of the times. Outside Ulster, east Ulster at that, few Protestants joined them, and there only a minority. Most 'political Catholics' were too prudent, too close to the clergy, too suspicious of the United Irish Protestant leadership, to join them. The countryfolk tended to join the movement very much on their own terms: closer to the ideology of William O'Driscoll of the Munster peasantry than to that of the society: for them, the rights of man were a vehicle of historic animosity, rather than an escape from it. The United Irishmen hoped after successful insurrection to mould a common post-sectarian nationality. Means and ends were thus inevitably set at odds. Protestantism collectively panicked in 1798. The British administration decided that insurrection was the stalking horse of a French revolutionary subversion of British liberties via Ireland and their own fleets, which had recently mutinied. The conservative Anglo-Irish party, led by John Fitzgibbon, Lord Clare, won complete control over its community, and determined on total repression. The green bough of liberty, early grafted with images of a remote American achievement, was left to instigate in the future an almost solely native popular nationalism, Irish and Catholic.

Logically, the ascendancy were then cajoled, frightened, beguiled and persuaded—some bought—into the extinction of the achievements of 1782. In 1800, an Act of Union determined that Ireland and Britain become one kingdom, its parliament in London. In the years after 1782, the ascendancy had demonstrated its incapacity, in a sense, to understand the meaning of its own victory: that nationality must become policy. To say, with one scholar, that "this is a Utopian idea . . . at a time when parliament was expected to represent property rather than people," is to deny that climates of opinion change by reason, choice and policy, rather than mechanistically. The American revolutionaries, largely patrician, showed a moral imagination capable of transforming the basis of politics in an orderly fashion. The Irish ascendancy was immobilized less by its situation than by its corruption: "an interested, selfish, savage race of harpies and plunderers," as Lord Rutland called them in 1785, whereas the Irish revolutionary Wolfe Tone was only seemingly more moderate: "They see Ireland only in their rent rolls, their places, their patronage, and their pensions." Most of the projected reforms assumed the primacy of property, and thus Protestant preeminence.

Strangely, such was the prestige of American example, that in selling the Union of Ireland and Britain to the literate public, one writer compared it with the progressive development of the United States from a confederation to a Federal Union. Doubtless many once reformist and now frightened Protestant admirers of America breathed amen to this balm to their sad inconsistency!

First Capital City: Second Street and Christ Church, Philadelphia.

Chapter 7

Aftermaths

Washington's and Jefferson's America: Social Revolution

The merits of Irish immigrants have several times been revealed below the crusts of prejudice in the crucible of national crisis: the famine generation was rescued from widespread obloquy by the Civil War of 1860–65, the diligent Irish American clerks and foremen of the twentieth century were thrust upwards by the New Deal and Second World War. Such crises generate solidarity and seem to sharpen perceptions of a common humanity. Obviously, too, men are brought together who would otherwise remain distant and hence estranged. The caricature gives way, that of all Irishmen as the wild, Indian-scalping Paxton Presbyterian, or later as the whisky-sodden gang-fighters of New York's Five Points of the 1850s. The process was not completed. If the Irish already in the country proved in close-up to be as prosaic, as self-regarding, as comfortable and as decent as most other Americans might wish, yet their assertive politics and religion still appeared threatening, so that further mass arrivals continuously fed the distinctiveness of Irish communities and thereby re-instigated waves of native incomprehension, misgiving and even hostility. Nonetheless, the promise made explicit in crisis times was always to remain implicitly present because America adhered broadly to the principles of her first crisis ideology, that of 1776: that all men are created equal, and that governments exist to provide for their common welfare in direct response to their needs.

For, however inspired, the principles of 1776 justified and secured on high grounds the gains of crisis times which might otherwise have remained fortuitous and precarious. There is considerable evidence that eighteenth century Irish Americans (of each kind) benefited from the War of Independence and the Revolutionary crisis as later Irish Americans did from the industrial and political upheavals of their times. There is evidence, too, that they related the security of those gains to firm maintenance of the principles of 1776 and of the constitutions and liberal religious and social legislation of those years. To canvass these developments in detail would be to write a full history of the post-Revolutionary Irish down to 1830: a few highlights must suffice. The other side of this is more important yet, and has never been adequately recognised. Among the truly revolutionary gains of the American Revolution was the first comprehensive enhancement of the status of Irish Presbyterians and of Irish Catholics within the English-speaking world, not excepting their condition in Ireland itself! In short, by 1785, Irishmen who were un-rich, un-landed and un-Anglican could attain high civil and military office, vote freely, practise law or medicine, accept the highest judicial appointments, and move in the highest social circles in Pennsylvania, Maryland, Delaware and Virginia (in order of their approximate openness). In the other nine colonies, although there were legal barriers remaining against Catholic office-holding, the real residual barriers were social: and these were giving away everywhere, rapidly in New York and the western territories, more slowly in New England and the South. By contrast, where the Crown still reigned, despite glacial improvement in the legal situation, Irish Presbyterians and Irish Catholics were still as such excluded from the dominant social and political élites, even in Ireland itself. Such a momentous change cannot be excluded from consideration of the 'American Revolution as a Social Movement,' even from its claims to a revolutionary character.

For if social conditions alone were ushering Irish immigrants upwards even before the Revolution, a psychological barrier remained to be breached: that erected by a culture (despite Tom Paine) rooted in Englishness and the prejudices of Englishness. Goethe, in now hackneyed lines, epitomised a glaring misconception about the America of his day:

You do not suffer
In hours of intensity
From futile memories
And pointless battles.

For the Anglo-Americans of New England and the southern plantations, although the leaders of the revolution, were hag-ridden by the monsters of the middle-brow English imagination of the seventeenth century. Right to the very eve of that event, Popery, Irishmen, continental monarchies, Frenchmen, Spaniards and servility were all linked in a grand arc of witchcraft threatening the frail light of liberty and pure religion. As a remote cultural inheritance, this played its part in deepening their suspicions of George III (was he a re-incarnated Stuart, bent upon tyranny and episcopacy?). The Quebec Act, annexing the Mississippi basin to Quebec while accepting its Catholicism, seemed a frightening confirmation (1774). Pointedly, these men sustained widespread penal legislation against Catholicism, prohibited of public practice everywhere except Pennsylvania, although tolerated in the other middle colonies; prevented Catholics from participation in political life (Charles Carroll's courageous anti-Stamp Act polemics apart); and effectively barred both general free Irish Catholic immigration, and the higher social mobility of such Irish Catholics as there were, by the maintenance of a general climate of mistrust and rejection. Rather than monotonously chronicle the restrictions and detail the prejudices of colonial America in these matters (effectively done by others), several incidents may be used to illustrate the change.

The day after St. Patrick's day, New York city 1741, a series of fires broke out, accompanied by robberies. Fort George (the 'Dublin Castle' of the colony) was itself consumed. Paranoia swept the city: slaves, black freedmen, and Irishmen were swept up for investigation. The conviction spread that these groups, in alliance with the Spanish, planned a conspiracy to destroy the city and/or turn it over to the King's enemies. The whole affair was probably really a rash of arson and theft by people generally ill-used and embittered. It centred on a circle of slave-thieves and their white 'fences'. It was far from a plot to slaughter all the town's inhabitants, but to New Yorkers a grouping of slaves and papists could only spell the worst, particularly as the empire was then at war with Spain. Twenty whites and one hundred and fifty blacks were arrested: the whites included Peter Connolly, Edward Kelly, William Kane, Andrew Ryan, Edward Murphy, John Corry, and John Coffin (none executed). We know most about Athlone-born Kane, a soldier, who professed himself an Anglican and "never was at any Roman catholic congregation in his life" (which *was* the danger!) but all appear to have been lowest-class Irish immigrants. The key white defendants were the members of two Hughson families (several of them executed), who may have been of Irish background; John Ury, also of unknown background, who was wrongly executed as a Catholic priest (then banned in the colony), was called by the Anglo-Irish name Jury by Kane. The incident generally throws a lurid light upon the wartime status of the colonial native Irish, both in social condition, and in civic position, and on their place in Anglo- and Dutch-American demonology. It incidentally suggests that more Irishmen forged links with blacks (as life would suggest) than runaway evidence indicates.

In 1810 the proceedings of the trial were re-published, with notes which emphasised the intervening transformation. Commenting on the anti-Catholicism of his Dutch forefathers in the city, the editor noted: "It was the policy of the English government, after the conquest (of the city), to cherish this animosity, and those of our readers who were born and educated before the American revolution, will recall how religiously they were taught to abhor Pope, Devil and Pretender". Of the anti-Catholic legislation which led to Ury's execution, he added, that it "will account, why so few of this profession existed in this city and colony before the revolution", and, of the hysteria of 1741, argued that "ignorance and illiberal prejudices universally prevailed" whereas, "the advantages of a liberal, indeed of the plainest education, were the happy lot of very few," in an isolated and hyper-provincial society. For the editor, such passions had departed in his own "more favoured and enlightened" time, so much so that the ethos of pre-Revolutionary times required careful explanation!

Official toleration of Catholicism, begun in wartime, and everywhere upheld by implication in the freedom-of-religion clauses of the new constitutions, or by new law (as in Virginia), worked a double revolution where the Irish were concerned. It enabled them to emerge to collective visibility, to organise and associate as such, and to build the Catholic institutions which for over a century were to be the principal instruments of their cohesion. Secondly, it enabled the Catholic Church itself to come out from the corners of a side-show toleration, into the arena of growth, order, and increasing populousness in the port cities of the nation. If to other Americans, the relations between the two groups (Irish and Catholic) were so clear as to become identical, this was not so to either Irish laymen, or to Catholic leaders. Active Catholics in the past had been disproportionately Anglo-American (in Maryland, where descendants of the old English Catholic settlers were a twelfth of the inhabitants), or German (in Pennsylvania). The tone of the Church, under the new and first bishop John Carroll (consecrated 1790) of Baltimore, despite his remote Irish descent, was strongly Anglo-American. Possible tensions arising from the possession of Irish servants by the Maryland gentry have never been examined: but tension of a more general nature there certainly was. To John Carroll, Irish priests were useful only when others were unobtainable: he wrote Archbishop Troy of Dublin that they were greedier for a higher standard of living than America could afford. On the other hand, the rapid Americanisation of Irish immigrant laymen, their initiative in the establishment of many congregations and their crude or broad familiarity with Protestant theories of lay status, caused them to seek power in their congregations to a degree then quite unacceptable in canon law, and intrusive of bitter nationality issues into essentially pastoral questions: a problem which mushroomed into controversy over whether Catholic churches should have 'Lay Trustees' in legal control of their property.

Nonetheless, the establishment and growth of the Catholic Church can be seen as the first realisation of (native) Irish America's collective future: within a decade, John Carroll himself accepted the connection quite fully. In 1785 there were few more than 25,000 practising Catholics in the colonies, apparently few of them Irish. Thereafter, the institution of new parishes became a mapping of native Irish emergence, largely by immigration, but also probably because thousands long in America now renewed their past, making themselves known to Church authorities. Thus in New York, St. Peters in 1783, in Boston, a parish in 1788, in Baltimore, St. Peters in 1775, St. Patricks in 1795, and St. Johns in 1799, in Alexandria, St. Marys in 1795, in Albany, St. Marys in 1797, in New Castle, Delaware, St. Marys in 1790 (although unorganised services dated back beyond 1772), in Charleston, St. Marys in 1788. These were established before the turn of the century as the availability of priests allowed; all were in port cities (even Albany was a strong river port). Others were of course added to those existing in Philadelphia since around 1730. Thereafter there was something of a pause, despite the 1808 sub-division of Carroll's gargantuan all-America Baltimore archdiocese into additional diocese of dioceses of Boston, New York, Philadelphia and Bardstown (Kentucky). Rapid further expansion began with the heavy immigration after 1815. This too suggests that erstwhile unpractising ex-indentured servants were the nucleus of the first 'Irish expansion' in the immediate post-revolutionary decades. The availability of such religious and community life can hardly be separated from the re-definition of America as a popular and hospitable

The first Cabinet: Knox, Jefferson, Randolph, Hamilton, Washington, 1790

republic when one considers the attractions that would draw more Irish attention toward America. Coupled with improved communication of its economic opportunities *outside* of bondage, the message, once received, would be a forceful one. Community, livelihood and religious freedom, all were waiting in one society,—the same attraction that had already been drawing Ulstermen to the middle colonies for over fifty years.

For Ulster Presbyterian Americans, all this should have meant the beginning of the end of *their* Irish America. But only in Philadelphia was this realised, and even there not until after 1800. For in the short term, the American Revolution brought the recognition and prosperity which the Scotch-Irish had only marginally possessed before it. Office-holding offers one key to this. If the Revolution brought most Catholic Irish acceptance and opportunity, rather than wealth or influence, it brought the Scotch-Irish and the pro-American Anglo-Irish integration within the power structures of those colonies where they had the connections or popular base to sustain it. Almost exactly a century would pass before the Catholic Irish would stake such a bold claim. We have seen the state-by-state situation where the Scotch-Irish were powerful (or the Anglo-Irish well connected as in the Carolinas). Nationally, the gains were important, although not so secure: it was, I believe, partly to sustain them, that the Scotch-Irish became so rancorously involved in the politics of the Washington and Adams presidencies. It is an axiom among historians that revolutions telescope development which otherwise occur more slowly. The mass of nineteenth century Irish Americans had to wait three or four decades until they achieved substantial municipal power in the 1870s and 1880s, five or six decades until they gained important congressional representation in the 1890s and permanently after 1912, and almost a century until they were fully integrated into the national power structure and the federal judiciary, after 1932: the exceptions, such as California in the 1850s, or token national office under Cleveland, McKinley, and Wilson, only emphasise the overall pattern. The American revolutionary era ensured that the Scotch-Irish and Anglo-Irish made these gains all but simultaneously: local state power, congressional representation, national office and high judicial appointment, all came between 1773–1783, and were confirmed thereafter. Considering that the bulk of the immigrants (although *not* of their representative office-holders) came between 1760–1775, such gains were a dramatic vindication of their support of the revolution. Furthermore, even Irish Catholics gained a disproportionate prominence in the American Revolutionary era which would not return to them for a century.

A full chronology of office-holders would be tedious, but the well-known highlights may be briefly summarized. Charles Thomson was Secretary to the Continental Congress from 1775–1790, both because of previous expertise, and because of his role in revolutionary Pennsylvania, "the life of the cause of liberty," as John Adams put it. George Bryan chaired key legislative committees in Pennsylvania from 1779, was vice-president of the commonwealth 1777-9, president in 1778, and a justice of its supreme court from 1780–1791. George Taylor was a member of Pennsylvania's assembly, its representative to the Continental Congress and a member of its Supreme Executive Council between 1775–77, his career terminated only by ill-health. James McHenry served as Washington's secretary 1778–80, as a member of the Maryland senate, 1781–86, as a member of Congress, 1783–86, and as a Maryland delegate to the Constitutional Convention of 1787. William Irvine, Anthony Wayne, William Thomson, Edward Hand, Richard Montgomery and Richard Butler were respectively commissioned brigadier-, major- and full generals in the Continental armies by Congress, and saw important service in the middle colonies and northern campaigns: they not unnaturally tended to be pro-Federalist nationalists after 1787. On the other hand, the Pennsylvania militia forces were likewise heavily Irish in generalship: John Armstrong, James Ewing, James Potter and Andrew Porter were their key generals, and became zealous partisans of Scotch-Irish Pennsylvania particularism and opponents of Federalism after 1787. All these figures were Irish-born. But the second generation was likewise powerfully represented: of Thomas McKean, member of the Delaware Assembly, and of Congress from 1774–83 (its president in 1781), ultimately Chief-Justice of Pennsylvania, 1777–99, it was rightly said of him by John Adams that he "saw more clearly to the end of the business" of independence than any other member of Congress. George Read was Delaware delegate to Congress throughout the period, and to the 1787 Convention and Joseph Reed, of the third generation, was president of Pennsylvania. Taylor, McKean and Read signed the Declaration of Independence, together with Irish-born James Smith, another Pennsylvania assembly member and militia leader. Irvine and Armstrong also served in Congress. Such names are not fortuitous: they represent the points of prominence of a movement elevating all the Protestant Irish in the middle colonies. William Paterson of New Jersey and John McKinly of Delaware likewise interlock with the pattern.

Elsewhere, there is a more random character to the elevation: it is less a matter of the upgrading of a community, so much as the fact of Irishmen and their children being beneficiaries of the general opportunities of American life as offered more notably in revolution. Nonetheless, one does have a sense that previous patterns of prejudice were giving way to enable even such cases to occur. In short, in the Carolinas or in newer or post-frontier New England, one senses something of the California of Senator David Broderick in the 1850s: men were taken at their merits, and the exigencies of creating a new political society gave the main chance to the boldest of them. Note Wicklow-born Matthew Lyon from Vermont, an adjunct commander to Ethan Allen, Montgomery and Gates in the northern campaigns. He became an industrialist and pioneer politician, active in Vermont's committee of public safety, and the chief developer of Fair Haven. Thus too the droll and dark little Limerick-born physician, Matthew Thornton, chairman of the revolutionary committee in Londonderry, New Hampshire, speaker of the state's assembly, chairman of its constitutional convention, associate justice of its superior court, and delegate to Congress for one year, 1776: a term well-chosen to give him some immortality as one of the signatories! Most vital of all were the Sullivans, James (1744–1808) and John (1740–1795), brothers from northern New England, where their immigrant father was a schoolmaster in Maine. James was active in revolutionary committees in Maine (then the northern part of Massachusetts), a member of the state's legislature and justice of its supreme court, 1776–83. In that year he was elected to Congress, and widened the scope of his political connections, while building a practice as one of the state's most skilled and wealthy lawyers. His brother John, the more famous, also a lawyer, was perhaps less disciplined. Active in New Hampshire revolutionary politics, he was commissioned by Congress (after election to it), and saw service in the major campaigns from Boston, 1775, through Brandywine, Germantown, and Valley Forge, 1777–78. In 1779, he burnt himself out in the western Pennsylvania campaigns and returned to politics: to Congress, to New Hampshire's constitutional convention and the attorney-generalship of the state, 1782–86, and its governorship, 1786–90. The Sullivans and Thornton were far from conformists: their traits were generally seen as Irish, again suggestive of the tolerance induced even among the Yankees by the Revolution. More attuned to New Englander styles was General Henry Knox, together with Wayne and Montgomery the most prominent of all Irish American generals, himself an American born Boston bookseller of Ulster parentage. Knox was as methodical and controlled as Sullivan was brash and spirited.

In the south, major Anglo-Irish revolutionary careers were those of Pierce Butler, John and Edward Rutledge and the Thomas Lynches of the Carolinas in politics; and among Scotch-Irish military careers those of Francis Marion, Daniel Morgan, Andrew Pickens and Andrew Lewis, key subordinates to Washinton and Greene in the southern campaigns. The former like the New England examples, were very much their own men; the latter, however, played key roles in swinging the Scotch-Irish backcountry into active and continuous armed opposition to the British (which insensitive American commanders like Charles Lee might otherwise have jeopardised).

None of the foregoing were Catholic, despite, in the case of Lyon and the Sullivans, Catholic background and clearly native Irish antipathies to the English. Yet the revolution, as noted, extended to a more open perception of Catholics, although never an enthusiastic one. It is indeed the *partial* quality of the new attitudes that helps explain the caution and diffidence with which Irish Catholics seemed to receive their new status. Consistency to the principles of 1776; the necessities of a united patriot front in the middle colonies; the importance of weaning indecisive indentured Irishmen to the revolution; a knowledge among a minority in Virginia and Pennsylvania that the European Catholicism of the Enlightenment was not that of the Austrian or Spanish Counter-Reformation; the impossibility of creating a new freedom for Baptists, Presbyterians and others without extending it to Catholics (lest the revolution be accused of hypocrisy); the chance to win Quebec to the revolution; the danger that the new toleration towards Catholicism shown in English, Irish and Canadian legislation turn Catholic Americans and immigrants to Tories; above all, the effect of alliance with France and Spain, all these factors made for a new atmosphere. Yet since for most uneducated and semi-educated Americans, the vast majority, Popery remained a symbol of tyranny (we would say, of the totalitarian), rather than the living religion of anyone they actually knew, the issue was more academic than Catholic historians have allowed. Now that liberty could be affirmed in arms and constitutions, it was no longer necessary to affirm it negatively by attacking an imaginary Romanism. The central use of anti-Popery, a not ignoble one as such (although bearing little relationship to Catholicism), was thus removed at a stroke.

Unfortunately, very little is known about the attitudes of the Scotch-Irish revolutionaries in Pennsylvania to these new exigencies. For them alone, Maryland apart, Catholicism had a real dimension, although one inextricably linked into their political past. It is notable, however, that there seems to have been no opposition from them to the extension of full civic and political rights to Catholics in 1775–6. But on the other hand, it is significant that the Catholic appointed to the inter-denominational Board of Trustees of the Presbyterian-controlled University of Pennsylvania was Fr. Ferdinand Steinmeyer, alias Farmer, a German: the Scotch-Irish had few difficulties getting along with the German Catholics of Lancaster county and Germantown (the Philadelphia suburb); it was the native Irish they drew back from. (Indeed in 1844, in largely Irish Orange riots in Philadelphia against Catholic churches, German Catholic churches were always left alone). In short, there is no reason to believe that the revolutionary Scotch-Irish commitment to universal civic rights for whites was insincere. Just as later in Belfast (after 1783) the Ulster Protestant Volunteers drew back from the full implications of their rhetoric, so in Pennsylvania the tragic constraints of hereditary hatreds proved too much for them. They helped negate Joseph Reed's hope, (written to the ex-Catholic *philosophe*, Abbé Guillaume Raynal), that the revolutionary state's new university be founded "on Principles of universal catholicism, embracing all Professions of the Christian Religion which are formed and organised among us".

Cautionly patriotism seems to have been the hall-mark of the careers of the Catholic Irish involved in the revolution. Not that they were backward. Garrett and George Meade and John Mease were among the first signatories of Philadelphia's 1765 non-importation agreements. In character they were very different: George Meade was self-sacrificingly patriotic, contributing and even lending on the never-never large sums to sustain the revolutionary cause, and feed and clothe its armies; Mease, by contrast, was a war profiteer. Yet neither sought the public office taken as a matter of course by most men of their means at that time. Thomas FitzSimons, the Meade's brother-in-law, did serve: on the Philadelphia Council of Safety and its Navy Board, in Congress from 1782 and in the Constitutional Convention in 1787 as a strong

Federalist. He had joined with Robert Morris and others in 1781 in establishing the Bank of North America and was the brain of patriotic finance among eastern Irishmen (as Ulsterman Oliver Pollock was in the west). The many services of Charles Carroll to the cause of revolution in Maryland from its beginnings, to the move for independence, to Congress from 1776–78, and to the attempt to win Quebec to the revolution, are often given as the pre-eminent Irish-American participation of the era; but Carroll was thoroughly assimilated to the mores of Maryland's Anglo-Catholic and Americanised community, and several generations removed from Ireland. It could be said that his own diffidence (he unquestionably could have achieved more prominent offices nationally and locally), set the pattern for the explicitly Irish Catholics: there was a certain common sense, but also a certain irony, in the pen-name of his revolutionary-era polemics: 'Second Citizen.' Ironically, too, he survived a very long life to become an initiator of the Baltimore-Ohio railroad, thus in himself a link between the aristocratic Irish emigrés of the seventeenth century, the revolutionary era, and the hordes of Irish labourers who built America's rail network in the nineteenth century.

Carroll joined with Thomas FitzSimons, Dominick Lynch (the wealthiest of New York's Irish merchants) and his cousins Daniel Carroll and Bishop John Carroll to send the "Address of the Roman Catholics" to George Washington in 1790. Strongly Federalist in tone, conservative too in its assumption that a handful of near-aristocrats could speak for all Catholics, the document epitomised the cautious sense of second citizenship. However unacceptable today, then it was a positive breakthrough from the pariah status which had been the formal lot of Irish Catholics almost everywhere (outside continental Europe) until then: it was the citizenship, they realised, was the gain, and the secondary status a small price to pay for it. Clearly they believed it to be as yet a precarious gain, for the Address was a strangely old-fashioned bid, like an appeal to a monarch, to have George Washington set his protection over them (to which Washington replied in kind. Continue to earn it!):

> whilst our country preserves her freedom and independence, we shall have a well-founded title to claim from her justice equal rights of citizenship as the price of our blood spilt under your eyes, and of our common exertions for her defence, under your auspicious conduct; rights rendered more dear to us by the remembrance of former hardships. When we pray for the preservation of them, where they have been granted, and expect the full extention of them from the justice of those states, which still restrict them . . . we conceive that no human means are so available to promote the welfare of the united states, as the prolongation of your life and health.

For the Protestant Irish, then, the revolution was complete; for the Catholic Irish, it was but a beginning, at once precarious and welcome.

Yet the ordinary Irish immigrant Catholic, then less religious than his leaders or his successors, had more interest in his day-to-day status. This too markedly improved as a result of the revolution. As slavery fell into question with the ideals of 1776 and the dangers of British propaganda among blacks, so too did indentured servitude. In an unnoted pamphlet, "Observations on the Slaves and Indented Servants, inlisted in the Army, and the Navy of the United States" (Philadelphia, 1777), an anonymous thinker, 'Antibiastes' argued that both forms of bondage were inconsistent with the genius of the revolution and the exigencies of active and courageous military service: they should be abolished. Thomas Jefferson's well-known ruminations on the same problem where blacks were involved were painfully turned to the question of bond servitude by a persistent French editor. Jefferson's prose, here as often constrained by his conscious need to put a good face upon America (something few American historians admit of their philosopher king), reveals a strange mixture of injured rectitude, genuine thought, and shrewd common sense. It also illuminates the intensification of the process of migration from Ireland after 1783:

> So desirous are the poor of Europe to get to America, where they may better their condition that, being unable to pay their passage, they will agree to serve two or three years on their arrival there, rather than not go. During the time of that service they are better fed, better clothed, and have lighter labour than while in Europe. Continuing to work for hire for a few years longer, they buy a farm, marry, and enjoy the sweets of a domestic society of their own. The American gov[ernments] are censured for permitting a species of ser[vitude] which lays the foundation of the happiness of these people . . . Those who know the situation of the poor in Europe and America would say that this is the alternative that humanity dictates.

Others were not so sure. In 1784, citizens of New York purchased the freedom of a cargo of servants, since "the traffick of White People, heretofore countenanced . . . under the arbitary control of the British Government, is contrary . . . to the idea of liberty." And around the same time, the Irish of Philadelphia (of all kinds, probably) prevented the purchase of Irish bond servants by two affluent free blacks, and forced the legislature there to pass a law preventing such a situation from arising again. However, reports in Irish newspapers in 1788 of the ill-treatment of servants in America, and the availability of other work there (as probably of relatives to pay passages) cut heavily into the proportions of Irish immigrants coming as redemptioners and bondsmen in that decade, and after 1800, although not formally abolished, the trade trickled away.

With the decline of servitude at one end of the social scale, came a remarkable opening up of opportunity for the native Irish at the other. Already by the turn of the century, towns such as Albany and New York were developing the beginnings of an Irish Catholic mercantile élite, created as such by non-Catholics. Although difficult to prove, it seems likely that wider recognition that these rich Irish could so Americanize, helped make the poorer immigrants more acceptable: the coincidence of chronology is otherwise too striking between the emergence of such a middle class and the beginnings of mass free Catholic immigration. For Philadelphia, of course, this pattern had long existed.

Party Politics, 1787–1800

We can but summarise this theme very briefly. If the American Revolution had re-defined man as a self-directed political being in his very nature, rather than a spiritual or cultural being incidentally political, then the Irish were only too well suited to this realistic if overly narrow re-definition of life. Politicised to the core, it is hardly surprising that they became involved in the politics of the new nation to the virtual exclusion of everything else at first (1780s–90s). Thereafter they began to relax somewhat. Past experience, the bucketloads of wartime propaganda, the anxieties of an unsettled economy, the uncertainties of a rapidly changing collective status, the impact of secularisation (or worldliness!), all predisposed the Irish (of every kind) to see the political issues of the period in somewhat starker terms than other Americans. For them, the matter was intensified by the brightening hopes and savage disenchantment of the politics of Ireland in those two decades. If they had played the part of actors rather than creators during the revolutionary period, the very vitality of their embroilment in post-revolutionary politics helped shape the one central political institution not envisaged by the state and federal constitutions: the party system. Likewise they helped mould the accoutrements of that system, above all that of a strident and partisan journalism, with a rhetoric designed to shake apathetic voters into the belief that their future happiness and security depended upon returning a few individuals to power for one year, two, four, or at most six (depending upon the office).

The Irish, (Scotch, Anglo- and ordinary), split greviously over the question of replacing the loose and ineffective articles of Confederation with a new constitution. The central split was unrelated to the Irish past: that which fissured the Scotch-Irish pro-revolutionary bloc for good. Roughly put, it seems that the eastern, commercialised and more educated Scotch-Irish were strong protagonists of the Federal Constitution of 1787, but that the countrymen either opposed it or were apathetic. The Constitution replaced the loose E.E.C.-style confederation of sovereign states, which further lacked an executive, a civil service, and any independent tax base. In its place came the present system, at least in germ, with strong executive centring upon a national presidency, a federal judiciary, and a potentially powerful national legislature in command of a national tax base, of national commerce and of the future of the vast western territories. Everywhere the Scotch-Irish divided, as the new American political theory expected they should, according to where they saw their interests lie. McKean of Pennsylvania, Paterson of New Jersey, George Read of Delaware, Henry Knox of Massachussetts, and James McHenry of Maryland (he had removed to Baltimore from Pennsylvania) were among the leaders of the pro-Federalist Scotch Irish. All were professional men and professional politicians to whom the Revolution, as well as their business interests, had given wide, national horizons. All believed in a society in which elders had the decisive leadership, while earning it by attention to the public good and by unremitting industry. Yet they divided on specifics. As delegates to the Federal Convention from small states, Paterson and Read fought

William Paterson (1745-1806)

against any system which shared national power according to population distribution. Paterson also took the lead in insisting upon a clear division of powers within the constitution. McHenry, another delegate, was somewhat inactive. Anomalously among western territories, the Valley of Virginia also supported the new constitution, for it was linked by trade with the eastern ports via the Great Road and the navigable James and Potomac rivers, which they hoped to see improved: William Fleming, William McKee and Andrew Moore were its chief Scotch-Irish Federalist leaders, although not unopposed. Elsewhere inland, the Scotch-Irish were generally anti-Federalist or indifferent, with the exception of a handful of educated officers such as William Thompson and William Irvine of the continental forces. The anti-Federalists were led by James Smith and by the militia generals, Armstrong, Potter and Ewing, together with the newer leaders of the Ulster American westerners, Findley and Whitehill. It was very much a battle both of principles and of styles, and difficult to know where one left off and the other began: to the western and militia leaders, it seemed as though a pretentious new élite was attempting to build an arrogant ascendancy on the ruins of local liberties. One suspects too, knowing Ulstermen, that local leaders envied and mistrusted the acceptance which the easterners and continental officers had found with sophisticated Anglo-Americans such as Washington and Adams, as they did in Ulster those who found favour with the ascendancy. But Federalism was closer to the political science of Alison, as to the social prejudices he gave most of his students.

Because of Pennsylvania's peculiar polarisation during the revolution, as well as because of their generally more national, conservative and even élitist horizons, the bulk of the Anglo-Irish were pro-Federalist: Wayne, Hand, Ormsby, and others. The exception was George Bryan, who unlike them did not come from a background which benefited from a stratified society and a concentrated government in Ireland, but from the southern Irish dissenters who suffered from these. He and his son inspired a series of *Centinel* papers (the same title Alison had given his anti-episcopacy papers twenty years before) which, in the defence of states' rights pointed precisely to the abuse of national power in Ireland. Elsewhere, the Anglo-Irish and those assimilated to their mores strongly supported the new Constitution: the Rutledges in South Carolina, and even Pierce Butler, despite his championship of the back-country. Those elements of the Anglo-Irish merchant communities of New York and Philadelphia represented in the local Societies of St. Patrick, and their offshoots elsewhere, were likewise Federalist.

So too, generally, were the Catholic Irish. They mistrusted the tendency of local politics to turn sectarian and demagogic, and trusted the wider horizons of national politicians who stood above such concerns and kept an eye on international opinion. In Pennsylvania, for example, the very fact that the local revolutionary militia (quite apart from its Presbyterian tang) was named the Associators, may have suggested echoes of the anti-Catholic militia of Jack Coode's uprising in Maryland in the 1690s; and the Sons of St. Tammany,

William Irvine (1741-1804)

radically democratic, were also passively anti-Catholic. On the other hand, Washington had made such gestures as banning 'Pope Day' in the army, dining with the Sons of St. Patrick, befriending Stephen Moylan in his distant way and ensuring some other Catholic commissions. The very conservatism of the Catholic community, its vertical organisation and the transAtlantic outlook of its leaders, likewise inclined it to Federalism. FitzSimons was a delegate to the 1787 convention. Immigrant journalist Mathew Carey supported the ideal of a strong and natively industrialised American republic, and hence supported the new Constitution. The Carrolls helped to ensure its ratification in Maryland.

Although in 1787–90 some Scotch-Irish leaders, notably Smith and Potter, were bitter about the new constitution, there was never a concerted opposition to it among them. Had there been a general get-out-the-vote campaign in their constituencies, it is possible that ratification might have been prevented. Most voters apparently believed it immaterial to their local concerns and liberties. The real party feeling came later, with the actual development of the new Federal system in the presidencies of Washington and Adams. The former was not insensitive to Irish claims: James McHenry, Ballymena-born soldier and politician, was made secretary of war in 1796 and given considerable influence over patronage appointments. Anthony Wayne and Henry Knox received major military assignments. James Cathcart became a consul in the Mediterranean. From amongst the Catholics, John Barry was appointed senior captain of the reconstituted American navy in 1794. But this was not enough.

The Jay treaty normalising relations with Britain was bitterly opposed by many Irish at a time when Ireland's political needs remained unmet. But it was crucial to the Federalists' design of a reconstructed national economy. Even the powerful Thomas McKean, ever Anglophobic, abandoned them over it, despite his deepening social conservatism. In 1798, the coincidence of the United Irish insurrection, worsening relations with revolutionary France, and deteriorating political feeling in America swung almost the entire Irish community behind the new opposition of Jefferson and Madison. Only the élite of Anglo-Irish officers and merchants and the Catholic mercantile group of the seaboard cities stayed with the Federalists. Mathew Carey, despite his preference for a strong national economy went over to the 'Republicans' as the opposition was called. It seems clear that New Englander John Adams (1796–1800) lacked that inter-ethnic political touch Washington had gained as early as the Seven Years War. His problems were compounded when he supervised the passage of the Alien and Sedition Laws, permitting the deportation of unwanted aliens and extending the period necessary for naturalisation up to fourteen years. Maldwyn A. Jones has estimated that between 1783–1815, at least 100,000 immigrants came from Ireland at a time of intense anti-English feeling amongst almost all sections of the lower classes, Protestant and Catholic, from whom most immigrants were drawn. The Federalist vision of society (élitist, strongly nationalist, with a good understanding with Britain and distrust of revolutionary France) must have

James McHenry, Federalist Secretary for War. (1753-1816)

chilled somewhat their vision of America, and the application of the Alien and Sedition Laws did even more so. Ironically, amongst the first to be prosecuted for seditious libel was Matthew Lyon, now a Republican congressman from Vermont: the guilty verdict served to make him a hero to the urban crowds of the middle colonies. Shortly afterwards, Irish America became convinced that the Adams administration intended to keep United Irish refugees out of the country: this sealed their general drift to the Jeffersonian Republicans. So bitter was feeling that the lower class Protestant Irish Philadelphians mobbed the sedate congregation of Catholic St. Mary's when its more prominent Federalist laity (headed by FitzSimons) refused to sign petitions against the Alien and Sedition Acts.

By 1800 and the election of Jefferson, the bulk of the lower and middle class Scotch Irish and Irish Catholics were Republican: and the arriving United Irish leadership furnished them unparalleled (if not fully knowledgeable!) political leadership in its support, though various Hibernian societies and the re-constituted Tammany societies of New York and Philadelphia. James Mac Nevin, Thomas Addis Emmett, David Warden, Robert Patterson, Rowan Hamilton, and others were among them, managing to steer a cautious course over the potentially divisive Catholic/Protestant issue, (which proved lethal in Philadelphia), by stressing common American goals and exploiting a common American Irish nostalgia for the broken dream of a United Irishry. Meantime a host of able if almost rabid Irish immigrant journalists savagely lampooned the Federalists and praised the Jeffersonians: John Daly Burk, William Duane, Thomas Branagan, and, more moderately, Carey and Robert Walsh. It is difficult not to conclude that United Irish ideals and revolutionary democratic ideology did make sense to these men: as though in the context of America, the dreams which continuously broke upon the intractable ground of Ireland, took flesh amidst the perpetual motion and constant intercourse with strangers that *was* America. If closer acquaintance, such as in Philadelphia's Tammany society, proved such dreams socially inadequate to inherited antagonism, this does not negate their force at the time. There was plenty of room in America for two different kinds of Irish people with mutual, if distant, respect and with the one shared party and ideology, the Republican. And much of their exiled United Irishism seemed rooted in the hope that a roominess of spirit could achieve in Ireland what a roominess of space and opportunity achieved in America: a dubious proposition, but only amidst general poverty and ignorance then endemic.

It also reflected something else: the beginning of a synthetic yet legitimate Irish American culture, in part a response to the more clearly defined American nationality which the post–1783 immigrants encountered. Presbyterian immigrants were among its chief creators for on balance (being better educated) they were more conversant with the post-Ossianic romantic revival of Celticism and yet far enough away from Gaelic culture (unlike the native Irish immigrants) to romanticise it. The United Irishmen had logically been drawn to noble and spurious glues with which to cement an emergent

Robert Smith, Jeffersonian Secretary of the Navy, (1757-1842)

Irish nationality: French republican civic religion, a broad cultural nationalism. The first found fruitful soil in their politics in America, the second took off into fairyland, not without attracting such sober Americans as John Quincy Adams on the way. A Larne-born hunchback physician, merchant, novelist and poet was its chief manifestation: the *other* James McHenry (1785–1845).

Jefferson recognised all this support to a greater degree than has been noticed. He, and not Presidents Buchanan or Cleveland, began the technique of rewarding the Irish vote, but in sensibly oblique ways consonant with his policies. Perhaps he recognised that the American children of the Scotch-Irish were regarded amongst themselves as their own still. Robert Smith, son of Strabane-born John Smith, became Secretary of the Navy in 1801; his brother Samuel, a more powerful figure politically (and like Robert a Baltimore merchant), was Jeffersonian Senator from Maryland. Robert Patterson, the mathematician, United Irish exile and vice-president of the University of Pennsylvania, was appointed director of the federal mint in 1805. Meanwhile McKean had turned from his judicial office to politics again, winning the governorship of Pennsylvania successively from 1799–1809, once again moderating the radical thrust of his new party and swinging the state to Jefferson in two national elections: a Scotch-Irish encore!

For a period, through the inauguration of Andrew Jackson perhaps, it seemed as though the two Irelands might even coalesce in a spacious America. But mass southern immigration, beginning around 1830, doomed that possibility. Intensifying job competition amongst the over-supplied Irish handloom weavers of Philadelphia, Protestant and Catholic, fanned the dying embers of sectarian animosity. In 1844, the Ulster Protestants of Kensington, a Philadelphia suburb, exploded against their Irish Catholic neighbours. The vast famine immigration was only three years away. When it subsided, after ten years innundation, little was left of the Ulster America and Irish America brought into focus by the revolutionary era, and into coalescence by the politics of Jefferson and the United Irish exiles. Nor did the bewilderment, excitement, and raw manipulation which the Irish newcomers found in an industrialising America make their adjustment to the new land an easy one. That so many of them were countrymen, often Irish speaking, compounded their task. Yet the inheritance of an older and revolutionary America mitigated the strains of their earlier years: of exploitation, casual labour, and nativist American hostility. It provided them with the ideology and instruments of self-respect, social advancement and political power, and found them more friends among native Americans sensitive to their grade-school lessons in American ideology than has often been thought. It even helped to recruit to their defence a not inconsiderable minority of Protestant Irish emigrés. It is scarcely surprising that the Irish immigrants were among the most virulent enthusiasts of the revolutionary heritage during the first centennial in 1876, a time of recession and violence. Correctly, they saw in it the promise of civic equality in face of the inequities unleashed by industrialism. Their descendants in 1976,

Winter Scene in Brooklyn, 1810

beneficiaries of a suburban transformation, have been notably more restrained, even muddled, in their celebration.

Promises Fulfilled and Expectant: The United States after 1800

The conventional wisdom in the new United Kingdom of Great Britain and Ireland, and in the United States of America, was not dissimilar in certain broad respects. Thus men in both countries had certain similar expectations of the Act of Union on the one hand, and the accession to power of Thomas Jefferson on the other. Many hoped that in each case a sweeping solution had been found for the ills of a society distracted by incessant division, sectional bitterness, and élitist pretensions at the expense of the common good: a description certainly applicable to Ireland before 1800, and believed to be true of the Federalists' America by the over-heated Jeffersonian Republicans. A politics of suspicion and self-protection, believed both William Pitt and Thomas Jefferson, could now be replaced by less fevered activities of national development. In America, the return of considerably more autonomy to states and localities after the tentative centralising of the Federalists would allow the private energies of the new nation full play, and ensure that farmers and artisans gained the full measure of their productive labour. In Ireland, by contrast, many believed that Catholics and Protestants could now exercise their energies under the auspices of a fair umpire, the British government, in the challenging free marketplace of a great empire. Many, particularly Catholic leaders, assumed that Catholic Emancipation would follow Union, as Pitt had promised, and exaggerated its economic benefits. In both cases, élites supposedly had impaired the beneficent workings of the natural order which otherwise would thereby produce wealth and diffuse its effects naturally: in Ireland, the Ascendancy through its control of separate institutions in Dublin in a narrow interest; in America, a mercantile group in Philadelphia and New York by turning federal government to their own advantage. These groups had now been ousted from power in Dublin and Washington, D.C.

Despite the vast differences between the conservatism of the ministry of the younger William Pitt, and the optimistic republicanism of Jefferson's party; despite the real paralysis of Ireland's élite against the constructive merits of America's (the Jeffersonians could not see the latter); despite the obvious gulf between a solution which relocated and reconcentrated power, from Ireland to London, and one which dismantled and redistributed it, in effect if not law, in America, yet the analogy could hold more meaning for a generation convinced that most constructive human activity was non-political than it does for our own. Politics would now be tamed, simplified; in both instances, an era of good feelings might hopefully ensue. That a new century was dawning intensified the hope. Hamilton Rowan, the exiled United Irishman, vainly trying to establish a calico-printing business on the Delaware, who feared America's Federalists and sympathised with the Republicans, believed that the Act of Union might have good effects, curtailing aristocracy and liberating talent; if few other emigrants agreed with him ("I am almost sent to Coventry here by the Irish, for my opinion"), such grounds were more commonly held in Ireland amongst all creeds.

But the nineteenth century was to betray that hope. Political institutions do affect the scope of even the more unpolitical human capacities, and those established under the Union helped ensure that nineteenth century Ireland could not draw the world's eyes to a continuing contribution to modern learning towards which its real and wide interest in arts and science might otherwise have led. On the other hand, the institutions of the United States helped foster a range of Irish activity unparalleled at home, the more remarkable when it is remembered that the mass of Irish emigrants continued to be countrymen of only basic skills, and that even the majority of their high achievers in the United States were of a sort who at home should have remained constrained to the routine tasks of an impecunious gentry and middle class. Several examples in the period before 1820 illustrate these ideas, which were to become commonplace even at that time, yet no less persuasive for that.

Christopher Colles, a man of "the most diminutive frame and the most gigantic conceptions, the humblest demeanour and the boldest projects," born in Dublin in 1739, was something of a visionary in his driving determination to wed America's future to technology. Educated by Richard Pococke in Kilkenny in maths, geography, engineering and science, and advanced by his teacher when the latter became Protestant bishop of Ossory, Colles worked on the Kilkenny-Inistioge Canal and directed the building of the Limerick Customs House. In 1771 he came to Philadelphia, lecturing for awhile, and early publishing his conviction that America must systematically, rather than haphazardly, develop labour-saving devices (*Pennsylvania Packet*, 22 September 1773). John Dunlap from Strabane published his *Syllabus . . . in Natural Experimental Philosophy* the same year, a compendium of hydrostatics, hydraulics, mechanics, pneumatics and geography. His lectures increasingly emphasised the need to transform the theory of these fields into practice. He was completing a project to supply New York City with fresh water by a system of reservoirs, conduits and steam engines when interrupted by the war of the revolution. Fleeing the approaching British, he lent his services to the Patriots, training John Lamb—deputy to Henry Knox who was commander of the Continental Artillery—in gunnery principles; he probably served as an artillery adviser himself. His revolutionary travels and experiences re-awakened his interest in canals. He suggested the improvement of the Ohio river system for full navigation, writing George Washington on the subject. The next two years, 1784–85, he developed his grand scheme of *Proposals for the Speedy Settlement of the Waste and Unappropriated Lands on the Western Frontiers of New York*, which envisaged the construction of a system of internal waterways linking Albany on the Hudson with Oswego on Lake Ontario. He argued further that this would transform New York city into the entrepot for the Great Lakes basin. Thus the city would expand, upstate regions be settled and the lakes area developed. Incredibly, the New York legislature turned down the proposal, although the Clinton family supported it: perhaps George Clinton, the anti-Federalist governor, was sympathetic to Colles since his own father was an Anglo-Irish immigrant from Longford. Ultimately his son, in turn also governor, De Witt Clinton, was to act upon Colles' vision, which he acknowledged. In 1816, he attended Colles' funeral. The next year he encouraged the state legislature to approve such a scheme, and between 1818 and 1826 the Erie Canal was built, linking the Hudson (and thus the Atlantic) with Lake Erie. Colles thus lost credit for his scheme, and his importance has only lately been re-established. A man inured to rebuff, he turned his attention elsewhere, he planned a survey of the roads of America. In 1790, the U.S. Congress turned the idea down, but he went ahead with the aid of private subscribers who included Washington and Jefferson, eventually producing a road survey and atlas patterned on Taylor and Skinner's *Maps of the Roads of Ireland* of 1778. Further continuing his schemes to accelerate American development by annihilating distance, he planned a semaphoric telegraph system to link Maine to New Orleans, and hoped that the exigencies of the War of 1812 would secure its adoption. Again he was disappointed: only a fragment of the system was made to link New York City and New Jersey in 1816. This and the improvement of the Connecticut river navigation were the sole life-time material achievements of the man, whose restless and practical enthusiasms presaged the later development of the American spirit. So different were Americans then, that at his death, the *New York Gazette* noted that "notwithstanding his mechanical eccentricities" he was "respected by all who knew him". A contemporary, Dr. J. W. Francis, noted that "his cavernous gray eyes . . . betokened a resigned spirit," for the "little weather-beaten old man" remained "naturally cheerful and bouyant, at times pensive, yet free from any corrosive melancholy". It may well have been that Colles was sustained by the admiration in which he was held by men like De Witt Clinton and Cadwallader Colden, and understood that ultimately his talented designs would find their fulfilment, prompted as they were by profound consideration of America's environment.

Colles' counterpart among Catholic Irish enthusiasts for the new nation was Mathew Carey. The son of a Dublin businessman and army contractor, Mathew worked as a journalist in Dublin between 1779–84, his radicalism bringing him within the outer limits of the political ferment of those years. Fleeing to America, he at once immersed himself in the world of Philadelphia's newspapers, this time at the conservative end of a very different political spectrum, allied with Catholic and other mercantile proponents of federalism. Maturing and marrying, he launched himself as a precarious publisher. Gradually he built himself toward real success. His determination to redesign his Irish trade of publisher/writer to the demands of a vast country paralleled that of Colles. He understood the country's trifold urge for literature which was practical, moral and escapist (preferably all together), launched scores of

Mathew Carey (1760-1839), *Henry C. Carey* (1793-1879), *H. C. Baird* (1825-1912).

writers to provide for it and spread his wares by promotion and peddling across the country, perhaps in the remembrance of Irish chap-book distribution. In all this he was aided by the most famous of his hacks, parson Mason Weems. A competence secured for his wife, Bridget Flahavan and their nine children, Carey then launched himself into almost as many fields of activity as Colles, and, like him if with less originality, unified them with an overall view of America's needs and possibilities. He understood too, that America was a country under construction and hence one that need not be bound by the narrow orthodoxies of the past. He ceaselessly attacked as irrelevant to America the views of British conventional wisdom about poverty and class stratification, about industry and free trade. He provided the theoretic foundations for the 'American System' proposed after 1818 by Henry Clay and others, supporting national communications, federal banking, protective tariffs, industrialisation, and the retention of America's staples, flour, cotton and tobacco. He pressed these ideas repeatedly in a series of books and pamphlets between 1810-1830. That he sometimes used the pseudonyms 'Colbert' and 'Hamilton' is partly suggestive of the lineage of his thought. That he worked for Franklin at Passy during his first exile from Ireland and returned to Ireland when the debate over Irish economic nationalism was at its height were both also important influences upon him. Franklin at that stage had abandoned his agrarian model of America's future and was looking toward its economic self-sufficiency, naturally stimulated by the hostilities against Britain and by French economic thought. Irish politicians had been moving in a similar direction in 1779–84. Nonetheless, Carey pursued his examination of America's advantages and the international workings of 'liberal' and 'restrictive' trade systems and, with a forceful logic which was largely his own, subordinated them to the ideal goal of a prosperous community benefiting all its citizens. Not surprisingly he early attempted to convert his fellow Republicans to the merits of many ideas of their Federalist opponents (*The Olive Branch,* 1814), although in the party divisions of the 1790s he had followed the Irish over to Jefferson, rather than pursue his Hamiltonian inclinations. In a batch of Philadelphia organisations he worked for his economic programmes, not merely writing for them. Later he tried in his works to defuse mounting tension with the anti-tariff, pro-slave south; supported Sunday and infant schools; was an early railroad enthusiast; encouraged prison reform; promoted Noah Webster's attempts to create a clear American usage of English; and gave considerable attention to the vindication of Catholicism, publishing the Douai Bible in Philadelphia, and organising an anti-defamation society.

Few other immigrants equalled Colles or Carey in the scale and imagination of their Americanisation of their Irish education. Yet other careers are indicative of patterns later more widely followed. Few men in America, few immigrants to it, could rise to a searching view of its possibilities and a consequent estimate of their own future capacities. Most simply followed the bent of their talents; this alone in a still rudimentary and expanding country was sufficient to bring them a reputation. Carrickfergus-born Robert Adrain, after in-

volvement with the United Irishmen, fled to Philadelphia, where he became a
teacher, if, like many able minds, a sarcastic and impatient one. Between
1809–1834 he taught mathematics and sciences at Rutgers (then Queen's College), Columbia, and the University of Pennsylvania, effectively establishing
the advanced study of mathematics in America, founding journals to further
this aim. Largely self-developed, and working in isolation from European
scholars, his achievements went unnoted by them, such as his independent
demonstrations of the exponential law of error, the first to appear. Ironically,
the erstwhile rebel was forced from the office of vice-provost in Philadelphia
because he could no longer discipline rebellious students! James Hoban, born
in Callan, Kilkenny (then Irish speaking) in 1762, was educated as a craftsman
and draftsman under the schools of the Royal Dublin Society as a youth, and
worked on the Royal Exchange and the Custom's House between 1781–84.
By 1785 he was in Philadelphia, advertising himself as a designer, joiner and
carpenter. In 1791 he designed the State Capitol at Columbia, South Carolina,
and the next year the White House in Washington D.C., the construction of
which he supervised; he later re-built it after its burning in 1814 by the British.
The commission and later spin-offs turned him into the first of Irish America's
many construction magnates; architecturally his work was derivative, if
creditable for one without advanced training. Of an entirely different type was
George McClure who came from rural Derry to upstate New York after training as a carpenter. Where Colles and Carey, Adrain and Hoban brought the
sophisticated skills of urban Ireland to the growing towns, McClure continued
the tradition of the frontier entrepreneur common amongst the pre-
Revolutionary Scotch-Irish, but his opportunities were enhanced by an expanding national economy. He developed distilling, flour milling, yarn
manufacture, shipping and wholesaling in Steuben county, New York, linking
the then remote area via the Susquehanna to Baltimore, and again followed
classic patterns in serving as a militia general in the War of 1812 and a county
politician and state legislator for the remainder of his New York years: when
sixty four, he moved on to the Illinois frontier, fleeing age as he had once fled
rural Irish poverty. Also a westerner and developer from Ulster, John Mullanphy of St. Louis was a very different sort. An educated Catholic veteran of
the Irish Brigade of France, socially conservative yet enterprising, he came to
Philadelphia in 1792 in his mid-thirties, and went west in 1798, engaging in
business in Kentucky, then moving to St. Louis; speculated heavily in land and
development, made a fortune 'cornering' the cotton production of the Mississippi Valley in 1815, and became a major civic leader in St. Louis and leader
and philanthropist to nascent western Catholicism. Yet he avoided major
political office, in the reticent tradition then still general amongst Catholics. He
died in 1833, reputedly the wealthiest man in the entire Valley. In his benefac-
tions he had fought the levelling spirit of the times by requiring that the
Catholic orphanages he endowed neither educate nor spoil their wards beyond
their expected state in life!

The variety of such lives, and instances could be multiplied, underscores the transtitional patterns of the period 1800–1850: if the successes of men were Americanised, their personalities still diverged as widely as the worlds which overlapped Irish lives—the eighteenth century worlds of French aristocracy, of urban Irish trade, of improving skills, the new nineteenth century of bolder enterprise, of territorial expansion, of liberal politics. Mullanphy would have found impossible the confident national planning on behalf of the common good which came naturally to Colles or Carey: with the O'Haras of industrial Pittsburg, Daniel Clark and Maunsel White in New Orleans, Dominick Lynch of New York, and others elsewhere, he formed the beginnings of a mercantile Irish élite in the new national economy, which buried its aggressive opportunism in the mannered trappings of an earlier age. Such careers invited emulation, and Anglo-Irishman Clements Burleigh warned prospective newcomers in 1818, as a "countryman and friend":"There is a number of young men who leave Ireland and go to America intending to be clerks or merchants. Of all classes of people I can give these the least encouragement. We have ten people of this description where we cannot get employment for one". The Shamrock Society of New York, in a publication of 1817, was more encouraging to them, but agreed that they would find themselves less advantaged than native Americans.

In this period, however, all authorities in America agreed that the demand for skilled labour and even more, for unskilled labourers, was certain and growing. Although most middle class writers had few illusions about labouring life (particularly during winter, when construction ceased, the gangs were laid off, rents were high and fuel prohibitive), yet they recognised that summer work at four dollars a week on the canals and turnpikes now beginning to network America, would seem irresistible to Irish peasants faced with mounting rural destitution. After Waterloo, and the collapse of wartime agricultural prosperity, Ireland rapidly became (in Oliver MacDonagh's phrase), "a land without employment for wages". Emigration to the United States began to climb, particularly from those areas whence many indentured servants had come in the past, Ulster, Munster and Leinster. It is important to stress this, since most authorities write as though the flow after 1815 was entirely new and unprecedented, the beginning of the great Irish emigration of the nineteenth century. It certainly was the latter, but its connections with previous patterns would repay fuller study. There is evidence too that a marginally better-off class of person was involved: in short, that as these regions became affected by the downward spiral of living standards (or the threat of it), caused by falling prices, the contraction in domestic textile production, rising rents, the consolidation of estates for grazing and the retraction of leases, and above all by rising population, the sons of smaller farmers, even tenant farmers themselves, looked toward migration as a solution, to Canada (from whence they could re-migrate to the United States), or directly to the States if they could afford the more expensive fees. In short, the Ulster pattern of the eighteenth century was spreading through other parts of the country. The Erie Canal drew thousands of Irish immigrants to New

York, as the reclamation of the Mill Dam area in Boston drew many more south from Newfoundland and Nova Scotia. Weavers, said Dr. William Murphy of Cork around 1825, were drawn to Philadelphia.

Precise statistics are unavailable for the earlier immigration to the United States. Considering that later Irish emigration (post–1851) has been considerably underestimated, despite better sources, and that (as we have seen) so too has eighteenth century migration, it is likely that the flow after 1815 was heavier than once believed. Certainly 260,000 came between 1820–1840 direct from Ireland, with scores of thousands more re-migrants from Canada and Britain. Data on the earlier period 1800–1820 is even less secure, with at least 210,000 immigrants in general to the United States, of whom a third were Irish, and perhaps as many as a half. Certainly contemporaries were aware of a rapid growth of the Irish population: Hibernian, Irish Emigrant, or Shamrock societies were established in New Orleans, St. Louis, New York, Philadelphia and Baltimore by 1818, the latter three petitioning Congress for the establishment of land grants for Irish colonisation in Illinois in that year. These societies addressed themselves to the problems of the new immigrants. Unlike older social and business Irish societies, they seem to have consisted largely of established Catholic merchants and artisans, concerned at the problems encountered by the new style of emigrant, the countryman turned labourer. Carey, Mullanphy, Dominick Lynch and their type were heavily involved in such societies. The population impact was considerable: New York, for example, had an Irish population of around 12,000 before 1817, by the 1830s, it was over 50,000, with another 50,000 in the upstate communities. We shall come back to other figures.

Reliable information on these early communities of mass free migrants from Ireland is also skeletal (unlike those of post-Famine years). Even at this period, residential segregation was developing in the eastern cities (newcoming labourers in New York city being concentrated in 1824 in then separate Greenwich village, for example). The established Irish were well aware of the new patterns. They were unhappy about them, did what they could, but too many feared to jeopardise their more assimilated and comfortable position by a too-close identification with the newcomers. It was recognised that not only was labouring precarious, but that what we should term culture shock was a real danger to immigrants. Burleigh warned that fifteen of twenty Irish immigrants were so taken aback by their first experience of America, that they failed to plan their futures, and became moody, and were thus dragged down to labouring, forge, and furnace work, and thus after thirty years could not put a good coat on their back. The New York Emigrant Society admitted in 1817 that for the want of advisers and congenial homes, "they remain perplexed, undecided, and dismayed by the novelty and difficulty of their situations," many turning to drink as a result. The Shamrock Society seemed impatient at the Irish labourers' difficulty in turning from digging and ditching to lumbering and fencing.

Gradually, however, the adjustment to labouring as a short term route to family sufficiency was achieved. Disorientation, rather than underpayment, was the main threat to it. Mathew Carey was never inclined to underestimate the difficulties of the poor, or of the mass of his fellow-countrymen, but he nonetheless argued in 1830 that "there is scarcely any limit to the number of labourers, who are now and probably will be for twenty years to come, needed in this country," a route thus being open "from the most abject state of existence, to superabundance of food, good clothing and the prospect—honesty, frugality and industry presumed—of acquiring independence and wealth in due season". With remarkable swiftness, mature communities of Irish Americans were constructed along the line of the Erie Canal, for example, many of their leaders lacking the advantaged backgrounds of the earlier elite of the seaport cities. Harry O'Reilly, a poor immigrant from Carrickmacross, became a Jacksonian leader in Rochester, editor of its first daily newspaper, and ultimately the great rival of Samuel Morse in networking the eastern states with telegraph lines.

The Famine emigration has so dominated accounts of Irish American development, that it might be best to understand it afresh as a grotesque interruption of a normal and accumulating pattern of emigration/immigration which was a barometer of America's economic expansion, and of the pressures of poverty and of rising expectations in Ireland. It was to break down for a time the usual patterns whereby the more flexible and responsive Irish absorbed themselves into many varied and changing jobs in America, after initial stints as labourers and after they brought out their families. Most of them remained working people, while ensuring more diverse chances for their children. These patterns seem to have been established already in the years between 1820–1840, and had roots going back beyond that. On the other hand, there is no question too that the 'residual sediment' of Irish Americans which Jacob Riis detected in the 1890s, a group victimised by the worst stresses of industrial life and economic debasement, likewise had their roots in this period. There were those for whom labouring on canals and turnpikes was a sordid and fragmentary hold upon a new life they could not cope with at all. Yet the proportions of these (the immediate Famine aftermath apart) have been revealed by careful study to have been considerably less than believed, and constantly declining, from 1850–1900; hence it seems probable that the optimism of Mathew Carey with regard to labouring and the immigrant is at least as close to the truth as the pessimism of Clements Burleigh. To American commentators, the coincidence of large numbers of the poor living together with Irish accents and manners told its own story: but many Irish were scattered more generally across urban societies, wearing American dress, decently housed, and already brushing shoulders with ordinary Americans whom they might address with an Americanised twang. These escaped reflective notice.

As they noted, the emigration from Ireland after 1800 was very considerable, and little is known as to either precise figures, or to the religious

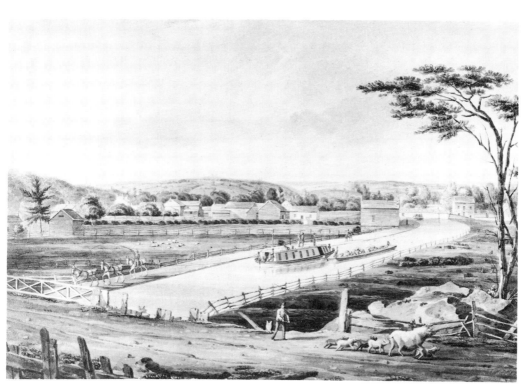

The Erie Canal (1818-1825) *in* 1830

breakdown of the flow. Figures before 1815 are more uncertain, although it is certain that there was an important drop by late 1803, when legislation sharply increased passenger fares to the United States. In 1801–2, several thousand weavers had emigrated from Cavan alone. In 1811, John Chambers reported from New York that "The Emigrants from every part of Ireland, are pouring in here, in unexampled number". But in June 1816, the Dublin *Evening Post* found the mass migration from England then under way remarkable, although within months the same movement, if smaller, began from Ireland. Between 1815–1834, 400,000 left Ireland for North America, well over half of these for Canada. It is probable that most of these re-migrated to the States: in the fortnight ending 3 September 1819, 200 immigrant arrivals at New York from Waterford were reported, 163 from Cork, 279 from Belfast, 55 from Derry, 38 from Limerick, 813 from Liverpool and 889 from Halifax and St. John; Liverpool and the British American ports being the usual embarkation points for the Irish coming to the States. Between 1835–1844, another 400,000 were to emigrate from Ireland to North America, and by 1840 the majority were going direct to United States ports. Analysis of skeletal reports from Irish landlords suggested that this included a heavy outflow from the disturbed areas of north Cork, Limerick, Kerry and the midlands generally. More recent and careful study of population changes points to the bulk of new flow as coming from the counties of Ulster and adjacent areas of north Leinster and Connacht: counties such as Longford, Leitrim and Roscommon losing as many as a fifth of their young people in migration. This does confirm continuity with eighteenth century Ulster patterns. In these areas, the competition of England's mechanised textile industry after 1800, especially after 1815, progressively destroyed the supplemental domestic textile economy that had made possible the heaviest population densities in rural Ireland and the sale of a farmer's interest or improvement in his holding ('tenant right'), enabled would-be emigrants to afford the passage money. The Orange/Catholic riots in New York, Philadelphia and elsewhere in 1824, 1831, 1844 and lesser affrays at other times are illuminated by supposing the virtual transference of the tensely competitive situation of these areas to the textile and labouring sections of the seaboard cities. At the same time, there was a significant secondary flow from Cork, as well as a light flow from all eastern sections of the country. Thus the most severe of all intra-Irish construction riots of the 1830s was between Corkmen and Longfordmen in 1834 on the Chesapeake and Ohio Canal at Williamsport on the Potomac. If Ulster emigrants were divided amongst themselves, they were also distanced by the Munstermen, who organised in Whiteboy societies, modelled on the agrarian movements at home, to protect their hold on jobs and to ensure their payment by sub-contractors. Not for another two generations, until the 1870s, would thousands from the western seaboard of Ireland follow those of Ulster, Munster and Leinster to America, for their response to intensifying population pressure was to reclaim and subdivide land for potato production which no landlords found it worthwhile to clear or to thin of people, since the soils were

Commodore Thomas Mac Donough (1783–1825)

Liberty in 1886, that symbol which pre-eminently links the theory for which he stood with the later vast migrations to America. An uncritical advocate of *laissez-faire* as the instrument of democratic prosperity, yet he had his counterparts on the other side. John P. Kennedy of Baltimore, 1795–1870, son of a wealthy Ulster immigrant merchant of the city, was scarcely less devoted to popular welfare, himself a theorist of the effect of the absence of an hereditary plutocracy in America. But for him, government must be directive and creative, and the end was more than merely social equality: "It is a great and beautiful problem to study in this country the great and the immediate interest which, as a nation, urges us to the melioration of the condition of the working classes. Every improvement which they experience is instantly national: they are the people; their suffrage elects, their will determines, their power directs and executes. Give them education, competence, affluence, and straightaway you give to the nation intelligence, vigour and virtue, depress them, and you sink the national character. . ."

Twentieth-century commonplaces, these sentiments were revolutionary in the world of 1834. The Irish and Scotch-Irish, Irish Americans and Ulster Americans, could still understand, with peculiar force, how revolutionary America was. Even the cumulative tragedies of the immediate postFamine years, those of "the long and dark probation" in city slums, did not erase this sense, born in a country where economic privation and gross inequality fed each other, the mental survivals of which still haunt political calculation and economic competition, and once flourished despite their anachronism. To those who hold that history is neither the sum of the typical, of mass advancement and mass livelihood, nor yet the story of the dynamic and the talented alone, but rather the study of their unity, the manner in which America's people constructed a politics and a society between 1775–1830s which attempted a fidelity to both insights, remains remarkable, however flawed, partial and continuously incomplete and recomposed. The mass of the Irish, Protestant and then Catholic, were the beneficiaries and hence naturally tribunes of the establishment of popular power, worth and opportunity; the capable and creative amongst them were singularly aware of America's promise, and yet attuned to the benefits which their own pursuits might lend to ordinary people, particularly their own. The recipes of that time which were thought to produce so happy a result may never have been fully apposite to a cramped and sectionalised island, though generations of Irish nationalists were to believe so. These included local subdivision in overall unity, to accommodate the maximal interests and energies of the nation; the diffusion of a republican ideal in which the common good is explicitly popular; the constriction of governmental power and the enhancement of private activity; the assertion of common religious principles as the basis of social improvement and of ordered liberty; the praise of creative energies coupled with hostility to passive wealth and solicitude for the poor; the artificial overstimulation of the political sense, and general education and enlightenment. To Irish Americans these seemed the foundation of their well-being. The spirit behind them was spacious, comprehensive, openly

Corner of Greenwich St., N.Y., 1810

elusive on many particulars, yet assured as to fundamental convictions. Its certainty was that just and well-made political institutions would give energies play which should surprise men and assure their friendship.

SOURCES AND REFERENCES

[The general sources for each section are given. Page citations are sometimes added for direct quotations and certain key incidents. Certain sources are held over until the section in which they are most generally used, and minor references sometimes excluded. Chapter 5 is so extensive that specific references are referred to page, not section].

ABBREVIATIONS

DAB Dictionary of American Biography.
DNB Dictionary of National Biography.
Econ. Hist. Rev. Economic History Review.
IHS Irish Historical Studies.
Jour. Econ. Hist. Journal of Economic History.
JPH Journal of Presbyterian History.
MG Maryland Gazette.
Mss. manuscripts.
NYJ New York Journal.
PC Pennsylvania Chronicle.
PG Pennsylvania Gazette.

PICHC Proceedings of the Irish Catholic Historical Committee.
PMHB Pennsylvania Magazine of History and Biography.
PP Pennsylvania Packet.
r. reprinted edition.
Va.Mag. Virginia Magazine of History and Biography.
VG(P&D) Virginia Gazette (Purdie and Dixon, printers).
VG(R) Virginia Gazette (Rind).
WMQ William and Mary Quarterly, third series.
WPMH Western Pennsylvania Magazine of History.

Prelude

Roger Lamb, *An Original and Authentic Journal of Occurences During the Late American War* (Dublin, 1809), 114-5, 193-4, 306 and his *Memoirs of His Own Life* (Dublin, 1811), 6-7, 45-48, 61ff., 167-70, 176-79, 190, 201ff., 222, 252-4; Marquis James, *Andrew Jackson: Border Captain* (New York, 1933), 1-34; P. S. Dineen, ed., *Amhráin Eoghain Ruaidh Uí Shúilleabháin* 2nd ed. (Dublin, 1902); R. Ó Foghludha, *Eoghan Ruadh Ó Súilleabháin* (Dublin, 1937): his poem in English, "Rodney's Glory" in K. Hoagland ed., *1000 Years of Irish Poetry* (New York, 1947), 349-51: interpretations of him are as many as the facets of the man; J. H. Parry, *Trade and Dominion* (London, 1971), 151, 216-18; *Dict. Nat. Biog.*, 9:117-22, 7:191-2, 14:755-56 and 15:1005-1012; *Hist. Mss. Comm., 9th Report*, Part iii, Stopford Sackville Mss., Cornwallis to Lord George Germain, 21 August 1780, Camden, S.C., p. 104; "Letters of Charles O'Hara to the Duke of Grafton", *South Carolina Historical Magazine* 65 (1964), 158-80; Richard Fitzpatrick Mss., letters from Pennsylvania to the Earl of Upper Ossory, 1777-78, copies in National Library, Dublin.

Chapter 1

IRELAND

Sources: Edmund Burke, *Correspondence*, vols. I-IV (Cambridge, 1959–63); John Carr, *The Stranger in Ireland* (London, 1806); W. H. Crawford and B. Trainor, eds. *Aspects of Irish Social History* (Belfast, 1969), 90-91, 175; W. H. Crawford, ed., *Domestic Industry in Ireland* (Dublin, 1971); De LaTocnaye, *A Frenchman's Walk Through Ireland, 1796–97* (ed. J. Stevenson, Belfast, 1917), 18-19, 145, 177, 221, 265, 285; Oscar Handlin, ed., *This was America* (New York, 1964), 45-46 (Crevecoeur on Irish); K. H. Jackson, ed., *Celtic Miscellany*, 2nd ed. (Penguin, 1973), 224; G. Holmes, *Sketches of Some of the Southern Counties of Ireland . . . 1797* (London, 1801); Pádraig Ó Canainn, *Filidheacht na nGaedheal* (Dublin, 1940); Enri Ó Muirgheasa, *Céad de Cheoltaibh Uladh* (Dublin, 1915), 99, 133, 256; Enri O Muirgheasa, *Dhá Chéad de Cheoltaibh Uladh* (Dublin, 1934); R. Slade, *Narrative of a Journey to the North of Ireland . . . 1802* (London, 1803); Stopford Sackville Mss., cited above, John Hotham to Lord Germain, Dublin, 1 Dec., 1777, *Hist. Mss. Comm.,* 9:iii:p.59; R. Twiss, *A Tour in Ireland in 1775* (London, 1776), 9, 31, 33, 41, 48–9, 74, 107; Arthur Young, *A Tour in Ireland (1776/79)*, 2 vols., ed. A. W. Hutton (London, 1892; Shannon, 1970), I:20–21, 59–60, 85–90, contrast 119–136 (n. Armagh, e. Down), with 138–143 (Ards, Lecale), and 150–1, on poverty of linen counties as a whole in Ulster, also 189–91 (Fermanagh); v.II:7, 60–72 for his views on the whole question of Anglican ascendancy as a political economy which would do justice to the analytical standards of a Eugene Genovese! Edward Wakefield, *An Account of Ireland, Statistical and Political*, 2 vols., (London, 1812); G. D. Zimmermann, *Songs of Irish Rebellion . . . 1780–1900* (Dublin, 1967), 27 n49, 29–30; Anon., *Ancient Irish Prophecies translated from Original Parchments* (n.p., n.d.: bound with pamphlets of the 1780s and 1790s, Irish Folklore Department Library, University College, Dublin), "Prophecy of Maoltamhlacta," p. 49; Boston *Pilot*, 1847, quoted in George Potter, *To the Golden Door* (Boston, 1960), 83.

Secondary Authorities: J. C. Beckett, *Making of Modern Ireland* (London, 1966), 138–86, with 178–81 the only serious misreading of matters; John Brady and Patrick Corish, *The Church under the Penal Code* (Dublin, 1971); L. M. Cullen, *An Economic History of Ireland since 1660* (London, 1972), 50–133, *Life in Ireland* (London, 1968), and "Hidden Ireland: Re-Assessment of a Concept" *Studia Hibernica* (1969), 7–47; K. H. Connell, *The Population of Ireland, 1750–1845* (London, 1950) and *Irish Peasant Society* (Oxford, 1963), 1–86; F. G. James, *Ireland in the Empire, 1688–1770* (Harvard, 1973), 190–250; L. M. Cullen and T. C. Smout, eds., *Comparative Aspects of Scottish and Irish Economic and Social History, 1600–1900* (Edinburgh, 1977); W. H. Crawford, "The Social Structure of Ulster in the Eighteenth Century" and David Dickson, "Evolution of Social Structure in Eighteenth Century South Munster", papers given at a Franco-Irish historical conference, March, 1977; E. M. Johnston, *Ireland in the Eighteenth Century* (Dublin, 1974), 19; R. B. McDowell, ed., *Social Life in Ireland, 1800–45* (Dublin 1957, 1973), especially 53–66; R. B. McDowell, *Irish Public Opinion, 1750–1800* (London, 1944), 5–6; Constantia Maxwell, *Country and Town in Ireland Under the Georges* (Dundalk, 1949) and *Dublin Under the Georges, 1714–1830* (London, 1956); A. P. W. Malcomson,

"Absenteeism in Eighteenth Century Ireland," *Irish Economic and Social History*, 1 (1974), 15–35; Maureen Wall, "The Rise of a Catholic Middle Class . . ." *Irish Historical Studies* 9 (1958–9), 91–115, but cf. her further study in *Reportorium Novum* (1959–60), 298–323; also Maureen Wall, *The Penal Laws, 1691–1760* (Dundalk, 1967), and *"The Whiteboys"* in T.D. Williams, ed., *The Secret Societies* (Dublin); J. G. Simms, "Connacht in the Eighteenth Century", *Irish Historical Studies*, 9 (1958–59), 116–133. For Catholicism, see also, David Miller, "Catholicism in Ireland Before the Great Famine" *Journal of Social History*, December 1975; Cathaldus Giblin, *Irish Exiles in Catholic Europe* (Dublin, 1971), checked against R. R. Palmer, *Catholics and Unbelievers in Eighteenth Century France* (Princeton, 1939); Fr. Charles Carmody, Loyola University, Chicago, unpublished cathechetical studies and forthcoming studies by W. J. Lowe (Irish church-going in Lancashire, 1840s–60s), Seán Connolly (Irish religion and society, 1800–1850), D. N. Doyle (1851 religious census and Irish in U.K.), and Patrick J. Corish (Irish Catholicism, 17th and 18th centuries); W. H. Crawford, "Landlord-Tenant Relations in Ulster, 1609–1820" *Ir. Econ. and Soc. Hist.*, 2 (1975), 5–21; Richard Hayes, *Biographical Dictionary of Irishmen in France* (Dublin, 1949); F. R. Bolton, *The Caroline Tradition of the Church of Ireland* (London, 1968): Louis Bouyer, *Orthodox Spirituality and Protestant and Anglican Spirituality* (London, 1969).

AMERICA

Sources: (I have deliberately used those sources available to Irish opinion in the 1780s–1820, to stress that the sense of contrast was even then available):
    The Constitutions of the Several Independent States of America . . . (Dublin 1783); Francois Jean de Chastellux, *Travels in North America in the Years 1780, 1781, and 1782* (Dublin, 1787); Hector St. John [Crèvecoeur] *Letters from an American Farmer* (Belfast, 1783); Thomas Cooper, *Some Information Respecting America* (Dublin, 1794); Benjamin Franklin, *Two Tracts: Information for Those who would Remove to America* (Dublin, 1784); Gilbert Imlay, *A Description of the Western Territory of North America . . .* (Dublin, 1793); Roger Lamb, *Original and Authentic Journal* and *Memoirs*, cited above; Richard Price, *Observations of the Importance of the American Revolution* (Dublin, 1795); David Ramsay, *The History of the American Revolution* (Dublin, 1793); J.F.D. Smyth, *A Tour in the United States of America* [c. 1775] (Dublin, 1784); Charles Stedman, *The History of the Origins, Progress and Termination of the American War* (Dublin, 1794); Banastre Tarleton, *A History of the Campaigns of 1780 and 1781 in the Southern Provinces of North America* (Dublin, 1787).
    Secondary Authorities: Much of the growing literature is indicated elsewhere but here Jackson Turner Main, *The Social Structure of Revolutionary America* (Princeton, 1965); Carl Bridenbaugh, *Cities in Revolt, 1743–1775* (New York, 1955); James Lemon, *The Best Poor Man's Country* (Baltimore, 1972); and Aubrey C. Land, ed., *Bases of a Plantation Society* (New York, 1969) are noteworthy as congruent with the primary accounts yet up-to-date. For what appears to me, notwithstanding slavery and servitude, an imbalanced emphasis, see Gary Nash, "Poverty and Poor Relief in Pre-Revolutionary Philadelphia", *WMQ*, 33 (1976), 3–28, and the overall tenor of his collection *Class and Society in Early America* (1970). Despite exceptions, America then generally lacked the class structure and seas of poverty which shaped major events from the Pugachov outburst in Russia to the *jacqueries* in France, of which

Whiteboyism and Steelboyism in Ireland were local manifestations. Nonetheless since Irish ex-servants did tend to be numbered disproportionately among such poor as there were, Nash's article is useful here, as is Raymond A. Mohl, "Poverty in Early America: A Reappraisal," *New York History*, 50 (1969), 5–27. Franklin's views on Ireland are detailed in J. Bennett Nolan, *Benjamin Franklin in Scotland and Ireland* (Philadelphia, 1938) and excerpted and set in the context of his political economy in Paul Conner, *Poor Richard's Politicks* (New York, 1965), 24, 45, 85, 87, 143.

Chapter 2

General framework and the American colonies: Charles Andrews, *The Colonial Period of American History, 4: England's Commercial and Colonial Policy* (Yale, New Haven, 1938); Bernard Bailyn, *The Origins of American Politics* (New York, 1968) and *The Ideological Origins of the American Revolution* (Harvard, 1967); Thomas C. Barrow, *Trade and Empire; The British Customs Service in Colonial America, 1660–1775* (Harvard, 1967); Stuart Bruchey, ed., *The Colonial Merchant* (New York, 1966); Jack P. Greene, "Changing Interpretations of Early American Politics," in Ray A. Billington, ed., *The Reinterpretation of Early American History* (New York, 1966); Jack Greene, *Quest for Power: The Lower House of Assembly in the Southern Royal Colonies* (Chapel Hill, N.C., 1963) and his *Great Britain and the American Colonies, 1606–1763* (Columbia, S.C., 1970); Lawrence A. Harper, *The English Navigation Laws* (New York, 1939); Michael Kammen, *Empire and Interest* (Philadelphia, 1970); Stanley Katz, *Newcastle's New York: Anglo-American Politics, 1732–1753* (Harvard, 1968); Leonard W. Labaree, *Royal Government in America* (Yale, 1930); Paul Lucas, "A Note on the Comparative Structure of Politics in Mid-Eighteenth Century Britain and Its American Colonies", *WMQ*, 27 (1971), 301–309, a gem of clarification; Curtis Nettels, "British Mercantilism and the Economic Development of the Thirteen Colonies," *Jour. Econ. Hist.* 12 (1952), 105; Alison Olson and R.M. Brown, *Anglo-American Political Relations, 1675–1775* (New Brunswick, N.J., 1970); I.K. Steele, *Politics of Colonial Policy: The Board of Trade* (Oxford, 1968). P.D.G. Thomas, *British Politics and the Stamp Act Crisis* (Oxford, 1975).

Ireland in the Imperial System: James, *Ireland in the Empire, op. cit.* was my chief guide; see also (apart from the works cited for the previous chapter), Raymond Barrett, "A Comparative Study of Imperial Constitutional Theory in Ireland and America . . ." unpubl. Ph.D., Trinity College, Dublin, 1953, which stresses the differences and anticipates much of the recent work cited above on the distinctiveness of colonial development; as also does John P. Reid, *In A Defiant Stance* (University Park, Pa., 1978); and additionally, L.M. Cullen, *Anglo-Irish Trade, 1660-1800* (Manchester, 1968); F.G. James, "The Irish Lobby in the Early Eighteenth Century", *Eng. Hist. Rev.*, 81 (1966), 543–577; Edith Johnston, *Great Britain and Ireland, 1760–1800* (Edinburgh, 1963); Hugh Kearney, "The Political background to English Mercantilism, 1695–1700", *Econ. Hist. Rev.* 2nd ser. 9 (1959), 484–496; J.L. McCracken, *The Irish Parliament in the Eighteenth Century* (Dundalk, 1971) and "The Conflict Between the Irish Administration and Parliament, 1735–56," *IHS*, 3 (1942–3), 159–79. Especially aiding contrast is J.C. Beckett, "Anglo-Irish Constitutional Relations in the Late Eighteenth Century," *IHS*, 14 (1964–5), 20–38.

The argument as to Irish precedent for Anglo-colonial activities, government and race attitudes is to be found in such works as David B. Quinn, *The Elizabethans and the Irish* (Ithaca, N.Y., 1966) and his "Ireland and Sixteenth Century European Expansion" in T.D. Williams, ed., *Historical Studies*, 1, (London, 1958) and "The First Pilgrims", *WMQ*, 23 (1966) 359–366 and is fully developed in N.P. Canny, "The Ideology of English Colonization: From Ireland to America", *WMQ*, 30 (1973), 573–598; it seems quite inconsistent with the drastic differences obtaining between the conquest of a European society (Ireland) and settlement in the Americas, where imagined or real Spanish precedents, if anything, had greater impact upon English practice and attitudes: see, e.g., Howard Peckham and Charles Gibson, eds. *Attitudes of Colonial Powers Towards the American Indian* (Salt Lake City, 1969), and Winthrop Jordan, *White Over Black* (Chapel Hill, N.C., 1968). Howard Mumford Jones, in *A Strange New World* (New York, 1964) gave the analogy an undeserved currency. A dispassionate reading of the standard works on 17th c. Ireland and the Americas should correct it.

For the 1670s precedents, see A.P. Thornton, *West India Policy Under the Restoration* (Oxford, 1956), 5, 163, 173,186–7, and for the later precedent of the application of the principles of the 1719 Irish Declaratory Act to the Colonies, see Owen Edwards, "The American Image of Ireland", *Perspectives in American History*, 4 (1970), 206–07, 212-215.

For Cosby, Herbert Osgood, *The American Colonies in the Eighteenth Century*, 4 vols. (New York, 1924), 2:443 ff.; for Dobbs, Desmond Clarke, *Arthur Dobbs, Esquire, 1689–1765* (Chapel Hill, N.C., 1957); for Johnson, Arthur Pound, *Johnson of the Mohawks* (New York, 1930) and J.T. Flexner, *Mohawk Baronet: Sir William Johnson of New York* (New York, 1959); for Croghan, Nicholas B. Wainright *George Croghan, Wilderness Diplomat* (Chapel Hill, 1959); A.T. Volwiler, "George Croghan and the Westward Movement, 1741–1782", *PMBH*, 46 (1922), 273–311 and Margaret P. Bothwell, "The Astonishing Croghans", *WPMH*, 48 (1965), 119–137; for Ward, see Bothwell, "Edward Ward", *WPMH*, 43 (1960), 97–127. For Warren, Hillsborough, Murray and Sterling, see *DAB* and *DNB*. For Hillsborough's 1770 appointments, R.M. Brown, *The South Carolina Regulators*, 107–08. Katz, *Newcastle's New York*, provides the background for the Cosby-Warren-Murray-Johnson advancements. Clearly there is badly needed a Namierite study of the inter-actions of the Irish, colonial and metropolitan "connections", but the dismal predictability of the results would probably deter any student! For Irish Loyalists in South Carolina and New York, see Wallace Brown, *The King's Friends* (Providence, R.I., 1965): with 97 Loyalist Irish claimants in N.Y., and 72 in S.C., the next nearest being Pennsylvania with 23. Such figures are clearly related to the foregoing patterns, for they bear no relationship to the density of Irish immigration.

Merchants and Sailors

Trade: James F. Shephard and Gary M. Walton, *Shipping, Maritime Trade and the Economic Development of Colonial North America* (Cambridge, 1972), 107–13, 138, 160–3; Francis G. James, "Irish Colonial Trade in the Eighteenth Century", *WMQ*, 20 (1963), 574–84; Clarence Gould, "Economic Consequences of the Rise of Baltimore", in *Essays in Colonial History . . . Charles Andrews* (New Haven, 1931), 239; Stuart Bruchey, *The Colonial Merchant* pp. 183–193; Bruchey, *Robert Oliver, Merchant of Baltimore, 1783–1819* (Baltimore, 1956), 3–98; A. L. Jensen, *The Maritime*

Commerce of Colonial Philadelphia (Madison, 1963), 85–87, a distorted judgement; Virginia Harrington, *The New York Merchant on the Eve of the Revolution* (New York, 1935), 359–64; Edward C. Papenfuse, *In Pursuit of Profit . . . the Annapolis Merchants, 1763–1805* (Baltimore, 1975), 239–42; Charles G. Sellers, "Private Profits and British Colonial Policy: The Speculations of Henry McCulloh," *WMQ,* 8 (1951), 535–51; Clarence B. Coulter, "The Import Trade of Colonial Virginia", *WMQ,* 2 (1945), 298–9, 311–12; G.S. Wood, *William Paterson of New Jersey* (Paterson, 1933), 1–2; Robert A. Davidson, *Isaac Hicks, New York Merchant and Quaker, 1767–1820* (Harvard, 1964), 46, 68–73, 89, 112–16; Albert Myers, *Immigration of the Irish Quakers into Pennsylvania, 1682–1750* (Swarthmore, 1902), 262–7; J. A. Ernst and H. R. Merrens, " 'Camden's Turrets': Urban Process in the South," *WMQ,* 30 (1973), 549–74; Julian Gwyn, *Enterprising Admiral: The Personal Fortune of Sir Peter Warren* (Toronto, 1974); M. S. Morriss, *Colonial Trade of Maryland, 1689–1715* (Baltimore, 1914), 71, 100, 110–13, 118, 139ff.; Byron Fairchild, *Messers. William Papperrell* (Ithaca, N.Y., 1954); F. G. James, "Irish Smuggling in the Eighteenth Century," *Irish Historical Studies,* 12 (1961), 299–317; L. M. Cullen, "The Smuggling Trade in Ireland in the Eighteenth Century," *Proc. Royal Irish Academy,* v. 67 (1969); James A. James, *Oliver Pollock* (New York, 1937); John Roche, *Joseph Reed* (New York, 1957), 3–6; Ruth Kistler, "William Allen, Provincial Man of Affairs", *Pa. Hist.* 1 (1934), 165–74; Frederick Tolles, *James Logan and the Culture of Provincial America* (Boston, 1957); Olive Goodbody ed., "The Letters of Benjamin Chandlee," *Quaker History,* 64 (1975) 110–115; Thomas Truxes "Connecticut in the Irish American Flaxseed Trade, 1750–1775," *Eire-Ireland,* 12 (1977), 34–62.

The Irish side of this trade has been little investigated, but see several of the documents in Trainor and Crawford, *Aspects of Irish Social History,* 64–67, 70; Mary McNeill, *Mary Ann McCracken* (Dublin, 1960), 37–40, and other incidental information in George O'Brien, *Economic History of Ireland in the Eighteenth Century* (Dublin, 1918) and Walter O'Sullivan, *Economic History of Cork City* (Cork, 1937); and in L. M. Cullen, ed., *Merchants, Ships and Trade* (Dublin, 1971). For the American market and its changes, David Gilchrist, ed., *The Growth of Seaport Cities* (Charlottesville, Va., 1967); Gordon C. Bjork, "The Weaning of the American Economy: Independence, Market Changes and Economic Development", *Jour. Econ. Hist.* 24 (1964), 541–66; John Coatsworth, "American Trade with European Colonies in the Caribbean . . . 1790–1812", *WMQ,* 24 (1967), 242–66; Curtis Nettels, *The Emergence of a National Economy* (New York, 1962) and Jacob Price, "The Rise of the Port of Glasgow in the Chesapeake Tobacco Trade, 1707–1775," *WMQ,* 11 (1954), 179–99, detail the vast changes which few Irish businessmen (unlike Scottish) seemed able to handle.

For statistics, see the series by Lawrence Harper and his associates in *Historical Statistics of the United States* (Washington, D. C., 1975), series Z 268–278, Z 294 and the additions in James, "Colonial Trade", 578, 581 and 582, and Shephard and Walton, *Shipping, Maritime Trade,* 217–19. Stella H. Sutherland, "Colonial Statistics", *Explorations in Entrepreneurial History,* 5 (1967), 58 ff. for comment. There is an unstudied mass of information and statistics on the trade, 1763–1797 in the Massereene Foster MSS, Public Records Office, Northern Ireland.

Sailors: Cullen, *Merchants, Ships and Trade,* 46–55; Pauline Maier, "Popular Uprisings and Civil Authority", *WMQ,* 3rds., 27 (1970), 17; S. E. Morison, *The Maritime History of Massachussetts* (Boston, 1922) 107nl; VG (P & D), 9 February, 1 June 1769, 3 Jan. 1771, 11 Nov. 1773, 26 July 1776; PG, 15 Sept, 1773; PP, 9 Jan. 1775; NYJ, 31 March 1768; MG, 14 June and 19 July 1745 are examples of many

Irish sailor runaways; for men indentured to mariners, see "Account of Servants Bound and Assigned before James Hamilton," (1745–46), in *PMHB*, 31 (1907), 83ff., 195ff., 351ff., and 461ff., John Stewart on 25 Oct. 1745, Daniel McDaniel on 28 Feb. 1746, Robert Murphy on 23 April, Daniel Welsh on 28 May, Robert Campbell on June 16 and Timothy Scannell on 15 July, all 1746, among others. Most persuasive of all, apart from the combination of a floating poor Irish port population with English ships victualling there, is the number of Irish ships built and registered in Philadelphia (and presumably other American ports), John McCusker, "Ships Registered at the Port of Philadelphia, before 1776" unpubl. manuscript deposited at the Historical Society of Pennsylvania (College Park, Md., 1970), which lists not only the Irish-owned vessels, but scores of vessels owned by Philadelphia's two Irish communities: ten by Blair McClenachan, over twenty by John Mease, eight by George Meade, six by Thomas FitzSimons, many others by Hugh Williamson, Christopher Marshall and others. The revolutionary Irish captains were captains of these vessels, as a check on the names provided by McCusker in one instance, and Michael O'Brien in the other, shows. The crews of the Ulster Americans' and Irish Americans' vessels thus were probably also Irish. For the merchant communities, see John H. Campbell, *History of the Friendly Sons of St. Patrick and the Hibernian Society* (Philadelphia, 1892); and Richard C. Murphy and Lawrence J. Mannion, *The Society of Friendly Sons of St. Patrick in the City of New York* (New York, 1962), 1–234; for the *King's Meadow* mutiny, MG, 17 Jan. 1745.

Chapter 3

R. J. Dickson, *Ulster Emigration to Colonial America, 1718–1775* (London, 1966) and Audrey Lockhart, *Some Aspects of Emigration from Ireland to the North American Colonies between 1660 and 1775* (New York, 1976) are the key secondary sources for this chapter. The works are based almost entirely upon exhaustive readings of available British and Irish evidence and are especially complete for the period 1760–1775. Dickson's work covers northern, and Lockhart's southern emigration. Public Record Office, Northern Ireland, *18th Century Ulster Emigration to North America* (Education Facsimiles, no. 121–40, Belfast, 1971–74); Trainor and Crawford, *Aspects of Irish Social History*, 49–55; T. W. Moody, "Irish and Scotch–Irish in Eighteenth Century America", *Studies*, 35 (1946), 84–90; W. T. Latimer, "Ulster Emigration to America", *Jour. Royal Soc. of Antiquaries of Ire.*, 32 (1903), 385–92; and especially E. R. R. Green, "Scotch–Irish Emigration: An Imperial Problem", *WPHM*, 35 (1952), 193–209, "The 'Strange Humors' That Drove the Scotch–Irish to America, 1729", *WMQ*, 12 (1955), 113–123, and "Queensborough Township: Scotch–Irish Emigration and the Expansion of Georgia, 1763–1776," *WMQ*, 17 (1960), 183–99 provide further interpretation and documentation from Irish and British sources. Remarkably little has been done with complementary American sources since H. J. Ford, *The Scotch–Irish in America* (Princeton, 1915) and Albert C. Myers, *Immigration of the Irish Quakers into Pennsylvania, 1682–1750* (Swarthmore, 1902): they are far from exhaustive; but see also Robert L. Meriwether, *The Expansion of South Carolina* (Kingsport, Tenn., 1940), 79–88; Patricia G. Johnson, *James Patton and the Appalachian Colonists* (Verona, Va., 1973), 3–15; and Wayland Dunaway, *Scotch–Irish of Colonial Pennsylvania* (Chapel Hill, N.C., 1944), 33–49, using the Logan and Dickinson papers.

On the subsequent settlement patterns of the Scotch-Irish, James G. Leyburn, *The Scotch–Irish: A Social History* (Chapel Hill, N.C., 1962), c. 13, 184–223, 231–255 is good, and the best part of his book; see also Dunaway, *Scotch–Irish of Col. Penn.*, 50–117 and his "Pennsylvania as an Early Distributing Centre of Population", *PMHB*, 55 (1931), 134–56; Solon and Elizabeth Buck, *The Planting of Civilization in Western Pennsylvania* (Pittsburg, 1939), 135–55 and 204–228 (strangely ignored by Dunaway, yet scholarly); Robert Ramsey, *Carolina Cradle: Settlement of the Northwest Carolina Frontier, 1747–1762* (Chapel Hill, N.C., 1964), and the aforecited work of Green, Meriwether and Johnson. The work of Buck and Ramsey corrects the false impression created by Leyburn, Dunaway and others that the Scotch–Irish settled in self-contained communities: ex-Quakers, Quakers and Anglicans, largely native Americans, were not only amongst them, but disproportionately office-holders and traders, a point also stressed throughout Freeman Hart, *The Valley of Virginia* (Chapel Hill, 1942).

For the mixed composition of Ulster before the migration, Dickson, *Ulster Emigration*, 3–4; Ulster Folk Museum, *Ulster Dialects* (Belfast, 1964), especially the maps; Séamas Pender, *A Census of Ireland Circa 1659* (Dublin, 1939) which reveals ratios of Scots and English (combined) to Irish at 1:1.5 in Ulster, 1:5.5 in Leinster and 1:10 in Munster and Connacht.F. J. Byrne, T. W. Moody and F. X. Martin, ed.s *A New History of Ireland, III: 1534–1691* (Oxford, 1976), provides the fullest critical background to the 17th c. bases of population intermixture.

For Anglo-Irish migration (including converted native Irish, and Ulster English elements), see the sources cited p. 235, and William A. Hunter, "Thomas Barton and the Forbes Expedition," *PMHB*, 95 (1971), 431–36 and Marvin Buxbaum, *Benjamin Franklin and the Zealous Presbyterians* (London, 1975), 243n72 and 252n50; Walter Kemprad, "John Ormsby, Pittsburg's Original Citizen", *WPHM*, 23 (1940), 203ff.; Lawrence Oriil, "General Edward Hand", *WPMH* 25 (1942), 99–112; Nelson Rightmyer, *Maryland's Established Church* (Baltimore, 1956), 176–220; Nelson R. Burr, *The Anglican Church in New Jersey* (Philadelphia, 1954), 618–25; Michael Malone, "North Carolina Clergy, 1765–1776", *Hist. Mag. of the Protestant Episcopal Church*, 39 (1970), 150–53, 414–16; for Searson, PC, 4 Dec. 1769; for Butler, Edward Williams, "The Journal of Richard Butler, 1775," *WPMH*, 46 (1963), 381–95; R. J. Purcell, 'The Irish Contribution to Colonial New York," *Studies*, 29 (1940), 596, 600–03 and 30 (1941), 107, 109, 114, 116–17, 118–19; although Prof. Purcell had little wish to stress the fact, it is clear that the pre-Revolutionary New York immigration was largely Anglican!

Apart from Lockhart, the books on southern Irish servant immigrants will be cited in the next chapter; for important sidelights, see Benjamin Marshall to Barney Egan, 9 Nov. 1765 and 7 June 1766 and to Thomas Murphy, 9 Nov. 1765 in F. R. Diffenderfer, *German Immigration into Pennsylvania*, Part II (Lancaster, Pa., 1900), 228–30. Marshall, a Dublin Quaker immigrant, used Egan and Murphy as agents in his servant importing trade, and stated "the less women the better as they are very troublesome" (to Murphy). The usual reward for male Irish runaways varied from 40/– to £5; for girls, from 20/– to as low as sixpence: PP and PC, 1771–76 *passim*.

The inadequacies of Lockhart and Dickson on the pre-Seven Year War patterns were established by correlating the indentures of arriving Irish passengers 1745–46 (which gave the name of the incoming vessel), with the ship ownership listings provided by McCusker, and the actual arrivals as noted in the *American Mercury* (Philadelphia), 1741–46. Correlation of later series of indentures, and of ship arrivals in the *Pennsylvania Packet* and *Pennsylvania Chronicle* for 1771–6 confirms the almost exhaustive completeness of their work for that decade: see (apart from the *Mercury* and *Packet*), "Account of Servants Bound and Assigned Before James Hamilton, Mayor of Philadelphia," *PMHB*, 30 (1906), 428 ff., 31 (1907), 83–102, 195–206, 351–67, 461–73, 32 (1908), 88–103, 237–49, 358–70; McCusker. "Ships Registered at the Port of Philadelphia", *op. cit.;* "Record of Indentures . . . Before Mayors John Gibson and William Fisher, Oct. 1771–Oct. 1773", Pennsylvania German Society, *Proceedings,* 16 (1907), *passim.* The material in these sources also makes clear the pattern of southern Irish and native Ulster immigration. Other specific evidence of continuing southern Irish immigration is contained in Thompson Westcott, ed., *Names of Persons who Took the Oath of Allegiance to the State of Pennsylvania, 1777–1789* (Philadelphia, 1865), which usually contains trade and birthplace information: all immigrants and British deserters (many Irish) were required to take it. For evidence of Irish re-migration (by floating elements) from Britain, see M. and J. Kaminow, eds., *Original Lists of Colonists in Bondage sent over from London, 1719–1744* (Baltimore, 1967) for obviously Irish transportees (Bernard McCoy, Ferdo O'Neale, Ann O'Hara etc.) and such runaway examples as James Mooney, Irish-Liverpool blacksmith, PP, 14 Feb. 1774, John Wilson, a former soldier, MG, 31 March 1747 or Thomas Adair, PP, 9 Jan., 1775: for background, Dorothy Marshall, *The English Poor in the Eighteenth Century* (London, 1941), *passim;* and Dorothy George, *London Life in the Eighteenth Century* (London, 1925), *passim;* Edward McQuilk, a Kilkenny labourer who died in Salem co. N. J., was well known for his part in the Brentford (Middlesex), Wilkes riots, and his subsequent acquittal of murder, although "In this country he behaved very quietly". PP, 2 Jan. 1775.

Since this was written, T. H. Mullin, *Coleraine in Georgian Times* (Belfast, 1977), 13–29, provides evidence that there *was* a significant Scotch-Irish—West Indies—Georgia connection.

The Tom Paine and Henry Whistler quotations are from Jordan, *White Over Black,* 65 and 337; Young's on Ulster's crisis from *A Tour in Ireland,* 1:146, 150; Hugh Jones, from the *Present State,* (r., New York, 1865), 53–4, also excerpted in Land, *Bases of the Plantation Society,* 57.

Further detail on the Irish generally in colonial America can be pursued in two works which underestimate their numbers and presence (to correct previous exaggerations): John Tracy Ellis, *Catholics in Colonial America* (Baltimore, 1965), part 3; and in Charles H. Metzger, *Catholics and the American Revolution: A Study in Religious Climate* (Chicago, 1962), 1–176, on pre-revolutionary situation, together with a series of detailed, but often contextless local studies, such as Richard Madden, "Catholics in Colonial South Carolina", *Records of the Amer. Cath. Hist. Soc.* 73 (1962), 10–44; Richard Purcell, "Irish Colonists in Colonial Maryland", *Studies,* 23 (1934), 279ff., ". . . of Colonial Rhode Island", *Studies,* 24 (1935), 289ff.; ". . . in Early Deleware," *Pennsylvania History,* 14 (1947), 94ff.; "Education and Irish Teachers in Colonial Maryland", *Catholic Educational Review,* 32 (1934), 143ff., one of a long series on Irish colonial teachers in that periodical by Purcell, who was professor at the Catholic University of America, reliable as to data, if loose in interpreting it: certainly he is in a different category than Michael O'Brien, and his virtual exclusion by Ellis, and complete exclusion by Metzger, difficult to understand, apart from his failure to make denominational distinctions. Richard D. Doyle, "The Pre-Revolutionary Irish in New York", Ph.D., St. Louis, 1932, and George Francis Donovan, *Pre-Revolutionary Irish in Massachussetts,* Menasha, Wisconsin, 1931, are also careful, if old-fashioned. A new standard for such work is established in James O'Beirne, "Some Early Irish in Vermont," *Vermont History,* 28 (1960), 63–72. It has recently been shown that J.

Franklin Jameson, president of the American Historical Association, who did much to discredit the work of Michael O'Brien in 1920, was descended from Ulster emigrants of 1746, and visited their home area in 1913 and 1921, during the high-tide of Unionist agitation, T. H. Mullin, *Coleraine in Georgian Times,* 15. Was their quarrell a matter of rival filiopietisms?

Chapter 4

"Ulster America". This section attempts a new reading of chiefly well known sources, in the light of our developing understanding of eighteenth century rural Ulster, on which see the works cited below and c.1; material in John Mogey, *Rural Life in Northern Ireland* (London, 1947) and E. Estyn Evans, *Irish Folkways* (London, 1947), is also retrospectively useful. On Scotland, John Galt's classic *Annals of a Parish* depicted the emergence of the "improving" spirit as being as late as the 1770s in Ayrshire, origin of many Ulster emigrants a century and more before, and is now generally sustained by Scottish historians: e.g., C. T. Smout, *A History of the Scottish People,* 1560–1830 (London, 1969). A full social and economic history of the Scottish Lowlands, 1600–1800, and of northern Ireland in the same period, is lacking. For the American experience: Leyburn, *Scotch-Irish,* 256–72 is weak; Dunaway, *Scotch-Irish in Col. Penn.,* 165–200, better; Buck, *Planting of Civilisation in Western Pennsylvania,* 127–34, 204–217, 229–400, although ostensibly on the period 1763–1790s, is probably the best full account of Scotch-Irish settlement, culture and economy, valid for the whole century in outline; Carl Bridenbaugh, "The Back Country", in *Myths and Realities: Societies of the Colonial South* (Baton Rouge, 1952), 119–96, congruent with Buck, is remarkable, and Freeman Hart, *Valley of Virginia,* 3–32, 149–69, valuable. There is too little recent work upon Pennsylvania farming, but James Lemon, *Best Poor Man's Country,* and A. C. Lord, "The Pre-Revolutionary Agriculture of Lancaster County, Pennsylvania", *Lancaster County Historical Journal,* 79 (1975), 23–42, are indispensable, as is E. Estyn Evans, "The Scotch-Irish: Their Cultural Adaption and Heritage in the American Old West," in E. R. R. Green, *Essays in Scotch-Irish History* (London, 1969), 69–86. For the maturing middle class seaboard community, Bridenbaugh, *Cities in Revolt,* and Gilchrist, *Growth of Seaport Cities,* set the urban context; John Munroe, *Federalist Delaware, 1775–1815* (New Brunswick, 1954), 21–67 and John Neuenschwander, *The Middle Colonies and the Coming of the American Revolution* (London, 1973), 9–27 were suggestive, and the picture amplified with biographical material cited on Scotch-Irish revolutionary leaders in chapters six and seven, and on traders cited in chapter two: considerably more is available in such works as the county histories of eastern and central Pennsylvania, and the county historical journals: see below, pp. 248 for examples. On the South, Ramsey, *Carolina Cradle* and Meriwether, *Expansion of South Carolina,* were useful, John A. Caruso, *The Appalachian Frontier* (New York, 1959), weak.

Primary Sources: I had time only to examine the patterns of correspondence in the vast Historical Society of Pennsylvania Collections, which, properly and exhaustively used, would transform our conception of Ulster and Irish America: none of the Scotch-Irish chroniclers, not excepting scholars such as Klett, Dunaway and Leyburn, have done so. Papers available are the Bryan, Hand, Irvine, Lamberton, Logan, McHenry,

McKean, Marshall, Strettell, Thomson and Wayne (Logan, Strettell and Marshall being Irish Quakers), and those of George Meade and Mathew Carey, John Keating, Thomas FitzSimons and James Mease on the native Irish connection. Diaries and travels are also useful: William Fisk, ed., "The Diary of John Cuthbertson, Missionary to the Covenanters of Colonial Pennsylvania", *PMHB*, 73 (1949), 441–58; Joshua Gilpin, "Journal of a Journey to Bethlehem [1802]," *PMHB*, 46 (1922), 21, 143 and "Journey of a Tour from Philadelphia [1809]" *PMHB*, 50 (1926), 71; L. H. Butterfield, ed., "Dr. Benjamin Rush's Journal of a Trip to Carisle in 1784", *PMHB*, 74 (1950), 443–56; Fortescue Cumming, *Sketches of a Tour to the Western Country* (Pittsburg, 1810); J. F. D. Smyth, *A Tour*, 1:61–186, 2:116–62; Hunter D. Farish, *Journal and Letters of Philip Vickers Fithian: Journal, 1773–4* (Williamsburg, 1943) and Robert G. Albion and Leonidas Dodson, *Philip Vickers Fithian: Journal, 1775–76* (Princeton, 1932); Charles Woodmason, *The Carolina Backcountry on the Eve of the Revolution. The Journals . . .* ed. Richard J. Hooker (Chapel Hill, N.C., 1953); Hugh T. Lefler, ed., *North Carolina History Told by Contemporaries* (Chapel Hill, 1965); Patrick McRoberts, "Tour through Part of the North Provinces of North America, 1774–75", ed. C. Bridenbaugh, *PMHB*, 59 (1935), 134–80.

For comparable material on Ulster backgrounds, W. H. Crawford, *Domestic Industry in Ireland* (Dublin 1972); T. H. Mullin, *Coleraine in Georgian Times* (Belfast, 1977); Denis C. Rushe, *Monaghan in the Eighteenth Century* (Dundalk, 1916); W. G. Simpson, ed., *Ordnance Survey Memoir for the Parish of Antrim* (Belfast, 1969); and the *Statistical Surveys* of Sir Charles Cooke for *Armagh* (1804) and *Cavan* (1802), of J. Dubourdieu for *Antrim* (1812) and *Down* (1802), of J. McParlan for *Donegal* (1802) and G. V. Sampson for *Derry* (*Survey*, 1802; *Memoir*, 1814).

Unpublished dissertations: Eugene R. Fingerhut, "Assimilation of Immigrants on the Frontier of New York, 1764–1776", Columbia U., New York, 1962, covers the settlement of Orange and Ulster counties; George W. Franz, "Paxton: A Study of Community Structure and Social Mobility in the Colonial Backcountry of Pennsylvania", Rutgers, New Brunswick, 1974. Both of these valuably detail the dynamic, cumulative and middle-class-led patterns of frontier and post-frontier life.

The section has been derived from these materials, except with regard to the patterns of women's lives in which there is scattered detail in Dunaway, *Scotch-Irish*, 188–9, and Julia C. Spruill, *Women's Life and Work in the Southern Colonies* (Chapel Hill, 1938, r. New York, 1972); on folk-music in George P. Jackson, *White Spirituals of the Southern Uplands* (1933, r. New York, 1965) and in the mis-named Cecil Sharp, *English Folksongs from the Southern Appalachians* (London, 1932), both by musicologists, as are David D. Buchan, *The Ballad and the Folk* (London, 1972) on the Scottish background and Herbert Hughes, *Irish Country Songs*, 4 v. (London, 1909–36), for many Sharp songs from Ireland; on church life, Guy Klett, *Presbyterians in Colonial Pennsylvania* (Philadelphia, 1937); Ernest Trice Thompson, *Presbyterians in the South, 1607–1861* (Richmond, 1963), 18–125; L. J. Trinterud, *The Forming of an American Tradition* (Philadelphia, 1949), supplemented by Howard Miller, "A Contracting Community: American Presbyterians, Social Conflict and Higher Education, 1730–1820", Ph.D., University of Michigan; Martin Lodge "The Crisis of the Churches in the Middle Colonies, 1720–1750," *PMHB*, 95 (1971), 195–220, and many others in *JPH*. For background J. C. Beckett, *Protestant Dissent in Ireland, 1687–1780* (London, 1948) and J. S. Reid, *History of the Presbyterian Church in Ireland* (Belfast, 1851).

Quotations in the section are as follows: Dunaway, *Scotch-Irish in Col. Penn.*, 165, 181, but contrast Leyburn, *Scotch-Irish*, 151–53; "The frontiersman . . ." T. W.

Moody, "The Ulster Scot in Colonial and Revolutionary America", *Studies*, 34 (Dublin, 1945), 86; Bridenbaugh, "Back Country", in *Myths and Realities*, 135; Lord, "Pre-Revolutionary Agriculture", *passim;* Woodmason, quoted Bridenbaugh, 177; Huidekoper, in Buck, *Western Pennsylvania*, 212–213; Spruill, *Women's Life and Work*, 59; Matthews (1798), in Buck, *Western Pennslyvania*, 330; on early marriage, Spruill, 139, from Lawson, 1718, slightly differently reported in Land, *Bases of the Plantation Society*, 198, from Brickell, 1737: the latter may have plagiarised Lawson (common then as now!), yet in doing so revealed his own agreement. Dennis O'Bryan, from Buck, *Western Pennsylvania*, 328, and McAdooe in Spruill, 181; Miss Steel's tombstone in Klett, *Presbyt. in Col. Penn.* 182; J. F. D. Smyth, *Tour*, 1:102–04 and 2:162 on Scotch-Irish business.

Youthful Bondage

General and Middle Colonies: The indenture records from Philadelphia, 1745–46, and 1771, in *PMHB*, v. 30–32 (1906–08), op. cit., and in the Penn. German Soc. *Proceedings, 16 (1907)*, op. cit., and runaway advertisements from the *American Mercury*, 1741–46, and the *Pennsylvania Chronicle, Pennsylvania Packet, New York Journal,* and *Pennsylvania Gazette*, 1768–75 (all in microform at Columbia University Libraries) were the prime sources, together with Gottlieb Mittleberger, *Journey to Pennsylvania in the Year 1750*, ed. John Clive and Oscar Handlin (Harvard, 1960): other travel accounts of the middle colonies have virtually nothing to say on so major an institution, which was the German's main concern. Secondary material is good, but strangely oblique upon the Irish as such, although they constitued the bulk of the servants: F. R. Diffenderfer, *The German Immigration into Pennsylvania, 1700–1775.* Part II, *The Redemptioners*, op. cit., has scattered Irish material; Karl F. Geiser, *Redemptioners and Indentured Servants in Pennsylvania* (New Haven, 1901); Cheesman A. Herrick, *White Servitude in Pennsylvania* (Philadelphia, 1926, r. New York, 1969); Marcus W. Jernegan, *Laboring and Dependent Classes in Colonial America, 1607–1783* (Chicago, 1931); Samuel McKee, *Labour in Colonial New York, 1664–1776* (New York, 1935), 89–113; Richard Morris, *Government and Labor in Early America* (New York 1946), 341–3, 448n; and Margaret Cowden, "Lost Americans: On the Trail of some New York Indentured Servants", Masters essay, Columbia University. For the Irish rural and urban background, see the citations to chapter one.

Southern Colonies: There is considerable source material in Ulrich B. Phillips, ed., *Plantation and Frontier*, v. I of J. R. Commons et al., *Documentary History of American Industrial Society* (Cleveland, 1910), 339–75, and some in Lord, *Bases of the Plantation Society*, op. cit.; William Eddis, *Letters From America, Historical and Descriptive* (London, 1772, r. Harvard, 1969), 35–46; and John Brickell, *Natural History of North Carolina* (Dublin, 1737, r. New York, 1969), 30–46, 258–9, 267–71, with the harsher colours painted by the former (on Maryland, 1769–77) perhaps affected by the hostilities of the Revolution, although scholars have not said so; and runaway advertisements in the *Maryland Gazette*, 1745–47 and the *Virginia Gazettes* (Rind's and Purdie and Dixon's), 1768–1773. Secondary material is good, but (despite the vast expansion of the field recently), detailed studies of the related institution of black slavery, abundant for 1800–65, do not exist for 1700–75 and could conceivably alter our view of other servitude forms in that period: see Smith, *Colonists in Bondage*, esp. 131, 167, 220, 228–35, 239–41, 250, 265–7; J. C. Ballagh, *White Servitude in the*

Colony of Virginia (Baltimore, 1895); John S. Bassett, *Slavery and Servitude in the Colony of North Carolina* (Baltimore, 1896); E. I. McCormac, *White Servitude in Maryland, 1634–1820* (Baltimore, 1904) and Warren Smith, *White Servitude in Colonial South Carolina* (Columbia, S. C., 1961), this last, with Herrick, being the fullest upon the Irish. Freeman Hart, *Valley of Virginia*, op. cit., 15–18, 25, 55, adds detail, as does Russell Menard "From Servants to Slaves", *Social Studies*, 16 (1977), 355–90, on Md.

For Irish status in contrast to black, see Smith, *Colonists in Bondage*, 171; Jordan, *White Over Black*, 85–88; Morris, *Govt. and Labor*, 341–43; McCormac, *White Servitude in Maryland*, 67–69, 75; and Phillips, *Plantation and Frontier*, 316–17, for specific instances, and also MG, 16 Aug. 1745, VG (P & D), 7 February 1771 for exceptions. See also below, pp.253–4. The fullest account of an Irish plantation workforce is William D. Hoyt, "White Servants at 'Northampton', 1772–74", *Maryland Historical Magazine*, 33 (1938), 126–133. Quotations on the South Carolina situation are from *The Papers of Henry Laurens* (Columbia, S.C., 1976), 5:567, 629–30, 700, and from *A State of the Province of Georgia* (London, 1740), 18 (actually on South Carolina). There seems to have been some fluctuation in the proportions of native and Protestant Irish in South Carolina, to judge by somewhat contrasting tables in Warren Smith, *op. cit.*, 23–26, 46–47.

Smith, *Colonists in Bondage*, 162–74, rightly stresses the important precedents of Irish 17th c. indentured servitude in the Caribbean; since the developing history of American black slavery is conceding the crucial importance of the Anglo-West Indian precedent, these may prove to be even more significant: see various articles and documents on the 17th c. West Indian Irish by Aubrey Gwynn in *Analecta Hibernica*: "Documents Relating to the Irish in the West Indies" IV: 139–236, and in *Studies*, 18 (1929), 377–93 and 648–63, 19 (1930), 279–94, 607–23, and 20 (1931), 291–305. Black slavery elevated the Hiberno–West Indian population as it did that elsewhere: for a portrayal by one of its members, Patrick Browne, *The Civil and Natural History of Jamaica* (London, 1789), and Irene Neu, "From Kilkenny to Louisiana, Eighteenth Century Irish Immigration", *Mid-America*, 49 (1967), 101–114, a study of immigration via that community.

Instances of cruelty, running away and mass-breakaway cited in the text are from MG, 5 July 1745 (Hogan, Jolly, Kirk), 27 May 1746 (Kirk, Jolly and Flanagan), 22 April 1746 (Horney), 2 and 30 Sept. 1746 (Magee, then Haily): cf. 16 June 1747, for Edward Charleton, "born in Ireland . . . was very bare of Cloaths", an indication of ill-treatment never found in the middle colonies, and the editorial, 4 August 1747, against cruelty causing servant suicide; for later, VG (P & D), 3 and 24 Jan. 1771 (Campbell, then Carey), 26 August 1773 (Farrell); VG (R), 23 August 1770 (Ruark), 15 June 1771 (Clerk), 10 Dec. 1772 (Savage), 9 Dec., 1773 (Drwer); for the Egg's Island breakaway, VG (P & D), 21 and 28 Jan. 1773, and "A Picture of Europe", VG (P & D), 26 Dec. 1771. Evidence of continuing servant trade to the area, sometimes in British vessels unlisted in Lockhart, which called in Ireland, can be found to the eve of the revolution: VG (P & D), 24 Jan. 1771, 28 March 1771, 25 March 1773 (Industry, Jenny and Justitia). The 1741 N. Car. Act is reproduced in Land, *Bases of a Plantation Society*, 209.

For the contested aftermath, Smith, *Colonists in Bondage*, 285–306; Herrick, *White Servitude in Pennsylvania*, 267–85; Brickell, loc. cit.; Mosley, quoted in Robert Walsh and W. Lloyd Fox, *Maryland: A History* (Baltimore, 1974), 92; McKee, *Labor in Colonial New York*, 112–113, quoting Moore; Hart, *Valley of Virginia*, loc. cit.; for the Scotch–Irish, Leyburn, *The Scotch–Irish*, 176–79, 244–45; he assumes that the great numbers discoverable in the documentation cited above simply melted into the general Ulster Scots community, but there has never been detailed evidence of the process. See generally, further, pp.142–3, 190–1 and 253–4. On Western Maryland, J. F. D. Smyth, *Tour*, 2:116–19, and O'Brien, *Washington's Associations with the Irish*, 244–48, and, more generally on patterns of advancement and repression affecting the Irish: Catherine Crary, "The Humble Immigrant and the American Dream,"*Jour. Am. Hist.*, 46 (1959), 55, 58–9, 60–61 for examples from the 1770s; and A. C. Lord, *The Dulanys of Maryland* (Baltimore, 1955), 1–42 for earlier ones. However, Donnell Owings, *His Lordship's Patronage: Offices of Profit in Colonial Maryland* (Baltimore 1953), shows how exceptional the Macnemara, Carroll Sr. and Dulany Sr. cases were: the Baltimores had enough difficulty finding office for Anglo-American Catholics! Mary Augustina Ray, *American Opinion of Roman Catholicism in the Eighteenth Century* (New York, 1936) and Emberson Proper, *Colonial Immigration Laws* (New York, 1900), detail barriers.

Chapter 5

P. 109: These works mention the Scotch–Irish only incidentally or not at all, and can be taken as representative: John R. Alden, *The American Revolution, 1775–1783* (New York, 1954) and *A History of the American Revolution* (New York, 1975); Douglas Freeman, *George Washington*, 7 vols. (New York, 1948–57); Merrill Jensen, *The American Revolution Within America* (New York, 1974) and *The Founding of a Nation* (New York, 1968); Dumas Malone, *Jefferson,* 5 vols. (Boston, 1948–74); Gordon Wood, *The Creation of the American Republic, 1776–1787* (Chapel Hill, N.C., 1969). The work of pre-war scholars was somewhat more attentive, e.g., Evarts Greene, *The Revolutionary Generation, 1763–1790* (New York, 1943), 48–9, 69–71, 157–60, 224, 247.

P. 110: Ambrose Serle, *The American Journal*, ed. Tatum (San Marino, Cal., 1940), 209, 256–259, and his report to Dartmouth in D. F. Stevens, *Facsimiles of Manuscripts . . . Relating to America, 1773–1783,* 26 vols. (London, 1889–95), 24: 2045, 2057, reprinted in O'Brien, *A Hidden Phase of American History* (New York, 1919), 107; *Diary of Frederick Mackenzie*, 2 vols. (Harvard, 1930), 1:81; Joseph Galloway, *Letters to a Nobleman on the Conduct of the War in the Middle Colonies* (London, 1779, 1780), 25, and the report of his examination before a House of Commons committee of inquiry, *The Examination of Joseph Galloway . . . Before the House of Commons . . .* (London, 1779), as further reported in the N.Y. *Royal Gazette*, 27 Oct. 1779; *The Narrative of Lieutenant General Sir William Howe . . . relative to his conduct . . . in North America* (London, 1781), as made before the same committee on 29 April 1779; Sir Henry Clinton to Lord George Germain, 23 October 1778, W. L. Clements Library, University of Michigan; Major General James Robertson before the same inquiry, as reported, *Parliamentary Register* (London, 1779), vol. 13:276, 305 for 8 June 1779. Some of these, and the journal of Captain Pell, are quoted uncritically and poorly cited in Michael O'Brien, *A Hidden Phase of American History*, 75–85, 102–115. The Galloway *Royal Gazette* report and the Clinton/Germain letter are reproduced in the facsimile packet *Ireland and Irishmen in the American War of Independence* (Dublin, 1976). Heinrichs is quoted in almost all accounts of the Scotch–Irish and Pennsylvania, as in those of Thayer and Ireland following.

P. 110–12: For "Old Countrymen" see Clinton to Germain, *op. cit.*, and J. P.

Martin, *Private Yankee Doodle: A Narrative of a Revolutionary Soldier*, ed. G. F. Scheer (Boston, 1962), 145. The views of Franklin and Rush are cited in Owen Ireland, "The Ethnic-Religious Dimension of Pennsylvania Politics, 1778–1779", *WMQ*, 30 (1973), 424–425, and those of other Americans, John Allen, Jonathan Sergeant and Uriah Tracy to the same effect in Theodore Thayer, *Pennsylvania Politics and the Growth of Democracy, 1740–1776* (Harrisburg, 1953), 184–85. For further views, David Ramsay, *The History of the American Revolution*, 2 vols. (London, 1793), 2:597 and Marquis de Chastellux, *Travels in North America* (Dublin, 1787), 2:36–38. The following offer only negative evidence: John C. Fitzpatrick, *The Writings of George Washington*, 39 vols. (Washington, D.C., 1931–44); Lyman H. Butterfield ed., *The Diaries of John Adams*, 5 vols. (Harvard, 1961–66); Julian C. Boyd, ed., *The Jefferson Papers*, 18 vols. (1950–1971); A. H. Smyth, *The Works of Benjamin Franklin*, 10 vols. (New York, 1905–07), but the full-scale Franklin *Papers*, ed. Leonard W. Labree et al., 19 vols. (1959–75), have yet to reach and cover the revolutionary period and should somewhat redress the balance, as does Lyman H. Butterfield ed., *Benjamin Rush: Letters*, 2 vols. (Princeton, 1951). Contrast Lincoln's concern: William Hanchett, *Irish: Charles G. Halpine* . . . (Syracuse, 1970) and Robert Athearn, *Thomas Francis Meagher* (Boulder, 1949). George III and Walpole are cited in Leyburn, *Scotch-Irish*, 305, but inattention is paid the nature of their warped sources, which played upon their prejudices. Apart from Galloway, other exiled Loyalists were plying the same line: Douglas G. Adair and John A. Schurtz, eds., *Peter Oliver's Origin and Progress of the American Rebellion: A Tory View* (San Marino, Cal., 1961). For Baurmeister, his letters and journals edited by Bernhard A. Uhlendorf, *Revolution In America* . . . *Carl Leopold Baurmeister* (New Brunswick, N. J., 1957), 593.

P. 112: John Neuenschwander, *The Middle Colonies and the Coming of the American Revolution* (Port Washington, N.Y. 1973).

P. 113: J. G. Simms, *Colonial Nationalism, 1698–1776, Molyneux's "Case of Ireland* . . . *Stated"* (Dublin, 1976); Caroline Robbins, " 'When It Is That Colonies May Turn Independent'. . . Francis Hutcheson (1694–1746)," *WMQ*, 11 (1954), 214–251, with quotation, 216. For the background, see Robbins, *The Eighteenth Century Commonwealthman* (Harvard, 1959); Bernard Bailyn, *Ideological Origins of the American Revolution* (Harvard, 1967); H. Trevor Colburn, *The Lamp of Experience* (Chapel Hill, N. C., 1967); and David Lovejoy, *The Glorious Revolution in America* (New York, 1974). For the Dublin twist to these traditions see the works cited in Simms' book.

P. 114: Elizabeth A. Ingersoll, "Francis Alison, American *Philosophe*, 1704–1799", unpubl. Ph.D., Univ. of Delaware, 1974; James L. McAllister, "Francis Alison and John Witherspoon: Political Philosophers and Revolutionaries", *JPH*, 54 (1976), 33–60; John Coleman, *Thomas McKean* (Rockaway, N.J., 1975); William C. Lehmann, *Scottish and Scotch-Irish Contributions to Early American Life and Culture* (Port Washington, N.Y., 1977); Douglas Sloan, *The Scottish Enlightenment and the American College Ideal* (New York, 1971) and Donald R. Cone, "The Influence of Princeton on Higher Education in the South before 1825," *WMQ*, 2 (1945), 359–396.

P. 114–15: Coleman, *McKean*, 169–70; Wayland Dunaway, *Scotch-Irish of Col. Penn.*, 157–60; Robert L. Scribner, ed., *Revolutionary Virginia: The Road to Independence*, 2 vols. (Richmond, 1975), 2:298–302; Ernest T. Thomson, *Presbyterians in the South, 1607–1861* (Richmond, 1963), 89–90, is the most judicious conclusion on the Mecklenburg resolves.

P. 115–16: A full bibliography is inappropriate here. Jensen, *The American Revolution Within America*, and Elisha Douglass, *Rebels and Democrats* (Chapel Hill, N.C. 1955) are the best recent 'internal revolution' interpretations. Why such views seem no longer so persuasive can be gauged from major collections such as David Jacobson, ed. *Essays on the American Revolution* (New York, 1970), and Jack Greene, ed., *The Reinterpretation of the American Revolution* (New York, 1968). More pointed re-appraisals include "The Two Revolutions" by R. B. Morris in his *The American Revolution Reconsidered* (New York, 1967), 43–91.

P. 117: A. N. Sheps, "English Radicalism and the American Revolution", unpubl. paper, Anglo-American Conference of Historians, Univ. of London, July 1974; Joyce Appleby, "America as a Model for the Radical French Reformers of 1789", *WMQ*, 28 (1971), 267ff; John Brewer, *Party Ideology and Popular Politics* (Cambridge, 1976); 201–216; Colin Bonwick, *English Radicals and the American Revolution* (Chapel Hill, N.C., 1977).

P. 118: Dunaway, *The Scotch-Irish in Col. Penn.*, 120. His whole account, 118–138, has now only limited value. The works upon which he drew included J. P. Selsam, *The Pennsylvania Constitution of 1776* (Philadelphia, 1935); and C. H. Lincoln. *The Revolutionary Movement in Pennsylvania* (Philadelphia, 1901), with perspectives derived from F. J. Turner, *The Significance of the Frontier in American History* (r. New York, 1966). P. L. Paxson, *The Frontier in American History 1763–1893* (Boston, 1924), 4, *passim*, offered the fullest argument on Scotch-Irish democracy.

P. 118–33: The following account is based upon these works, *The Pennsylvania Packet*, 1775–1778. Wayne Bockelman and Owen Ireland, "The Internal Revolution in Pennsylvania: An Ethnic-Religious Interpretation", *PH*, 41 (1974), 16ff. Wayne Bockelman, "Local Politics in Lancaster County in Pre-Revolutionary Pennsylvania", *PMHB*, 97 (1973), 45–74. J. P. Gleason, "A Scurrilous Colonial Election and Franklin's Reputation", *WMQ*, 18 (1961) 68–84. Robert Gough, "Notes on the Pennsylvania Revolutionaries of 1776", *PMHB*, 96 (1972), 89–103. Owen Ireland, "The Ethnic-Religious Dimension", *op. cit.* C. S. Rowe, "Thomas McKean and the Coming of the Revolution", *PMHB*, 26 (1972), 3–37. John J. Zimmerman, "Charles Thompson, 'The Sam Adams of Philadelphia',", *Jour. Am. Hist.*, 45 (1958), 464–80. Carl Bridenbaugh, *Mitre and Sceptre* (New York, 1962), 252–342. Robert Brunhouse, *The Counter-Revolution in Pennsylvania, 1776–1790* (Harrisburg, 1942). Marvin H. Buxbaum, *Benjamin Franklin and the Zealous Presbyterians* (Penn. State, 1975). John M. Coleman, *Thomas McKean, op. cit.* John R. Dunbar, ed. *The Paxton Papers* (The Hague, 1957). Arthur Graeff, *The Relations between the Pennsylvania Germans and the British Authorities* (Norristown, 1939), pp. 189–254 on their convergence with Scotch-Irish. David Hawke, *In the Midst of Revolution* (Philadelphia, 1961). James H. Hutson, *Pennsylvania Politics, 1746–1770* (Princeton, N.J., 1972). Burton A. Konkle, *George Bryan* (Philadelphia, 1922), 42–263. John Neuenschwander, *The Middle Colonies and . . . the American Revolution, op. cit.* John F. Roche, *Joseph Reed* (New York, 1957). Dietmar Rothermund, *The Layman's Progress: Religion and Political Experience in Colonial Pennsylvania, 1740–1770* (Philadelphia, 1961). In the rest of this section, sources are given only for quotations or special points.

P. 120: George Ross's "Report", *Delaware History*, 10 (1962), 129; Fingerhut, "Assimilation of Immigrants on the Frontier of New York", *op. cit.*, 294.

P. 124: Carl Bridenbaugh, *Cities in Revolt, 1743–1776* (New York, 1955), 87; James Hutson, "An Investigation of the Inarticulate: Philadelphia's 'White Oaks',", *WMQ*, 3 (1971), 3–25, and Zimmerman, "Charles Thompson", *op. cit.*; see pp.

96–97 for evidence of Irish and Scotch-Irish penetration of the urban workforce.

P. 124: Alison to Stiles, 1 Aug. 1769, reprinted *JPH*, 52 (1974), 344–46.

P. 126: Thomson to Franklin, 24 Sept. 1745, in Zimmerman, "Charles Thomson", 468.

P. 127: Reed to Dartmouth, 27 Dec. 1773, in Roche, *Reed*, 39.

P. 128: Alison to unidentified party, 20 Aug. 1776, in Brunhouse, *Counter-Revolution*, 13. The characterisation of Assembly policy is Howard Miller's: see his "Grammars of Liberty", *JPH*, 54 (1976), 157.

P. 130: McKean is quoted in Rowe, "McKean and the Coming of the Revolution", *op. cit.*, 37; Reed to Wayne, 13 June 1781, in Roche, *Reed*, 187.

P. 130–3: Bryan's own description of those now opposing the revolutionary constitution he helped establish, is revealing: Konkle, *Bryan*, 304–05; for Findley, see Samuel Harding in Amer. Hist. Ass., *Report*, 1894, 393, and Brunhouse, *Counter-Revolution*, 225–7, 297.

P. 133: For the South, see above pp. 82–3, 100–1, and John R. Alden, *The South in the Revolution, 1763–1789* (Baton Rouge, 1957), together with the works cited below.

P. 133–34: Freeman Hart, *The Valley of Virginia in the American Revolution, 1763–1789* (Chapel Hill, N.C., 1942), 28, 33–101; for shrewd, uncelebratory background, Patricia G. Johnson, *James Patton and the Appalachian Colonists* (Verona, Va., 1973), and on politics, see Robert Detweiler, "Political Factionalism and the . . . Virginia House of Burgesses, 1730–1776", *Va. Mag.*, 80 (1972), 267–285.

P. 134–35: Richard M. Brown, *The South Carolina Regulators* (Harvard, 1963); Richard Walsh, *Charleston's Sons of Liberty* (Columbia, S.C., 1959); Edward McCrady, *The History of South Carolina in the Revolution*, 2 vols. (New York, 1901–02, r. 1969); M. F. Treacy, *Prelude to Yorktown: The Southern Campaign of Nathanael Greene, 1780–81* (Chapel Hill, N.C., 1963).

P. 135–37: Alan S. Brown ed., "James Simpson's Reports on the Carolina Loyalists, 1779–1780", *Jour. of Southern Hist.*, 21 (1955), 513–515; Caldwell, "The Character and Doom . . ." reprinted in *JPH*, 52 (1974), 388–92 with the Alison and others circular, *ibid.*, 392–96; Robert O. De Mond, *The Loyalists in North Carolina During the Revolution* (Durham, N.C., 1944); Elisha Douglass, *Rebels and Democrats*, 111ff.; Robert Gaynard, "Radical and Conservative in Revolutionary North Carolina", *WMQ*, 24 (1967), 568ff.; E. R. R. Green, "The Scotch-Irish and the Coming of the Revolution in North Carolina", *Irish Historical Studies*, 7 (1950), 77–86; Miller, "Grammar of Liberty", op. cit., 146–49; Charles Sellers, Jr., "Making a Revolution: The North Carolina Whigs, 1765–1775", in J. C. Sitterson ed., *Studies in Southern History* (Chapel Hill, N.C., 1957), 25ff.; Durward Stokes, "Adam Boyd, Publisher, Preacher, Patriot," *N. Car. Hist. Record*, 49 (1972), 1–21; Charles Woodmason, *The Carolina Backcountry*, ed. R. Hooker (Chapel Hill, N.C., 1953), 190ff.; and for an Anglo-Irish view that the whole province was anti-British, and that its invasion was 'quixotic', see "Letters of Charles O'Hara to the Duke of Grafton", *So. Car. Hist. Mag.*, 65 (1964), 158–180, an estimate borne out in Burke Davis, *The Cowpens-Guilford Campaign* (Philadelphia, 1962) and especially as regards the Scotch-Irish in Lynam C. Draper, *King's Mountain and Its Heroes* (New York, 1929). *The Roster of Soldiers from North Carolina in the American Revolution* (Durham, N.C., 1932), is also suggestive in that regard, if not conclusive as to actual service.

P. 137: Michael O'Brien, *A Hidden Phase of American History*, 443–526 for lists, and 385–92 for part of his motivation; see J. Franklin Jameson, *American Historical Review*, 26 (1920), 797–99, and the critical yet sensitive study by John Rodechko in *New York Historical Society Quarterly*, 54 (1970), 173–192: "Michael J. O'Brien".

P. 137, 142: Ella Lonn, *Foreigners in the Confederacy* (Chapel Hill, N.C., 1940) and *Foreigners in the Union Army and Navy* (Baton Rouge, 1952); Blanche McEniry *American Catholics and the War with Mexico* (Washington, D.C., 1937); Doyle, *Irish Americans, Native Rights and National Empires*, 165–223; R.B. McDowell, "Ireland in the Eighteenth Century British Empire", *op cit.*, pp. 61–62; William Riordon, *Plunkitt of Tammany Hall* (New York, 1963), 15.

P. 142: Charles Metzger, *The Quebec Act* (New York, 1936), *passim;* M.A. Ray, *Opinion of Catholics, op. cit., passim;* John Brickell, *loc. cit.*

P. 142: Mackenzie, *Diary*, 1:81.

P. 142–44: John Shy, *A People Numerous and Armed* (New York, 1976); Herrick, *White Servitude in Pennsylvania*, c.XIII, 233–51; O'Brien, *George Washington's Associations with the Irish* (New York, 1937), 244–48 and 249–54 for Virginia soldiers generally in 1754–58; Smith, *Colonists in Bondage*, 279–283; McCormac, *White Servitude in Maryland*, 80–91.

P. 143: Herrick, *White Servitude in Pennsylvania*, 251–253; McKee, *Labor in Colonial New York*, 175.

P. 144: See above pp.48–9; O'Brien, *Washington's Associations*, 241–43 lists probable Irish captains in American privateering service, many of which tally with ships masters' names listed by McCusker for Philadelphia pre-war registration. Not all were of native stock, some of them such as James Cathcart and Gustavus Conyngham were of settler stock. The tradition remained, however, and in 1853 Archbishop Bedini, as Papal Delegate, reported to the Vatican that whereas high army rank was closed to Catholics, naval rank was more open: McAvoy, *Hist. of Am. Cath. Church*, 173.

P. 146: Green, "The Scotch Irish and the Coming of the Revolution", *op cit.*, 77.

P. 146: This paragraph is based upon a reading of the journals concerned for part of the 1770s and the later ones for most of the 1890s: see my *Irish Americans, Native Rights and National Empires*, 1890–1901, 342–50 and also W.L. Joyce, *Editors and Ethnicity: The Irish American Press, 1848–1883* (New York, 1976). On Boyd, see Stokes "Adam Boyd", *op. cit.*: on Dunlap, *DAB*, 5:514–15, and on Gaine, *DAB*, 7:92–93.

P. 146–7: Contrast Ralph Wood ed., *The Pennsylvania Germans* (Princeton, 1942) with John A. Hawgood, *The Tragedy of German America* (London, 1940). The collections of the German American Society and the *Proceedings* of the Pennsylvania German Society on the depth of language and folklore survival in rural Pennsylvania before 1914 especially are a revelation as to possibilities of cultural tenacity. For the Ulster quotations, Hart, *Valley of Virginia*, 87, 166; Bridenbaugh, *Mitre and Sceptre*, 185.

P. 147: Oscar Handlin, ed., *Children of the Uprooted* (New York, 1966), xvii–xix, *passim*. But Brown, *Irish American Nationalism*, 63–4; Doyle, *Irish Americans, Native Rights, National Empires*, 1–89; and a forthcoming study of Kerby Miller reveal more inter-generational coherence in 19th c. Irish America than Handlin's thesis would allow, based upon the absence of a linguistic breach, upon the church, on the political machines and upon the general need of the community for a leadership conversant with the ropes of Amerian life. Most Tammany and most Church leaders were American born in the 1880s–1910: see the biographies in Bernard Code, *A Biographical Dictionary of the American Hierarchy* (New York, 1940), and in E. Vale Blake, *History of the Tammany Society, 1789–1900* (New York, 1901), 294–325. For the absorption of new Ulster immigrants into already established families, see Coleman, *McKean*, 10–11 (a genealogy), and the genealogies in many such works as Anon.,*The Scotch Irish of Northampton County, Pennsylvania* (Easton, Pa.,

Northampton Co. Hist. and Genealogical Soc., 1926) and the Bucks Co. Hist. Soc. *Papers,* 8 vols. (Doylestown and Riegelsville, Pa., 1908–1940). It is possible that as with a later Irish America, a sense of slight, and of difference, impelled American-born Ulster Americans back into the leadership of their communities. G. S. Rowe argues that Thomas McKean was driven by the ethnic envy he faced in college: "McKean and the Coming of the Revolution", *op. cit.* 3–10. For the common culture of Ulster immigrants and America, certainly among literate people, see Michael Kraus, *The Atlantic Civilization: Eighteenth Century Origins* (Ithaca, N.Y., 1949); Ralph Barton Perry, *Puritanism and Democracy* (New York, 1944); Sloan, *Scottish Enlightenment and American College Ideal;* Tolles, *Logan and the Culture of Provincial America;* and Lehmann, *Scottish and Scotch-Irish Contributions.* Rothermund, *Layman's Progress, passim,* argues that retention of European culture and religion did not retard *political* Americanisation, but rather hastened it by rendering inevitable a politics of interplay and laicism, a view sustained by the studies completed since his work.

P. 148: Alice Baldwin, "Sowers of Sedition: The Presbyterian Clergy and the American Revolution", *WMQ,* 5(1948), 52–76; Leonard Kramer, "Presbyterians Approach the American Revolution", and "Muskets in the Pulpit, 1776–83", *JPH,* 31(1953), 71–86, 167–80, 229–44 and 32 (1954), 37–52; Klett, *Presbyterians in Col. Penn.,* 242–266.

P. 148: Clinton to Lord George Germain, New York, 23 Oct. 1778, *op. cit.*

P. 148: Ambrose Serle, *Journal,* ed. Tatum, p. 259 for 18 Oct. 1777; T.N. Brown, *Irish American Nationalism, 1870–1890* (Philadelphia, 1966), *passim.*

P. 148–9: Francis von A. Cabeen, "The Society of the Sons of St. Tammany in Philadelphia", *PMHB,* 25(1901), 442, 26(1902), 216–18 and 27(1903), 43–45; the citation is from the (Philadelphia) *Freeman's Journal,* 10 April 1805. Although all but one of the ceremonial figures of the orders' rites or games were pseudo-Indians, the exception was also perhaps a take-off: that of a speaker called Captain O'Beal. The Scotch-Irish Tammanyites certainly knew sufficient Irish to so consciously name him "Captain Mouth!"

P. 150: In the middle colonies, runaway notices distinguish Irish dialects: Scotch-Irish are often noted as talking "broad", Anglo-Irish Ulster immigrants as talking "good English" and all other Irish as talking "much" or "little" "on the brogue", (the preposition was usually used) *or* as having bad English, the latter an indication of Irish as first language. Exceptions to such patterns were usually noted as remarkable. In the southern colonies, where there were proportionately fewer opportunities for a scattered population to become familiar with various Irish immigrants, planters inclined to record every Irish accent (even the then broad Scots of East Ulster) as a "brogue!" For evidence of Irish language usage or background, see PP 4 July 1774 and 7 March 1774; VG (R), 27 April 1769 and 22 Dec. 1768, 14 Feb. 1771; VG(P&D), 16 May 1771; PG, 7 July 1768; PC, 12 June 1769. For Gardiner, *Parliamentary Register* (Dublin, 1784), 3:125.

P. 150–51: *DAB,* 3:336 (Richard Butler), 3:364–5 (Pierce Butler), 8:223–4 (Hand), 11:523–24 (Thomas Lynch, Sr. and Jr.), 13:98–99 (Montgomery), 16:257–60 (Edward and John Rutledge) and 19:563–64 (Wayne). The same applies to other immigrants of upper-class background: James Cathcart, *DAB,* 3:572. Lower class Anglo-Irish immigrants may have been more radical, such as carpenter Thomas Proctor, artillery commander at Brandywine and Germantown: Cabeen, "Sons of St. Tammany", *PMHB,* 26 (1902), 344. Rev. Devereux Jarratt's family (poorer immigrants) in Virginia were Patriot: *The Life* (1806, r. New York, 1972).

P. 151: Konkle, *George Bryan,* 20–21, 189–98 and *passim;* Myers, *Immigration of*

Irish Quakers, 274; for Marshall, William Duane ed., *The Diary of Christopher Marshall* (Albany, 1877) and *DAB,* 12:306–307; for the common background, Thomas C. Hall, *The Religious Background of American Culture* (New York, 1930, r. 1959), on English dissenting culture, has not been replaced yet.

Chapter 6

Given the historiography of this period for the other nations affected by the "Atlantic revolution", the literature for Ireland remains surprisingly thin, virtually every problem which has exercised French, British and American historians recently remaining largely untouched: popular movements, ideology, the rising middle class, literacy, regionalism. The exceptions are those of political structure and landlord economy. I have attempted to re-shape some of the fragmentary information given often incidentally, in studies focused elsewhere, to at least suggest that such dimensions also existed in the Irish situation, and deserve much fuller study. Pioneering suggestions have been made by Gearóid Ó Tuathaigh, in extracted form in John Brady, ed., *Catholics and Catholicism in the Eighteenth Century Press* (Maynooth, 1965), in Caoimhín Ó Danachair, "The Penal Laws and Irish Folk Tradition," *PICHC,* 1961, pp. 10–16, and in Philip O'Connell, "The Plot Against Father Nicholas Sheehy," *PICHC,* 1965–7, 49–61. Compare these with Patrick O'Donoghue, "The Holy See and Ireland, 1780–1803," *Archivium Hibernicum,* 34 (1976/7), 99–108.

J. C. Beckett, *The Making of Modern Ireland* (London, 1966), 187–288, and his "Anglo–Irish Constitutional Relations in the Late Eighteenth Century" in his *Confrontations: Studies in Irish History* (London, 1972) 123–141; Owen Dudley Edwards, "The Impact of the American Revolution on Ireland", in R. R. Palmer, ed., *The Impact of the American Revolution Abroad,* (Washington, D.C., 1976), 127–159 and his "The American Image of Ireland: A Study of Its Early Phases", *Perspectives in American History,* 4 (1970), 314–41; R. Dudley Edwards, ed. "The Minute Book of the Catholic Committee (1770–93)"*Archivium Hibernicum,* 9 (1942), 3–172; F. G. James, *Ireland in the Empire* (Harvard, 1973), 251–312; Edith M. Johnston, *Great Britain and Ireland, 1760–1800* (Edinburgh, 1963) and *Ireland in the Eighteenth Century* (Dublin, 1974); W. E. H. Lecky, *A History of Ireland in the Eighteenth Century,* 5 vols. (London, 1892), masterfully abridged by L. P. Curtis, 1 Vol. (Chicago, 1972); R. B. McDowell, *Irish Public Opinion, 1750–1800* (London, 1944) and his "Ireland in the Eighteenth Century British Empire" in John Barry, ed., *Historical Studies,* 9 (Belfast, 1974), 49–63, which confirms that Catholics entered the British Army officially only from 1784, unofficially constituting 20% of soldiers during the American War; Mary MacNeill, *The Life and Times of Mary Ann McCracken* (Dublin, 1960), 23–26, 59–77, 86–192; T. H. D. Mahony, *Edmund Burke and Ireland* (Oxford, 1960); Constantia Maxwell, *Dublin Under the Georges, 1714–1830* (London, 1936), 24–45, 123–4; Thomas F. Moriarty, "The Irish Absentee Tax Controversy of 1773: A Study in Anglo–Irish Politics on the Eve of the American Revolution", *Proceedings* of the American Philosophical Society, 118 (1974), 370–408; Michael Kraus, "America and the Irish Revolutionary Movement", in Richard Morris, ed., *The Era of the American Revolution* (New York, 1965), 332–348; M. R. O'Connell, *Irish Politics and Social Conflict in the Age of the American Revolution* (Philadelphia, 1965); Michael J. O'Brien, *A Hidden Phase of American History* (New York, 1919), 1–73, critically used, provides useful material, which I have re-checked against the sources, esp. pp. 41, 43, 47–8; Patrick Rogers, *The Irish Volunteers and Catholic Emancipation, 1778–1793* (London, 1934), which, in the absence of anything else, is also fullest on parliamentary reform, with McDowell, *Public Opinion*, 97–219. On the later developments, Gearóid Ó Tuathaigh, *Ireland before the Famine, 1798–1848* (Dublin, 1972); Thomas Pakenham, *The Year of Liberty* (London, 1969) and Richard Hayes, *The Last Invasion of Ireland* (London, 1937) on 1798, and G. C. Bolton, *The Passing of the Irish Act of Union* (Oxford, 1966) on the finale. The English background is best co-ordinated through J. Steven Watson, *The Reign of George III, 1760–1815* (Oxford, 1960), despite his patrician contempt for Defenderism: "The underground peasant organization for arson and destruction", 383, n3 and other lapses, with Herbert Butterfield, *George III, Lord North and the People, 1779–1780* (London, 1949), on a key crisis. There is wanting a full account of the American revolutionary impact on Britain. David Freeman Hawke, *Paine* (New York, 1974), esp. 130–1, 226–33, 265–66, and Ray B. Browne, "The Paine-Burke Controversy in Eighteenth Century Irish Popular Songs" in his *The Celtic Cross*, ed. with W. J. Roscelli and R. Lofthus (Purdue, 1964), 80–97, are important, and Eric Foner, *Tom Paine and Revolutionary America* (New York, 1976), suggestive of his appeal elsewhere. Irish dissenter attitudes to the revolution emerge in Kenneth L. Carroll, "Irish and British Quakers and their American Relief Funds, 1778–1797," *PMHB*, 102 (1978), 437–57; Ernest Moyne, "The Reverend William Hazlitt," *WMQ*, 21 (1964), 288 ff.; W. D. Bailie, "W. Steele Dickson, D.D." *Irish Booklore*, 2 (1976), 239–67.

Unpublished theses include Raymond Barrett, "A Comparative Study of Imperial Constitutional Theory in Ireland and America in the Age of the American Revolution," Ph.D., Trinity College, Dublin, 1958, which perhaps unduly labours the now secure point that the Irish ascendancy were seeking to establish in fact parliamentary rights they enjoyed in theory, whereas the Americans were trying to re-adjust imperial relationships to match the legislative freedom they enjoyed in fact, but not in theory, before the 1760s: but does usefully point up how the threat of taxation to America did underscore to the Commons in Ireland the restrictions on its own trade, and the dangers of encroachment on its jealously regarded freedom of financial appropriation, however formal it was. However the older tendency of Charles McIlwain and Robert Schuyler to take seriously the legal comparisons between the two societies in relation to Britain, deserves more attention. Also Theresa O'Connor, "The more Immediate Effects of the American Revolution in Ireland", M.A., Queen's University, Belfast, 1937.

For popular manifestations, apart from above, see specifically E. Ó Muirgheasa, *Céad de Cheoltaibh Uladh*, 152; Zimmermann, *Irish Political Songs, 1789–1900* (Geneva, 1966); Gearóid Ó Tuathaigh, "Gaelic Ireland, Popular Politics and Daniel O'Connell", *Journal of the Galway Archaeological and History Society*, 74 (1974–5), 21–34, and Gréagoir Ó Dughaill, "Ballads and the Law, 1830–32", *Ulster Folklife*, 19 (1973), 38–40.

The books published in Ireland on America are listed above, p. 233. To these should be added Paine's *Letter Addressed to the Abbé Raynal Concerning Affairs in North America* (Dublin, 1782); William Robertson, *The History of America*, 2 vols. (Cork, 1792); Jean P. Brissot de Warville, *A New Journey in the United States* (Dublin, 1792). Among works preparing the public mind for parallels were such as Anon., *Liberty Boys—The True Friends of Liberty* (Cork, 1763). Examples of protective middle class Catholic thought include Arthur O'Leary, *Miscellaneous Tracts* (Dublin, 1791), others used are cited in McDowell, *Public Opinion*. See John T. Gilbert, *The History of Dublin*, 3 vols. (Dublin, 1854–59), 3:103–05 on rioting.

For the Irish poems on Washington, with texts and translations by Tom Peete Cross, F. N. Robinson and Douglas Hyde, see "Communication by George L. Kittredge, Feb. 1911 Meeting: An Irish Song Relating to Washington," *Publications of the Colonial Society of Massachusetts*, XIII (1910–11), 254–59. The O'Conor and Laffran letters are in the O'Conor Don Papers, 8.4.143, consulted and quoted with permission from the Trustees of the Estate of O'Conor Don. I am grateful to Mr. John Smith, Trinity College, and Prof. Kerby Miller, Uni. of Missouri, for reference to these materials. For Ó Miodhchain's views, see further Brian O'Looney, ed., *A Collection of Poems by the Clare Bards* (Dublin, 1863).

On the continental connection, the pioneer work Richard Hayes, *Ireland and Irishmen in the French Revolution* (Dublin, 1932), is essential, although the whole subject needs more critical re-examination. Hayes corrected Lecky on the politics of the key officers, but only in broadest terms. W. S. Murphy, "The Irish Brigade at the Siege of Savannah," *Irish Sword*, 2 (1955), 95–102 and "The Irish Brigade of Spain at the Siege of Pensacola, 1781," *Florida Historical Quarterly*, 38 (1960), 216–225, show that by this time, the "Irish" presence in the Spanish and French Irish units was largely that of their officers, with continentals making up the rank-and-file, which might help explain the officers lack of sympathy for democratic theory. This ethos is also apparent in Jack D. Holmes, "Some Irish Officers in Spanish Louisiana," *Irish Sword*, 6 (1964), 234–47. See also Marcus de la Poer Beresford, "Ireland in French Strategy During the American War of Independence, 1776–1783", *Irish Sword*, 23 (1976), 285–297 and 23 (1977), 20–29.

Documentary material on this period is contained in the facsimile collections published by the Northern Ireland Record Office, Belfast, 1973–4: *The Volunteers, 1778–84; Irish Elections, 1750–1832; The United Irishmen; The Act of Union; The '98 Rebellion;* and in its *Aspects of Irish Social History*, ed. Trainor and Crawford, 153–192. Much of the material is clearly chosen to point up deficiencies in the extant generalities, and is thus invaluable.

Since this work was written the following have appeared. R. B. Mc Dowell, *Ireland in the Age of Imperialism, 1760–1801* (Oxford, 1979), encapsulating older views. The following begin the task defined at the outset of this note: M. R. Beames, "Peasant Movements in Ireland, 1785–1795", *Journal of Peasant Studies*, 2 (1975), 502–06; James S. Donnelly, "The Whiteboy Movement, 1761–5," *IHS*, 21 (1978), 20–54. and "The Rightboy Movement, 1785–8", *Studia Hibernica*, 17 (1978), 120–202; W. Benjamin Kennedy, "The Irish Jacobins", *ibid.*, 16 (1976/7), 108–21; Marianne Elliott, "Origins and Transformation of Early Irish Republicanism", *International Review of Social History*, 23 (1978), 405–428; T. Bartlett and D. W. Hatton, eds., *Penal Era and Golden Age* (Belfast, 1979), articles by W. H. Crawford and M. Elliott; A. P. W. Malcolmson, *John Foster: The Politics of the Anglo-Irish Ascendancy* (Oxford, 1978).

Chapter 7

Washington and Jefferson's America. Generally, see Charles H. Metzger, *Catholics and the American Revolution* (Chicago, 1962) and Thomas McAvoy, *History of the Catholic Church in the United States* (Notre Dame, 1970), 6–91; the establishment of parishes data is taken from the various diocesan accounts in the *New Catholic Encyclopedia*, 15 vols. (New York, 1967); for the 1741 conspiracy, Daniel Horsmanden, *The New York Conspiracy* (1810, r. Boston, 1971), 1–3, 278–83, 443, 477 and passim; Ellen Hart Smith, *Charles Carroll of Carollton* (Cambridge, Mass., 1942) and Peter Guilday, *Life and Times of John Carroll, Archbishop of Baltimore* (1735–1815), 2 vols. (New York, 1922), offer much detail on the Catholic and Irish communities of the time. The Address to Washington is in O'Brien's *Washington's Associations with the Irish*, reproduced from the *Virginia Herald*, 1 April 1790, together with a facsimile of the reply (between pp. 66–67); information on the growing Irish communities of the time will be found in Dennis Clark, *The Irish in Philadelphia* (Philadelphia, 1974, 3–27; in W.C. Abbott, *New York in the American Revolution* (New York, 1929), 4; in George Potter, *To the Golden Door* (Boston, 1960), 175–226, Carl Wittke, *The Irish in America* (Baton Rouge, 1956), 75–30; W.E. Rowley, "The Irish Aristocracy of Albany, 1798–1878", *New York History*, 52 (July, 1971), 275–304, and in the various diocesan histories: Robert Lord, J.E. Sexton and E.T. Harrington, *Hitory of the Archdiocese of Boston* 3 vols. (New York, 1944), 1:347–72, for example.

The history of the Scotch-Irish has not been carried beyond the revolution, quite falsely in my view, but partly due to the comforting mythology that they rapidly became more American than the Americans; a view hardly sustainable: as late as the mid-19th c. Philadelphia had a Scotch-Irish connection, which put John MacMannes into power as city boss. On continuing immigration, Maldwyn A. Jones, "Ulster Emigration, 1783–1815", in Green, *Essays in Scotch-Irish History*, 46–68 and W.F. Adams, *Ireland and Irish Emigration to the New World from 1815 to the Famine* (New Haven, 1931). John Coleman is working upon a second volume on McKean's later career which should illuminate the connections somewhat.

On the politics of early party, see in addition to the standard accounts of the presidencies by Freeman, Malone, John C. Miller and others: Edward C. Carter II, "A 'Wild Irishman' Under Every Federalist's Bed: Naturalizations in Philadelphia, 1789–1806", *PMHB*, 94 (1970), 331–46; Rex Syndegaard, " 'Wild Irishmen' and the Alien and Sedition Acts", *Eire-Ireland*, 9(1974), 14–24; James M. Smith, "The *Aurora* and the Alien and Sedition Acts", *PMHB*, 77(1953), 123–155; Lewis Leary, "Thomas Branagan: Republican Rhetoric and Romanticism in America", *PMHB*, 77(1953), 332–352: Arthur Shaffer, "John Daly Burk's *History of Virginia* and the Development of American National History", *Va. Mag. Hist. Biog.*, 77(1969). 336–346; Joseph I. Shulim, *John Daly Burk: Irish Revolutionist* (Philadelphia, 1964); Bernard Fay, "Early Party Machinery in the United States: Pennsylvania in the Election of 1796", *PMHB*, 60(1936), 375–390; James H. Peeling, "Governor McKean and the Pennsylvania Jacobins", *PMHB*, 54(1930), 320–54 and Callista Schramm, "William Findley in Pennsylvania Politics", *WPMH*, 20(1937), 31-40 for their later careers.

On Washington's or Congress's appointees, I have usually followed the *DAB* for the information contained herein, but North Callahan, *Henry Knox, Washington's General* (New York, 1958) and Charles P. Whittemore, *A General of the Revolution: John Sullivan of New Hampshire* (New York, 1961) are interesting. For the key Irish Americans who remained Federalist, see Bruchey, *Robert Oliver, passim* (he became son-in-law of Nicholas Biddle), Wood, *William Paterson*, 125–199, and B.C. Stainer, *The Life and Correspondence of James McHenry* (Cleveland, 1907), *passim*. It is notable that they did not remain interactive with the new, or even older, Ulster American communities. Where there was heavy fresh immigration, as in New Castle co., Delaware, there was a marked swing to the Jeffersonian Republicans: Munroe,

Federalist Delaware, 198–231, 261, an excellent account which ought long since to have been developed for elsewhere

For Reed to Abbé Raynal, see Roche, *Reed,* 163.

The United States after 1800: The material cited immediately above is again relevant, additionally, biographical material is from the *Dictionary of American Biography,* and from Christopher Colles, *A Survey of the Roads of the United States* [1789], ed. Walter Ristow (Harvard, 1961); Mathew Carey, *Autobiography* (Brooklyn, New York, 1942), *Appeal to the Wealthy of the Land* (Philadelphia, 1833), *Letters on the Condition of the Poor* (Philadelphia, 1835), and K. W. Rowe, *Mathew Carey* (Baltimore, 1933); T. A. Emmet, *Memoirs of Thomas Addis and Robert Emmet,* 2 vols. (New York, 1915); Archibald Hamilton Rowan, *Autobiography,* ed. R. B. McDowell (Dublin, 1972); R. R. Madden, *The United Irishmen, their Lives and Times* 4 vols. (Dublin, 1857–60); John Binns, *Recollections of the Life of John Binns* (Philadelphia, 1854); Alice L. Cochran, *Saga of an Immigrant Family: Descendants of John Mullanphy* (New York, 1976); David B. Warden, *A Statistical, Political and Historical Account of the United States,* 3 vols. (Edinburgh, 1819). On emigration, and settlement, Edith Abbott, ed., *Historical Aspects of the Immigration Problem* (Chicago, 1926), is unusually good on early nineteenth century Irish migration, especially 22, 34, 68–72, 75, 80–1, 90, 227–30, 253–56, 615–6, 718–24, 727, 732–3 for documentary material on which I relied heavily; see also her *Immigration: Select Documents and Case Records* (Chicago, 1924); W. F. Adams, *Ireland and Irish Emigration to the New World from 1815 to the Famine* (New Haven, 1832), a crucial work; Marcus Hansen, *The Atlantic Migration, 1607–1860* (Harvard, 1940), 69–225; John F. Maguire, *The Irish in America* (London, 1968, reprint, New York, 1969); Oscar Handlin, *Boston's Immigrants* rev. ed. (Harvard, 1959), 1–52; Earl F. Niehaus, *The Irish in New Orleans, 1800–1860* (Baton Rouge, 1965), 3–36 and *passim;* David Montgomery, "The Working Classes in a Pre-Industrial American City, 1780–1830", *Labor History,* 9 (1968), 3–22; John T. Smith, *The Catholic Church in New York,* 2 vols. (New York, 1905); Alfred Young "The Mechanics and Jeffersonians: New York, 1789–1801". *Labor History,* 5 (1964), 247–76. On religion, Daniel Callahan, *The Mind of the Catholic Layman* (New York, 1963), 3–51; Thomas McAvoy, "The Formation of the Catholic Minority in the United States, 1820–1860", *Review of Politics,* 10 (1948), 13–34; John T. Ellis *American Catholicism* (Chicago, 1955), 40–81 and Andrew Greeley, *The Catholic Experience* (New York, 1967), 19–101 all "Americanise" this period, and refer to more detailed studies; Potter, *To the Golden Door,* 175–216, 344–371 is a useful corrective. The Ulster component in American Presbyterianism, ill-served in eighteenth century studies, disappears entirely from those of early nineteenth century American Presbyterianism, despite an immigration of over 200,000 from Ulster, 1783–1830s, about one half Presbyterian, and probably more stalwartly so than many of their predecessors: M. W. Armstrong, L. A. Loetscher, C. A. Anderson, *The Presbyterian Enterprise* (Philadelphia, 1956); H. R. Niebuhr, *The Kingdom of God in America* (New York, 1937); Sidney Mead, *The Lively Experiment* (New York, 1963); Elwyn Smith, *The Presbyterian Ministry in American Culture* (Philadelphia, 1962); W. W. Sweet, *The American Churches* (New York, 1948), all stress, however differently, the convergence of an Americanised Presbyterianism with the 'calvinist' and more liberal elements in the culture generally, disregarding any continuing immigrant influence. Studies of Irish Catholicism and Presbyterianism, 1780s–1830s, however, are required before such gaps can be filled with any confidence. Guides and bibliographies for later themes in Irish American history referred to in this section are Lawrence J. McCaffrey, *The Irish Diaspora in America*

(Bloomington, 1976) and D. N. Doyle and O. D. Edwards eds. *American and Ireland, 1776–1976* (Westport, CT., 1980), and fuller materials are contained in McCaffrey, Margaret Connors, James Walsh and David Doyle, *The Irish Americans*, 42 vols. (New York, 1976).

On the decline of indentured servitude, see William Miller, "The Effects of the American Revolution on Indentured Servitude," PH, 3(1940), 131–141; the "Antibiastes" pamphlet in the Historical Society of Pennsylvania Collections; Boyd, ed., *Papers of Thomas Jefferson*, 10:30–32; Maldwyn Jones, "Ulster Emigration," pp. 53–54; cf. Abbott, *Historical Aspects*, 210–18 [popular revulsion after 1800: German cases]; on the Pa. incidents of 1783, Carl Leopold Baurmeister to Colonel von Junken, 23 Oct. 1783: "This occurrence was very provoking to the old Irish settlers. They threatened to kill the bold negro if he did not immediately free the two Irishmen upon having the purchase price refunded to him and if the governor did not immediately proclaim a law that a freed slave could never hold slaves. The incident stirred Philadelphia for two days and moved the governor to enact a law . . ." in Baurmeister, *Revolution in America: Confidentrial Letters and Journals, 1776–1783*, trans. Bernard Uhlendorf (New Brunswick, N.J., 1957), 593; cf. a Va. law to same effect passed 1785 or 1792 (Jordan, *White Over Black*, 407); for N.Y. incident, McKee, *Labor in Colonial N.Y.* For examples of its persistence, on a larger scale than Miller believed, see J.K. Trimmer's evidence in 1812: "as lately as last year I witnessed an American vessel freighted with nearly three of these poor deluded self-sold men," and press reports from Cork for 1818, both cited Nicholas Nolan, "Irish Emigration," Ph.D., University College, Dublin, 1935, p. 37; Mathew Carey, in "Emigration from Ireland and Immigration into the United States", as late as 1828, who assumes servitude the normal passage-method of poor immigration still, and sought reduction its term to six months, the labor-value of the average passage (*Miscellaneous Essays*, Philadelphia, 1830, p. 321–24); and Dennis Clark, "Babes in Bondage: Indentured Irish Children in Philadelphia in the Nineteenth Century," *PMHB*, 101 (1977), 475–86. Indeed it resumed at once following peace in 1783, e.g., "Just Arrived in the ship Sophia, Alexander Verdeen, Master, from Dublin, Twenty stout, healthy Indented MEN SERVANTS . . ." MG, 27 Dec. 1785. See also John Palmer and William Priest, c. 1800, cited Mesick, *English Traveller*, 44–46.

Recent attempts to soften our images of the trade, following similar techniques used by Fogel and Engerman on slavery, contradict the Irish evidence of Carey, Trimmer, etc., of this study, and those cited p. 242–3. They do usefully point up its economic rationale, and its greater tolerability, in the middle states/colonies: Robert O. Heavner, "Indentured Servitude: The Philadelphia Market, 1771–1773, " *Jour. of Econ. Hist.*, 38 (1978), 701–713; David W. Galenson, "British Servants and the Colonial Indenture System in the 18th Century," *Journal of Southern History*, 44 (1978), 41–46 and "Immigration and the Colonial Labor System: An Analysis," *Explorations in Economic History*, 14 (1977), 360–377. These studies confirm by implication that British servants (their subject) were better treated than German or Irish.

That the revolution had a conscious effect on Irish images of America as a future haven was early made clear to American leaders: e.g. "L'esprit d'émigration en Europe, en Amérique, favorise la population de ces contrées. Le Juge Supréme de la Pennsylvanie, Mr. McKean, a dit au G. Washington que dépuis la paix quatre mille âmes ont descendu l'Ohio à Pittsburg. Un Irlandois est venu trouver le Gén. [Washington] à Princeton et lui a parlé de cinquante à cent familles Irlandoises prétes à passer en Amérique." G.K. von Hogendorp, report of Jefferson's comments, 11 April,

1784; Boyd, *Papers,* 7:218–219; see also, Jefferson to Démeunier, 24 Jan. 1785, ibid., 10:13.

On politics at local level in Ireland see especially Peter Jupp, *British and Irish Elections, 1784–1831* (New York, 1973), 142–185 and K. T. Hoppen, "National Politics and Local Realities in Mid-Nineteenth century Ireland," in Art Cosgrove and Donal McCartney, eds., *Studies in Irish History Presented to R. Dudley Edwards* (Dublin, 1979), 190–227. T. N. Brown, "The Political Irish: Politicians and Rebels," in Doyle and Edwards, pp. 133–49, discusses the transition to American styles.

For the changing educational background of emigrants, increasing if unevenly after 1800, see Mary Daly, "Development of the National School System, 1831–1840," in Cosgrove and McCartney, esp. 151–54; David Kennedy, "Education and the People," in R. B. McDowell, ed., *Social Life in Ireland, 1800–1845* (Dublin, 1957), 53–66; Harold O'Sullivan, "Emergence of the National System of Education in Co. Louth," *PICHC,* 1968, 5–26; but contrast Seosamh Ó Dufaigh, "James Murphy, Bishop of Clogher, 1801–1824," *Clogher Record,* 6 (1968), 23–25. Before available funding, schooling depended upon relative rural surpluses, and hence fluctuated by region. It was *marginally* more available to Presbyterians, not greatly so: see sources p. 241. In 1821, only a minority of children were in schools: 20% of those from 5 to 15 yrs. in Munster, 30% in Co. Antrim, but due to staggered schooling, 40%–50% gained some literacy. See a forthcoming study by Mary Daly, David Dickson and John Logan.

Quotations are from: Robert Simms papers, Public Record Office of Northern Ireland, John Chambers to Simms, New York, 24 May 1811 and 6 June 1818; T.A. Emmet to A.H. Rowan, 3 Jan. 1827, in T.A. Emmet, *Memoirs,* 1:467; Rowan to Mrs. Rowan, 15 April 1799, *Autobiography,* 342; MacNeven in the *Enquirer,* Madden, 3:236; Richard Fitzpatrick to John, Earl of Ossory, 31 Jan. 1781, copy in National Library of Ireland, reproduced in *Ireland and Irishmen in the American War of Independence* (facsimile collection, Dublin, 1976); John O'Hanlon, *The Irish Emigrant's Guide for the United States,* ed. Edward J. Maguire (New York, 1976), from original (Boston, 1851), 12–13, 14; O'Sullivan and Kennedy, in George Probst, ed., *The Happy Republic, A Reader in Tocqueville's America* (New York, 1962), 11–12, 593, 597; Tocqueville, *Democracy in America,* ed. Phillips Bradley (New York, 1945), 2:105–06; Anthony Doyle to Andrew Doyle, 31 May 1819, in Richard Wade, *The Urban Frontier* (Harvard, 1959), 119–120; John Gamble, in T.H. Mullin, *Coleraine in Georgian Times,* 29; I. Holmes, Clements Burleigh, Mathew Carey, Harvey Fearon, the Irish societies and the Massachusetts Commission on Lunacy (1855), are in Abbot, *Historical Aspects,* 230, 239–42, 256, 615, 716–18, 722–4, 727.

That travellers were aware of the persistence of a Scotch-Irish culture in the backcountry deserves emphasis. Speaking of observations by John Melish, C. H. Wilson, Wilson, William Faux, C. W. Janson and others, Jane L. Mesick noted: "The western Virginians and their Western neighbors, the Kentuckians, were looked upon by Englishmen as types parallel to the wildest kind of Irishmen, and it is interesting to see how often the similarity in open-heartedness, rude hospitality, generosity, wit and love of lawless behavior, is emphasized": *The English Traveller in America, 1785–1835* (New York, 1922), 69. Only closer study could establish whether Jefferson's train of though linking fresh Irish migration with McKean's description of movement down the Ohio to these regions betokens a real direct movement, which might have reinforced these traits; A "Western Pennsylvania Emigrant Society" encouraged it in 1826: Abbott, *Hist. Aspects,* 733.

For discussions of patterns of Irish assimilation, see Miller, "Emigrants and Exiles," 176–308, and for later periods, John Duffy Ibson, "Will the World Break Your Heart?

A Historical Analysis of the Dimensions of Irish American Assimilation," Ph.D., Brandeis University, 1976; Dale Thomas Knobel, "Paddy and the Republic: Popular Images of the American Irish, 1820–1860," Ph.D., Northwestern University, 1976; and William Ryan, "Assimilation of Irish Immigrants in Britain, "Ph.D., St. Louis University, 1973.It could well be that the virulence of Pennsylvania attitudes in the War of 1812 owed a considerable amount to coherence of a reinforced Ulster American community, as argued here: see Victor A. Sapio, *Pennsylvania and War of 1812* (Lexington, Ky., 1970).